T0406913

The Future of
Catholic Biblical
Interpretation

The Future of Catholic Biblical Interpretation

Marie-Joseph Lagrange and Beyond

Edited by James B. Prothro and
Isaac Augustine Morales, OP

William B. Eerdmans Publishing Company
Grand Rapids, Michigan

Wm. B. Eerdmans Publishing Co.
4035 Park East Court SE, Grand Rapids, Michigan 49546
www.eerdmans.com

Published 2024

Book design by Leah Luyk

Printed in the United States of America

30 29 28 27 26 25 24 1 2 3 4 5 6 7

ISBN 978-0-8028-8291-2

Library of Congress Cataloging-in-Publication Data

A catalog record for this book is available from the Library of Congress.

In memoriam
Father Donald P. Senior, CP
Robert D. Miller II, OFS

Contents

Acknowledgments ix

List of Abbreviations xi

Catholic Biblical Interpretation 1
James B. Prothro and Isaac Augustine Morales, OP

Biblical Interpretation and the Community of Faith 19
Donald P. Senior, CP

***Dei Verbum*, Historical Criticism, and Theological Exegesis** 24
Brant Pitre

Reading Beyond the Horizon 44
Laurie Brink, OP

Père Lagrange and the Criticism of Criticism 60
Isaac Augustine Morales, OP

Why Did Marie-Joseph Lagrange Abandon the Old Testament? 79
Mark Giszczak

Lagrange's *Religions Sémitiques* a Century Later 92
Robert D. Miller II, OFS

Foreshadowings of the Kingdom 120
Nina Sophie Heereman

Eucharistic Hermeneutics 143
Kelly Anderson

Memory and the Human Dimension of Inspiration 161
Michael Patrick Barber

Jesus as God and Man in the Gospels 184
Anthony Giambrone, OP

A Postcolonial Latino/a Catholic Biblical Interpretation in the Americas 211
J. L. Manzo

Catholic Biblical Interpretation 227
Kathleen P. Rushton, RSM

What Does It Mean to Read Scripture as the Word of God? 246
Luke Timothy Johnson

Biblical Inspiration and Textual Criticism 266
James B. Prothro

Bibliography 287

List of Contributors 323

Index of Authors 327

Index of Subjects 333

Index of Scripture 341

Index of Other Ancient Sources 348

Acknowledgments

This collection of essays grew out of an online conference in 2022, organized by James B. Prothro and John A. Kincaid. We the editors are grateful to the contributors of this volume for their collaboration, patience, and hard work and to John Kincaid for his work in the original conference. We are thankful also to James Ernest, Trevor Thompson, and the team at Eerdmans for their efforts in bringing this volume to print and to Sr. Laurie Brink, OP, and the Passionists for their help with Fr. Senior's essay.

Throughout the chapters below, translations of the Bible are those of the author unless otherwise noted, and versifications follow the standard critical texts.

Abbreviations

AAS	*Acta Apostolicae Sedis*
AB	Anchor Bible
ABRL	Anchor Bible Reference Library
AnBib	Analecta Biblica
ANES	*Ancient Near Eastern Studies*
ANET	*Ancient Near Eastern Texts Relating to the Old Testament.* Edited by James B. Pritchard. 3rd ed. Princeton: Princeton University Press, 1969
ANF	*Ante-Nicene Fathers*
ANTC	Abingdon New Testament Commentaries
AOAT	Alter Orient und Altes Testament
ASJ	*Acta Sumerologica*
AYBRL	Anchor Yale Bible Reference Library
BEATAJ	Beiträge zur Erforschung des Alten Testaments und des antiken Judentum
BECNT	Baker Exegetical Commentary on the New Testament
BETL	Bibliotheca Ephemeridum Theologicarum Lovaniensium
Bib	*Biblica*
BTB	*Biblical Theology Bulletin*
BZAW	Beihefte zur Zeitschrift für die alttestamentliche Wissenschaft
CBC	Cambridge Bible Commentary
CBET	Contributions to Biblical Exegesis and Theology
CBQ	*Catholic Biblical Quarterly*
CCC	*Catechism of the Catholic Church.* 2nd rev. ed. Rome: Libreria Editrice Vaticana, 2019

ConBNT	Coniectanea Neotestamentica
COS	*The Context of Scripture.* Edited by William W. Hallo. 3 vols. Leiden: Brill, 1997–2002
EANEC	Explorations in Ancient Near Eastern Civilizations
EBib	Études bibliques
ECL	Early Christianity and Its Literature
EDB	*Eerdmans Dictionary of the Bible.* Edited by David Noel Freedman. Grand Rapids: Eerdmans, 2000
EDNT	*Exegetical Dictionary of the New Testament.* Edited by Horst Balz and Gerhard Schneider. ET. 3 vols. Grand Rapids: Eerdmans, 1990–1993
EKKNT	Evangelisch-katholischer Kommentar zum Neuen Testament
EstBib	*Estudios Bíblicos*
ExpTim	*Expository Times*
FAT	Forschungen zum Alten Testament
FOTL	Forms of the Old Testament Literature
Fran	*Franciscanum*
HBAI	*Hebrew Bible and Ancient Israel*
HBS	History of Biblical Studies
HR	*History of Religions*
ICC	International Critical Commentary
JAAR	*Journal of the American Academy of Religion*
JANER	*Journal of Ancient Near Eastern Religions*
JANES	*Journal of the Ancient Near Eastern Society*
JBL	*Journal of Biblical Literature*
JBQ	*Jewish Bible Quarterly*
JFSR	*Journal of Feminist Studies in Religion*
JISMOR	*Journal of the Interdisciplinary Study of Monotheistic Religions*
JSHJ	*Journal for the Study of the Historical Jesus*
JSNT	*Journal for the Study of the New Testament*
JSNTSup	Journal for the Study of the New Testament Supplement Series
JSOTSup	Journal for the Study of the Old Testament Supplement Series
KEK	Kritisch-exegetischer Kommentar über das Neue Testament
KTU	*Die keilalphabetischen Texte aus Ugarit.* Edited by

	Manfried Dietrich, Oswald Loretz, and Joaquín Sanmartín. Münster: Ugarit-Verlag, 2013
LD	Lectio Divina
LNTS	The Library of New Testament Studies
NBL	*Neues Bibel-Lexikon*
NCE	*New Catholic Encyclopedia*
NEchtB	Neue Echter Bibel
NICNT	New International Commentary on the New Testament
NIGTC	New International Greek Testament Commentary
NJPS	*Tanakh: The Holy Scriptures: The New JPS Translation according to the Traditional Hebrew Text*
NovT	*Novum Testamentum*
NTS	*New Testament Studies*
NTTS	New Testament Tools and Studies
NTTSD	New Testament Tools, Studies, and Documents
PG	*Patrologia Graeca*. Edited by Jacques-Paul Migne. 162 vols. Paris, 1857–1886
PHSC	Perspectives on Hebrew Scriptures and Its Contexts
PL	*Patrologia Latina*. Edited by Jacques-Paul Migne. 217 vols. Paris, 1844–1864
ProEccl	*Pro Ecclesia*
RB	*Revue biblique*
RBS	Resources for Biblical Study
ResQ	*Restoration Quarterly*
RevistBSup	Revista Bíblica Supplements
RIBLA	*Revista de Interpretación Bíblica Latinoamericana*
RJFTC	The Reception of Jesus in the First Three Centuries
SAC	Studies in Antiquity and Christianity
SBLDS	Society of Biblical Literature Dissertation Series
SBS	Stuttgarter Bibelstudien
Sem	*Semitica*
SemeiaSt	Semeia Studies
SNTSMS	Society for New Testament Studies Monograph Series
SP	Sacra Pagina
ST	*Studia Theologica*
STI	Studies in Theological Interpretation
StPatr	*Studia Patristica*

SubBi	Subsidia Biblica
TB	Theologische Bücherei: Neudrucke und Berichte aus dem 20. Jahrhundert
TBN	Themes in Biblical Narrative
TDNT	*Theological Dictionary of the New Testament.* Edited by Gerhard Kittel and Gerhard Friedrich. Translated by Geoffrey W. Bromiley. 10 vols. Grand Rapids: Eerdmans, 1964–1976
THKNT	Theologischer Handkommentar zum Neuen Testament
ThSt	Theologische Studiën
UF	*Ugarit-Forschungen*
VT	*Vetus Testamentum*
VTSup	Supplements to Vetus Testamentum
WBC	Word Biblical Commentary
WUNT	Wissenschaftliche Untersuchungen zum Neuen Testament
ZAW	*Zeitschrift für die alttestamentliche Wissenschaft*
ZNW	*Zeitschrift für die neutestamentliche Wissenschaft und die Kunde der älteren Kirche*
ZTK	*Zeitschrift für Theologie und Kirche*

Catholic Biblical Interpretation

Lagrange and Beyond

James B. Prothro and Isaac Augustine Morales, OP

This book had its birth in an online conference of several Roman Catholic biblical scholars in the spring of 2022. The participants discussed current and future prospects for our own work in biblical studies from the perspective of our identity as Catholics and anchored in the figure of Père Marie-Joseph Lagrange, OP. That group both grew and shrank as our reflections developed in the essays printed together in this volume. Despite the definite article in the title—"the" future of Catholic biblical interpretation—one will not find a single prescribed future in this volume. The scholars who participated in our online meeting and those featured in the pages below are not homogenous in focus or methods. Though this book's editors have training primarily in New Testament, the contributors represent different fields within biblical studies, engaging variously in historical, theological, narrative, postcolonial, comparative, ecological, and other modes of interpretation and representing both Old Testament/Hebrew Bible and New Testament. We also have different relationships to the institution of the Catholic Church as priests, religious, and laypeople. Nonetheless, amid such differences, the authors here all have a vested interest in the project of biblical interpretation as it is carried out by and for God's people in Catholic contexts. It is out of that shared identity and concomitant shared goals—represented not only by authors in this volume but also by thousands of others engaged in the effort—that the future of Catholic biblical interpretation will be determined.

This essay collection participates in a long-standing conversation that encompasses diverse interests and methods within a common interpretive endeavor. Indeed, at the very beginning of Christian biblical interpretation, within the New Testament itself, one finds a diversity of interests and methods among writers united by common goals and convictions. Though these reading strategies would be pitted against each other in the modern period, Paul engages in both typology and allegory as he reads and applies Israel's Scriptures to his churches (1 Cor 10:10–11; Gal 4:21–31). One also finds differences in the focus and interest different authors have on different texts. A book like Proverbs seems less influential in the New Testament until one turns to Hebrews and the Catholic Epistles (Heb 12:5–6; Jas 4:6; 1 Pet 4:18; 5:5), and beyond the canon of Scripture, Jude is heavily influenced by the otherwise marginal 1 Enoch (Jude 14–16). Some texts seem to have taken on a common Christian interpretation, as one sees in the messianic reading of Psalm 110 connected with Jesus's ascension and lordship, though this is developed differently in different contexts (e.g., Mark 12:35–37; Acts 2:32–36; Eph 1:20–22; 1 Pet 3:22). Other texts receive different or apparently opposing interpretations by different authors: Paul makes a diachronic argument that Gen 15:6 shows Abraham being justified even before his circumcision (Rom 4:3–10), while James argues that this verse is truly "fulfilled" long after, in Abraham's obedience at the binding of Isaac (Jas 2:21–23).

Nonetheless, the New Testament authors appear to share the conviction expressed by Paul that "whatever was written beforehand was written for our instruction, that by endurance and by the encouragement of the Scriptures we might have hope" (Rom 15:4; cf. 1 Cor 10:11; 2 Cor 1:20). They read the ancient Scriptures as speaking not merely about the distant past but into the present, and they applied its words to the life and theology of their communities through various hermeneutical modes. The same continues also in later periods of emerging Catholic biblical interpretation, in which a common purpose remained and a shared identity was forged and reforged in controversy. Naturally, there are noticeable differences and even flash points of argument. Jerome and Augustine are instructive examples regarding translation and texts, the former striving for accuracy (and favoring a Hebrew base for Christian readings of the Old Testament) and the latter prioritizing a hermeneutic of charity and esteeming the Septuagint. Nevertheless, both were motivated by their interest in the biblical authors' words as divine revelation. Hermeneutical lenses and cultural engagements differed as well. Second-century Christianity provided a home for both Tertullian's insistence that Athens has nothing to do with Jerusalem and Clement of Alexandria's use of what today we might call "secular" Hellenistic and Platonic learning to understand and explain the faith. The third century saw in Origen a bibliophile who sought insight from the rabbis while following in Clement's footsteps, and in the thirteenth century Thomas Aquinas drew on Aristotle—to the dismay of some—to understand and explain the truth of God and the words of Scripture.

One also notes differences in approach between more doggedly "literal" and more imaginatively "spiritual" interpretations not only in the (sometimes exaggerated) differences between Antiochene and Alexandrian exegesis but also in later centuries. A notable example of difference and unity here comes from Hugh of St. Victor (d. 1141). Hugh felt that his contemporaries too quickly jumped from the texts to follow their allegorical and anagogical fancies. He writes, "I am amazed with what boldness teachers boast of their allegories when they do not know this first signification of the letter. 'We read Scripture,' they say, 'but we do not read the letter. We do not care about the letter, but we teach allegory.' How then do you read Scripture and not read the letter? For if the letter is taken away, what is Scripture?"[1] His refutations of such attitudes are strident. Nonetheless, his criticisms were not meant to oppose such allegories outright. Rather, he wanted to ensure that allegorical interpretation was done well and that interpreters would be conscious of the moves they were making and of the warrants for their legitimacy in the "letter" or, in another of his terms, the "history" (*historia*) of what is directly narrated or proposed. "To ignore the letter is to ignore what the letter signifies and what is signified by the letter."[2] He offers as an example an allegorical interpretation of the word *leo* (lion) as Christ. Hugh approves of the ultimate results of this application, but he insists that *leo* does not simply refer to Christ but first to a kind of animal, particular characteristics of or associations with which can be interpreted with reference to Christ "by a certain similitude." Hugh wants interpreters to slow down lest they follow their own fancies rather than the text and end in potential error. "So do not make the leap, lest you fall on your face."[3]

Whether Augustine or Aquinas or Bonaventure or Bernard, the great lights that illuminate the history of Christian exegesis throughout and beyond its first millennium differ in much yet still possess a common goal of interpreting the Bible to hear the word of God and proclaim and apply it within the church. The exegetical landscape in Catholicism today is in many ways similar. Questions of translation are still current, though perhaps with

1. Hugh of St. Victor, *De Scripturis* 5 (PL 175:13; our translation throughout).

2. Hugh of St. Victor, *De Scripturis* 5 (PL 175:13).

3. "Noli ergo saltum facere, ne in praecipitium incidas." Hugh of St. Victor, *De Scripturis* 5 (PL 175:14).

different suppositions than in Jerome's day.[4] Reminiscent of Origen, one sees Catholic interest in learning ecumenically from non-Christian Jews—both ancient and modern—though with (hopefully) greater respect for the integrity of their texts and their faith.[5] Reminiscent of moves made by figures like Clement and Aquinas, modern trends in understanding truth and advances in the sciences are likewise being used to aid theological interpretation and cultural application.[6]

In other respects, however, the landscape of Catholic biblical interpretation today might appear distant from its heritage. Much of what is identified as Catholic biblical *scholarship*—which overlaps but is not coterminous with Catholic biblical *interpretation*—has become institutionally decoupled from the context of prayer and preaching shared by Aquinas and Origen to the extent that some have alleged in print (and many more have said the same off the record) that the academic enterprise of biblical scholarship has lost and must recover its own "soul."[7] Some Catholic exegetes, even when aiming to address the church, seem simply uninterested in the use or application of the Bible among the faithful, while other interpreters actively oppose interpreting Scripture with any theological or practical interest. In reaction, one can find biblical commentaries today intentionally written by theologians to edify readers' faith, and yet they appear nearly devoid of attention to "literal sense" matters of language, genre, or history that the Catholic magisterium maintains are essential elements of the human communication God inspired.[8]

4. E.g., Emil A. Wcela, "What Is Catholic about a Catholic Translation of the Bible?," *CBQ* 71, no. 2 (2009): 247–63.

5. See Vatican Council II, Declaration *Nostra aetate* (October 28, 1965). More recently, see the Pontifical Biblical Commission, *The Jewish People and Their Sacred Scriptures in the Christian Bible* (Rome: Libreria Editrice Vaticana, 2002). For appreciation of these developments and critiques showing what work is still needed here, see Amy-Jill Levine, *The Misunderstood Jew: The Church and the Scandal of the Jewish Jesus* (San Francisco: HarperOne, 2006), 93–95, 111–14, 227–28.

6. Such advances pertain, for instance, to semiotics and enculturation, recent trends in social memory, and anthropology. E.g., John F. Haught, *Resting on the Future: Catholic Theology for an Unfinished Universe* (New York: Bloomsbury Academic, 2015); Sandra M. Schneiders, IHM, *The Revelatory Text: Interpreting the New Testament as Sacred Scripture*, 2nd ed. (Collegeville, MN: Liturgical Press, 1999); Michael Patrick Barber, *The Historical Jesus and the Temple: Memory, Methodology, and the Gospel of Matthew* (Cambridge: Cambridge University Press, 2023).

7. E.g., Luke Timothy Johnson and William S. Kurz, SJ, *The Future of Catholic Biblical Scholarship: A Constructive Conversation* (Grand Rapids: Eerdmans, 2002), 39, 61, 91.

8. One might see these commentaries as latter-day counterparts to the objects of Hugh of St. Victor's criticisms.

In many cases, conversations remain collegial and reflect attempts at rapprochement. But some conversations in the public sphere suggest an outsider could be forgiven for wondering if all these exponents of "Catholic biblical interpretation" in fact share a common identity or goal.

The polarities are in part accentuated by conflicts over what came to be known as "the biblical question" in the nineteenth and twentieth centuries. The Enlightenment drew readers to consider the world behind the biblical text and in many cases denied the possibility of the divine in history, reducing theology to personal experience and rejecting many of the Bible's claims. Some faithful Catholics took up data and legitimate insights from new historical studies to provide nuance, defend, and further develop an understanding of divine revelation in history and in the production of Scripture—many in ways that closely anticipated the Second Vatican Council.[9] Nonetheless, many within the church responded simply by rejecting all elements of the new criticism as irreducibly irreligious, and they saw their position vindicated by the infamous example of Alfred Loisy, a priest who studied archaeology and antiquity, but whose work eventuated in a radical skepticism regarding Jesus and the church.[10] Catholicism in the late nineteenth and early twentieth centuries saw itself fighting a rear-guard action against a faithless rationalism and an anti-traditional modernism, not merely outside but within the walls of the church, and history and biblical criticism came to be a center of debate over Catholic identity and fidelity.[11] In 1893, Pope Leo XIII's encyclical on biblical studies, *Providentissimus Deus*, affirmed historical inquiry, archaeology, the original languages, and ancient manuscripts as aids to defend and explicate the Scriptures, but it also insisted—following the Council of Trent—that exegetes should be sure not to depart from the "consensus of the fathers" in their interpretations.[12] As the crisis continued, however, exegetes who employed "profane" methods of historical study or who pressed for the notion of development (even continuous, organic de-

9. Those associated with Tübingen are especially notable here. See James Tunstead Burtchaell, CSC, *Catholic Theories of Biblical Inspiration since 1810: A Review and Critique* (Cambridge: Cambridge University Press, 1969); Johannes Beumer, *Die katholische Inspirationslehre zwischen Vaticanum I und II*, SBS 20 (Stuttgart: Katholisches Bibelwerk, 1966).

10. See Jeffrey L. Morrow, *Alfred Loisy and Modern Biblical Studies* (Washington, DC: Catholic University of America Press, 2019).

11. See Marvin R. O'Connell, *Critics on Trial: An Introduction to the Catholic Modernist Crisis* (Washington, DC: Catholic University of America Press, 1994).

12. Leo XIII, Encyclical Letter *Providentissimus Deus* (November 18, 1893).

velopment) in church doctrine came increasingly under suspicion. In 1907, Pius X's *Pascendi dominici gregis* offered a scathing directive against "modernism." Clearly targeting figures like Loisy, it associated historical criticism and even textual criticism with philosophical agnosticism, calling ultimately for the censorship of such views.[13]

Happily, amid conflict, the polarities drew toward a synthesis in the decades following. In 1943, Pius XII issued a new encyclical on biblical studies, *Divino afflante Spiritu*, which Raymond E. Brown calls a Catholic "Magna Carta for biblical progress."[14] The encyclical amplified Leo XIII's summons to biblical studies, urging Catholics that recent advances in the knowledge of biblical languages, texts, and environment constituted a gift of divine providence that they must not ignore; he called on exegetes to engage recent studies and discoveries not only to reject error but for their positive value to aid us in understanding the genre and intended meaning of the biblical texts, emphasizing the foundational importance of the "literal sense" for all spiritual interpretation.[15] Pius XII still called for spiritual interpretation and deference to tradition, but he also urged the faithful to be patient with legitimate but perhaps unfamiliar analyses that would soon be published, and he freed exegetes with a salutary reminder that there is no "consensus of the fathers" on many particularities of inquiry.[16] Further progress was achieved at the Second Vatican Council, whose Dogmatic Constitution on Divine Revelation *Dei Verbum* offered a deeper synthesis of divine revelation, inspiration, and human history: God is revealed within history through words and deeds, and the Scriptures are inspired by God to communicate through the medium of human language within historically embedded conventions and communities, the analysis of which is therefore requisite for theology and spiritual application within the living tradition of the Catholic faith.[17]

13. Pius X, Encyclical Letter *Pascendi dominici gregis* (September 8, 1907) §§9, 13–14, 22, 26, 30–34. See further Morrow, *Alfred Loisy*, 11–30.

14. Raymond E. Brown, SS, and Thomas Aquinas Collins, OP, "Church Pronouncements," in *The New Jerome Biblical Commentary*, ed. Raymond E. Brown, SS, Joseph A. Fitzmyer, SJ, and Roland E. Murphy, OCarm (Englewood Cliffs, NJ: Prentice Hall, 1990), 1167. On some of the progress and debates during this period, see Robert Bruce Robinson, *Roman Catholic Exegesis since Divino afflante Spiritu: Hermeneutical Implications*, SBLDS 111 (Atlanta: Scholars Press, 1988), 1–55.

15. Pius XII, Encyclical Letter *Divino afflante Spiritu* (September 30, 1943).

16. See Pius XII, *Divino afflante Spiritu* §§11–19, 46–48.

17. See Vatican Council II, Dogmatic Constitution *Dei Verbum* (November 18, 1965), esp. §§11–13.

The same positions have been repeated in papal and conciliar directives since Vatican II, calling for both history and theology in the interpretive task as well as the use of other perspectives and methods. Even so, inasmuch as group identity is reinforced in controversy, the suspicions and censorship of the modernist crisis cast a long shadow. A few still decry the implementation of historical methods as still inescapably faithless, and the Pontifical Biblical Commission still finds a need to warn against fundamentalism in interpretation.[18] Even in recent decades, some Catholics have felt a need to defend the use of historical criticism and its value for interpretation.[19] On the other hand, exegetes espousing traditional positions (even for nontraditionalist reasons) or calling for retrieval of the spiritual goods of premodern interpretation can find themselves decried by their peers as magisterial toadies. Tensions remain between theology and history and between tradition and free inquiry.[20] All the while, other interpreters are struggling to gain a hearing for modes of fruitful interpretation that prioritize the world and people addressed by the word of God today more than the world behind the texts.

The twenty-first century is clearly a time for renewed conversation. With the major developments of the twentieth century behind, it is a time ripe for retrieval and synthesis. It has also been a time of fresh and friendly ecclesial encouragement for biblical study. The papacy of Benedict XVI saw renewed interest in Scripture, in part simply because of his private interest in and study of the "biblical question" as a theologian but even more because of his public leadership in the Synod on the Word of God and his Apostolic Exhortation *Verbum Domini*.[21] Pope Francis, likewise, has issued apostolic letters encouraging all the faithful to engage personally, prayerfully, and liturgically with the God who speaks through Scripture.[22] Biblical and theological scholars are setting

18. Pontifical Biblical Commission, *The Interpretation of the Bible in the Church* (Rome: Libreria Editrice Vaticana, 1993) §§I.F; II. B.1.

19. E.g., Joseph A. Fitzmyer, SJ, *The Interpretation of Scripture: In Defense of the Historical-Critical Method* (New York: Paulist, 2008); James B. Prothro, "Theories of Inspiration and Catholic Exegesis: Scripture and Criticism in Dialogue with Denis Farkasfalvy," *CBQ* 83, no. 2 (2021): 294–314.

20. Johnson's call for retrieval of premodern perspectives notes some of these tensions (in Johnson and Kurz, *Future of Catholic Biblical Scholarship*, 25). Note the review and response to Johnson and Kurz by Viviano, who frames the issue in terms of freedom and oppression in Benedict Thomas Viviano, OP, *Catholic Hermeneutics Today: Critical Essays* (Eugene, OR: Cascade, 2014), 29–33, 51–52.

21. Benedict XVI, Post-synodal Apostolic Exhortation *Verbum Domini* (September 30, 2010).

22. Francis, Apostolic Letter *Scripturae sacrae affectus* (September 30, 2020); Francis,

new eyes on old questions regarding biblical inspiration.[23] Theologians and philosophers are seeking to re-source perspectives on the "biblical question" in figures like Thomas Aquinas and the recent work of Ratzinger/Benedict XVI.[24] And the exegetical guild has hardly been idle, as one can see in the massive and international tome *The Jerome Biblical Commentary for the Twenty-First Century*, which has a foreword by none other than Pope Francis.[25]

The present volume aims to join this renewed conversation about Catholic biblical interpretation and its possible futures. And it aims to do so particularly by centering the conversation not around more recent figures, nor indeed around ancient ones, but around a central and even founding figure of Catholic biblical studies in the modern era, the Dominican priest Marie-Joseph Lagrange.

Marie-Joseph Lagrange: Founder of Modern Catholic Biblical Studies

Born in Bourg-en-Bresse, France, on March 7, 1855 (the feast day of St. Thomas Aquinas according to the old liturgical calendar), Albert La-

Apostolic Letter issued "motu proprio" *Aperuit illis* (September 30, 2019). Indeed, a large part of Francis's *Fratelli tutti* is an extended interpretation—though perhaps not a detailed historical exegesis—of Jesus's parable of the Good Samaritan. See Francis, Encyclical Letter *Fratelli tutti* (October 3, 2020).

23. E.g., Gerald O'Collins, SJ, *Inspiration: Towards a Christian Interpretation of Biblical Inspiration* (New York: Oxford University Press, 2018); William M. Wright IV and Frances Martin, *Encountering the Living God in Scripture: Theological and Philosophical Principles for Interpretation* (Grand Rapids: Baker Academic, 2019); Denis Farkasfalvy, OCist, *A Theology of the Christian Bible: Revelation, Inspiration, Canon* (Washington, DC: Catholic University of America Press, 2018); Angelo Tosato, *The Catholic Statute of Biblical Interpretation*, ed. Monica Lugato (Rome: Gregorian & Biblical Press, 2021).

24. E.g., Olivier-Thomas Venard, *A Poetic Christ: Thomist Reflections on Scripture, Language and Reality*, trans. Kenneth Oakes and Francesca Aran Murphy, Illuminating Modernity (London: T&T Clark, 2019); Wilhelmus G. B. M. Valkenberg, *Words of the Living God: Place and Function of Holy Scripture in the Theology of St. Thomas Aquinas*, Publications of the Thomas Instituut te Utrecht 2/6 (Leuven: Peeters, 2000); Aaron Pidel, SJ, *The Inspiration and Truth of Scripture: Testing the Ratzinger Paradigm*, Verbum Domini (Washington, DC: Catholic University of America Press, 2023); Matthew J. Ramage, *Jesus, Interpreted: Benedict XVI, Bart Ehrman, and the Historical Truth of the Gospels* (Washington, DC: Catholic University of America Press, 2017).

25. John J. Collins et al., eds., *The Jerome Biblical Commentary for the Twenty-First Century*, 3rd ed. (London: T&T Clark, 2022).

grange attended minor seminary and earned a doctorate in law before joining the Dominicans in 1879, taking the name Marie-Joseph Lagrange. He was ordained to the priesthood in 1883 and became Père Lagrange—Father Lagrange—a name by which he would become known the world over.

Lagrange is regularly regarded as a founding father of Catholic biblical studies in the modern era.[26] His prodigious output attests to his mind and productivity; his bibliography includes 1,786 entries.[27] He was a voracious reader and researcher throughout his life, publishing reviews of major works of scholarship as well as (especially faith-related) literature, with research articles on everything from ancient inscriptions to Israelite religion to literary criticism to Jesus and Paul, biblical commentaries on both Old and New Testament books, and analyses and refutations of theological and academic movements. Even more significant are the enduring institutions that he established to promote biblical studies in the Catholic Church.[28] In 1890, then in his midthirties, Lagrange was tasked with founding the École biblique, which has become an enduring center for research on Scripture under the aegis of the Dominican order. Its facilities have expanded, as has its library—in no small part due to Lagrange's efforts—and the school is now licensed to grant doctoral degrees as the École biblique et archéologique française de Jérusalem. But from Lagrange's day until now, it has been a practical school of exegesis, as indicated in its original name, École pratique d'études bibliques, where instruction can be received by apprenticeship, training "on the job" in ancient texts and quite literally "on the ground" in the Holy Land.[29] The École and its mission became a hub not only for instruction but also for research and publication in the same spirit. The journal *Revue biblique* was quickly launched in 1892 as a venue in which biblical studies could be pursued positively and academically by the École's professors and other contributors and in which Catholic exegetes could meet head-on some of the intellectual challenges of the day.[30] The journal continues today as an

26. So, indeed, the title of one of his biographies: Bernard Montagnes, OP, *The Story of Father Marie-Joseph Lagrange: Founder of Modern Catholic Bible Study*, trans. Benedict Viviano, OP (New York: Paulist, 2006).

27. F.-M. Braun, OP, *The Work of Père Lagrange*, ed. and trans. Richard T. A. Murphy, OP (Milwaukee: Bruce, 1963), 163–253.

28. On Lagrange's activity as "founder" see Braun, *Work of Père Lagrange*, 3–34; Montagnes, *Story of Father Marie-Joseph Lagrange*, 20–52.

29. On the "practical" nature of the school, see Montagnes, *Story of Father Marie-Joseph Lagrange*, 32–35.

30. Braun cites Lagrange's printed response to objections to giving too much press,

academic periodical, with a supplemental monograph series (Cahiers de la Revue Biblique), alongside the series Études bibliques, which Lagrange launched to encompass biblical commentaries and monographs as well.

Lagrange's founding of the École, the *Revue*, and the series Études bibliques are, however, not the only or even the primary respects in which he can be called the founder of modern Catholic biblical study. His significance goes beyond the institutions he set up to the spirit and goals for which he set them up, the struggles he faced as an exegete and the spirit in which he endured them, and the impact of his teaching and example on Catholic exegesis worldwide.

Lagrange's work blazed a trail, employing and developing methods of inquiry that would come to dominate much of twentieth-century biblical criticism. He saw the benefits of new discoveries and methods in historical study being utilized by "profane" academics, and he also saw the damage they had done to the intellectual credibility of the church. At a time when some employed history against faith and others sustained faith by rejecting the critical study of history, Lagrange saw his work as both positively and defensively necessary. As he wrote in the foreword to the first issue of the *Revue*, the divine inspiration of Scripture through human writers called for Catholic readers to attend to the latter not only to understand and show forth the divine message but also to defend it against rationalist "attacks."[31] Inasmuch as the Bible could become a battleground subject to rationalist or modernist attack, he wrote, "We must not use a crossbow against a cannon; that is, we are invited to rival our adversaries in competence; to recognize in the Bible the word of man, written as history, and at the same time, to receive the Bible as the *Word of God*, bearer of transcendence."[32] His attention not only to apologetics but also to the understanding of the transcendent in the earthly set him apart from some others. Lagrange studied and taught everything from comparative religion to the history of religions to textual criticism to epigraphy to genre criticism to philology, but he did so neither

in a Catholic periodical, to anti-Catholic and secularist positions: "Draw the blinds as tightly as you like. . . . If error spreads first in special works, and then in periodicals and newspapers, who can hope to keep it shut up behind curtains?" (Braun, *Work of Père Lagrange*, 24). See Marie-Joseph Lagrange, OP, "Avant-propos," *RB* 1, no. 1 (1892): 10.

31. Braun, *Work of Père Lagrange*, 6, 24. One also notes Lagrange's prayer, printed in Montagnes's biography, to be able to defend truth at its core rather than engage in intramural quibbles: "'O, very pure Mary,' Brother Marie-Joseph prayed, 'teach me to combat heresies, not Catholics'" (Montagnes, *Story of Father Marie-Joseph Lagrange*, 17).

32. Quoted in Montagnes, *Story of Father Marie-Joseph Lagrange*, 29.

as a mere apologist nor as a pure historian. Anticipating what would receive magisterial formulation in *Divino afflante Spiritu* and *Dei Verbum* (both published after his death), Lagrange took up historical studies because of his own thick understanding of divine revelation *in* history in God's inspiration of Scripture and preservation of the church. As he explains in the lectures that became his *Historical Criticism and the Old Testament*, God's transcendent revelation is given and promulgated through human communication, and the historically conditioned aspects of such human communication and authorship (such as language, genre conventions, memory, etc.) are therefore components of divine revelation.[33]

As Robinson summarizes, emphasis on the human author was "Lagrange's major hermeneutical contribution." Yet this was not intended to reduce Scripture's import only to the human plane or reduce all interpretation to history: "The author for Lagrange was the inspired instrument by which revelation was conveyed to the Church. The emphasis fell on what the author intended to say, in which could be found the inspired testimony to divine revelation."[34] Père Lagrange's preoccupation with the historical and literal in exegesis was hardly exclusive of "spiritual" interpretation. He writes, "Once a man accepts the Scriptures as inspired, he must grant that they contain more than the obvious and purely literal sense," but what he refers to as *supraliteral* significance.[35] Like Aquinas and others, he insisted that spiritual interpretations and applications have to be grounded in the literal sense and guided by the rule of faith and the biblical canon. As he explained when proposing the series Études bibliques, he did not envision technical commentary as replacing further theological interpretation and application. And he himself engaged in writing that was self-consciously philosophical, such as his refutations of German Lutheran systems of thought on the one hand and of Loisy on the other.[36] Even so, he saw his own competency and

33. See Marie-Joseph Lagrange, OP, *Historical Criticism and the Old Testament*, trans. Edward Myers (London: Catholic Truth Society, 1905). Note also the discussion in Joseph Chaine, "The Old Testament – Semitism," in *Père Lagrange and the Scriptures*, trans. Richard T. A. Murphy, OP (Milwaukee: Bruce, 1946), 11–53, esp. 11–22.

34. Robinson, *Roman Catholic Exegesis*, 22.

35. Quoted in Braun, *Work of Père Lagrange*, 59. See Marie-Joseph Lagrange, OP, "Bulletin: L'interprétation de la Sainte Écriture par l'Église," *RB* 9, no. 1 (1900): 135–42. See further Raymond E. Brown, SS, "Père Lagrange and the *Sensus Plenior*," *CBQ* 17, no. 3 (1955): 451–55; and Brown's rejoinder to an objector, John P. Weisengoff, in Raymond E. Brown, SS, "Counterreply," *CBQ* 18, no. 1 (1956): 47–53.

36. Marie-Joseph Lagrange, OP, *Le sens du christianisme d'après l'exégèse allemande*,

the needs of the church dictating that his gifts be focused on understanding the biblical "letter," its world, and its history. Matters such as history, background, and literary and textual commentary were "the chief preoccupation of non-Catholics and basic to almost all of the problems raised in our days," and those with special training had a duty to attend to these problems for the good of the church.[37] Here Lagrange pointed to the need for collaboration in the task of published academic interpretation so that he could focus on laying a foundation on which others might build.[38]

Indeed, Père Lagrange's life betrays a deep theological and devotional sensibility that was nourished by regular prayer and liturgy from which his studies were never divorced. His biographer and student F.-M. Braun writes that throughout his life "there runs, like a thread of gold, an ardent desire to serve the Church and the good of souls by a selfless defense of revealed truth."[39] And later in the same work: "The spirit which emanated from his strong personality manifested itself in his daily life. It was a spirit of service toward the Church, of devotion for the good of souls, of serene piety sustained by the monastic office, and of persistence in work."[40] He saw his own work of defending and expounding Scripture, even in the particular academic forms that it took, as a needed contribution for the "good of souls."[41] If Scripture needed to be brought out from the hallowed confines of ecclesial traditions and endure scrutiny from skeptics in the academy, this was consistent with and necessitated by the Bible's sacramental character, which Lagrange compared to the Eucharist. "This 'holy thing' [Scripture] is *a light for souls*, and I must make it shine in them, even if this means that it must go forth from the sanctuary."[42]

Lagrange had no interest in bracketing faith from his work, for himself or

EBib (Paris: Gabalda, 1918); Marie-Joseph Lagrange, OP, *Monsieur Loisy et le modernisme: A propos des "Mémoires"* (Paris: Éditions du Cerf, 1932).

37. Quoted in Braun, *Work of Père Lagrange*, 27. See Marie-Joseph Lagrange, OP, "Projet d'un commentaire complet de l'Écriture Sainte," *RB* 9, no. 3 (1900): 414–23.

38. "Strictly dogmatic theology may take little interest in this. . . . It may appear that what is principal is being sacrificed to what is secondary. . . . All very true, but as there are different tasks in God's house, and as a division of labor is of prime necessity if overwork and confusion are to be avoided, a man should be permitted to apply himself, when necessary, to the humblest of needs, and to delimit his efforts" (quoted in Braun, *Work of Père Lagrange*, 27).

39. Braun, *Work of Père Lagrange*, 4.

40. Braun, *Work of Père Lagrange*, 16.

41. Lagrange, "Avant-propos," 1–2.

42. Lagrange, "Avant-propos," 2 (as quoted in Braun, *Work of Père Lagrange*, 126).

for his students: "The study of holy scripture without a great spirit of faith is very dangerous, as proven by numerous apostasies, and I do not want to work in order to arrive at that sort of result for myself and for others."[43] Further, in his view, such faith was inseparable from the Catholic Church. And this brings us to another important aspect of Lagrange as a figurehead of modern Catholic biblical scholarship: his spirit of hope and his long-suffering obedience to the ecclesial hierarchy. Lagrange hardly escaped popular detraction for his adoption of historical-critical methods, and he was often hit by the rhetorical missiles aimed at Loisy. The *Revue biblique* was forbidden in some circles, and Lagrange's own views of the Pentateuch's composition—though he thought it helpful to faith in light of biblical data—occasioned suspicion and reprimand from the magisterium.[44] Naturally, Lagrange complained at various points that there would be no progress in the defense or understanding of the Bible without academic freedom. Yet he knew no service to the truth apart from obedience to those he believed God had entrusted with the care of his and others' souls. He protested to the head of the Dominicans that "a strong, armed, powerful Catholic exegesis . . . seems impossible to me without a certain freedom of discussion that would allow us to put the best arms of our enemies to use in the service of faith." But he insisted in the same missive: "I possess a blind faith in obedience. . . . If the time has not yet come, I will wait, and it will only be time for me when I have the full consent of my superiors."[45] Patiently he obeyed, at points offering to cease teaching or hand over his life's work, the École, and he encouraged colleagues and students as well in the same spirit of submission. "To submit and then to start all over again in the same vein would be to imitate Loisy," he wrote.[46] He was allowed, with some restrictions, to continue and found some solace in turning from the Old Testament to less controversial work on the New. But a sketch of his life is lined with the collateral damage he endured as a soldier in the battles over Scripture.

Lagrange's spirit of obedience demonstrated a clear difference between him and other dissident critics, and it made perhaps as great an impact as

43. Quoted in Montagnes, *Story of Father Marie-Joseph Lagrange*, 25. Note also Montagnes's own summary: "Father Lagrange does not put faith in parentheses; he does not practice a secularized reading of the Bible." Lagrange, rather, practiced and taught "a *believing* reading" (Montagnes, 39).

44. See Montagnes, *Story of Father Marie-Joseph Lagrange*, 53–115.

45. This letter of April 11, 1897, is printed in Montagnes, *Story of Father Marie-Joseph Lagrange*, 57.

46. Quoted in Montagnes, *Story of Father Marie-Joseph Lagrange*, 107.

his arguments and apologies for his methods. He was never excommunicated, nor were his books placed on the infamous *Index*.[47] The *Revue* and the École biblique endured. When he died on March 10, 1938, a "spiritual testament" was found written for this occasion in his desk. It reads, in part, as follows:

> I declare before God that it is my intention to die in the Holy Catholic Church to which I have always belonged with my whole heart and soul since the day of my baptism, and to die there faithful to my vows of poverty, chastity, and obedience, in the Order of St. Dominic. . . . I declare also most expressly that I submit to the judgment of the Apostolic See all that I have written. I believe that I can add that I have always had the intention, in all my studies, of contributing to the good, and by that I mean: to the reign of Jesus Christ, to the honor of the Church, to the good of souls.[48]

Père Lagrange embodied his own proposal of "using the science of criticism without losing sight of the authority of the Church."[49] And he did not fail in his life's work, not in his own generation, nor in the generations affected by his students, nor in the worldwide and posthumous effects of his teaching, nor in the example of his piety *in*—and not despite—his work as a rigorous and embattled exegete. As we write this, the cause of beatification of Servant of God Marie-Joseph Lagrange is open.

Looking Back, Looking Forward: Lagrange and Beyond

Lagrange blazed a trail on which modern Catholic exegetes progress toward whatever futures God's providence and our own efforts lead. He is also a figure in whom one sees united the tensions of inquiry and obedience, of history and theology, and of ministry and scholarship. Those looking to the future can see in him not merely a founder but an icon of a love for serious study of God's word always carried out within the church and for the good of souls.

47. Some of Lagrange's work was declared unsuitable for seminarians, but only vaguely. See Braun, *Work of Père Lagrange*, 92–94.

48. In Braun, *Work of Père Lagrange*, 127.

49. Lagrange, *Historical Criticism and the Old Testament*, 37.

As conversation about Catholic biblical interpretation looks ahead, there is much to be learned and much that can be considered through the icon of this figure from the past. His own biography is instructive and inspiring, and much is to be learned by revisiting—in the context of today's debates and advances—his own contributions and viewpoints on matters of history, theology, and exegesis. But his spirit of inquiry and discovery would hardly restrict our future to matters he himself dealt with in the past. Lagrange's call for interpretation that serves the good of souls and attends to developments in both science and theology likewise inspires and embraces interpretive considerations that he, pioneering though he was in his own day, did not countenance.

In the pages that follow, readers will find Catholics reflecting with and beyond Lagrange on the nature of Catholic interpretation and on its future expressions. The first essays set the stage for the others, as they address the sweep of Catholic magisterial teaching on Scripture and major conflicts and trends in recent history, particularly those by Donald P. Senior, CP, and Brant Pitre. Those that follow treat Lagrange and his legacy more directly. Laurie Brink, OP, considers the unity of study and prayer in Lagrange's Dominican life and the shared task of interpretation for the good of souls by the global people of God. Isaac Morales, OP, considers Lagrange's use and critique of philosophical principles in comparison with the more recent work of Joseph Ratzinger/Benedict XVI. Next follows Mark Giszczak's biographical reflection on Lagrange's struggles and the fate of his Genesis commentary, which considers the nature and some of the difficulties particular to Old Testament scholarship in the church. Robert Miller, OFS, engages in a comparative exercise in the spirit of and beyond Lagrange, considering African Traditional Religions as a useful heuristic for understanding Israelite monotheism and for engaging in interreligious dialogue. Next, and still related to Old Testament studies, Nina Heereman offers an essay in historically thick and canonically fruitful biblical theology. The final contributions center on the New Testament and hermeneutical perspectives. Kelly Anderson brings literary and liturgical-theological skill to offer a "eucharistic hermeneutics" of the Gospel of Mark. Michael Barber brings Lagrange and magisterial teaching about the human authorship of Scripture into dialogue with modern memory research and the historical Jesus. Anthony Giambrone, OP, likewise considers a Catholic perspective on the historical Jesus through the lens of Lagrange's interaction with a literary *Life of Jesus* by Mauriac. The next two essays press into hermeneutics for the good of created souls: J. L. Manzo surveys the history and state of Catholic interpretation especially in Latino/a postcolonial modes, and Kathleen P. Rushton, RSM, argues for interpretation that attends to the "cry of the earth and the cry of the poor." The final two essays return to a topic central not only to Lagrange's work but also to the development of Catholic thinking about the nature of Scripture and its interpretation: the mediation of the divine word through the inspired text. Luke Timothy Johnson asks what it means to read and affirm Scripture as God's word among the faithful, and James Prothro considers the task of textual criticism in light of the inspiration of Scripture.

Readers will not find represented here every issue that touches on Lagrange's work and biography, much less every issue or perspective that should be addressed as one looks to the next century. There are too many, and even to attempt such a comprehensive project would be erroneous twice over: feigning comprehensiveness and stifling the many other voices—exegetical and theological, professional and lay—who must determine the future of Catholic biblical interpretation. "The future is not one to be charted by any one person or any single committee."[50] What one will find in this book is a collection of voices and views that pay tribute to a founding figure of the past while looking squarely ahead, a group of scholars who, amid differences, share a Catholic identity and a vision for interpretation that serves the good of souls.

In Memoriam: Donald P. Senior, CP, and Robert D. Miller II, OFS

One final note is in order here. The progress of time from present to future always brings with it meetings and partings. Since we have been at work on the contents of this volume, the guild of Catholic scholarship has seen the parting of many of its company from this life for the next. Close and dear to this project, two souls now faithfully departed are Fr. Donald P. Senior, CP, and Robert D. Miller II, OFS.

Father Don Senior was an enthusiastic correspondent and participant in this project from its beginning, when he presented his essay "A View from the Top," surveying magisterial teachings on the Bible and its interpretation. Before finishing expansions he had hoped to make on that essay for the published volume, he succumbed to illness and died on November 8, 2022, at the age of eighty-two. He brought a fatherly and caring spirit of love and service to all that he did. Ordained to the priesthood in 1967 as a Passionist, he earned a licentiate and then a doctorate in New Testament

50. Johnson and Kurz, *Future of Catholic Biblical Scholarship*, 33.

studies from KU Leuven in 1972. He taught for fifty years at the Catholic Theological Union in Chicago, serving for twenty-three of those years as its president. He authored several academic works aimed at scholars and students, wrote commentaries and introductions to the Gospel of Matthew and Jesus studies, and was an editor of and contributor to *The Jerome Biblical Commentary for the Twenty-First Century*.[51] He also wrote books aimed at a nonprofessional readership and edited study Bibles for popular use.[52] And he penned a monumental biography of another founding figure in modern Catholic biblical studies, *Raymond E. Brown and the Catholic Biblical Renewal*.[53] His influence will live on through his prayers, his writings, and especially the students and friends whom he so charitably encouraged and mentored throughout his career.

A year after Father Senior's passing came that of Robert Miller, another major figure in American Catholic biblical studies. Bob earned an MA and PhD in biblical and Near Eastern studies at the University of Michigan (PhD, 1998). He taught at West Virginia University, Mount St. Mary's Seminary in Maryland, and then The Catholic University of America from 2008 until he lost his battle with cancer at the age of fifty-seven on November 22, 2023. A secular Franciscan, Bob was a devoted husband and father and a mentor of many students. Bob's excellence in teaching matched his impressive range as a polymath. He taught and published on numerous topics related to the Old Testament and theology, from Israelite history to oral tradition, from royal treaties and covenants to mythical traditions and theological imagination, ranging across corpora from Judges to the Song of Songs and across disciplines from biblical studies and archaeology to comparative religion.[54] His

51. Donald Senior, CP, *The Gospel of Matthew*, Interpreting Biblical Texts (Nashville: Abingdon, 1997); Donald Senior, CP, *Matthew*, ANTC (Nashville: Abingdon, 1998); Donald Senior, CP, *Jesus: A Gospel Portrait*, rev. ed. (New York: Paulist, 1992).

52. For example, see Donald Senior, CP, *The Landscape of the Gospels: A Deeper Meaning* (New York: Paulist, 2020); Donald Senior, CP, John J. Collins, and Mary Ann Getty, eds., *The Catholic Study Bible*, 3rd ed. (New York: Oxford University Press, 2016).

53. Donald Senior, CP, *Raymond E. Brown and the Catholic Biblical Renewal* (New York: Paulist, 2018).

54. E.g., Robert D. Miller II, OFS, *Chieftains of the Highland Clans: A History of Israel in the 12th and 11th Centuries B. C.* (Grand Rapids: Eerdmans, 2005); Robert D. Miller II, OFS, ed., *Between Israelite Religion and Biblical Theology: Essays on Archaeology, History, and Hermeneutics*, CBET 80 (Leuven: Peeters, 2016); Robert D. Miller II, OFS, *The Dragon, the Mountain, and the Nations: An Old Testament Myth, Its Origins and Afterlives*, EANEC 6 (Winona Lake, IN: Eisenbrauns, 2018); Robert D. Miller II, OFS, *Oral Tradition in Ancient Israel*, Biblical Performance Criticism 4 (Eugene, OR: Cascade, 2011);

interest in the project of Catholic theological exegesis is evident particularly in his *Many Roads Lead Eastward: Overtures to Catholic Biblical Theology.*[55] Bob's capacious range and interest are reflected in his essay in this volume treating African Traditional Religion, Israelite religion, and interreligious dialogue today.

These men, like Lagrange, were moved by a love of God to study and interpret Scripture for the good of souls. They are dearly missed, but their influence on the present and future of Catholic biblical interpretation is keenly felt. We dedicate this book to them.

Robert D. Miller II, OFS, *Covenant and Grace in the Old Testament: Assyrian Propaganda and Israelite Faith*, PHSC 16 (Piscataway, NJ: Gorgias Press, 2012); Robert D. Miller II, OFS, *Finding Beauty in the Bible: An Aesthetic Commentary on the Song of Songs*, McMaster Biblical Studies Series (Eugene, OR: Pickwick, 2023).

55. Robert D. Miller II, OFS, *Many Roads Lead Eastward: Overtures to Catholic Biblical Theology* (Eugene, OR: Cascade, 2016).

Biblical Interpretation and the Community of Faith

A View from the Top

Donald P. Senior, CP

Père Marie-Joseph Lagrange, OP, stood in the nexus between critical biblical scholarship and the expectations of the community of faith. This essay traces the evolution and significance of official Roman Catholic teaching on the role of the exegete in the life of the church from Pius XII's *Divino afflante Spiritu* to Vatican II's *Dei Verbum*, Benedict XVI's *Verbum Domini*, and Francis's *Evangelii gaudium*.

Over the past few years, I have had the occasion to trace the evolution of official Catholic responses to the use of historical-critical methods in biblical interpretation that emerged particularly in the late nineteenth century.[1] I note that certain key Catholic biblical scholars had a pivotal role in enabling the church to move from a primarily defensive posture to a nuanced acceptance. Through their unimpeachable loyalty to the church and its magisterium, these scholars were able to counter the prevailing view that the use of historical-critical methodology in interpreting the Scriptures was inherently rationalistic and reductionist and, therefore, a danger to Catholic biblical interpretation and the community of faith.

1. See Donald Senior, CP, *Raymond E. Brown and the Catholic Biblical Renewal* (New York: Paulist, 2018); Donald Senior, CP, "Interpreting the Scriptures – the Church and the Modern Catholic Biblical Renewal," in *The Jerome Biblical Commentary for the Twenty-First Century*, 3rd ed., ed. John J. Collins et al. (London: T&T Clark, 2022), 1923–49.

Editors' note: Father Senior presented this essay orally at the online conference from which this book was born in 2022. He had intended to expand this overview for printed publication but succumbed to illness and departed this life before having the opportunity to do so. We are grateful to be able to print it here in an essentially unaltered form as one of his last writings. Though brief, this chapter provides an overview into which fit the stories and further details of the subsequent essays, where the events and documents mentioned here receive further elaboration.

From Leo XIII to Pius X

Père Lagrange's work is an evident example of a faithful Catholic appropriation of historical methods in the critical period from Leo XIII's *Providentissimus Deus,* which amid cautions acknowledged some validity to historical inquiry into the Scriptures, to the decrees of the early Pontifical Biblical Commission, which was founded under Leo XIII but took on more of a monitoring function under Pius X's more stringent opposition, as expressed in his decree *Lamentabili sane exitu* (1907) and his encyclical *Pascendi dominici gregis* (1907). This challenging period coincided with the founding of the École biblique and subsequently its journal, *Revue biblique.* During this period, Lagrange came under severe attack, but he remained a consultor on the Biblical Commission, and for a time the *Revue biblique* was used as the official organ of the Commission. He was not permitted to publish his commentary on Genesis, and there were strong attacks on the École as a supposed hotbed of radical historical inquiry. Yet despite this opposition and the suffering it caused Lagrange, he maintained loyal ties with Roman authorities and, importantly, with his Dominican religious community, which provided shelter.

Lagrange's loyalty to the magisterium and his deft diplomacy with Roman authorities stood in contrast to the situation of his contemporary Alfred Loisy, who paid less attention to the concerns of church authority and found himself isolated and ultimately excommunicated.

From Pius X to Pius XII

The chill imposed on Catholic biblical scholarship in Lagrange's era dissipated with the groundbreaking 1943 encyclical of Pius XII, *Divino afflante Spiritu.* Even though World War II was raging at the time, Pius, not unlike Leo XIII, was a man of strong intellect and wide experience. He was personally aware of advances in biblical archaeology and linguistics and sensed their impact on biblical interpretation. And here again the influence of prominent Catholic biblical scholars played a key role. Augustin Bea, SJ, became both the rector of the Pontifical Biblical Institute (which had been founded at the time of Pius X and played something of a rival role with the École) and, at the same time, the personal confessor and confidant of the pope. Simultaneously, the Belgian scholar Jacques-Marie Vosté, OP, was the secretary of the Pontifical Biblical Commission. Both men were Roman insiders and respected scholars and were viewed as thoroughly loyal to the church and its magisterium. There is no question that their combined influence—and particularly that of Bea—made it possible for historical-critical methodology to break through into accepted Catholic biblical scholarship.

The impact of *Divino afflante Spiritu* would ultimately not only unleash a popular biblical movement that prepared the way for Vatican II; it would also encourage a whole generation of Catholic scholars (at this time, primarily priests and religious men) to take up biblical studies. This was particularly true for the church in the United States, where many began graduate work in Scripture, even at non-Catholic or secular universities. The chill on historical inquiry at the time of Pius X had a direct impact on the American scene. A particularly prominent case was that of the Dutch scholar Henri Poels, a professor of exegesis at Catholic University of America, who was severely—and unfairly—censored, leaving an impact on future generations there. This negative atmosphere affecting American Catholic biblical scholarship was lightened considerably—but not entirely—with the advent of Pius XII's Magna Carta encyclical calling for Catholics to engage in serious study of the Bible by means of archaeology, philology, history, and literary criticism.

From *Dei Verbum* to *Verbum Domini*

In many ways, the "triumph" of historical-critical methodology as an integral part of Catholic biblical scholarship took shape in the period between the Second Vatican Council, with its important constitution on divine revelation, *Dei Verbum* (1965), and Benedict XVI's post-synodal exhortation *Verbum Domini* (2010). Even though on the eve of the Council there were still skirmishes between some Roman authorities and some Catholic biblical scholars (Stanislaus Lyonnet, SJ, and Maximilian Zerwick, SJ, of the Biblical Institute were both attacked), the preparation for and enactment of the Second Vatican Council carried the day. A surge of Catholic biblical scholars served as *periti* for the Council fathers, and strong biblical motifs were woven into most of the Council's documents. The negative reaction to the more rigid preparatory schema on divine revelation and Pope John XXIII's intervention led to a mature dogmatic constitution, *Dei Verbum*, that forthrightly endorsed the proper use of the historical-critical method in Catholic biblical interpretation.

This absorption of historical inquiry continued into the postconciliar era, particularly through the statements of the Pontifical Biblical Commission, which Paul VI transformed into a consultative body composed of twenty international biblical scholars to advise the Office for the Doctrine of the Faith and, through this Congregation, to advise the pope himself on matters of biblical interpretation. The Commission had already exerted such profound influence through its document *Sancta Mater Ecclesia* ("Instruction on the Historical Truth of the Gospels," 1964), setting forth a historical vision for the reliability and interpretation of Gospel tradition, which was referenced in the constitution *Dei Verbum* itself. Later, in 1993, the Commission released a much fuller and longer document on the nature and tools of the interpretation of all the Scriptures entitled *The Interpretation of the Bible in the Church.*

American Catholic biblical scholars such as Raymond Brown, SS, Joseph Fitzmyer, SJ, Roland Murphy, OCarm, and others were recognized not only by church authorities but by their Protestant and Jewish peers. This same post–Vatican II period also saw an explosion of popular use of the Bible in religious education, liturgy, and spirituality.

A New Moment

The "triumph" of historical-critical methodology has been tempered in important ways in more recent years, both in the Catholic community and more broadly. While recognizing the validity and importance of historical methodology, many church leaders and biblical interpreters began to question the adequacy of the historical approach and the need for other methodologies to both complement and move beyond historical inquiry. This new phase was triggered in part by advances in the hermeneutics of textual interpretation and also by pastoral concerns. Some purely historical-critical interpretations could lead to very narrow results, focusing on minutiae or treating the Bible as an interesting historical and religious artifact at the expense of any significance or meaning of the biblical text for contemporary Christian life. Some such studies were used to cast doubt on current Catholic tradition and practice by appearing to set it in contrast to the original historical context of Scripture. What was the contribution of historical methods for the community of faith?

Here again, the role of Catholic scholars who were loyal to the church's teaching authority and sensitive to the meaning of Scripture for the community of the faith was key. A famous example was the so-called debate between then Cardinal Joseph Ratzinger and Fr. Raymond E. Brown at the theology conference following Ratzinger's Erasmus Lecture in 1988. Ratzinger warned of the limits and even the deviant qualities of historical methodology exercised apart from the community of faith. Brown emphasized the positive results of historical approaches for church reform and renewal. At that same conference, Ratzinger famously refused to portray Brown as anything but a loyal and effective Catholic scholar—a position he would maintain. Brown, for his part, considered himself a scholar at the service of the church and, in the spirit of Lagrange, maintained close ties with church authorities in the United States and in Rome (he served two different stints on the Biblical Commission). There is no doubt his writings and his evident Catholic sensibilities contributed to the post–Vatican II biblical renewal in the United States.

A final chapter might be the 2010 publication of the post-synodal exhortation of Pope Benedict XVI, *Verbum Domini*, which captures much of the spirit of official Catholic biblical interpretation. That exhortation strongly endorses historical-critical inquiry as foundational and, with equal strength, refutes fundamentalism. It emphasizes the need to supplement historical interpretation with other methodologies, stresses the proper place of the Scriptures in the church rather than simply in the academy, and affirms the responsibility of the Catholic interpreter of Scripture to be at the service of the community of faith and in harmony with Catholic teaching. A constant reference point for grounding the interpretation of Scripture in history is the comparison to the incarnation itself: just as Jesus, the incarnate Word, was both divine and human, so also the Scriptures, while rooted in a divine origin, are at the same time fully human writings and thus subject to both historical and literary analysis.

A coda on all this is found in the writings of Pope Francis, especially in his reflections on homiletical preparation in his 2013 exhortation *Evangelii gaudium*, and exemplified in the strong and pervasive use of Scripture in virtually all his encyclicals and writings.

It is inconceivable that the Catholic Church would ever reject the use of historical-critical methodology in biblical interpretation. A case can be made that such a position was arrived at not simply on the basis of rational inquiry and the accumulation of academic wisdom but also because key Catholic biblical scholars, in their writings and in their comportment, demonstrated the validity of a historical approach and its compatibility and coherence with a Catholic interpretation of Scripture.

Dei Verbum, Historical Criticism, and Theological Exegesis

The Future of Catholic Interpretation

BRANT PITRE

Over a hundred years have passed since the great Dominican biblical scholar Marie-Joseph Lagrange, OP, penned his classic and controversial book *Historical Criticism and the Old Testament*.[1] In it, Père Lagrange set out to demonstrate both that there is a pressing "need of historical criticism, particularly as applied to the study of the Old Testament" and that "no Catholic exegetical scholar can claim to withdraw himself from the dogmatical judgement of the Church."[2] In other words, Lagrange set forth a vision of Catholic exegesis that embodied what he referred to as "the twofold spirit" of "respect for dogma" and "regard for sound conscientious work."[3] Regarding this twofold approach, Lagrange triumphantly (but perhaps somewhat prematurely) declared: "All Catholics hold that such a combination is possible: the future will show that it has been realized."[4] As is well known, Lagrange's little book set off a firestorm of criticism, which continued unabated throughout the whole of his scholarly and ecclesial life.[5] Indeed, even though more than a century has passed since the publication of *Historical Criticism*

1. Marie-Joseph Lagrange, OP, *Historical Criticism and the Old Testament*, trans. Edward Myers (London: Catholic Truth Society, 1905). Originally published as *La méthode historique, surtout à propos de l'Ancien Testament* (Paris: Lecoffre, 1903).

2. Lagrange, *Historical Criticism and the Old Testament*, 7, 16.

3. Lagrange, *Historical Criticism and the Old Testament*, 17.

4. Lagrange, *Historical Criticism and the Old Testament*, 17.

5. For biographical accounts of the trials Père Lagrange faced as the result of his historical-critical work, see Bernard Montagnes, OP, *The Story of Father Marie-Joseph Lagrange: Founder of Modern Catholic Bible Study*, trans. Benedict Viviano, OP (New York: Paulist, 2006), 81–130; F.-M. Braun, OP, *The Work of Père Lagrange*, ed. and trans. Richard T. A. Murphy, OP (Milwaukee: Bruce, 1963), 66–100.

and the Old Testament, the historical-critical method continues to be the subject of widespread and often intense debate.

On the one hand, various aspects of historical criticism, if not the entire method, have been seriously called into question by prominent Catholic scholars. For example, in 2002, in *The Future of Catholic Biblical Scholarship*, Luke Timothy Johnson provocatively described "the historical-critical method" as "bankrupt"—especially in "its incapacity to feed the life of faith in a positive fashion."[6] Although Johnson has qualified his position somewhat in more recent publications, his initial critique of the historical-critical method set off something of its own firestorm of discussion and controversy.[7]

In response to such critiques, equally prominent Catholic scholars have published staunch defenses of the historical-critical method. For example, in 2008, Joseph Fitzmyer published a volume subtitled *In Defense of the Historical-Critical Method*.[8] The fact that a scholar of Fitzmyer's stature felt the need to publish *any* defense of historical criticism after a lifetime of engaging in historical-critical work shows that the controversy is far from

6. Luke Timothy Johnson and William S. Kurz, SJ, *The Future of Catholic Biblical Scholarship: A Constructive Conversation* (Grand Rapids: Eerdmans, 2002), 14–15. Here, Johnson is following the earlier description of historical criticism as "bankrupt" by Walter Wink, *The Bible in Human Transformation: Toward a New Paradigm for Biblical Study* (Philadelphia: Fortress, 1973).

7. See the response of Benedict Thomas Viviano, OP, in his *Catholic Hermeneutics Today: Critical Essays* (Eugene, OR: Cascade, 2014), 1–13. More recently, Johnson has drawn a distinction between the "historical method" (which he deems "entirely appropriate" for recognizing the "historical dimension" of the biblical texts) and "the historical model" (which he critiques as "an overarching model for understanding the NT"). Luke Timothy Johnson, *The Writings of the New Testament: An Interpretation*, 3rd ed. (Minneapolis: Fortress, 2010), 6–7. Johnson's commitment to the historical method as he understands it is on full display in his prominent contributions to the prestigious Anchor Bible Commentary (now known as the Anchor Yale Bible Commentary) series. See, e.g., Luke Timothy Johnson, *The Letter of James*, AB 37A (New York: Doubleday, 1995); Luke Timothy Johnson, *The First and Second Letters to Timothy*, AB 35A (New York: Doubleday, 2001). Notably, Johnson's critique is much more nuanced and much less harsh than that levied by some Catholic theologians, such as René Laurentin, who referred to the historical-critical method as "the excrement of historical research." See René Laurentin, *Les évangiles de l'enfance du Christ: Vérité de Nöel au-déla des mythes; Exégèse et sémiotique, historicité et théologie*, 2nd ed. (Paris: Desclée, 1983), 439. I owe this quotation to Robert D. Miller II, OFS, *Many Roads Lead Eastward: Overtures to Catholic Biblical Theology* (Eugene, OR: Cascade, 2016), 12.

8. Joseph A. Fitzmyer, SJ, *The Interpretation of Scripture: In Defense of the Historical-Critical Method* (New York: Paulist, 2008), 115.

over.[9] In his conclusion, Fitzmyer states that the goal of the book was to argue that "the future of biblical interpretation" can "*never dispense* with the historical-critical method."[10]

There is of course an enormous difference between bankruptcy (Johnson) and indispensability (Fitzmyer). In light of such competing views, what role *should* historical criticism play in the future of Catholic biblical interpretation? And what role (if any) should theology play in the task of exegesis? The goal of this essay is to answer these questions by revisiting the teaching of the Second Vatican Council's Dogmatic Constitution on Divine Revelation *Dei Verbum*, with a particular focus on its directives for exegetes in §12, and the reception of the Council's teaching in Pope Benedict XVI's Apostolic Exhortation *Verbum Domini* (2010).

This essay will consist of three basic points: (1) Although the first half of *Dei Verbum* §12 does not explicitly speak of "historical criticism" or "the historical-critical method," it does describe the basic *tools* of historical criticism—the study of language, literature, history, and culture—as essential for Catholic exegesis. (2) The second half of *Dei Verbum* §12 also calls biblical scholars to engage in exegesis that is properly theological by paying equal attention to the canon of Scripture, the tradition of the church, and the analogy of faith. (3) In *Verbum Domini*, Pope Benedict XVI interprets Vatican II as teaching *both* that "historical-critical exegesis" is "indispensable" *and* that Catholic exegetes must interpret Scripture in light of "three fundamental criteria": the canon of Scripture, the living tradition, and the analogy of faith.[11] However, the pope

9. For example, among many other publications, Fitzmyer almost single-handedly brought the prestigious Anchor Bible Commentary (now the Anchor Yale Bible Commentary) on the New Testament to fruition by authoring massive and authoritative historical-critical commentaries on some of the most important books in the New Testament. See Joseph A. Fitzmyer, SJ, *The Gospel according to Luke: A New Translation with Introduction and Commentary*, 2 vols., AB 28–28A (New York: Doubleday, 1981–1985); Joseph A. Fitzmyer, SJ, *Romans: A New Translation with Introduction and Commentary*, AB 33 (New York: Doubleday, 1993); Joseph A. Fitzmyer, SJ, *The Acts of the Apostles: A New Translation with Introduction and Commentary*, AB 31 (New York: Doubleday, 1998); Joseph A. Fitzmyer, SJ, *The Letter to Philemon: A New Translation with Introduction and Commentary*, AB 34C (New York: Doubleday, 2000); Joseph A. Fitzmyer, SJ, *First Corinthians: A New Translation with Introduction and Commentary*, AB 32 (New Haven: Yale University Press, 2008).

10. Fitzmyer, *Interpretation of Scripture*, 115 (emphasis added).

11. Benedict XVI, Post-Synodal Apostolic Exhortation *Verbum Domini* (Sept 30, 2010) §§32, 34. Hereafter, this source is cited as *VD* in the text.

suggests that though contemporary Catholic exegesis has done an excellent job of implementing the directives in the *first* half of *Dei Verbum* §12, it has not yet fully implemented the directives in the *second* half of *Dei Verbum* §12, and it must do so if it is to achieve what Benedict refers to as "theological exegesis" (*VD* §34).[12] According to *Verbum Domini*, only this kind of theological exegesis can do justice to the fully human and fully divine character of Scripture and thereby overcome the extremes of both rationalism and secularism on the one hand and fideism and fundamentalism on the other.

In short, what is needed is precisely the kind of twofold historical and theological approach to Catholic exegesis that was modeled by the pioneering work of Marie-Joseph Lagrange and which, I submit, was eventually enshrined in the teaching of *Dei Verbum*.[13] Only when both of these dimensions are combined can a fruitful way forward be charted for the future of Catholic biblical interpretation. In order to see this clearly, however, we need to go back to the text of the Second Vatican Council's Dogmatic Constitution on Divine Revelation and reread it carefully.

Historical-Critical Exegesis Is Indispensable

The first point that needs to be made is this: although *Dei Verbum* never explicitly utilizes the terms "historical criticism" or "the historical-critical method," it nevertheless clearly teaches that the basic tools of historical criticism are necessary for discovering the meaning of Scripture as set forth through its human authors. Here is the first half of *Dei Verbum* §12, with key phrases emphasized:

> Seeing that, in sacred scripture, God speaks through human beings in human fashion, it follows that *the interpreters of sacred scripture*, if they are to ascertain what God has wished to communicate to us, should carefully search out the meaning which the sacred writers really had in mind, that meaning which God had thought well to manifest through the medium of *their words*.

12. For fuller discussion, see the essays in Scott Carl, ed., *"Verbum Domini" and the Complementarity of Exegesis and Theology*, Catholic Theological Formation Series (Grand Rapids: Eerdmans, 2015).

13. Cf. Lagrange, *Historical Criticism and the Old Testament*, 17.

> In determining the intention of the sacred writers, *attention must be paid*, inter alia, *to literary genres*. The fact is that truth is differently presented and expressed in the various types of *historical writing*, in prophetical and poetical texts, and in other forms of *literary expression*. *Hence the exegete must look for that meaning which the sacred writers, in given situations* and granted *the circumstances of their time and culture*, intended to express and did in fact express, through the medium of *a contemporary literary form*. Rightly to understand what the sacred authors wanted to affirm in their work, due attention must be paid both to *the customary and characteristic patterns of perception, speech and narrative* which prevailed in their time, and to *the conventions which people then observed* in their dealings with one another.[14]

Notice here that this entire paragraph is directed specifically to "interpreters of sacred scripture" (*interpres Sacrae Scripturae*). The Council is giving directives to exegetes for how exegesis is to be done. With this in mind, one can single out at least four tools that Catholic interpreters must utilize in their attempts to discover the meanings intended by the human authors of Scripture:

1. **Language**: "their words"; "customary and characteristic patterns of . . . speech"
2. **Literature**: "literary genres"; "literary expression"; "contemporary literary form"
3. **History**: "historical writing"; "given situations"; "circumstances of their time"
4. **Culture**: "circumstances of . . . culture"; "conventions which people then observed" (*DV* §12).

Once again, although the words "historical criticism" are not utilized, these four areas of inquiry are precisely what modern Catholic historical critics have devoted an almost incalculable amount of effort to studying.[15]

14. Vatican Council II, Dogmatic Constitution *Dei Verbum* (November 18, 1965) §12. Hereafter, references to this source are cited as *DV* in the text. Translations of *Dei Verbum* in this essay are drawn from Austin Flannery, OP, ed., *Vatican Council II: The Basic Sixteen Documents*, rev. ed. (Northport, NY: Costello, 1996).

15. See Pontifical Biblical Commission, *The Interpretation of the Bible in the Church* (Rome: Libreria Editrice Vaticana, 1993) §I. A.1–4, for a detailed description of the historical-critical method and its various components. For recent monuments to the wealth

Other commentators on *Dei Verbum* have come to similar conclusions. For example, in the early and highly respected commentary on *Dei Verbum* coauthored by Joseph Ratzinger, Alois Grillmeier, and Béda Rigaux, Grillmeier interprets this section of *Dei Verbum* in just this way: "In this first part of the hermeneutical rules the Constitution recommends ways of establishing what the sacred writers intended to say—and hence ways of *critical historical research*."[16] Grillmeier then goes on to identify four key "ways" that are substantially identical with my fourfold summary above—(1) language, (2) literature, (3) history, and (4) culture.[17] More recently, Ronald Witherup sees in *Dei Verbum* §12 what he refers to as a "'qualified endorsement' of the historical-critical method, especially form and redaction criticism."[18] Along similar lines, Francis Martin interprets "the second paragraph [of *Dei Verbum* §12]" as a description of "the historical work of the exegete."[19] Finally, in his biography of the eminent American New Testament scholar Raymond E. Brown, Donald Senior writes, "The affirmations of *Dei Verbum* . . . were, in fact, a decisive confirmation of the acceptance of the historical-critical methodology of biblical exegesis by the official church."[20]

---

of linguistic, literary, historical, and cultural insights enshrined in twenty-first-century Catholic biblical scholarship, see especially John J. Collins et al., eds., *The Jerome Biblical Commentary for the Twenty-First Century*, 3rd ed. (London: T&T Clark, 2022); José Enrique Aguilar Chiu et al., eds., *The Paulist Biblical Commentary* (New York: Paulist, 2018).

16. Alois Grillmeier, "Chapter III, The Divine Inspiration and the Interpretation of Sacred Scripture," in *Commentary on the Documents of Vatican II*, ed. Herbert Vorgrimler, trans. William Glen-Doepel et al. (New York: Herder and Herder, 1968), 3:224–25 (emphasis added).

17. See Grillmeier, "Chapter III," 225: "1) '*inter alia*' the investigation of the literary forms in the various texts; 2) the establishing (a) of the particular situation (of the *determinata adiuncta*) in which the writer and his statement are placed; (b) the particular temporal and cultural conditions of this statement, which can be expressed in various literary forms; 3) the study of inherited or native ways of feeling and thinking (forms of thought), of language in the spirit of language, the various modes of narration; 4) attention to the forms of ordinary daily social intercourse."

18. Ronald D. Witherup, SS, *Scripture: Dei Verbum*, Rediscovering Vatican II (New York: Paulist, 2006), 62. Here, Witherup is following the work of Jerome Neyrey, SJ, "Interpretation of Scripture in the Life of the Church," in *Vatican II: The Unfinished Agenda; A Look to the Future*, ed. Lucien Richard, OMI, with Daniel Harrington, SJ, and John W. O'Malley, SJ (New York: Paulist, 1987), 33–46.

19. Francis Martin, "Revelation and Its Transmission," in *Vatican II: Renewal within Tradition*, ed. Matthew L. Lamb and Matthew Levering (Oxford: Oxford University Press, 2008), 68.

20. Donald Senior, CP, *Raymond E. Brown and the Catholic Biblical Renewal* (New York: Paulist, 2018), xxv.

Should there be any doubt that Vatican II was implicitly affirming the use of historical criticism by Catholic exegetes, it is important to note that the footnote at the end of the first paragraph in *Dei Verbum* §12 explicitly cites the section of Pope Pius XII's 1943 encyclical *Divino afflante Spiritu*—sometimes called "the Magna Carta" of biblical studies[21]—in which Pius XII directs the Catholic exegete not to neglect any insights from contemporary research, especially in three areas:

> Let the interpreter, then, with all care and without neglecting any light derived from recent research, endeavor to determine [1] the peculiar character and circumstances of the sacred writer, the age in which he lived, [2] the sources written or oral to which he had recourse, and [3] the forms of expression he employed. Thus can the exegete better understand who was the inspired author and what he wishes to express by his writing.[22]

There seems little reason to doubt that by each of these expressions, Pius XII is referring to *historical criticism* ("the peculiar character and circumstances of the sacred writer, the age in which he lived"), *source criticism* ("sources written or oral to which he had recourse"), and *literary or form criticism* ("the forms of expression he employed"). If this is correct, then the footnote in *Dei Verbum* is not accidental or incidental. Rather, it explicitly anchors the Second Vatican Council's directives in the great encyclical of Pius XII, who explicitly enjoined Catholic exegetes to "unite the greatest reverence for the sacred text with an exact observance of all the rules of criticism."[23]

In sum, according to the Second Vatican Council and the teaching of Pius XII on which the Council built, the use of historical criticism by Catholic exegetes is a requirement, not an option.

21. Raymond E. Brown, SS, and Thomas Aquinas Collins, OP, "Church Pronouncements," in *The New Jerome Biblical Commentary*, ed. Raymond E. Brown, SS, Joseph A. Fitzmyer, SJ, and Roland E. Murphy, OCarm (Englewood Cliffs, NJ: Prentice Hall, 1990), 1167.

22. Pius XII, Encyclical Letter *Divino afflante Spiritu* (September 30, 1943) §33. In Dean P. Béchard, SJ, ed. and trans., *The Scripture Documents: An Anthology of Official Catholic Teachings* (Collegeville, MN: Liturgical Press, 2002), 128. This is noted by Witherup, *Scripture: Dei Verbum*, 37.

23. Pius XII, *Divino afflante Spiritu* §19 (trans. Béchard, *Scripture Documents*, 123).

Theological Exegesis Is Equally Essential

With that said, the second key point that needs to be made is that *Dei Verbum*'s directives for exegetes do not stop at the door of historical criticism. Although it is often overlooked, Vatican II also taught that equal attention must be given to the divine authorship of Scripture and to what Alois Grillmeier refers to as "the principles of *theological* exegesis."[24] By this expression, Grillmeier refers to an approach to Scripture in which "the meaning of Scripture [is] to be investigated in the light of the whole, i.e., within the unity of all the books, but especially of the Old and New Testaments within each other, and further with the aid of tradition and the analogy of faith."[25] In this vein, here is the second half of *Dei Verbum* §12, once again with key phrases emphasized:

> But since sacred scripture *must be read and interpreted* in the light of the same Spirit through whom it was written, *no less attention must be devoted to the content and unity of the whole of scripture, the tradition of the whole church* and *the analogy of faith*, if we are to derive their *true meaning* from the sacred texts. *It is the task of exegetes to work, according to these rules,* towards a better understanding and explanation of the meaning of sacred scripture in order that their research may help the church to form a firmer judgment. (*DV* §12; Flannery's translation slightly adapted here)

Three aspects of this important passage need to be underscored.

First, notice that *Dei Verbum* uses the language of necessity to describe this kind of theological exegesis: "*must* be read and interpreted" and "*must* be devoted to" (*DV* §12; emphasis added). These are not just suggestions. According to Vatican II, it is necessary to read Scripture in light of its divine authorship and not merely its human authorship.

Second, and even more importantly, in addition to the study of human language, literature, history, and culture, "no less attention" must be given by interpreters to three other "rules" (*regulas*) of Catholic biblical interpretation, which can be summarized and identified as follows:

24. Grillmeier, "Chapter III," 225.

25. Grillmeier, "Chapter III," 225. It should be noted here that Grillmeier does not seem to use the expression "theological exegesis" in contrast to "critical historical work" but rather as a completion or perfection of it (see "Chapter III," 222).

1. **Canon of Scripture**: "the content and unity of the whole of scripture"
2. **Tradition**: "the tradition of the whole church"
3. **Magisterium**: "the analogy of faith" (*DV* §12)

Obviously, much could be said about each one of these three loci in Catholic theology.[26] For our purposes here, I would simply highlight that *Dei Verbum* §12 is once again drawing directly (although inexplicitly) on the so-called Magna Carta of biblical studies—Pius XII's 1943 encyclical *Divino afflante Spiritu*[27]—and that each of these three "rules" of interpretation is formulated with a distinctively *universal* emphasis. That is, according to Vatican II, Catholic interpreters must pay attention to "the *whole* of Scripture" (*totius Scripturae*) and "the tradition of the *whole* Church" (*totius ecclesiae traditionis*; *DV* §12; emphasis added).[28] Indeed, even the "analogy of faith" (*analogia fidei*) is implicitly universal in scope since Pius XII (and Leo XIII before him) used the expression to refer to the entirety of "Catholic doctrine, as authoritatively proposed by the Church."[29] In its exposition of *Dei Verbum* §12, the *Catechism of the Catholic Church* makes this universal emphasis explicit when it defines "the analogy of faith" as "the coherence of the truths of faith among themselves and within the whole plan of Revelation [*totum Revelationis propositum*]."[30] Notice here that Vatican II is proposing a distinctively *Catholic* (καθολικός) form of exegesis that always attempts, insofar as is humanly possible, to interpret any given biblical passage "according to"

26. See, e.g., Denis Farkasfalvy, OCist, *Inspiration and Interpretation: A Theological Introduction to Sacred Scripture* (Washington, DC: Catholic University of America Press, 2010); Francis A. Sullivan, SJ, *Magisterium: Teaching Authority in the Catholic Church* (New York: Paulist, 1983); Yves M.-J. Congar, OP, *Tradition and Traditions: A Historical and Theological Essay* (London: Macmillan, 1967).

27. Compare Pius XII, *Divino afflante Spiritu* §24: Biblical "commentators" should "no less diligently take into account explanations and declarations given by the teaching authority [Latin: *magisterium*] of the Church, as likewise the interpretation given by the holy Fathers, and even 'the analogy of faith'" (trans. in Béchard, *Scripture Documents*, 125).

28. Francis Martin rightly notes that the expression "the living tradition of the entire church" here "must refer to the fathers and liturgies of both East and West, as well as the living faith practice of the members of the Church" ("Revelation and Transmission," 68).

29. See Pius XII, *Divino afflante Spiritu* §24, quoting Leo XIII, Encyclical Letter *Providentissimus Deus* (November 18, 1893) §28: "In other passages, the analogy of faith should be followed, and Catholic doctrine, as authoritatively proposed by the Church" (trans. in Béchard, *Scripture Documents*, 48).

30. *CCC* §114. See also Martin, "Revelation and Transmission," 68, who points out that this "traditional phrase" refers to interpreting the Scripture "as deriving from and contributing to an understanding of the whole."

(κατά) "the whole" (ὅλος)—that is, the *whole* of Scripture (i.e., both Old and New Testaments), the *whole* of the living tradition (i.e., both East and West), and the *whole* of Catholic doctrine on faith and morals proposed for universal belief by Christians (i.e., ancient, medieval, and modern teachings of the living magisterium).[31] As Ronald Witherup, SS, rightly puts it, "Interpretation from a Catholic perspective always takes place in this broader context."[32]

Third and finally, but by no means least significantly, note well that *Dei Verbum* §12 does *not* say that it is the duty of dogmatic or systematic *theologians* to pay attention to these three rules of theological interpretation. Rather, the Dogmatic Constitution singles out *biblical scholars* in particular and teaches that it is the task of "exegetes" (*exegetarum*) to work according to these three "rules" by giving equal attention to Scripture, tradition, and the analogy of faith in the task of biblical interpretation.[33] In short, Catholic exegesis, while remaining thoroughly historical and critical, must be equally and explicitly theological.

Summarily, according to Vatican II, Catholic exegetes must not remain at the level of the human authors but must go beyond them to a properly theological mode of interpretation.

Verbum Domini, Vatican II, and Theological Exegesis

In support of these two main points regarding the teaching of Vatican II, it is important to note that the longest magisterial document on Scripture ever penned—Pope Benedict XVI's Apostolic Exhortation *Verbum Domini*—explicitly interprets *Dei Verbum* §12 as teaching *both* that historical-critical exegesis is "indispensable" *and* that Catholic exegetes must interpret Scripture in light of these "three criteria" of the canon, tradition, and the analogy of faith (*VD* §§34, 32).[34]

31. Cf. Grillmeier, "Chapter III," 226: "The *analogia fidei* is . . . nothing but the consciousness of the unity of the revelation of God in its *whole history* and in its development in the Church" (italics added).

32. Witherup, *Scripture: Dei Verbum*, 37.

33. See Grillmeier, "Chapter III," 226, for background on the development of this section of *Dei Verbum* regarding "the task of exegetes."

34. Here, the pope is quoting his own previous statements during the Synod. See Benedict XVI, "Intervention in the Fourteenth General Congregation of the Synod" (October 14, 2008), in *Insegnamenti* 4, no. 2 (2008): 492.

Regarding the necessity of historical-critical work on the Bible, the pope writes in *Verbum Domini*:

> Before all else, we need to acknowledge the benefits that *historical-critical exegesis* and other recently-developed methods of textual analysis have brought to the life of the Church. *For the Catholic understanding of sacred Scripture, attention to such methods is indispensable,* linked as it is to the realism of the Incarnation: "This necessity is a consequence of the Christian principle formulated in the Gospel of John 1:14: *Verbum caro factum est.* The historical fact is a constitutive dimension of the Christian faith. The history of salvation is not mythology, but a true history, and it should thus be studied with *the methods of serious historical research*". *The study of the Bible requires a knowledge of these methods of enquiry and their suitable application.* (*VD* §32; emphasis added)

Notice here that, unlike Vatican II, Pope Benedict explicitly refers to "historical-critical exegesis" (Latin: *exegesi historico-critica*) and describes attention to such methods as "indispensable" (*necessaria*). Here, the pope is drawing the language of indispensability directly from the Pontifical Biblical Commission's 1993 document, *The Interpretation of the Bible in the Church.*[35] This shift from an implicit affirmation of historical criticism in *Dei Verbum* to an explicit affirmation of its necessity in *Verbum Domini* represents, in my view, a significant development of Catholic teaching. Notice also that Benedict's rationale for the necessity of historical-critical exegesis is not just historical but also theological: it is rooted in "the realism of the incarnation" (*VD* §32). Because Christianity makes historical claims about foundational events like the incarnation and bodily resurrection of Jesus, it not only must not flee from history but "demands" that Scripture be studied with "the methods of serious historical research" (*VD* §32). It is hard to imagine a stronger magisterial affirmation of the necessity of historical-critical exegesis or a stronger refutation of any attempt to reject historical research in favor of an exclusively spiritual exegesis or a fideistic fundamentalism.[36]

35. See Pontifical Biblical Commission, *Interpretation of the Bible* §I.A: "*The historical-critical method* is *the indispensable method* for the scientific study of the meaning of ancient texts. Holy Scripture, inasmuch as it is the 'word of God in human language,' has been composed by human authors in all its various parts and in all the sources that lie behind them. Because of this, its proper *understanding not only admits the use of this method but actually requires it*" (in Béchard, *Scripture Documents*, 249; emphasis added).

36. For a fuller exposition of what follows here, see Brant Pitre, "*Verbum Domini* and Historical-Critical Exegesis," in Carl, *"Verbum Domini" and the Complementarity of Exegesis*

At the same time, Pope Benedict also insists that Vatican II itself taught that Catholic exegetes must go beyond historical criticism to a properly theological form of exegesis. In a section of *Verbum Domini* entitled "The Council's biblical hermeneutic: a directive to be appropriated," Pope Benedict writes:

> Against this background, one can better appreciate *the great principles of interpretation proper to Catholic exegesis* set forth by the Second Vatican Council, especially in the Dogmatic Constitution *Dei Verbum*. . . . On the one hand, the Council emphasizes the study of literary genres and historical context as basic elements for understanding the meaning intended by the sacred author. On the other hand, since Scripture must be interpreted in the same Spirit in which it was written, *the Dogmatic Constitution indicates three fundamental criteria* for an appreciation of the divine dimension of the Bible: 1) the text must be interpreted with attention to *the unity of the whole of Scripture*; nowadays this is called canonical exegesis; 2) account is be taken of the *living Tradition of the whole Church*; and, finally, 3) respect must be shown for *the analogy of faith*. "*Only where both methodological levels, the historical-critical and the theological, are respected*, can one speak of *a theological exegesis*, an exegesis worthy of this book." (*VD* §34; some emphasis added)[37]

Three aspects of this consequential passage are worth highlighting.

First, Pope Benedict is not speaking about the methods to be utilized in systematic or dogmatic theology but "the principles of interpretation" proper to "Catholic exegesis" (*exegesis catholicae*; *VD* §34). This is in direct continuity with the teaching of Vatican II, where the directives in *Dei Verbum* §12 are specifically identified as a task to be carried out by Catholic biblical scholars.

Second, Benedict describes (1) the whole of Scripture, (2) the living tradition of the whole church, and (3) the analogy of faith as "three fundamental criteria" or, more literally, "three fundamental methodological elements" (*tria elementa methodologica fundamentalia*) of Catholic biblical interpretation (*VD* §34). None of these three is dispensable or optional; they all play an essential role in the kind of scriptural interpretation Vatican II was calling Catholic exegetes to engage in.

---

and Theology, 26–40. For an important critique of the fundamentalist approach to Scripture, see *VD* §44 as well as the Pontifical Biblical Commission, *Interpretation of the Bible* §I. F.

37. Here, the pope is again quoting his own statements from the Synod. See Benedict XVI, "Intervention," 493.

Finally, and perhaps most significantly, Benedict describes this synthesis of historical-critical and theological interpretation as "theological exegesis" (*de exegesi theologica*) and insists that it is only this form of exegesis that is truly "worthy" of Sacred Scripture (*VD* §34). This is an intriguing expression, for it holds together both the human ("exegesis") and divine ("theological") aspects of biblical interpretation but puts the emphasis on exegesis. It is also the exact expression used many decades earlier by Joseph Ratzinger's co-commentator on *Dei Verbum*, Alois Grillmeier, to describe the kind of exegesis called for by Vatican II.[38]

One reason this formulation is so important is that a case can be made that although modern Catholic exegetes have expended an enormous amount of energy on the *first* half of *Dei Verbum* §12, we have not given adequate attention to the *second* half of *Dei Verbum* §12. For example, in the final official propositions of the world Synod on the Word of God in the Life and Mission of the Church in 2008, the bishops dedicated a remarkably long paragraph to both the benefits gained and challenges faced by contemporary Catholic exegesis. According to the Synod fathers:

> The positive fruits borne by the use of modern historical-critical research are undeniable; at the same time, however, it is necessary to look at the current state of exegetical studies with an attentive eye also to its difficulties. *While current academic exegesis, including Catholic exegesis, operates on a very high level with regard to historical-critical methodology, including its happiest and most recent integrations* (Pontifical Biblical Commission, "The Interpretation of the Bible in the Church"), *one cannot say the same regarding study of the theological dimension of the Biblical texts. Unfortunately, the theological level indicated by the three elements of* Dei Verbum *12 very often appears to be absent. . . .* The synod fathers, while they sincerely thank the many exegetes and theologians who have given, and who are still giving, an essential help in discovering the deep sense of the Scriptures, invite all to an increased commitment so that the theological level of Biblical interpretation can be reached with greater strength and clarity. In order to truly arrive at the deepened love for the Scriptures hoped for by the Council, the principles that *Dei Verbum* exhaustively and clearly indicated must be applied with greater care.[39]

38. Grillmeier, "Chapter III," 225.
39. Synod of Bishops, "The Word of God in the Life and Mission of the Church"

This is a remarkable statement, both for its balance in praising the fruits of historical-critical interpretation and for its frankness in recognizing the need to fully implement the exegetical directives of the Second Vatican Council. Significantly, in his Post-synodal Apostolic Exhortation, Benedict XVI took this particular proposition of the Synod bishops and made it his own when he wrote:

> While today's academic exegesis, including that of Catholic scholars, is highly competent in the field of historical-critical methodology and its latest developments, it must be said that *comparable attention needs to be paid to the theological dimension of the biblical texts*, so that they can be more deeply understood in accordance with *the three elements indicated by the Dogmatic Constitution* Dei Verbum. (*VD* §34)

Notice once again that Benedict is absolutely clear about the positive fruits of historical criticism in contemporary Catholic exegesis and the real gains that have been made in implementing the *first* half of *Dei Verbum* §12, which emphasizes the need to investigate the human authors' language, literature, history, and culture. At the same time, he is clearly at pains to emphasize the importance of balancing these fruits with equal attention to the *second* half of *Dei Verbum* §12 and the need to interpret biblical texts in the light of the whole canon of Scripture, the whole living tradition, and the analogy of faith. Indeed, by my count, in *Verbum Domini*, the pope explicitly refers to "the criteria set forth in number 12 of the Dogmatic Constitution *Dei Verbum*" a total of five times (*VD* §34 [twice], 38, 39, 47)! We have already looked at the first two above; here are the three other instances:

> *The criteria set forth in Number 12 of the Dogmatic Constitution Dei Verbum* thus become clearer: this progression cannot take place with regard to an individual literary fragment unless it is seen in relation to the whole of Scripture. (*VD* §38; emphasis added)

> In this way we can understand *the words of Number 12 of the Dogmatic Constitution Dei Verbum*, which point to the internal unity of the entire Bible as a decisive criterion for a correct hermeneutic of faith. (*VD* §39; emphasis added)

(October 28, 2008), Final Propositions §26. The full text is available at https://www.ncronline.org/news/synod-final-propositions-synod-bishops-bible.

> Care must be taken to ensure that the study of sacred Scripture is truly the soul of theology inasmuch as it is acknowledged as the word of God addressed to today's world, to the Church and to each of us personally. *It is important that the criteria indicated in Number 12 of the Dogmatic Constitution Dei Verbum* receive real attention and become the object of deeper study. (*VD* §47; emphasis added)

Particularly important in this regard is the third quotation, in which Benedict links the use of the three "criteria" of theological exegesis in *Dei Verbum* with the ability for Sacred Scripture to take its place as "the soul of theology," as was also called for by the Second Vatican Council (see *Dei Verbum* §24).[40] Clearly, this full implementation of the directives of the Second Vatican Council is a matter that Benedict sees as one of pressing urgency for the future of Catholic exegesis.

Should there be any doubt about this, it is worth noting that in the foreword to volume 2 of his *Jesus of Nazareth*, Benedict—writing in a non-magisterial mode as Joseph Ratzinger—makes the same point even more strongly when he speaks of "finally putting into practice the methodological principles formulated for exegesis by the Second Vatican Council (in *Dei Verbum* 12), *a task that unfortunately has scarcely been attempted thus far*."[41] This is a remarkable claim: according to Benedict, over forty years after the Second Vatican Council, its complete vision of Catholic exegesis has still "scarcely been attempted," even by Catholic exegetes.

If we turn to the reception of *Dei Verbum* among Catholic biblical scholars, we can find support for Benedict's claim as well as positive signs of development. On the one hand, among the first generation of postconciliar Catholic exegetes, it is striking to note that influential commentaries on *Dei Verbum* 12 often passed over the three criteria of theological exegesis as if they were not part of the Council's teaching.[42] For example, in the influential 1990 edition of *The New Jerome Biblical Commentary*, the teaching of *Dei Ver-*

40. Cf. Joseph A. Fitzmyer, SJ, *Scripture, the Soul of Theology* (New York: Paulist, 1994).

41. Joseph Ratzinger (Pope Benedict XVI), *Jesus of Nazareth, Part Two: Holy Week; From the Entrance into Jerusalem to the Resurrection*, trans. Philip J. Whitmore (San Francisco: Ignatius, 2010), xv (emphasis added).

42. I owe the language of "generations" of postconciliar Catholic biblical scholars to Luke Timothy Johnson, though I have modified it to take into account the impact of the Second Vatican Council. See Johnson and Kurz, *Future of Catholic Biblical Scholarship*, 3–34.

bum on the essential role of the canon of Scripture, the living tradition, and the analogy of faith receives no discussion whatsoever.[43] Along similar lines, in Fitzmyer's otherwise excellent essay "The Second Vatican Council and the Role of the Bible," he makes no mention of the three criteria of theological exegesis in *Dei Verbum* §12; he simply skips over them as if they were not part of the conciliar directives for Catholic exegetes.[44] Such silence reflects a major lacuna in the first generation of postconciliar Catholic exegesis, one that needs to be filled by giving equal balance to both halves of *Dei Verbum* §12, to both historical-critical and theological exegesis.[45]

On the other hand, contributions by the second generation of postconciliar Catholic exegetes seem to be filling this gap. For example, in a 2018 essay on scriptural interpretation in the massive *Paulist Biblical Commentary*, Witherup summarizes "the teaching of the constitution" *Dei Verbum* on "the threefold way in which Catholics read the Scriptures" as follows:

1) Be especially attentive "to the content and unity of the whole Scripture," interpreting in context.
2) Read the Scripture within "the living Tradition of the whole Church" and not simply on our own.
3) Be attentive to the analogy of faith, that is, the coherence of the truths of the faith.[46]

According to Witherup, "These three principles help keep biblical interpretation in a proper ecclesial context, assisting us to avoid overly simplistic and individualistic interpretations that, taken out of context, can distort Scripture."[47] Along similar lines, in *The Jerome Biblical Commentary for the*

43. See Brown and Collins, "Church Pronouncements," 1169.

44. Cf. Fitzmyer, *Interpretation of Scripture*, 8–9.

45. For a helpful critique of this lacuna in the reception of *Dei Verbum* in the work of Brown and Fitzmyer, see especially Gregory Vall, *Ecclesial Exegesis: A Synthesis of Ancient and Modern Approaches to Scripture*, Verbum Domini (Washington, DC: Catholic University of America Press, 2022), 74–119.

46. Ronald D. Witherup, SS, "The Bible in the Life of the Church," in Chiu et al., *Paulist Biblical Commentary*, 1617. See also Witherup, *Scripture: Dei Verbum*, 74, where he gives attention to the way in which "a Catholic approach to Scripture" is animated by the "three principles from the dogmatic constitution" regarding the "'content and unity' of all of Sacred Scripture," the "church's 'living Tradition,'" and the "'coherence' of all the truths God has revealed."

47. Witherup, "Bible in the Life of the Church," 1617.

Twenty-First Century, published in 2022, Donald Senior also highlights the importance of the second half of *Dei Verbum* §12 when he writes:

> While emphasizing the need to analyze the literal sense of a particular book or passage, *Dei Verbum* also notes the importance of situating a particular text within the framework of the biblical canon and the ongoing tradition of the church—both characteristic hallmarks of a Catholic approach to biblical interpretation.[48]

Such statements seem to reflect a growing awareness among Catholic exegetes that the gains made in the wake of the Second Vatican Council involving the use of the tools of historical-critical exegesis need to be supplemented by placing "biblical interpretation within the living Tradition of the Church" and manifesting "the complex interrelationship between Scripture and Tradition that is at the heart of the Catholic faith."[49]

In my view, this growing emphasis on the second half of *Dei Verbum* §12 is a very positive and promising development, one that does justice to the fuller teaching of the Council. For according to Vatican II, Catholic biblical interpretation needs to be characterized not only by close attention to the language, literature, history, and culture of the human authors but also by "theological exegesis"[50]—an exegesis that interprets biblical texts in the context of the entire canon of Scripture, the living tradition of the whole church, and the analogy of faith.

The Future of Catholic Biblical Interpretation

With all of this in mind, we can sum up and conclude with three final points about the vision of Vatican II and the future of Catholic exegesis.

First and foremost, although the Second Vatican Council's Dogmatic Constitution on Divine Revelation did not directly employ the term "historical criticism," later magisterial documents have interpreted the Council as teaching that the historical-critical method is in fact indispensable. There

48. Donald Senior, CP, "Interpreting the Scriptures – the Church and the Modern Catholic Biblical Renewal," in Collins et al., *The Jerome Biblical Commentary for the Twenty-First Century*, 1934.

49. Witherup, *Scripture: Dei Verbum*, 75.

50. Grillmeier, "Chapter III," 225; *VD* §34.

is no going back, no turning back the clock, no room for a Catholic to retreat into spiritual, mystical, or fundamentalist biblical interpretation that does not engage in historical criticism. Catholic exegesis cannot fall prey to what Robert Miller II has rightly described as a "biblical Docetism," in which the inspired Scripture only *appears* to be fully human but is in fact only divine.[51]

Second, at the same time, though Vatican II did not use the language of "theological exegesis," it did clearly state that Catholic exegetes must give equal attention to the divine authorship of Scripture by paying close attention to the whole canon of Scripture, the tradition of the whole church, and all the doctrines of faith. I submit that the implementation of the second half of *Dei Verbum* §12 is where the challenge of our day and the future of Catholic biblical scholarship lies. I am not alone in this view; this was the unanimous opinion of the 2008 Synod fathers and of Benedict XVI, and Pope Francis has also recently emphasized the need for biblical exegesis in the twenty-first century to constantly rediscover the teaching of the Council:

> The Second Vatican Council gave great impulse to the rediscovery of the word of God, thanks to its Dogmatic Constitution *Dei Verbum, a document that deserves to be read and appropriated ever anew.*[52]

One implication of *Dei Verbum*'s emphasis on the need to pay attention to the whole canon of Scripture is that, while Catholic exegetes may (of course) continue to specialize in certain areas, we must also do our best to resist the contemporary tendency toward overspecialization. We must try to work, insofar as possible, as *biblical* scholars and not just as Old Testament or New Testament experts.[53] This is a challenging task that calls for collaboration across disciplines. Likewise, *Dei Verbum*'s call for attention to the living tradition demands that we make a greater effort to deliberately engage patristic,

51. Miller, *Many Roads Lead Eastward*, 14. Here, Miller is adjusting (I think rightly) Denis Farkasfalvy's terminology of "biblical 'monophysitism.'" See Denis Farkasfalvy, OCist, "The Case for Spiritual Exegesis," *Communio* 10 (1983): 332–50, who is himself following Louis Bouyer.

52. Pope Francis, foreword to Collins et al., *The Jerome Biblical Commentary for the Twenty-First Century*, vii (emphasis added).

53. Cf. Senior, "Interpreting the Scriptures," 1948: "The tendency toward specialization also has the effect of discouraging or overlooking the value of more synthetic studies that give attention to the broader meaning of a biblical text—and thereby provide an opening to its theological and spiritual significance."

medieval, and early modern exegesis in both Western and Eastern Christianity. Thankfully, the late twentieth and early twenty-first centuries have witnessed a veritable explosion of English translations of ancient Christian writings from both the East and the West, making the exegetical writings of antiquity and the Middle Ages easily accessible to Anglophone students and scholars.[54] It is no longer sufficient to rest content in an almost exclusive engagement with contemporary, mostly Western, mostly male, mostly Protestant or secular biblical scholarship. We must listen, as Laurie Brink puts it, to the "whole community" of scriptural interpreters from throughout the centuries and across the globe.[55] Finally, *Dei Verbum*'s teaching on respect for the analogy of faith means that we must also pay close attention to how biblical texts have been interpreted by the living magisterium of the church, especially in its most authoritative forms, such as the teachings of the twenty-one ecumenical councils.[56]

Finally, I submit that it is only when Catholic exegesis gives due weight to both the human and divine aspects of the text, to both historical-critical and theological insights, that we can avoid both the Scylla of rationalism and secularism that has given historical criticism a bad name in some ecclesial circles *and* the Charybdis of a fundamentalist interpretation that is founded upon fideism and so often leads to radical traditionalism, if not atheism. It is also the only way that Sacred Scripture will ever truly take its rightful place as "the soul of sacred theology" (*DV* §12). In the words of Pope Benedict XVI:

> *In a word, "where exegesis is not theology, Scripture cannot be the soul of theology*, and conversely, where theology is not essentially the interpretation of the Church's Scripture, such a theology no longer has a foundation." Hence we need to take a more careful look at the indications provided by

54. See, e.g., the continued publication of up-to-date translations of patristic and medieval exegesis in various multivolume series, such as several subseries within The Fathers of the Church (over 130 vols., published by Catholic University of America Press), Ancient Christian Commentary on Scripture (29 vols., published by IVP Academic), The Church's Bible (6 vols., published by Eerdmans), Ancient Christian Texts (18 vols., published by IVP Academic), and The Bible in Medieval Tradition (5 vols., published by Eerdmans) to name just a few.

55. I owe this expression to an oral presentation given by Laurie Brink in March 2022, now included as an essay in this volume.

56. Helpfully collected in their original languages with an English translation and a scriptural index in Norman P. Tanner, SJ, *Decrees of the Ecumenical Councils* (London: Sheed and Ward, 1990).

the Dogmatic Constitution *Dei Verbum* in this regard. (*VD* §35; emphasis added)

Ultimately, postconciliar Catholic exegetes should strive to embody the vision of historical and theological exegesis anticipated at the beginning of the twentieth century by Marie-Joseph Lagrange, when he spoke of "the twofold spirit" of "respect for dogma" and "regard for sound conscientious work."[57] This combination was indeed not only "possible" for "all Catholics"[58] but would eventually go on to be enshrined in the teaching of the Second Vatican Council and to help pave a path forward so that Lagrange's vision of the future of Catholic biblical interpretation will indeed one day be "realized."[59]

57. Lagrange, *Historical Criticism and the Old Testament*, 17.
58. Lagrange, *Historical Criticism and the Old Testament*, 17.
59. Lagrange, *Historical Criticism and the Old Testament*, 17.

Reading Beyond the Horizon

The Legacy of Lagrange through a Dominican Lens

Laurie Brink, OP

"I have contemplated the beauty of Sinai—the arid desert, the oases, the colored sandstone, the pink granite, the majesty of God's mountain bathed in celestial light; I could not begin to describe it," wrote Père Marie-Joseph Lagrange, OP, in 1926, reflecting on his travels some three decades before.[1] And nearly a hundred years after he first journeyed to Sinai, I stumbled enthusiastically up the same well-worn path to the summit. As I began my research for this article, I searched for a point of connection: Père Lagrange and I were both biblical scholars, both Dominican, but there was more.

After his initial experiences of the biblical lands, Lagrange wrote: "I was stirred, seized, gripped by this sacred land, given over to delights of historical sensations of far-off times. I had so loved the Book and now I contemplate the Land!"[2] Yes. *Yes!* Though I had not known of Lagrange before my own first trip to the Holy Land, I, too, came to the same revelatory insights. In the opening speech of the École pratique d'études bibliques (now known as the École biblique et archéologique française), Lagrange stated, "One cannot understand the Bible without placing oneself in its atmosphere, without consulting both Hebrew and other Semitic languages, and without seeing the monuments, elsewhere than in museums, and the customs, other than in travel narratives."[3]

1. Marie-Joseph Lagrange, OP, *Personal Reflections and Memoirs*, trans. Henry Wansbrough, OSB (New York: Paulist, 1985), 39.

2. Quoted in Bernard Montagnes, OP, *The Story of Father Marie-Joseph Lagrange: Founder of Modern Catholic Bible Study*, trans. Benedict Viviano, OP (New York: Paulist, 2006), 26.

3. Quoted in Montagnes, *Story of Father Marie-Joseph Lagrange*, 28.

History matters. Place matters. And faith is not diminished. In a nutshell, these are the insights I share with Lagrange.

Père Lagrange and I may share similar observations, but we have come from very different worlds. The Bible lands I encountered were part of a vastly different geopolitical reality than the Palestine of Lagrange's day. For me, the use of the historical-critical method is an expectation, not a scandal. And the church of Pope Francis is a quantum leap beyond the anti-modernist papacy of Pius X.

Indeed, Père Lagrange and I would see things differently. But as our brother Thomas Aquinas is purported to have said, "Seldom affirm, never deny, and always distinguish." This paper is a practice in affirming and distinguishing. I intend to reflect on biblical studies through a Dominican, ecclesial, and cultural lens so as to point toward the horizon first glimpsed by my brother Marie-Joseph. To that end, I will briefly introduce the architecture of Dominican life that so framed Lagrange's professional, personal, and spiritual life. I will contextualize the historical-critical method in light of the very different ecclesial tides that he and I have had to navigate. And finally, I will point toward the hermeneutical horizon extending beyond the historical-critical method.

The Architecture of Dominican Life

In the Middle Ages, the church had become very powerful and very removed from the daily life of most peasants. Out of this vacuum of pastoral care—between the priest in the cathedral and the peasant in the field—emerged various heresies. In the very early thirteenth century, Dominic de Guzman, a canon regular, accompanied Bishop Diego of Osma in his preaching mission against one particular sect of heretics. Not unlike earlier heretics, the Cathars in the region of Languedoc in southern France taught that the physical world was evil and that believers should shun the needs of the flesh.

Dominic recognized that in order to combat this heresy and bring people back to God, he needed help. And he needed his fellow preachers to be steeped in the Bible. Not just armed with an occasional knowledge, they had to be the experts if they were to successfully combat the heretics. Very early in the foundation of the Order, Dominic sent his brothers to study at the universities. This brings to mind an oft-quoted phrase from Aquinas that is considered the motto of the Dominican Order: "contemplata aliis tradere" (to hand on the fruits of contemplation).[4] As this quotation recognizes, study must be coupled with contemplation, for only then does knowledge—touched by the Holy Spirit—become wisdom. As the order developed, study became a hallmark of the Dominican way, for as Hugh of St. Cher stated, "First the bow is bent in study, then the arrow is released in preaching."[5]

Lagrange's Dominican vocation found its most public expression in study and the publications and teaching that resulted. But communal prayer and contemplation were inseparable partners to his call. As he writes, "I believe I have given proof of a true passion for study, but I declare that I do not understand it as possible, in our order, without assigning a large part of the office, to rest and light! . . . The study of holy Scripture without a great spirit of faith is very dangerous, as proven by numerous apostasies, and I do not want to work in order to arrive at that sort of result for myself and for others."[6]

Despite his assiduous study and the Dominican tradition of dispensation, Lagrange "fulfilled with meticulous care the demands of his religious life, and this was especially true during the periods when he was most bitterly attacked. He was devoted to conventual observance, and to the end attended choir every day to recite the Divine Office with the other professors of the School. To this childlike obedience and deep inner piety must be added a great humility."[7] It was said that whenever the censors of the Order criticized his work, he did not hesitate to make the necessary changes.

Lagrange recounts how he came to his call in this way:

> Ever since I had read . . . the [*Life of Saint Dominic*], the Dominican ideal dominated my thought. I gave myself to St. Dominic after reading the work of Father Lacordaire and after being completely captivated by the radiant image of the saint as seen in the Coronation of the Virgin by Blessed Angelico of Fiesole. I did not doubt the exactitude of this portrait. . . . Long before entering his order, I was his son.[8]

4. Thomas Aquinas, *Summa theologiae*, III, q. 40, art. 1, ad 2.

5. George Herring cites the thirteenth-century Dominican biblical scholar and continues, "Dominicans did not study just for its own sake; study had a purpose. And that was to produce the most highly skilled preachers, teachers or counsellors possible." *An Introduction to the History of Christianity: From the Early Church to the Enlightenment* (London: Continuum, 2006), 217.

6. Quoted in Montagnes, *Story of Father Marie-Joseph Lagrange*, 25.

7. Richard T. A. Murphy, OP, "Mémorial—Lagrange," *CBQ* 3, no. 2 (1941): 144.

8. Quoted in Montagnes, *Story of Father Marie-Joseph Lagrange*, 13.

Lagrange found his vocation at an intersection of text and art. It is no wonder his professional life would follow a similar trajectory. In a memorial published in the *Catholic Biblical Quarterly*, Richard Murphy noted that Lagrange believed "true exegesis based on sound theology had nothing to fear from true science . . . there was pressing need for Catholics to seek for the truth in new sources, to examine excavations and inscriptions at first hand, to make discoveries. . . . Never for an instant was it his purpose to devote his energies exclusively to a study of the sciences connected with the Bible; his goal was always single: to make the Bible better understood."[9]

In his "spiritual testament," Lagrange encapsulates his life as a faithful Dominican:

> I declare before God that it is my intention to die in the Holy Catholic Church to which I have always belonged with my whole heart and soul since the day of my baptism, and to die there faithful to my vows of poverty, chastity and obedience, in the Order of Saint Dominic. To that end I commend myself to my good Savior Jesus and to the prayers of His most holy Mother who has always been so good to me.
>
> I declare also most expressly that I submit to the judgment of the Apostolic See all that I have written. I believe that I can add that I have always had the intention in all my studies, of contributing to the good—I mean to the reign of Jesus Christ, to the honor of the Church, to the good of souls.[10]

Here was a true brother of Dominic and son of the church.

The Historical-Critical Method and the Ecclesial Tides

In his opening speech at the École biblique in 1890, Père Lagrange exhorted his fellows to the task of historical biblical study. As Montagnes summarizes his comments, "The Bible offers itself to a new investigation thanks to the resources of modern culture."[11] The usefulness of such study would not be purely academic but would deepen contemplation as well. "We are invited to rival our adversaries in competence; to recognize in the Bible the [human

9. Murphy, "Mémorial—Lagrange," 137.
10. Quoted in Murphy, "Mémorial—Lagrange," 144.
11. Montagnes, *Story of Father Marie-Joseph Lagrange*, 29.

word], written as history, and at the same time, to receive the Bible as the *Word of God*, bearer of transcendence. The two aspects are inseparable. In knowing it better as a history book, one enjoys it more as an inspired and divine book."[12]

Seventy-five years and eleven popes later, *Dei Verbum*[13] would echo the same sentiment:

> Since God speaks in Sacred Scripture through men [and women] in human fashion, the interpreter of Sacred Scripture, in order to see clearly what God wanted to communicate to us, should carefully investigate what meaning the sacred writers really intended, and what God wanted to manifest by means of their words. (*DV* §11)

> For the correct understanding of what the sacred author wanted to assert, due attention must be paid to the customary and characteristic styles of feeling, speaking and narrating which prevailed at the time of the sacred writer, and to the patterns men normally employed at that period in their everyday dealings with one another. (*DV* §12)

But between the opening of the École biblique and the closing of Vatican II, Catholic biblical scholarship struggled to gain the exegetical ground already tilled by Protestant scholars.

The Church at the Turn of the Twentieth Century

Lagrange began his academic work during a paradigm shift in scientific, philosophical, and political thought. "Beginning around 1850 research and progress in archaeology and philology had, with a speed unparalleled in any other branch of science, been steadily pushing back its horizon."[14] As part of a larger ethos of modernism, such scientific inquiry challenged a more traditional understanding of the Bible. "At stake was a sense that not only

12. Montagnes, *Story of Father Marie-Joseph Lagrange*, 29. On October 20, 1920, the Academy of Inscriptions and Belles-Lettres in Paris recognized the school as the École archéologique française de Jérusalem (French Archaeological School of Jerusalem) because of the quality of its achievements in this field.

13. Vatican Council II, Dogmatic Constitution *Dei Verbum* (November 18, 1965). Hereafter, this will be cited in the text as *DV*.

14. Murphy, "Mémorial—Lagrange," 136.

were doctrines specific to Roman Catholicism under attack, but Christianity itself was being undermined in heretical Christologies and assaults on scriptural inspiration and inerrancy. Moreover, the very future of religion itself was feared to be at risk, as critics naturalized the supernatural and rendered religion a merely human product."[15] Though Lagrange believed "the Catholic exegete's obligation to respect the authority of the church does not set any arbitrary limits to his research," the historical-critical method he espoused challenged "a certain type of literal exegesis practiced in the nineteenth century that theologians wrongly swallowed and endowed with an absolute value."[16]

Though Pope Leo XIII supported the creation of the *Revue biblique* and later named it the publication of the newly formed Pontifical Biblical Commission, his encyclical *Providentissimus Deus* (1893) "argued that a biblical text could not contradict the sense given it by the magisterium or by the unanimous consent of the fathers, and no exegete was allowed to interpret the text so as to contradict church dogma."[17] His successor, Pope Pius X, continued the anti-modernist tenor with the syllabus *Lamentabili sane exitu* and the encyclical *Pascendi dominici gregis* (1907), the latter condemning sixty-five modernist propositions. In §34 of the *Pascendi*, the work of the historical critic was attacked:

> The Modernists have no hesitation in affirming commonly that these books, and especially the Pentateuch and the first three Gospels, have been gradually formed by additions to a primitive brief narration—by interpolations of theological or allegorical interpretation, by transitions, by joining different passages together.[18]

No wonder Lagrange's commitment to rigorous exegesis enhanced with archaeological insights caused no little disturbance during the anti-modernist period. "During this time P. Lagrange serenely pursued his work, taking no direct part in the controversies, as his superiors had counselled. . . . [H]e promptly and sincerely signified his submission when

15. Charles J. T. Talar, "Modernism," in *New Catholic Encyclopedia: Supplement 2010*, ed. Robert L. Fastiggi (Detroit: Gale, 2010), 2:797.

16. Montagnes, *Story of Father Marie-Joseph Lagrange*, 74.

17. Kevin Madigan, "Catholic Interpretation of the Bible," in *The Catholic Study Bible*, 3rd ed., ed. Donald Senior, CP, John J. Collins, and Mary Ann Getty (New York: Oxford University Press, 2016), 84–85.

18. Pope Pius X, Encyclical Letter *Pascendi Dominici gregis* (September 8, 1907) §34.

in 1907 Pius X issued his *Lamentabili* and the *Pascendi*."[19] Lagrange was advised to refrain from Old Testament scholarship and focus his efforts on the New Testament, which he did with the same discipline and commitment. "Ultimately his deep Catholic faith and loyalty to the Church would quell his critics, but many of his scholarly initiatives were viewed with suspicion and he and other colleagues like him suffered as a result."[20] The Dominican scholar and son of the church now quietly wore the mantle of the suffering servant.

"Catholic biblical scholarship, which in some sense had been plunged into a dark age with [Pius X's] papal pronouncements, was reliberated in 1943 to do its work by another papal encyclical."[21] Pope Pius XII's *Divino afflante Spiritu* (1943) claimed to support *Providentissimus Deus*, but it actually countered some of Pope Leo's earlier points. "Pius . . . encouraged scholars, as Leo emphatically did not, to examine the original intention and circumstances of the authors of Scripture and thus to understand the context in which they wrote."[22] Coming five years after his death in 1938, Lagrange's historical method received papal affirmation:

> Let those who cultivate biblical studies turn their attention with all due diligence towards this point and let them neglect none of those discoveries, whether in the domain of archaeology or in ancient history or literature, which serve to make better known the mentality of the ancient writers, as well as their manner and art of reasoning, narrating and writing.[23]

Thus, "the name Lagrange is rightly associated with the twentieth century revival of Catholic interest in the Bible and almost alone lifted Catholic Biblical studies out of mediocrity."[24]

19. Murphy, "Mémorial—Lagrange," 140.

20. John J. Collins et al., introduction to *The Jerome Biblical Commentary for the Twenty-First Century*, ed. John J. Collins et al. (London: T&T Clark, 2022), ix.

21. Madigan, "Catholic Interpretation of the Bible," 85.

22. Madigan, "Catholic Interpretation of the Bible," 85. The hope of reliberation was short-lived. After the death of Pius XII, some Catholic biblical scholars suffered reprisals for their historical conclusions about the text. Despite this setback, Raymond E. Brown would call the document "the Catholic Magna Carta for progress in biblical study" (Madigan, "Catholic Interpretation of the Bible," 85).

23. Pope Pius XII, Encyclical Letter *Divino afflante Spiritu* (September 30, 1943) §40.

24. Richard T. A. Murphy, OP, "Lagrange, Marie Joseph," *NCE* 8:281.

The Church at the Turn of the Twenty-First Century

The seeds of hope for a Catholic biblical renewal planted with *Divino afflante Spiritu* would come to fruition with the publication of the Vatican II document the Dogmatic Constitution on Divine Revelation *Dei Verbum*.[25] "The decree ratified the use of modern methods of interpretation, insisting that in Scripture God revealed himself, not a collection of doctrines."[26] *Dei Verbum* also encouraged Catholic biblical scholars to make fresh translations in the vernacular:

> Catholic exegetes then and other students of sacred theology, working diligently together and using appropriate means, should devote their energies, under the watchful care of the sacred teaching office of the Church, to an exploration and exposition of the divine writings. (*DV* §23)

The word of God was to be accessible, thus encouraging personal contemplation and the study of Scripture among all the faithful.

In 1993, on the fiftieth anniversary of Pius XII's groundbreaking *Divino afflante Spiritu*, the Pontifical Biblical Commission further confirmed the historical-critical method in its publication *The Interpretation of the Bible in the Church*: "The historical-critical method is the indispensable method for the scientific study of the meaning of ancient texts. Holy Scripture, inasmuch as it is the 'word of God in human language,' has been composed by human authors in all its various parts and in all the sources that lie behind them. Because of this, its proper understanding not only admits the use of this method but actually requires it."[27] The insights and scholarly pursuits of

25. "While the Second Vatican Council has been characterized as a 'pastoral' council, concerned primarily with the life and mission of the church rather than with doctrine, in fact, in the area of the church's view of divine revelation and the Scriptures, the Council made a substantial doctrinal contribution. The 'Dogmatic Constitution on Divine Revelation' (*Dei Verbum*) was one of only two 'dogmatic constitutions' produced by the Council (the other was *Lumen Gentium*, the 'Dogmatic Constitution on the Church'). The composition and final approval of *Dei Verbum* stretched from the opening session of the Council in October 1962 until its final session in the Fall of 1965." Donald Senior, CP, "Interpreting the Scriptures – the Church and the Modern Catholic Biblical Renewal," in Collins et al., *The Jerome Biblical Commentary for the Twenty-First Century*, 1931–32.

26. John W. O'Malley, "Councils, Church," in *Encyclopedia of the Bible and Its Reception Online*, ed. Constance M. Furey et al. (Berlin: de Gruyter, 2012). https://doi.org/10.1515/ebr.councilschurch.

27. Pontifical Biblical Commission, *The Interpretation of the Bible in the Church* (Rome: Libreria Editrice Vaticana, 1993) §I. A.

Lagrange were confirmed as the method by which critical Catholic biblical scholarship was to proceed.

The second major trajectory of Catholic biblical interpretation, as I see it, is the fruit grown from the seeds of the *Ad gentes*. This 1965 Decree on the Church's Missionary Activity, also from Vatican II, recognized the vitality of faith developing in regions that heretofore had been considered "mission territory." These "young churches," as the document calls them, were encouraged to

> borrow from the customs and traditions of their people, from their wisdom and their learning, from their arts and disciplines, all those things which can contribute to the glory of their Creator, or enhance the grace of their Savior, or dispose Christian life the way it should be. To achieve this goal, it is necessary that in each major socio-cultural area, such theological speculation should be encouraged, in the light of the universal church's tradition, as may submit to a new scrutiny the words and deeds which God has revealed, and which have been set down in Sacred Scripture and explained by the Fathers and by the magisterium.[28]

Six decades later, these young churches have grown up. And they have trained their contextualized "theological speculation" on the biblical text, engaging various methodologies and hermeneutical perspectives, including postcolonial studies, empire studies, and intercultural criticism to mention a few. The use of the historical-critical method encouraged by *Dei Verbum* and the growth of diverse hermeneutical and theological perspectives supported by *Ad gentes* point to a new horizon in Catholic biblical studies.

The Hermeneutical Horizon

In Nehemiah 8, Ezra took the book of the law and "read from it facing the square before the Water Gate from early morning until midday, in the presence of the men and the women and those who could understand; and the ears of all the people were attentive to the book of the law" (Neh 8:3, NRSV). Something of the experience of those men, women, and children who listened to Ezra is how I imagine some Catholics enthusiastically embraced the Catholic biblical renewal. Suddenly, the Bible, which had heretofore been

28. Vatican Council II, Decree *Ad gentes* (December 7, 1965) §22.

the purview of the clergy, was now available to them—to us. "Then all the people began to eat and drink, to distribute portions, and to celebrate with great joy, for they understood the words that had been explained to them" (Neh 8:12, NABR). In the wake of Vatican II, a veritable cottage industry sprung up to provide for the growing interest—dare I say, fervor—for biblical studies. In my own congregation, summer Bible institutes were designed to train and update the sisters so that they might teach their students. Publications abounded. Catholic Bible study programs developed. A book once opened only to update the family history, the Bible was now at the center of family faith. Like Ezra's reading of the scroll before the people, this was a paradigm shift for scholars and indeed all the faithful.

As I understand it, the Catholic biblical renewal was not simply the academic acceptance of the historical-critical method, long practiced among Protestant scholars, but an affirmation that the word of God could be studied, critiqued, and engaged not only by professionals but also by people in the pew. In a sense, the Catholic biblical renewal, at its height, democratized access to the Scriptures.

As a member of the post–Vatican II generation, I have reaped the benefits of the Catholic biblical renewal without having laid its foundation or paid the costs. As a Catholic biblical scholar, I stand on the shoulders of Père Lagrange, Raymond E. Brown, and other noble women and men who suffered mightily to bring the firstfruits of critical exegesis to Catholic biblical study. I am thoroughly and unapologetically a general practitioner of the historical-critical method. But I hold that exegesis is always at the service of actualization, and so my hermeneutical lens is constructed from my identity as a white woman of privilege who is also a member of the Order of Preachers and who teaches a multicultural student body.

The trajectories that I would like to discuss derive from my social location, which the Pontifical Biblical Commission's *The Interpretation of the Bible in the Church* attests is significant in the process of deriving meaning from the biblical text: "The interpretation of a text is always dependent on the mindset and concerns of its readers. . . . It is inevitable that some exegetes bring to their work points of view that are new and responsive to contemporary currents of thought which have not up till now been taken sufficiently into consideration."[29] As I ponder the continuity and distinction between the Catholic biblical scholarship of Lagrange's day and my own, I will offer a critique, an affirmation, and an invitation: a critique of historical

29. Pontifical Biblical Commission, *Interpretation of the Bible in the Church* §E.

criticism, an affirmation of the maturation of the reader as exemplified by feminist and intercultural criticisms, and an invitation to a banquet where all are welcome.

A Critique of the Historical-Critical Method

When I walked the corridors of the Divinity School at the University of Chicago, you could have heard nary a word of dissent in discussions on biblical methodology. As the heirs of Edgar Goodspeed, Shirley Jackson Case, Robert Grant, and Norman Perrin—to name-drop a few—doctoral students were well and truly trained for and enamored of the higher criticism that investigated what would later be called the "world behind the text."

Not surprisingly, what the first generation develops, the next must critique. In *The Future of Catholic Biblical Scholarship*, Luke Timothy Johnson fears that "a too-eager assimilation to the dominant historical-critical paradigm has brought with it some unfortunate corollaries of the Protestant ethos of either/or and a weakening of the distinctive Catholic instinct for the both/and."[30] The historical-critical method is not without its detractors.

More recently and from a Protestant perspective, Dale Martin has also complained about the predilection for the historical-critical method being taught in seminaries. "Historical criticism may be useful," he writes, but "it need not be king."[31] Martin's concern is chiefly pastoral. Seminarians only trained in analyzing Scripture through the historical lens may be poorly prepared to draw wisdom and insight from those same texts when they preach and pastor. The bottom line for Martin is that "most students are not being taught to think critically about textuality and interpretation in general . . . with the result that they express naïve notions about interpretation and textual meaning."[32] Martin proposes that seminaries teach historical criticism as one among other ways of reading. He explains: "We may talk about 'what the text says.' We may refer to 'the world revealed or created by this text.' None of these expressions need be avoided. What must be avoided is allowing those metaphors of agency to fool us into forgetting our own

30. Luke Timothy Johnson and William S. Kurz, SJ, *The Future of Catholic Biblical Scholarship: A Constructive Conversation* (Grand Rapids: Eerdmans, 2002), 33.

31. Dale B. Martin, *Pedagogy of the Bible: An Analysis and Proposal* (Louisville: Westminster John Knox, 2008), 3.

32. Martin, *Pedagogy of the Bible*, 27.

agency in the construction of meaning in the reading activity. We must not allow human agency to be masked by the metaphorical or mythical agency of the text itself. Human beings must take responsibility for their interpretations."[33] Martin's admonition finds affirmation in the trajectory of Catholic biblical interpretation to which I now turn—the maturation of the reader.

An Affirmation of the Reader

One of the most significant benefits of the Catholic biblical renewal has been the turn toward the subject. Giving agency to a person in the pew, whether by vernacular translations of the Bible or easily accessible study programs or enlightening publications, has resulted in not only a more "biblical" Catholic faithful but a more mature one. In the fifty-plus years since *Dei Verbum,* we have moved from viewing the Bible as an object of reverence whose access was limited to a few to a subject of active engagement available to all.

This new privileging of the reader has coincided with developments in interpretive methods concerned with the locus of meaning. Where historical criticism often roots the meaning of the text in the world behind it (e.g., the intentions of the authors), contemporary literary criticism and reader-response methods propose that meaning resides elsewhere—either in the text itself or in the reader's encounter with the text. Sr. Sandra Schneiders, IHM, suggests an integration: "Appropriation of the meaning of the text, the transformative achievement of interpretation, is neither a mastery of the text by the reader (an extraction of its meaning by the application of method) nor a mastery of the reader by the text (a blind submission to what the text says) but an ongoing dialogue with the text about its subject matter. For the believer . . . this dialogue is rooted in the faith that this text is a mediation of transformative divine revelation."[34] Hermeneutics is the process by which one interprets the data culled through historical criticism so as to come to a valid understanding that is both true to the text and transformative for the reader. Two hermeneutical trajectories that uphold the text and the reader both as subjects and that have impact on US and global Catholicism are feminist biblical hermeneutics and intercultural criticism.

33. Martin, *Pedagogy of the Bible,* 38.

34. Sandra M. Schneiders, IHM, *The Revelatory Text: Interpreting the New Testament as Sacred Scripture,* 2nd ed. (Collegeville, MN: Liturgical Press, 1999), 177.

1. *Feminist biblical hermeneutics.* The Commission's *The Interpretation of the Bible in the Church* offers an affirmation and a critique of feminist hermeneutics. Affirmingly, it states: "Feminine sensitivity helps to unmask and correct certain commonly accepted interpretations which were tendentious and sought to justify the male domination of women." But the document also warns: "Feminist exegesis, to the extent that it proceeds from a preconceived judgment, runs the risk of interpreting the biblical texts in a tendentious and thus debatable manner."[35]

When this document was written in 1993, feminist biblical scholars employed a wide variety of methods and held varying opinions about the usefulness of an androcentric text for liberation. Today, thirty years later, the scholars who practice feminist methods and engage in hermeneutics recognize that the text is not neutral or objective, but nonetheless, it retains a liberating potential. From hermeneutics of suspicion to hermeneutics of retrieval,[36] feminist biblical scholars employ a variety of methods as they attempt to uncover the "good news" for both women and men.

Barbara Reid, OP, defines feminism as "a perspective and a movement that springs from a recognition of inequities toward women"; feminism "advocates for changes in whatever structures prevent full flourishing of the human community and all creation."[37] Feminists begin from the experiences and perspectives of women and acknowledge the role one's own social location plays in reading and interpreting the text. Foundational to any interpretation is acknowledging that "the Bible has been written for the most part by men, for men, about men, and to serve men's purposes. While the Bible is the revered word of God which authentically communicates God's desires for humanity, feminist scholars recognize the fallible human instruments that have shaped the traditions we have received" (WWH, 140).

An important question addressed to the text is, What does it do to its reader? Does it liberate, or reinforce domination? Reid describes the importance of engaging "all the powers of creative imagination to envision a world in which the equality and dignity of women is a fact" and "to remember

35. Pontifical Biblical Commission, *Interpretation of the Bible* §I. E.2.

36. Sandra M. Schneiders, IHM, *Written That You May Believe: Encountering Jesus in the Fourth Gospel*, rev. ed. (New York: Crossroad, 2003), 131.

37. Barbara E. Reid, "The What, Why, and How of Feminist Biblical Interpretation," *The Bible Today* 57, no. 3 (May 2019): 136. Hereafter, this source is cited as WWH in the text. For a fuller discussion, see her publication, *Wisdom's Feast: An Invitation to Feminist Interpretation of the Scriptures* (Grand Rapids: Eerdmans, 2016).

and reconstruct the past history of women's presence and participation in discipleship and mission" (WWH, 140).

A feministic critical reading of Scripture upholds the positive portrayals of women but also acknowledges the "terrible texts" that demean and destroy women. "Rather than rip these out of the Bible, it is important to remember and tell such stories, but with the purpose of exposing the way they sanction violence against women and with the insistence, 'Never again!'" (WWH, 140). Feminist biblical interpretation is not simply an intellectual exercise "but culminates in action aimed at transforming relationship patterns and systems toward a renewed world and church in which women and men and all creation thrive in the fullness of life envisioned by Jesus" (WWH, 141).

Feminist hermeneutics leads to the recognition of the value of women both in the biblical text and as readers of that text. Since the majority of those who identify as Catholic and the majority of those who regularly attend liturgy are women, a biblical hermeneutic that privileges a woman's perspective has the potential to deepen faith commitment while also calling forth action on behalf of liberation.

2. *Intercultural criticism.* In the last few decades, missiologists and postcolonial scholars have developed a vocabulary that better reflects the global diversity in our church. As Roger Schroeder, SVD, explains, "Interculturality is both *dialogical*—acknowledging and engaging God's presence in human experience, culture, history, and all of creation—and *prophetic*—witnessing to and announcing God's reign and the Gospel, and denouncing that which is contrary to it."[38]

I find the trajectory of intercultural criticism as espoused by New Testament scholar Fernando Segovia to hold much promise for the future of Catholic biblical scholarship.[39] Segovia's interpretive strategy, which he calls a hermeneutics of engagement and otherness, holds in creative tension the contextualized biblical text and the contextualized reader, in order to evaluate the contextualized interpretive results, reception, and aftereffects. "It opts for humanization and diversity—it resists both dehumanization, any

38. Roger Schroeder, SVD, "Interculturality as a Paradigm of Mission," in *Intercultural Mission*, vol. 2, ed. Lazar T. Stanislaus, SVD, and Martin Ueffing, SVD (Sankt Augustin: Steyler Missionswissenschaftliches Institut, 2015), 168.

39. Fernando Segovia, "Towards a Hermeneutics of Diaspora: A Hermeneutics of Otherness and Engagement," in *Social Location and Biblical Interpretation in the United States*, vol. 1 of *Readings from This Place*, ed. Fernando F. Segovia and Mary Ann Tolbert (Minneapolis: Fortress, 1995), 59.

divestiture of all those identity factors that constitute and characterize the reader as reader, and rehumanization, any attempt to force all readers into one and the same particular and contextualized discussion. Finally, it seeks to acknowledge, respect, and engage the other—it opposes any attempt, implicit or explicit, to overwhelm or override the other, to impose a definition upon it, to turn the other into an 'other.'"[40] Such a reading strategy upholds diversity as a value, not as a stumbling block. As Fr. Jean-Pierre Ruiz notes, "Embracing a hermeneutics of engagement and otherness . . . makes it possible to recognize that the diversity of readers in the world *in front of* the text . . . reflects analogous diversity in the world *behind* the text."[41] With this hermeneutical lens and reading strategy, the particularity of the text and the particularity of the reader meet across the divide of distance, allowing Scripture to truly speak to an intercultural community.

As with most reader-response methods and hermeneutical perspectives, a concern arises about the validity of meaning when many "others" are engaged in the task of biblical interpretation. The problem is determining whose meaning is most "meaningful." The potential relativism is limited by the presence of what Stanley Fish calls "an interpretive community."[42] Such a community validates the meaning that emerges between the reader and the text based on a shared reading strategy. According to the Pontifical Biblical Commission, our interpretive community is the church: "It is the believing community that provides a truly adequate context for interpreting canonical texts. In this context faith and the Holy Spirit enrich exegesis; church authority, exercised as a service of the community, must see to it that this interpretation remains faithful to the great tradition which has produced the texts."[43]

The writers of *Ad gentes* extended an invitation to the table, and now the representatives of these once "young" churches and underrepresented groups are taking them up on it. Carmen Nanko-Fernández warns that contextualized theologians must not be marginalized at the "kids' table" of the academy, and I would add, also of the church. She continues: "It can certainly be argued that to be represented at the table by others is unacceptable, to merely have a place at the table is inadequate, to tolerate separate and unequal tables

40. Segovia, "Hermeneutics of Diaspora," 72.

41. Jean-Pierre Ruiz, *Readings from the Edges: The Bible and People on the Move* (Maryknoll, NY: Orbis, 2011), 7.

42. Stanley Fish, *Is There a Text in This Class? The Authority of Interpretive Communities* (Cambridge: Harvard University Press, 1982).

43. Pontifical Biblical Commission, *Interpretation of the Bible* §I. C.1.g.

is abhorrent and destructive. But full participation requires elbow room for engagement as well as table manners."[44] Drawing on that metaphor, we are invited to a banquet at which the various trajectories of current biblical interpretation find a place at the table of the interpretive community of faith. A table around which—to recall again the text of Neh 8:12—all the people eat and drink, distribute portions, and celebrate with great joy because we all understand the words that have been explained to us.

Being Doers of the Word

Since the Catholic Church has fully embraced historical criticism as significant in the study of Scripture and concomitantly made that Scripture more accessible to the faithful, we have witnessed a turn from the Bible solely as an object of reverence to the word of God as subject of our faithful, critical, and prayer reflections. Truly, this is the realization of Lagrange's long-suffering efforts to open the word of God to the people of God.

Engaging history, linguistics, and archaeology, Lagrange and others explored the world behind the text in order to mine its riches as the revelatory word of God. In the decades since, biblical scholarship has begun to wear bifocals, viewing both the world behind the text and the world in front of the text. The turn to the hermeneutical horizon testifies to the success of *Dei Verbum* and *Ad gentes*. As *The Interpretation of the Bible in the Church* noted of liberationist approaches: "If a people live in circumstances of oppression, one must go to the Bible to find there nourishment capable of sustaining the people in its struggles and its hopes. The reality of the present time should not be ignored but, on the contrary, met head on, with a view to shedding upon it the light of the word. From this light will come authentic Christian praxis, leading to the transformation of society through works of justice and love. Within the vision of faith Scripture is transformed into a dynamic impulse for full liberation."[45] The word exegeted must lead to the word actualized; we must become "doers of the word" (Jas 1:22). Or in our Dominican tradition, "First the bow is bent in study, then the arrow is released in preaching."

44. Carmen Nanko, "Elbows on the Table: The Ethics of Doing Theology, Reflections from a U. S. Hispanic Perspective," *Journal of Hispanic/Latino Theology* 10, no. 3 (2003): 54.

45. Pontifical Biblical Commission, *Interpretation of the Bible* §E.1.

Père Lagrange and the Criticism of Criticism

The Philosophical Underpinnings of Modern Biblical Scholarship

ISAAC AUGUSTINE MORALES, OP

In his well-known 1988 Erasmus Lecture, "Biblical Interpretation in Crisis," the then Cardinal Joseph Ratzinger proposed an agenda for the renewal of biblical scholarship.[1] Lamenting the way that much biblical scholarship since the Enlightenment has left Scripture a tangle of disconnected threads, Ratzinger calls for an evaluation of historical criticism, sifting the wheat from the chaff. At the heart of Ratzinger's proposal lies what he refers to as "a criticism of criticism."[2] The primary source of the problem with much modern biblical scholarship, according to Ratzinger, is to be found in its philosophical presuppositions: "At its core, the debate about modern exegesis is not a dispute among historians: *it is rather a philosophical debate.*"[3] The key to moving biblical scholarship in a more fruitful direction, then, is a more deliberate assessment of the role that philosophical presuppositions play in exegesis.

In that same 1988 lecture, Ratzinger suggested that this task would require the efforts of an entire generation of biblical scholars.[4] The former head of

1. This lecture has been published in various forms over the years. In this essay, I will cite the original published version: Joseph Ratzinger, "Biblical Interpretation in Crisis: On the Question of the Foundations and Approaches of Exegesis Today," in *Biblical Interpretation in Crisis: The Ratzinger Conference on Bible and Church*, ed. Richard John Neuhaus (Grand Rapids: Eerdmans, 1989), 1–23.

2. "What we need might be called a criticism of criticism. By this I mean not some exterior analysis, but a criticism based on the inherent potential of all critical thought to analyze itself." Ratzinger, "Biblical Interpretation in Crisis," 6.

3. Ratzinger, "Biblical Interpretation in Crisis," 16 (emphasis added).

4. "Hardly anyone today would assert that a truly pervasive understanding of this whole problem has yet been found which takes into account both the undeniable insights uncovered by the historical method, while at the same time overcoming its limitations and disclosing them in a thoroughly relevant hermeneutic. At least the work of a whole

the Congregation for the Doctrine of the Faith is certainly correct to note the magnitude of the task. Paradigm shifts like the one he calls for rarely occur overnight. Nevertheless, the early history of modern Catholic biblical scholarship offers at least one fine model of how Ratzinger's agenda might be carried out. In the great Dominican biblical scholar, Marie-Joseph Lagrange, we have an exemplar of the kind of criticism Cardinal Ratzinger calls for. In particular, Lagrange's much neglected work *Le sens du christianisme d'après l'exégèse allemande*—published in English as *The Meaning of Christianity according to Luther and His Followers in Germany*—carries out many of the items on Ratzinger's 1988 agenda.[5] Like Ratzinger after him, Lagrange affirms the great gains of modern scholarship, particularly in philological and historical study. Moreover, he looks critically at many of the philosophical presuppositions that shaped German approaches to Scripture since the Enlightenment as well as the role that the Reformer Martin Luther played at the outset of that development.[6] Lagrange's argument, however, is not simply deconstructive. Rather, he sifts the material, holding fast to the good that has resulted from historical-critical scholarship and presenting a synthesis of the gains that it has offered. Like Ratzinger, Lagrange also approaches the task from an ecclesial context, arguing that Catholic exegetes are better situated to understand Scripture in the proper way.[7] Those searching for an example of what Ratzinger's project might look like in practice (besides his own subsequent writings), then, can benefit from turning to the work of the great founder of the École biblique.

A Catholic Approach to Scripture

The Meaning of Christianity originated as a series of ten lectures presented at the Institut Catholique de Paris at the invitation of the institute's rector,

generation is necessary to achieve such a thing." Ratzinger, "Biblical Interpretation in Crisis," 5–6.

5. Marie-Joseph Lagrange, OP, *The Meaning of Christianity according to Luther and His Followers in Germany*, trans. W. S. Reilly, SS (London: Longmans, Green, 1920). The title of the English translation is somewhat misleading. The French title more clearly indicates the primary subject of the work, namely, modern German exegesis and historical reconstruction, especially of the eighteenth and nineteenth centuries.

6. In this regard, the title of the English translation, even if it is deficient in other respects (see the preceding note), points to an important aspect of Lagrange's analysis.

7. In each of these areas, Lagrange anticipates Ratzinger's agenda. For Ratzinger's formulation of the points just mentioned, see Ratzinger, "Biblical Interpretation in Crisis," 21–23.

Msgr. Alfred-Henri-Marie Baudrillart.[8] Delivered in late 1917 and 1918 during the period in which Lagrange was forced to return to France because of the First World War, the lectures focus on German exegesis, particularly since the time of Martin Luther. As Vincent notes, Baudrillart chose the theme of the lectures in order to take advantage of Lagrange's learning as well as of his patriotism.[9] Although Lagrange's patriotism certainly shows through at times, he nevertheless treats his opponents with charity and sympathy. From the outset, however, he is clear about two things: his commitment to scientific exegesis and his equal commitment to approaching the text from the perspective of faith. In both these respects, his approach anticipates Ratzinger's 1988 proposal.[10]

In the preface to the published version of the lectures, Lagrange emphasizes the many advances that modern scholarship has provided for the study of Sacred Scripture. It was only as he was coming to the end of the lectures that he discovered a book covering the same material by the Sulpician Louis-Claude Fillion.[11] Fillion's book, Lagrange notes, is in fact more comprehensive, covering not only German scholarship but also the critical attacks against Christianity coming out of France and England. Among the reasons Lagrange offers for publishing his lectures despite the overlap with the work of Fillion is the different assessment the two works make of German scholarship. The title of Fillion's book, *Les étapes du rationalisme dans ses attaques contre les Évangiles et la vie de Jésus-Christ* (The stages of rationalism in its attacks against the gospel and the life of our Lord Jesus Christ), indicates the decidedly negative evaluation he offers of the scholarship he reviews, regarding it "as an engine of war against Revelation" (*MC*, 9). While Lagrange is no less critical of the figures he treats, he also seeks to uncover

8. For a very brief overview of the context in which Lagrange prepared and presented the lectures, see Louis-Hugues Vincent, *Le Père Marie-Joseph Lagrange: Sa vie et son œuvre* (Paris: Parole et silence, 2013), 413–15.

9. Vincent, *Le Père Marie-Joseph Lagrange*, 413. One of the more amusing lines in the book appears in the preface: "Happily, in exegesis as in war, Germany excels in preparation more than in execution." Lagrange, *Meaning of Christianity*, 18.

10. Ratzinger affirms that "philological and scientific literary methods are and will remain critically important for a proper exegesis" and that "[exegesis] must recognize that the faith of the church is that form of 'sympathia' without which the Bible must remain a *closed* book." Ratzinger, "Biblical Interpretation in Crisis," 22, 23.

11. Lagrange, *Meaning of Christianity*, 8; L.-C. Fillion, *Les étapes du rationalisme dans ses attaques contre les Évangiles et la vie de Jésus-Christ: Exposition historique et critique* (Paris: P. Lethielleux, 1914). Hereafter, *The Meaning of Christianity* will be cited in the text as *MC*.

ideas that can be salvaged from German Protestant scholarship once recontextualized in a Catholic setting: "But we would also tell the story of the immense effort made by the exegetes of Germany, and show how it may be of profit to Truth, if we know how to employ it in the service of a method which is more reliable, because it is divine" (*MC*, 12).

Lagrange laments a lack of industry on the part of Catholic biblical scholars, whose output in his day paled in comparison with that of the Germans: "The work of Catholic scriptural scholars in defense of the Church's interpretation has not equaled, either in intensity or in the copiousness of its products, that of independent critics" (*MC*, 13). The Germans excelled in philological and historical studies, making contributions to the understanding of etymology and syntax as well as to the religious environment of early Judaism and Christianity (*MC*, 14). In an exhortation that Ratzinger himself could have penned, Lagrange opines:

> We must have scholars of equal competence, able to discern between what is based on the scientific knowledge of language and of history and what is derived from the philosophical theories of the exegete; able to detect the subjective element which glides in between the technical explanation of words and sentences and the appreciation of their meaning, between exegesis in the strict sense and the exegetical system taken as a whole, with its presuppositions and assumptions. (*MC*, 14–15).[12]

In order to meet the challenges of Enlightenment criticism, Lagrange goes on, Catholic biblical scholars must be just as technically skilled as their Protestant counterparts, so that they can meet them on their own ground (*MC*, 15). At the same time, he argues, Catholic biblical scholars must also be willing to learn from the Germans, albeit with caution: "Even when one is on his guard against their conclusions, he cannot but learn something from fellow-workers who are patient and persevering, with a curiosity which is ever on the alert, with a useful mania for references and bibliographical indications" (*MC*, 18–19). Lagrange does not simply prescribe a program, however. In the lectures collected in *The Meaning of Christianity*, he models the approach he advocates, offering a fair-minded but critical assessment of roughly three hundred years of scholarship.

12. Cf. Ratzinger, "Biblical Interpretation in Crisis," 21: "Scientific exegesis must recognize the philosophic element in a great number of its ground rules, and it must then reconsider the results which are based on these rules."

Before turning his attention to Luther and his followers, however, Lagrange lays out some basic principles for Catholic exegesis, arguing that Catholics are in a better position to understand Scripture in the spirit in which it was written. In the process, he points out the impossibility of approaching the texts of Scripture with neutrality, the protests of Enlightenment critics notwithstanding.[13] In response to those who would argue that one can approach the Bible in the same neutral manner as one can read the works of Homer, he notes two important differences between the exegesis of Homer and that of Scripture. First, the events described by Homer predate his writing by several centuries. The same cannot be said of the writings of the New Testament, which has important implications for how one treats the miracles recorded therein. Whereas the distance between the writings of Homer and the events described in his works allows for the development of myths and legends, the same, Lagrange suggests, is not true of the New Testament. Those who wish to deny the reality of the miracles recorded in the texts must, therefore, argue that the writers were either deceived or deceivers. There is no legitimate third option (*MC*, 28–30). But this skepticism, he continues, necessarily leads one to read against the grain, seeking to find the "truth" behind the text, to "unmask the fraud" (*MC*, 30). Such exegesis, he suggests, will not be loyal to the text.

More importantly, however, the New Testament differs from the writings of Homer in its moral framework. The gods of Homer are morally reprehensible, which is why the early Christians cautioned against allowing children to read Homeric texts. The solution to this problem was often simply to separate the supernatural element from the morals of the stories, admiring the virtues while condemning the indiscretions of the gods (*MC*, 31). Such an approach does not work for Christianity, however, because in the New Testament, the supernatural and the moral are interwoven. Moreover, since the New Testament makes a claim on the reader, no one can approach the text neutrally: "The unbeliever, if he abandons practical skepticism to examine into [the New Testament] and to discuss it, must demolish its pretensions and its titles; and this places him very far from that elegant ivory tower where one may in peace relish the antique form while smiling at the childishness of the content" (*MC*, 33). This skepticism, as we will see, is a running theme

13. This is another point of affinity between Lagrange and Ratzinger. The latter writes, "Finally, the exegete must realize that he does not stand in some neutral area, above or outside history and the church. Such a presumed immediacy regarding the purely historical can only lead to dead ends." Ratzinger, "Biblical Interpretation in Crisis," 22.

in his critique of the German exegetes he considers, as it underlies their rejections of various parts of the New Testament record.

In contrast to the figures he analyzes, Lagrange suggests that Catholics are in a better position to interpret Scripture properly for several reasons. The most important of these reasons for Lagrange is the guidance of the Holy Spirit (*MC*, 34). But even setting aside this theological point, he notes other factors that make a Catholic approach to Scripture more suitable. First, he suggests, "The understanding of texts is easier when one is in the same state of mind as the author" (*MC*, 35). The Catholic Church, like the writers of the New Testament, believes in a transcendent God who intervenes in history, accepting miracles and the supernatural. Thanks to this mindset, Catholics do not have to explain away instances of the miraculous in the Scriptures (*MC*, 36).[14] Moreover, the church stands in continuity with the early Christians, and so it accepts the authority of their writings as reliable testimonies to "the original meaning of Christianity" (*MC*, 37).

While Catholics affirm this authority, at the same time, they also supplement their reading of the New Testament with the teaching of tradition. Whereas Protestants often see this as a drawback, Lagrange points to two advantages of reading Scripture with the aid of tradition. First, history itself makes clear that the writings of the New Testament comprise only a part of the deposit of faith. The early church transmitted these texts together with a framework for interpreting them (*MC*, 37–38). Perhaps more importantly, though, this reliance on tradition frees Catholic interpreters from forcing the texts to say what they want them to say. Trusting in the teaching of tradition under the guidance of the Spirit allows interpreters to let the texts speak for themselves: "If the formulas [of a certain dogma] are not in Scripture, we shall not feel obliged to read them into it. And thus we have the sincerity of exegesis guaranteed, at the same time as its freedom" (*MC*, 40). Although it may seem counterintuitive, tradition actually safeguards the integrity of the New Testament documents because the Catholic interpreter need not force an artificial harmony on them.[15]

14. Compare Ratzinger's assessment of modern criticism: "Modern exegesis, as we have seen, completely relegated God to the incomprehensible, the otherworldly, and the inexpressible in order to be able to treat the biblical text itself as an entirely worldly reality according to natural-scientific methods." Ratzinger, "Biblical Interpretation in Crisis," 17.

15. This is not to say that Catholic interpreters have never tried to harmonize texts at all expenses, a point that Lagrange acknowledges. Nevertheless, such attempts at harmonization do not stem from a reliance on tradition. On the contrary, as the church's

The Philosophical Underpinnings of German Exegesis

Having laid out some basic principles of Catholic exegesis, Lagrange turns his attention to the varied positions of German exegesis, especially of the eighteenth and nineteenth centuries. True to the words of the preface, he focuses on the philosophical presuppositions that underlie the conclusions of each of these exegetes. Unlike many histories of modern biblical scholarship, Lagrange's account is dotted with the names of modern philosophers such as Spinoza, Kant, and Hegel, to name a few. Although the specific philosophical influences on each of the exegetes considered vary, all of them (with the exception of Martin Luther) share one important assumption: the denial of the supernatural.[16] Lagrange's analysis of the philosophical presuppositions of the scholars considered exemplifies the "criticism of criticism" that Ratzinger has called for.[17]

In the aftermath of the Reformation, the pendulum of German engagement with Scripture swung relatively quickly from one side to the other. As Lagrange describes, before "free enquiry" took root in the German lands, there was a brief period of Pietism, which "intervenes between early Lutheranism and the complete emancipation of reason" (*MC*, 97). This period was characterized by readings of Scripture that anticipated more recent fundamentalist interpretations of the Bible. Disregarding the point St. Augustine had made centuries before, that the evangelists agree on the substance but not the exact phrasing of the words and deeds they narrate, the Pietists counted events that were related in different ways by the different evangelists multiple times (*MC*, 97).[18]

Before long, however, these proto-fundamentalist readings began to give way under the influence of deism, which had arrived in Germany from England. According to the deists of this time, most notably Edward, Lord Herbert of Cherbury (whom Lagrange considers the father of deism), all one

rejection of Tatian's Diatesseron (for example) shows, tradition has resisted a flattening out of the gospel. See Lagrange, *Meaning of Christianity*, 45–48.

16. Lagrange's focus on the denial of the supernatural is characteristic of his work more broadly. See Marie-Joseph Lagrange, OP, *Christ and Renan: A Commentary on Ernst Renan's "The Life of Jesus,"* trans. Maisie Ward (London: Sheed & Ward, 1928), 7–8, 54–55; Marie-Joseph Lagrange, OP, *L'Écriture en Église: Choix de portraits et d'exégèse spirituelle (1890–1937)*, ed. Maurice Gilbert, LD 142 (Paris: Éditions du Cerf, 1990), 159–69.

17. Ratzinger, "Biblical Interpretation in Crisis," 6.

18. Lagrange uses the example of Peter's denials of Jesus, which according to some Pietist readings amounted to eight rather than three.

needs to found a religion applicable to all human beings is reason (*MC*, 101). Lord Herbert's deism, however, was neither a religion nor based solely on reason. Deism as presented by Herbert had a strong individualistic streak and so could be said to be more a system of thought than a religion. There was no room for worship other than doing what is right and avoiding what is wrong—hence, it was not a religion (*MC*, 101–2). Neither, however, was it based (solely) on reason, as the deists had actually inherited many of the teachings they accepted, such as the immortality of the soul and judgment after death, from their Christian upbringing (103). Regardless of its sources, deism, which in France charged Christianity with imposture and fraud, made its effects felt in Germany through the work of Hermann Samuel Reimarus and his publisher, Gotthold Ephraim Lessing.[19]

Although Lessing at times defended Protestant orthodoxy over and against more recent theology (a defense Lagrange ascribes to Lessing's "opportunism"), in his heart the German philosopher was a deist for much of his life (*MC*, 108–9). In line with the deism of Lord Herbert, Lessing cared primarily about moral truths, and he used Christianity to support those morals, though he expected Christianity to disappear (*MC*, 109). Lessing's biggest impact on German exegesis, however, came not from his own writings but from his role in the posthumous publication of Reimarus's deist account of the origins of Christianity. Originally written under the title *Apologie oder Schutzschrift für die vernünftigen Verehrer Gottes*, the work remained unpublished at the time of Reimarus's death, and parts of it remain unpublished to this day. The fragments that Lessing did eventually publish caused a sensation, but they were also to exert a major influence on subsequent studies of Jesus in his historical context.[20]

What sets Reimarus's work apart from that of other deists, like Voltaire and Rousseau, is his historical approach to the question of Christianity's origins (*MC*, 113). Reimarus seeks to understand Jesus and his followers against the backdrop of first-century Judaism, but his deism leads him to deny the veracity of any of the miraculous events recorded in the Gospels, above all the resurrection. Jesus's aspirations to be Israel's messiah came to a crushing defeat on the cross. How, then, to account for the origins of Christianity? For

19. Lagrange (*Meaning of Christianity*, 104–5) cites Desmarais, a friend of Voltaire, and Boulanger as French figures who accused the early Christians of fraud.

20. Schweitzer's famous work on the historical Jesus was first published under the title *Von Reimarus zu Wrede* (From Reimarus to Wrede), implying that Reimarus's work marks the beginning of the "quest for the historical Jesus." Lagrange (*Meaning of Christianity*, 265n2) suggests that this title gives too much credit to both figures.

Reimarus, the key appears in the book of Daniel's vision of the son of man. The disciples, remembering this passage and not wanting to return to their former work, perpetuated a fraud about Christ's resurrection, promising that he would soon return in glory and taking advantage of Jesus's financial supporters, who had provided for the disciples during his lifetime (*MC*, 113–16). Thus, for Reimarus, Christianity was founded upon a lie told for financial gain and subsequently perpetuated for centuries.

As Lagrange notes, at least two arguments were marshaled to refute Reimarus's case. First, his understanding of Jewish messianism is deficient. Second, his reconstruction fails to take into account the spiritual dimensions of Jesus's teaching (*MC*, 119–21). But for Lagrange, far more important than the details of the historical argument is the deeper source of Reimarus's account. His rejection of the testimony of the New Testament stems not primarily from historical arguments but rather from his deism, which cannot accept the possibility of miracles. According to Lagrange, the scandalous, even sacrilegious, nature of Reimarus's argument gave a bad name to deism in Germany (*MC*, 118). Nevertheless, although many subsequent German exegetes rejected the charges of fraud, they shared with Reimarus his skepticism toward miracles and the supernatural.

Lagrange describes the years in Germany between the publication of Reimarus's *Fragments* and David Friedrich Strauss's *The Life of Jesus* as a "relatively tranquil" period marked by the rise of Enlightenment rationalism, particularly of a "Wolffian" strain (*MC*, 125). The effects of this philosophical school made their way into the efforts of exegetes who wished to adhere to Christianity but only insofar as it conformed to reason (*MC*, 126). These rationalists thus rejected traditional dogma and, like Reimarus, denied the possibility of the supernatural, whether in the form of prophecy or of miracles (*MC*, 127). Lagrange sees in this period a four-stage development unified only by this rejection of the supernatural. Despite this unifying feature, the rationalists explained the miracles in different ways. I will focus briefly on three of the figures Lagrange considers: Franz Volkmar Reinhard, Heinrich Paulus, and Friedrich Schleiermacher, each of whose approach represents a different strand of rationalism.

According to Reinhard, Jesus is the perfect exemplar of enlightened reason. Although Reinhard uses the language of miracles, revelation, and the like, Lagrange sees this as window dressing, maintaining traditional Christian language while evacuating it of its meaning (*MC*, 131). The heart of Jesus's message, in proper rationalist fashion, lies in moral instruction. For Reinhard, miracles simply refer to that which has not yet been explained:

> All that we call miraculous and supernatural is to be understood as only relatively so; it implies nothing further than an obvious exception to what can be brought about by natural causes, so far as we know them and have experience of their capacity. A cautious thinker will not venture in *any single instance* to pronounce an event to be so extraordinary that God could not have brought it about by the use of secondary causes, but only by direct intervention.[21]

Given how he explains away the miraculous in the Gospels, it comes as no surprise that Reinhard also downplays the messianic claims of the New Testament as well. For him, the kingdom of God is simply a moral institution, one guided by enlightened reason (*MC*, 132).

Reinhard similarly reinterpreted Lutheran practices like baptism and the Eucharist as symbols having no real supernatural effects. In this, Lagrange suggests, he simply reflected the conditions of his time: "Men could not refuse to accept light and culture; but it was deemed unnecessary to upset the old Christian edifice and openly to renounce dogmas, since a man could accept these dogmas in the sense that appealed to himself" (*MC*, 133). Rather than do away with the notion of revelation, Reinhard simply transferred the role of revelation to reason, making the Bible nothing more than "a source of excellent morality and particularly of charity" (*MC*, 133–34). As Lagrange notes, it was Reinhard's commitment to rationalism rather than any purely historical arguments that led to his attenuated account of Jesus (*MC*, 132).

A similar approach to the miraculous appears in the work of Heinrich Paulus, though his rationalism is of a different variety. Influenced by the writings of Benedict Spinoza, an edition of whose works he prepared, Paulus was a pantheist. This pantheism inevitably led Paulus to deny the supernatural character of the miracles in the Gospels. As Lagrange notes, "When one makes up his mind, as had [Spinoza], not to distinguish God from nature, there can be no question of miracle" (*MC*, 140). Given this rejection of the miraculous, Jesus's mission must then have been one in accord with reason (*MC*, 144).

How, then, does Paulus explain the miracle stories? He undertakes a concerted effort to offer naturalistic explanations for all these stories: "The Evangelists relate supernatural facts in order to arouse faith in supernatural doctrine; he [Paulus] must knock the support from under the supernatu-

21. Lagrange, *Meaning of Christianity*, 132 (emphasis added). Lagrange takes this quotation from Schweitzer, on whom he relies for the whole discussion of Reinhard.

ral doctrine by reducing miracles to natural events and pointing out their secondary causes" (*MC*, 144). Unlike many of his contemporaries and later critics, Paulus accepted the Gospels as reliable historical sources, even affirming that the accounts in Matthew and John came from eyewitnesses. The difficulty of maintaining this position is not hard to see, and it is unsurprising that his arguments were easily refuted (*MC*, 144–45). On his reading, in at least some cases, the evangelists did not intend to present stories as actual miracles. In others, they simply misunderstood the events they witnessed and so mistakenly offered miraculous interpretations (*MC*, 145). The "miracle" of the multiplication of the loaves was simply an instance of sharing; Jesus healed people by medical arts unknown to the evangelists; the people Christ allegedly raised from the dead were not actually dead but rather in a coma (*MC*, 146–47).

The obvious problem with Paulus's proposal is twofold. First, it ascribes far too much credulity to the disciples. As Lagrange notes, the Jews of the first century were not inclined to see the supernatural anywhere and everywhere (*MC*, 148).[22] More importantly, though, Paulus's reconstruction implies that Jesus, rather than disabusing them of their misunderstanding, allowed them to remain in their error. But perpetuating such misunderstandings hardly fits with Paulus's portrayal of Jesus as a paragon of moral instruction (*MC*, 148). For these and other reasons, Lagrange says of Paulus's reading that it is not even worthy of the name "exegesis." Paulus's philosophical presuppositions thus invalidate his interpretation of the New Testament witness (*MC*, 146, 148).

Although not a rationalist in the strict sense, Friedrich Schleiermacher also appears in Lagrange's survey of the rationalist lives of Jesus because of his dependence on the thought of Immanuel Kant, specifically Kant's subjectivism (*MC*, 153). Lagrange describes Schleiermacher's project as an attempt "to reconcile naturalism with the supernatural," resulting in a "theology of compromise" (*MC*, 151). In this "compromise," Lagrange suggests, Schleiermacher's rationalism "invades the domain of the supernatural to steal its formulas and to put on the appearances of a regenerated Protestantism" (*MC*, 151). Because of his Kantian subjectivism, Schleiermacher argues that the supernatural reveals itself only within the limits of human nature (*MC*, 153).

These philosophical presuppositions obviously color Schleiermacher's account of the life of Jesus. Unlike the rationalists who preceded him, how-

22. Lagrange points to Josephus, among others, as an example of the reticence with which first-century Jews accepted miracles.

ever, he neither explains away the miracles in naturalistic fashion nor denies them altogether. Instead, he simply dismisses the importance of whether they happened or not, including the resurrection:

> [Schleiermacher] carefully refrains from indicating how much of the miraculous he would keep in the Gospel; the word miracle remains, the reality disappears. He avoids, indeed, naturalistic explanations. He insists on the spiritual power of Jesus, which was capable of affecting even the body. And, anyhow, what matters it whether a miracle was wrought or not? That is said even of the Resurrection. (*MC*, 155)

Schleiermacher's account may preserve the importance of religious sentiment, but like the true rationalists, it dismisses the importance, and at least implicitly the reality, of miracles (*MC*, 155–56). Once again, it is philosophical presuppositions rather than historical analysis that shape the argument.

Before we turn to the constructive aspects of Lagrange's argument, one final example will suffice to show how he anticipates Ratzinger's "criticism of criticism." One of the most well-known instances of the philosophical tail wagging the exegetical dog is found in the writings of Ferdinand Christian Baur, the early nineteenth-century leader of the Tübingen school. The affinities between his reconstruction of the development of early Christianity and the philosophical schemes of Hegel have been recognized for some time. Like Reimarus, Paulus, and Schleiermacher before him, Baur's exegesis owes as much to his philosophical presuppositions as to historical investigation. On Lagrange's reading, Baur's approach sought to uncover the tendencies in early Christianity, but as he notes, "It is itself very clearly the product of a tendency" (*MC*, 196).

In contrast to the figures we have already discussed and to Baur's student David Friedrich Strauss (whom Lagrange deals with in an earlier lecture), Baur concerns himself not with the historical Jesus but rather with the development of early Christianity. More specifically, he asks how the early Christian movement gave rise to the lives of Christ we see in the Gospels. In the process, Baur offers an account of the dating of the various writings of the New Testament, fitting them into a schema that reflects the Hegelian trope of thesis, antithesis, and synthesis (*MC*, 196, 203).

Central to Baur's argument is an alleged conflict between two parties in the early church, the one led by Peter and the other by Paul.[23] The Petrine

23. That there were conflicts in early Christianity is beyond dispute—even a cursory

party held to a Judaizing view of Christ's message. It emphasized observance of the law of Moses, making this a requirement for membership in the Christian community and for salvation. The Pauline group, by contrast, had a more Hellenizing or universalizing understanding of early Christianity. Paul and his companions reached out to the gentiles, emphasizing the expiatory nature of Christ's death on the cross and not requiring his converts to observe the Mosaic law. When these two groups faced external pressure from the gnostics, they reached a compromise, resulting in what many German scholars call "early Catholicism" (*MC*, 197–200).

Having laid out this hypothesis for the rise of early Christian history, Baur then applies it to the writings of the New Testament, categorizing them as Petrine or Pauline. The so-called *Hauptbriefe* (Romans, 1–2 Corinthians, and Galatians) are the purest witnesses to Paulinism. The Gospel of Matthew, as well as the book of Revelation, represents the Judaizing tendencies of Petrinism. The Pastoral Epistles and the Acts of the Apostles reflect the reconciliation brought about by the external pressure of Gnosticism. With this reading, Baur dates these last writings to the second century. The Gospels of Mark and John also fall into this reconciling synthesis. Baur thus takes Mark to be a conflation of Matthew and Luke and considers John to be a much later writing, composed in the late second century (*MC*, 200–202).

Lagrange critiques Baur's reconstruction on two fronts. First, as other scholars had already noted, he points to Baur's imposition of the Hegelian system on the data: "The teaching of Hegel . . . is recognized by critics as one of the principal factors in the production of the system. Petrinism is set forth as a thesis; Paulinism is its antithesis; naturally the conciliation and the compromise are the synthesis. All takes place in the rhythm of the philosophy of Hegel" (*MC*, 203).[24] Moreover, Baur's system "is too much preoccu-

---

reading of the New Testament reveals the many disagreements that characterized the Christian movement in its infancy. Nevertheless, it is the way that Baur characterizes the nature of the disagreement between Peter and Paul that is problematic and that Lagrange, like many since, would critique.

24. Scholarship since the time of Lagrange has shown that characterizing Baur as a straight Hegelian is an oversimplification. For a brief recent discussion, see David Lincicum, "F. C. Baur's Place in the Study of Jewish Christianity," in *The Rediscovery of Jewish Christianity: From Toland to Baur*, ed. F. Stanley Jones, HBS 5 (Atlanta: Society of Biblical Literature, 2012), 137–66, esp. 151–52. For an older, fuller discussion, see Peter C. Hodgson, *The Formation of Historical Theology: A Study of Ferdinand Christian Baur*, Makers of Modern Theology (New York: Harper & Row, 1966). Nevertheless, the basic point that Baur's philosophical principles exercise a significant influence on his reconstruction of early Christianity remains.

pied about the intellectual evolution of doctrines" (*MC*, 210). He treats the New Testament writings, Lagrange continues, as representing two different schools of philosophy and the writers as controversialists (*MC*, 210).

Equally important, though, is Lagrange's close reading of the texts themselves. Baur's reconstruction fails not simply because of his reliance on Hegel but also because it does not adequately explain the data. The details of Lagrange's argument would take too long to elaborate. The key, however, appears in the testimony of Galatians 2. In the Jerusalem meeting as described by Paul, he and Barnabas reached an agreement with Peter, James, and John regarding the question of circumcision. Perhaps more importantly, Paul's disagreement with Peter at Antioch calls into question Baur's characterization of Peter as one who observed the Jewish law. For, as Paul points out, prior to the arrival of the men from James at Antioch, Peter was living "like a gentile," which suggests that he agreed with Paul on basic principles. What mattered for salvation was faith in Christ, not the rite of circumcision.[25] Moreover, with respect to Baur's dating of the New Testament documents, later scholarship showed significant problems with his schema. For example, whereas Baur understood the Gospel of Mark as a "synthesis" of the Paulinism of Luke and the Petrinism of Matthew, later scholars came to the conclusion that Mark is almost certainly the earliest Gospel. Additionally, Lagrange argues that Mark reflects the testimony of Peter and at the same time contains theological themes consonant with Paul's thought, which again problematizes the conflict Baur proposed between Petrinism and Paulinism (*MC*, 209).

As with the deists and the rationalists, then, Lagrange's treatment of Baur and the Tübingen school again anticipates elements of Ratzinger's call for biblical renewal. Not only does he show the inadequacies of Baur's account from the perspective of biblical scholarship; he also, and just as importantly, shows that the deeper problem with Baur's exegesis lies in the philosophical presuppositions that inevitably determine the conclusion.

Toward a Synthesis

Almost halfway through *The Meaning of Christianity*, Lagrange acknowledges that the first few lectures focus almost exclusively on the deficiencies

25. For Lagrange's full engagement with Baur's hypothesis, see *Meaning of Christianity*, 211–22.

of the figures treated. The reason for this is not, however, that Lagrange sees nothing to gain from German exegesis: "When we meet in the critical schools we are studying discoveries in philology or history which may be regarded as certain, we shall not hesitate to pay our homage to the indefatigable activity of the Germans" (*MC*, 156). Indeed, in the concluding lecture, Lagrange acknowledges that there is some truth in many of the systems the German exegetes have proposed. But one of the main problems with the German exegesis of the eighteenth and nineteenth centuries is its one-sidedness: The Germans "discover an idea, cling to it, give it free rein, unheedful of difficulties or even of contradictions. Everything is, whether or no, squeezed into the system, until it crumbles" (*MC*, 367–68). This one-sidedness, he argues, stems from the thought of Luther, who himself fixated on certain texts and sought to force the rest of Scripture into a schema based on them (*MC*, 368–69).[26]

In order to offer a satisfying account of early Christianity, then, it is necessary to combine the valid elements of different schools. Of the figures he treats, Lagrange sees the most promise in generating a synthesis of the compromise theology of the liberals and the messianism of the eschatological school. Both of these approaches, however, must first be stripped of the antisupernaturalism that runs through their accounts, as it does in nearly all the approaches discussed in *The Meaning of Christianity*.

The liberal theology of the second half of the nineteenth century was not without its problems. As Lagrange notes, though it was not driven by one particular school of philosophy, such as that of Hegel, it nevertheless maintained the common presuppositions of the time, namely, "the denial of the supernatural and of the miracle, together with an abuse of subjectivism" (*MC*, 240). The exegetes of this school, predominantly university professors, maintained ties with German Protestantism, seeking to propose theories palatable to their coreligionists (*MC*, 240).

Despite their denial of the supernatural, the liberals nevertheless sought to recover the Gospels as reliable historical sources, at least in part. Reacting against the excesses of Strauss, for whom the Gospels were entirely mythical, the liberals argued that at least Mark and the sayings source commonly known as Q had some connection to history. The liberals accepted that Mark had a connection with Peter and so used his account as the basic framework for the life of Jesus (*MC*, 250). The sayings source served as witness to Jesus's teaching, reporting that teaching "at least as faithfully as Xenophon and Plato

26. See also the earlier lecture on Luther on pp. 54–92.

reproduce the doctrine of Socrates" (*MC*, 251). This summary of the liberal position, as Lagrange himself notes, is an oversimplification (*MC*, 251). There were numerous disagreements over the details. Nevertheless, the basic point remains that, in contrast to Strauss (as well as the radical skeptic Bruno Bauer), the liberals sought to establish the Gospels as (somewhat) reliable sources for the life of Jesus.

Lagrange offers the work of Heinrich Julius Holtzmann as representative of the "middle" of the liberal school, though he intersperses other voices in his description of the Jesus of the liberals (*MC*, 257). In contrast to Strauss, the liberals had disavowed Holtzmann's mythological interpretation of the New Testament. Nevertheless, they, too, reject certain aspects of the New Testament record, such as the infancy narratives, as legends and so begin their account of Jesus with the baptism by John (*MC*, 258). Moreover, they deny the two most common interpretations of the messianic claims of the Gospels in the late nineteenth century, asserting that Jesus was neither a nationalistic redeemer nor an enthusiast expecting the radical inbreaking of a new world (*MC*, 259). Jesus's messianism was instead a spiritual one characterized by moral instruction. Central to Jesus's message, according to the liberals, is the fatherhood of God as well as the higher righteousness of his moral instruction (*MC*, 259–60).

Unsurprisingly, the liberals, like their deist, rationalist, and Hegelian predecessors, deny Jesus's divinity, and with it much of the Gospel tradition. Their Jesus receives his mission and identity at the baptism. He then keeps his identity secret from the crowds, for fear of being misunderstood. It is only toward the end of his life, when the kingdom had not come fully, that Jesus decides that he must bring it about through his death (*MC*, 260–61). Despite the superficial similarities between the liberal portrait and the one proposed later by Schweitzer, the liberals continued to eschew an eschatological interpretation of Jesus's mission and mindset. They either reject or reinterpret the title "Son of Man," much as they had done with the title "Son of God," leaving a Jesus who bears little resemblance to the Gospel records, even the Gospel of Mark, on which they based their reconstructions (*MC*, 263–65).

Despite the many flaws in the liberal accounts—flaws that, like those of their predecessors, stem largely from an a priori philosophical rejection of miracles—Lagrange credits the liberals with at least preserving "a historical residue of the Gospel" (*MC*, 263). Moreover, he notes that they were right in affirming the moral and religious aspects of Jesus's message. The liberals correctly recognize the spiritual center of his teaching, but they maintain it at the expense of too much of the Gospel record. Their portrait of Jesus remains one-sided (*MC*, 263–65).

The same can be said of the "eschatological messianism" of Johannes Weiss, Albert Schweitzer, and others. Whereas the liberals emphasize the moral instruction of Jesus and downplay the messianic claims of the Gospels, the "eschatologists" acknowledge these messianic claims as coming from Jesus himself, but they interpret them within the framework of an imminent expectation of the end of the world. In contrast to the liberals, figures like Weiss place Jesus more believably in his historical context: "Weiss, then, divests Jesus of the garb of a Liberal-Protestant pastor. He pictures Him as living and breathing only in the expectation of the intervention of God, of the salvation of which He Himself was to be the agent, as wholly immersed in the supernatural" (*MC*, 269). In some respects, the picture proposed by the eschatologists is more congenial to the Catholic faith, insofar as they acknowledge Jesus's messianic self-understanding. In other respects, however, the eschatological reconstruction of Jesus challenges the Catholic faith because of the sharpness with which they present Jesus's imminent expectation. Given that their Jesus focuses so much on the impending reign of God, there is no place in this account for the church (*MC*, 269). Like the liberals, then, the eschatological reconstruction leaves out much of the material in the Gospels.

The way forward, Lagrange suggests, is a synthesis of the liberal and the eschatological perspectives: "We conclude that both the system of the Eschatologists and that of the Liberals has a part of the truth; that we must unite what is true in both systems; that Jesus was conscious of His dignity [with the eschatologists] and that He was not deluded [with the liberals]" (*MC*, 280). Although they misconstrue Jesus's self-understanding, the liberals rightly acknowledge that he had a clear vision of his role. Moreover, they correctly emphasize the importance of his moral instruction, which was not, *pace* the eschatologists, merely an interim ethic (*MC*, 291).

The mistakes of the eschatologists, like those of the liberals, stem from a one-sided reading of the data. They rightly see that eschatology lies at the heart of Jesus's message, but they then mistakenly flatten it out into a single-minded focus on the end of the world. In order to do so, they must ignore or distort Gospel passages that do not fit their schema. Lagrange indicates two points of interpretation that problematize the imminent understanding of the eschaton in Jesus's teaching: the complex nature of the kingdom or reign of God and the message of the parables (*MC*, 279–97).

The reconstruction by the eschatologists fails to make sense of the multiple senses of the kingdom of God. While it is true that Jesus at times speaks of the kingdom coming, and even of it arriving soon, this is not the only way that he uses the phrase. In some cases, Jesus's kingdom language refers to a supernatural kingdom that is to come, a realm contrasted with gehenna, the place of punishment (*MC*, 289–90). Other passages—most prominently, Matt 12:28—seem to suggest that the kingdom has already come in some sense (*MC*, 291). But perhaps the most problematic passages for the thoroughgoing eschatological interpretation of Jesus's life are the growth parables. Several parables in the Synoptic Gospels use the imagery of gradual growth: the kingdom is like a sower who went out to sow (Mark 4:26), like a mustard seed that grows over time (Matt 13:31–32; Luke 13:18–19), or like weeds and wheat growing in a field (Matt 13:24–30).[27] According to the Gospels, Jesus repeatedly used this kind of imagery as well as that of imminent expectation. In order to maintain their understanding of the imminent expectation of the end, the eschatologists must either dismiss or misinterpret this part of the Gospel data.

In addition to this aspect of the parables, Lagrange notes that certain of Jesus's judgment oracles do not make much sense if he expected the world to end immediately. In particular, his warning to Jerusalem, "Your house shall be left to you desolate," makes less sense if Jesus expected the world to end soon (*MC*, 289). Lagrange points out that this saying does not go on to refer to a supernatural transformation—the desolation of Jerusalem will continue for some time. Given this apparent discrepancy, Lagrange concludes that Jesus spoke of two judgments, one imminent (the destruction of Jerusalem) and one later (that of the whole world). The evangelists brought together sayings relating to both judgments because of their shared theme of the judgment of God (*MC*, 289). Distinguishing these two judgments better accounts for other aspects of the Gospel tradition that otherwise make little sense, such as the warning that the disciples will be brought before governors and kings or the proclamation of the gospel to the gentiles (*MC*, 288, 295–96).

As one can see, while there are certainly philosophical presuppositions at work among the eschatologists, in this case Lagrange focuses more on historical arguments. No doubt, they, like their liberal predecessors, deny the possibility of the miraculous, which contributes to their conclusion that Jesus

27. Lagrange, *Meaning of Christianity*, 290. In pointing to these examples, Lagrange once again anticipates an aspect of Ratzinger's reading of early Christianity. Cf. Benedict XVI, *Jesus of Nazareth: From the Baptism in the Jordan to the Transfiguration*, trans. Adrian J. Walker (New York: Doubleday, 2007), 52: "Even texts that seemingly contradict this [eschatological] interpretation were somewhat violently made to fit it—for example, the growth parables about the sower (cf. Mk 4:3–9), the mustard seed (cf. Mk 4:30–32), the leaven (cf. Mt 13:33/Lk 13:20), and the spontaneously sprouting seed (cf. Mk 4:26–29)."

was mistaken. Nevertheless, Lagrange does not rely solely on philosophical critique. Rather, he shows how their account does not adequately explain the data of the Gospels. In his synthesis of the liberal and the eschatological lives of Jesus, we see most clearly how he brings together philosophical analysis with an appreciation of some of the genuine advances provided by modern scholarship. In this regard, he models the kind of scholarship that Ratzinger called for in 1988 and for which he advocated throughout his career.[28]

Learning from Lagrange Today

Much has changed in the century that has passed since Lagrange first delivered the lectures eventually published as *The Meaning of Christianity*. Perhaps the most obvious development is the explosion in methodologies. Lagrange's lectures cover the work of approximately seven schools or figures (the deists, the rationalists, Strauss, the Tübingen school, the liberals, the eschatologists, and the syncretists). The late twentieth century, by contrast, witnessed a proliferation of methods that resulted in what one scholar has called "a discipline in search of its identity."[29] Were Lagrange alive today to give a similar set of lectures, the task would be much larger than it was in 1917. It is not without reason that Ratzinger sees such a project as "at least the work of a whole generation."[30] Nevertheless, despite the magnitude of the task, its basic nature remains the same. Ratzinger was correct to note the crucial role that philosophical presuppositions play in so many exegetical approaches—a point Lagrange saw long before him with keen insight. Equally important, though, is the way Lagrange also wrestled with the historical data of the New Testament and showed how faith, far from being a hindrance to good scholarship, actually gives the interpreter an advantage in understanding Scripture in the spirit in which it was written. Philosophical critique, though important, is not enough. A robust Catholic biblical scholarship must bring faith, history, philosophy, and theology to bear on the texts in an integrated way. A return to the work of Père Lagrange can help point the way forward to a renewal of Catholic biblical interpretation for the service of both scholarship and the church.

28. See especially the foreword of Benedict XVI, *Jesus of Nazareth*, xi–xxiv.

29. See Markus Bockmuehl, *Seeing the Word: Refocusing New Testament Study*, STI (Grand Rapids: Baker Academic, 2006), 30 and the discussion on 30–39.

30. Ratzinger, "Biblical Interpretation in Crisis," 6.

Why Did Marie-Joseph Lagrange Abandon the Old Testament?

The Risk and Promise of Biblical Scholarship

Mark Giszczak

One of the best ways to forecast the future is to achieve a serious appreciation for the past. When we consider the future of Catholic biblical studies, reflecting on the fate of Père Marie-Joseph Lagrange, OP, will help us to think clearly and realistically. With his innovative style of biblical interpretation, he sought to provide a balanced, level-headed, and cautious application of new historical methods within the framework of the Catholic faith. Lagrange's career unfolded in the context of the modernist controversy and its titanic conflicts between scholars and the hierarchy, and that reality must color our perspective.

Biblical scholars have always worked within constraints—whether those be the limits of available evidence, the limits of our own knowledge, or the boundaries of confessional traditions—Jewish, Lutheran, Catholic, or "secularist." Yet the constraints under which scholars work can at times be more or less flexible. In Père Lagrange's case, the constraints were flexible until they were not. His docility to Roman authority was admirable, but, sadly, he was required to pivot based on the personality of the officeholder above him rather than on the basis of a reasonable and sustainable principle. The requirements imposed led him away from his early work and the questions it had raised, away from the Old Testament and toward the New. Lagrange himself says, "I entirely abandoned the study of the Old Testament except in function of the New."[1] The value of reflecting on what happened and why extends beyond Lagrange's biography to a larger question about how to engage in authentic religious scholarship on the Old Testament while inhabiting a New Testament–focused church. That is, why does Old Testa-

1. Marie-Joseph Lagrange, OP, *Personal Reflections and Memoirs*, trans. Henry Wansbrough, OSB (New York: Paulist, 1985), 133.

ment scholarship seem more dangerous to religious authorities than New Testament scholarship?

Religious Truth and Historical Method

The real problem is methodological. Here I do not mean whether one chooses literary criticism or comparative linguistics to arrive at conclusions but rather the method of conceiving of religious truth. That is, where does doctrinal authority truly reside? In the text of Scripture? In the tradition of the church? In the hands of the pope? Traditional Catholic thinking, especially in the wake of the definition of papal infallibility at Vatican I, upheld a high view of magisterial authority and of previous generations of Christian commentary on Scripture, adopting a pious but unnuanced veneration for the past. New modes of historical research have challenged such a view of authority from putatively objective vantage points—from archaeology, philology, and textual criticism. While modernist historians could be accused of having a pious but unnuanced veneration for present methods at the expense of the past, their methods could not be ignored. Basing arguments on external sources of evidence like comparative ancient literature, archaeological findings, and historical reconstructions gave not only a plausibility but also a semblance, at the very least, of evidence-based "scientific" objectivity to their arguments. To respond to serious historians with serious historical arguments, Lagrange supposed, one must first become one of them. Indeed, he describes his anxiety to offer "a critical and historical defense of truth" as "the only way, nowadays, of reaching certain minds."[2] The minds he was thinking of were those who had been exposed to modern practices of historical investigation.

Two different and seemingly opposed methods for determining truth appeared to be at loggerheads: unfettered historical inquiry versus magisterial authority and tradition, archaeology versus dogma. Does truth come down from the invisible God or does it come up from the collection and analysis of visible evidence? It seemed that science—in the form of evolution and historical study—was opposed to a religious faith that upheld the doctrines of creation and the resurrection. This conflict presented a significant chal-

2. Bernard Montagnes, OP, *The Story of Father Marie-Joseph Lagrange: Founder of Modern Catholic Bible Study*, trans. Benedict Viviano, OP (New York: Paulist, 2006), 97. Hereafter, this work is cited in the text as *Story*.

lenge for both sides of the debate between scientific study of history and conventional religious approaches. But in fact, there were three sides to the debate. First, traditional religious authority generally felt itself to be in the right and deemed all challenges to be secularist and opposed to faith. Second, some genuine secularists sought to disabuse thinking persons of religious notions and actually did oppose the faith and religious authority as outdated, superstitious, medieval, and erroneous. I think Père Lagrange, however, falls into a third category: a faithful churchman who recognized the severe challenge that historical methods posed to traditional ways of understanding religious truths and who sought to provide a helpful historical corrective as an antidote for the faithful against rationalist historians. One observer posits that Lagrange represented "a sound approach to Scripture that embodies the marriage of faith and reason central to the Dominican heritage."[3] Yet placing oneself in the middle of the era's ideological crossfire was not a good strategy for career success. Père Lagrange, it seems, was hoping to show both the secularists and the religious traditionalists a different mode of viewing history—one that is neither overconfident of its claims nor opposed to authentic faith. Sadly, his entreaties ultimately fell on deaf ears.

Père Lagrange's Early Success

Returning to the problem of Lagrange abandoning the Old Testament, it will be helpful to review what happened in Lagrange's career that led to his complicated ecclesiastical case. His early studies were in law and theology, and he was ordained to the priesthood in 1883. While he began teaching history and philosophy at the seminary at Toulouse, he continued working away at biblical study on an informal basis until 1888, when he was invited by his superiors to embark on a formal program of study.[4] He then spent three semesters at the University of Vienna studying languages, including Egyptian, Arabic, Assyrian (Akkadian), and rabbinic Hebrew (*Story*, 18). During the course of his training, he was stunned by a letter calling him away from studies and assigning him to open a new biblical faculty at Jerusalem. The Dominican priory of St. Étienne had been founded in 1882 by Fr. Matthieu Lecomte, OP,

3. Isaac Augustine Morales, OP, "Père Lagrange and the Historical Study of the Bible: Faith, Reason, and Sacred Scripture," *Dominicana* 57, no. 1 (2014): 18.

4. F.-M. Braun, OP, *The Work of Père Lagrange*, ed. and trans. Richard T. A. Murphy, OP (Milwaukee: Bruce, 1963), 4.

at the site of St. Stephen's stoning in Jerusalem. Lecomte died in 1887, and the house needed new leadership and a new direction. Lagrange was tasked with leading the house and setting up a new school of biblical studies there. He finally opened the École biblique et archéologique française de Jérusalem on November 15, 1890, at the age of thirty-five. His enthusiasm for new modes of Scripture study led him to extol the value of Semitic languages, to advocate for a "return to the Great Eastern Book which is the Bible" (*Story*, 28), and to call for progress in Catholic biblical studies.

Fortunately, Pope Leo XIII (1878–1903) shared Lagrange's enthusiasm for biblical study and for using the latest methods of historical research. The pope erected the Pontifical Biblical Commission in 1902, and Lagrange was soon after appointed to it as a consultor. His periodical, the *Revue biblique*, published by the École biblique, was set to become the official publication of the Commission at the direction of the pope himself. The pope also invited him to establish a new school of biblical studies at Rome. Things were looking up.

At the same time, Père Lagrange gave his famous Toulouse lectures in November 1902, which were quickly published with the imprimatur in March 1903 as *La méthode historique surtout à propos de l'Ancien Testament* (The historical-critical method and the Old Testament). These lectures would project his vision for the path of Catholic critical study of the Old Testament, a path that he would soon be required to give up. He decided to give these lectures "as simple talks, without scholarly footnotes, for a cultivated public" (*Story*, 73). This decision may have been a strategic error. Soon the leading Modernists were writing to one another about his "abominable style" (Duschesne to Loisy, quoted on *Story*, 78) and complaining that Lagrange "does not know how to write or think" (Laberthonnière to Loisy, quoted in *Story*, 78). Yet he also infuriated certain conservatives. His biographer Montagnes sums up the situation well: "By publishing *The Historical Method*, Father Lagrange definitively alienated himself from the conservative party without winning the support of the innovators" (*Story*, 79). If he had chosen a more abstruse academic style, certain conservatives would likely not have been so interested to read his views. Indeed, Lagrange said that "what attracted even more attention to this little book was that it was short and easy to read."[5] If he had chosen to leave the lectures unpublished, many critics would not have been able to inspect them. Yet Lagrange was a bold man with daring in his blood. He reflects on this book in his memoirs, saying, "I have

5. Lagrange, *Personal Reflections and Memoirs*, 106.

written nothing which gives a greater impression of independence in the face of dogma and theology, nor any propositions more liable to censure."[6] At the same time that Lagrange succeeded in distancing himself from both groups that could have been his supporters, Pope Leo XIII died in the summer of 1903. Storm clouds were gathering.

Lagrange's Major Old Testament Studies

Père Lagrange's efforts in the direction of Old Testament studies, while vast and varied, can be represented by two of his major works: the commentary on Genesis, which he finished in 1898, and an article he wrote on the patriarchs in 1905. To tell the story of these two works is really to tell the tragic story of Lagrange's intellectual aspirations under a paranoid hierarchy. Lagrange gives a sense of the climate by quoting from a letter he received from Master General of the Dominican Order Hyacinth M. Cormier, OP, who tried to console him regarding the severe tactics employed by the hierarchy. Cormier explained that "if one does not exercise a regime of terrorism, one is bound to be fearful, fearful for those young clerics weak in scholarship and in holiness who cry 'exegesis' to bolster independence and to mock tradition, just as they cry 'democracy' in the secret desire of seeing it contribute to the overthrow of Church discipline."[7] Cormier's pessimism about the state of young clergy and his negative characterization of the hierarchy's approach as "a regime of terrorism" give a sense of the institutional conflicts that would shape Lagrange's experience. With the background of such an ecclesial environment, Lagrange's major efforts may now be evaluated.

First is the *Commentary on Genesis*. Père Lagrange hoped to issue a series of monographs to accompany the *Revue*, entitled Études bibliques. The first volume of the series would appropriately be a commentary on Genesis penned by the editor himself, Lagrange. It is said that Lagrange "had worked for almost ten years"[8] on the commentary. In May of 1898, he was almost done and so requested that censors be appointed to read the volume. Yet he only sent off the first three chapters to Rome because he thought it was "useless to send it if the main lines of the work are not approved" (*Story*, 86). This statement alone is curious. Was he hoping to save on postage or type-

6. Lagrange, *Personal Reflections and Memoirs*, 106.
7. Lagrange, *Personal Reflections and Memoirs*, 125.
8. Braun, *Work of Père Lagrange*, 83.

writer paper? More likely, the statement shows that Lagrange knew some of his claims were daring and that he was not willing to share a complete copy, perhaps for fear of what might be said about his opinions expressed in later chapters. Surprisingly, the censors approved the manuscript in principle but sought to delay publication until Lagrange had published "articles on limited points" (*Story*, 87). In response, Lagrange swiftly published an article on Jacob's prophecy in the October 1898 edition of the *Revue biblique* while at the same time seeking permission from the master general, at that time Fr. Andreas Frühwirth, OP, to start typesetting the book.[9] He received the discouraging answer: "Wait" (*Story*, 87). Lagrange did not appear to perceive that the counsel of delay was in fact simply a tactic of those in charge—to seem to give him the approval he desired while in fact withholding it. The beleaguered scholar could only lament his fate along with the fate of Catholic biblical studies in a letter: "I cannot hide from you how unhappy I feel. . . . I cruelly feel our inferiority as to critical studies" (*Story*, 88). The Genesis commentary was shelved for the time being. He would have to wait.

Six years later, he would try again, asking the new master general, Cormier, "What about *my* Genesis? It is most important to me" (*Story*, 90). He resubmitted the manuscript. While the censor approved, Cormier responded in October 1905: "I think it is wiser . . . not to publish, just now" (*Story*, 91). In January of 1906, even Pope Pius X was brought into the discussion, but he judged it better to wait until the Biblical Commission finished issuing a statement currently under preparation about the Pentateuch. Again, the authorities employed the tactic of delay. Finally, on May 27, 1906, the Holy See communicated its decision that the *Commentary on Genesis* could not be published in any form (*Story*, 92). This decree arrived at about the same time that the Pontifical Biblical Commission issued its famous decision on the Mosaic authorship of the Pentateuch (on June 27, 1906)—the very one the pope had been alluding to in January. The issue of Mosaic authorship would also be used to dismiss Fr. Henry Poels from teaching at the Catholic University of America in 1910, even though he, too, was a consultor to the Pontifical Biblical Commission.[10] In essence, the final decision on Lagrange's Genesis commentary was premised on a rejection of his views of its origin and composition history. The policy of postponement finally gave way to refusal: Lagrange would not be permitted to publish the work.

9. Marie-Joseph Lagrange, OP, "La Prophétie de Jacob," *RB* 7, no. 4 (1898): 525–40.
10. See Gerald P. Fogarty, SJ, *American Catholic Biblical Scholarship: A History from the Early Republic to Vatican II* (San Francisco: Harper and Row, 1989), 96–119.

Sadly, Lagrange was never able to let go. After about ten years preparing the manuscript and an eight-year-long process of seeking approval only to be rejected, his *magnum opus* was destined for the dust bin. Later, after Lagrange professed his complete submission to the Holy See, he switched to writing mainly about the New Testament in works such as his commentary on the Gospel of Mark (1911) or his commentary on the letter to the Romans (1916).[11] Yet late in life, as an old man, Lagrange returned to the Genesis manuscript. Forty years after its 1898 completion and thirty years after its ultimate rejection, we find him "working actively to bring his commentary on Genesis up to date" (*Story*, 183). He would die in 1938 before completing the revision. It is disheartening to think that the church was deprived of the talents of one of its greatest minds and one of its most loyal sons by the ecclesial authorities themselves at the very time when church teaching was under attack from secularist forces.

Lagrange's other long-term effort in Old Testament studies began in 1905 with "an article entitled *The Patriarchs: How They Belong to History*, which the censors deemed unpublishable" because of its novel view of biblical historiography (*Story*, 89). The application of widespread historical methods to the revered figures of Genesis was not to be permitted. Later, after twenty years had passed, in 1928, Lagrange sought to publish the article and again was refused. Yet again, in 1937, after ten more years, he tried one last time and was refused by the vicar general. Finally, "he decided to give up his article" (*Story*, 189). Sadly, thirty years did not change the situation. Long after his death, the article was resurrected and finally published in 1998 by Maxime Allard in a collection of essays.[12]

The Abandonment

In addition to forbidding the publication of the commentary on Genesis, Cormier essentially forbade Lagrange from ever doing scholarship on the Old Testament again (*Story*, 93). The record is somewhat murky on whether Cormier commanded Lagrange to cease Old Testament publications or only strongly encouraged him to do so, but the master general clearly felt that the

11. Marie-Joseph Lagrange, OP, *Évangile selon saint Marc*, EBib (Paris: Lecoffre, 1911); Marie-Joseph Lagrange, OP, *Saint Paul: Épitre aux Romains*, EBib (Paris: Gabalda, 1916).

12. See Guy Couturier, ed., *Les patriarches et l'histoire: Autour d'un article inédit du Père M.-J. Lagrange, O. P.*, LD (Paris: Éditions du Cerf, 1998).

danger of allowing Lagrange to continue in Old Testament scholarship far outweighed the benefit. In his own memoirs, Lagrange recalls the sequence of events differently. From his vantage point, it was only after the publication of *Lamentabili sane* (July 3, 1907), that he reached a personal resolution. He says that despite his protestations of fidelity, the "suspicions did not go away. In order to render them ineffective, I entirely abandoned the study of the Old Testament except in function of the New, and since my superiors would not allow me to say goodbye to biblical studies, I devoted myself to the study of the Gospel."[13] Whether the abandonment was a command or a personal choice, it is clear that the scholar felt boxed in, forced to give up the subject to which he had been devoted, in order to placate the ecclesial authorities above him.

Learning from Lagrange's Life

Abstracting valuable principles for the present from such a complex biography is no easy task. Lagrange was determined to use the latest results of historical-critical study of the Bible for the benefit of the Catholic faith. Yet to do so in such a strict ecclesial framework risked alienating the very authorities he was hoping to defend. Two lessons stand out.

First, a scholar must recognize the constraints within which he or she operates. These constraints might arise from one's confession, one's institution, or even one's physical health. To have a lasting impact on the ongoing discussion, one must come to understand the nature of that discussion and its relation to the ecclesial environment. Without such awareness, one is likely to be caught flat-footed when opposition develops. Lagrange gained too much confidence during the reign of Leo XIII and misapprehended the forces in Rome that would inhibit exegetical publications. His strategy was not well-thought-out. Instead of making the right friends, he made many enemies needlessly. He also did not know when to give up. Though he had lost the game, he obsessed over the unpublished Genesis commentary for almost fifty years. Had he played his cards differently, the outcome might have been better.

The second lesson is that "wisdom is vindicated by her works" (Matt 11:19, NABR). The truth has a way of winning in the end. Long after all the major players of the modernist crisis left the stage of history, new forces at

13. Lagrange, *Personal Reflections and Memoirs*, 133.

Rome would bring about a new era in Catholic biblical studies. Lagrange did not live to see the publication of Pius XII's encyclical *Divino afflante Spiritu* (1943) nor the promulgation of the Second Vatican Council's *Dei Verbum* (1965)—documents that opened up Catholic biblical scholarship to the latest available methods. He did not live to see the rise of critical study of Scripture among Catholic scholars and the explosion of academic publications. Sometimes, perhaps, one must die in order to live. Lagrange's efforts paved the way for generations of biblical scholars. Without him, the dramatic changes in the hierarchy's attitude toward biblical studies and biblical scholars would not have been possible. So, it might be right to say that Lagrange had the last laugh.

The Risks of the Old Testament

As I suggested at the beginning of this chapter, and as is demonstrated by Lagrange's career, ecclesial authorities appear to be more nervous about Old Testament scholarship than New Testament scholarship. From my vantage point, it seems that developing a more complete explanation of why ecclesial authorities tend to regard Old Testament criticism as more risky than New Testament criticism might help us chart a path forward. While we could perhaps come up with a long list of reasons, I would like to propose four possibilities: (1) that the Old Testament is often regarded as secondary; (2) that diachronic claims are difficult for nonspecialists to comprehend; (3) that the Old Testament challenges simplistic approaches to biblical authority; and (4) that preconciliar hierarchical thinking about intellectual inquiry was often characterized by a "battlefield mindset."

First, the Christian interpretive tradition has tended to regard the Old Testament as secondary, merely pointing to Christ, but of little intrinsic value. This perspective has been turned on its head in recent magisterial declarations regarding the Old Testament as "an indispensable part of Sacred Scripture."[14] Amusingly, the magisterial statements use the exact same word—"indispensable"—to describe the historical-critical method.[15] The

14. *CCC* §121.

15. For example, note Benedict XVI, Post-Synodal Apostolic Exhortation *Verbum Domini* (September 30, 2010) §32 (emphasis added throughout this note): "Before all else, we need to acknowledge the benefits that historical-critical exegesis and other recently-developed methods of textual analysis have brought to the life of the Church. For the Catholic understanding of sacred Scripture, attention to such methods is *indispensable*,

documents are hinting that some ecclesial authorities in the past have regarded the Old Testament, like historical criticism, as in fact "dispensable." Though the statements have been encouraging, habits are hard to change. This fact is represented by the balance of the current Lectionary (where only 13.5 percent of the Old Testament, excluding the Psalms, is covered, while 71.5 percent of the New Testament is);[16] seminary curricula, which are heavily balanced in favor of the New Testament; and even the recent Pontifical Biblical Commission document *The Inspiration and Truth of Sacred Scripture* (2014), which devotes thirteen pages to the Old Testament and twenty-nine to the New Testament. Considering that the Old Testament comprises about 78 percent of the canon, giving it only 30 percent of the treatment seems disproportionately low. While a christological focus for Christian biblical interpretation is laudable, it can tend to reduce the books of the Old Testament to a mine for prophecies about Christ or for insights that are directly applicable to Christian spirituality rather than urging that they be read on their own terms. This treatment of the Old Testament as of secondary importance has made serious and nuanced assertions about it difficult to incorporate into mainstream theology. Complex historical arguments from reconstructed archaeological findings may never be easy to absorb into theological thinking, yet the rediscovery of the indispensable nature of the Old Testament books offers an opportunity for reflecting on their intrinsic value as Christian Scripture.

Second, the kinds of diachronic claims scholars make about the Old Testament cannot be easily understood by nonspecialist ecclesiastics. For example, arguments regarding the genre of Tobit, the date of Daniel, or the text of Sirach involve serious and complex problems. Discussions of sources, comparative literature, literary forms, and textual criticism tend toward technical matters. For nonspecialists to understand what is at stake, some level of simplification or generalization is necessary. Yet because the field is constantly fraught by controversy, distilling the scholarly discussion down

linked as it is to the realism of the Incarnation." See also Pontifical Biblical Commission, *The Interpretation of the Bible in the Church* (Rome: Libreria Editrice Vaticana, 1993): "The historical-critical method is the *indispensable* method for the scientific study of the meaning of ancient texts" (§I.A); "But diachronic study remains *indispensable* for making known the historical dynamism which animates sacred Scripture and for shedding light upon its rich complexity" (§I. A.4); "'Diachronic' research will always be *indispensable* for exegesis" (§Conclusion).

16. Felix Just, SJ, "Lectionary Statistics," updated January 2, 2009, https://catholic-resources.org/Lectionary/Statistics.htm.

for a nonspecialist audience is a difficult task in itself, one that few undertake. But without this type of "outreach" to the hierarchy, biblical scholars' concerns and claims will be perpetually misunderstood.

Third, the Old Testament challenges simplistic approaches to biblical authority. Over the past century and a half, we have learned a great deal about the ancient world that alters our understanding of what a book is, whether biblical books truly have authors in a conventional sense, the role of scribal tradents in editing and recomposing works, the influence of other ancient cultures, the mixed religious practices in Israel, and the ways in which ancient historiographical works make claims.[17] These types of observations seriously change the way in which conventional statements about biblical authority need to be nuanced and revised. In describing the editing of the biblical text, which scholars frequently observe in the Old Testament, John Walton and D. Brent Sandy warn their evangelical readers: "We should not view that activity as destructive, deceptive or subversive. It would have been activity that was approved by the community and considered not only legitimate but advantageous. They were not tampering with authority, because authority continued to reside in the authority figure who inaugurated the tradition and in the tradition that had been transmitted by the tradents in the community."[18] Scripture, then, should not be seen as a threat to authority, tradition, and community but rather as a result of a community tradition. The challenge is to rethink our definition of "book" and "author" in light of recent research on the nature of scribal tradition to arrive at a more nuanced view. Yet for nonspecialists in the hierarchy, the challenge will be to craft careful and thoughtful affirmations of biblical authority that neither jettison Scripture as hopelessly ancient and complex nor naively assert its authority without proper nuance. New eras uncover new insights, so it is important that the conversation between the scholarly community and church leadership be open to future revision.

Fourth, preconciliar hierarchical thinking about the nature of intellectual inquiry tended to be agonistic in conception. Leo XIII represents this perspective when he calls for "champions that are needed in so momentous a battle"[19] against "the enemies of religion . . . [who are] attacking and

17. E.g., Karel van der Toorn, *Scribal Culture and the Making of the Hebrew Bible* (Cambridge: Harvard University Press, 2007), 27–49.

18. John H. Walton and D. Brent Sandy, *The Lost World of Scripture: Ancient Literary Culture and Biblical Authority* (Downers Grove, IL: IVP Academic, 2013), 34.

19. Leo XIII, Encyclical Letter *Providentissimus Deus* (November 18, 1893) §10.

mangling the Sacred Books."[20] Pius X similarly refers to "Modernists" who "vent all their gall and hatred on Catholics who sturdily fight the battles of the Church."[21] The hierarchical authorities could conceive of the rationalist historians in the Europe of their time only as opponents on the doctrinal battlefield, whereas Lagrange welcomed them to the table as friends who were likewise pursuing truth. He was maligned for reading and quoting from their works. Sadly, the inherent weakness of a positivist magisterium indeed matches the inherent weakness of the positivist historian. Both are overconfident in the unrevisable certitude of their statements. The decree on Mosaic authorship forms a helpful case in point, since the very definition of "authorship" has itself been thoroughly revised since 1906.

Reflecting on the Nature of Authority

These observations bring us back to the discussion about the nature of religious authority and where it resides. In observing the progress of Catholic theology in the twentieth century, some have concluded that "by the 1980s . . . most of the modernists' program had been adopted. The 'synthesis of all heresies' had, for the most part, been incorporated into Catholic orthodoxy."[22] That might be an overstatement, but what the Modernist crisis in general and Lagrange's case in particular reveal is that the Catholic hierarchy was intellectually unprepared for a crisis of confidence of this magnitude. What began as faithful Catholic scholars trying to learn as much as possible about their sacred texts with the best available methods ended in a showdown between bishops and exegetes. The hierarchy felt its authority being questioned and even undermined by careful historical analysis of the Scriptures, of which it was supposed to be the sole interpreter. It was not ready for the confrontation. Ultimate authority resides neither in human beings nor in books, but in God. The fact that God has deigned to consign his self-disclosure to writing and its official interpretation to human beings does not simplify the problem. Texts are complex by nature—whether in their authorship, origins, historical circumstances, or linguistic features. Human beings are also complex. The exercise of authority is shaped by personalities,

20. Leo XIII, *Providentissimus Deus* §17.

21. Pius X, Encyclical Letter *Pascendi Dominici gregis* (September 8, 1907) §42.

22. Lester R. Kurtz, *The Politics of Heresy: The Modernist Crisis in Roman Catholicism* (Berkeley: University of California Press, 1986), 181.

circumstances, and personal objectives. Rome was right to see critical biblical exegesis as a challenge to business as usual. Exegetes like Père Lagrange were revealing fissures in the current Catholic thinking. After a century of growth in Catholic biblical studies, we now have more tools available than ever to confront such a crisis and achieve a more complete synthetic view of biblical and ecclesial authority.

In the end, Lagrange never really abandoned the Old Testament. Rather, the Old Testament was taken from him—at the behest of ecclesiastical authorities. Lagrange never lost interest in Genesis, but he was required to leave his work unpublished and unseen. His questions probed the very foundations of Christian belief, complicating the accepted picture of the past, and risked undercutting confidence in ecclesiastical authority. He was a man ahead of his time, seeking to solve historical and theological problems with nuance and discretion. He pushed hard for progress in Catholic study of Scripture, but his boldness did not pair well with the extreme caution of the hierarchy in his time. Nonetheless, his work and his example prepared the way for a great renewal in Catholic biblical studies that has happily continued down to our time.

Lagrange's *Religions Sémitiques* a Century Later

Israelite Heterodoxy's Implications for Interreligious Dialogue (and Vice-Versa)

Robert D. Miller II, OFS

In 1903, Marie-Joseph Lagrange published his massive 430-page *Études sur les religions sémitiques*, thirteen years after arriving in Jerusalem, two years after being named master of theology, and a year before his *Historical Method*, which marked the beginning of his troubles. *Religions sémitiques* was published, in fact, the year Pope Leo XIII died and Pius X assumed the Chair of Peter. It is by far his most substantial work of scholarship in his first period, before forced temporary withdrawal from Old Testament work.[1] It interacts with classical texts, Phoenician and Neo-Punic inscriptions, the Amarna letters, and Akkadian texts, including Gilgamesh, Enuma Elish, Anzu, Etana, and Adapa.[2] Yet the book is never mentioned even once in Bernard Montagnes's 2006 *The Story of Father Marie-Joseph Lagrange.*

Although *Religions sémitiques* is not a work of biblical scholarship, Lagrange's purpose was not merely to outline West Semitic religion but to illuminate the cultural background of the Old Testament, throwing light on its Rephaim and *massevoth*, the Asherah and soothsayer's oak (*RS*, 120, 173, 204, 273). Lagrange saw the Canaanites not merely as Israel's neighbors but Israel's "parents." He saw a growth from Canaanite *semina verbi* to "primitive revelation" and eventually to Scripture (*RS*, 1). He wanted to examine that growth to understand the relationship of "pagan" religion to the broader

1. *Historical Criticism and the Old Testament* is exactly the same number of pages, but they are much smaller pages.

2. Marie-Joseph Lagrange, OP, *Études sur les religions sémitiques*, EBib (Paris: Lecoffre, 1903), 22, 121, 167, 270, 289. Hereafter, citations from this work will appear in notes in the text as *RS*. Note also that Lagrange found that descriptions of Canaanite paganism in the church fathers had been strongly influenced by Hellenism. The Amarna letters showed him that what was showing up in cuneiform literature was no doubt far closer to the ancient reality (*RS*, 37–39).

dispositions of the human heart (*RS*, 4). This remains a need today, as Angelo Tosato writes: "This scriptural 'incarnation' of the divine Word took place in well-determined times and places of a distant past. . . . As such, it cannot be understood except by understanding the concrete humanity, historicity and culture of the writings that compose it."[3] Lagrange used concepts like "religion," "myth," and "magic" in dialogue with the foremost theories of his time and in comparison with primary ethnographic data (*RS*, 4–5, 11, 13–14, 18–19, citing Tylor, Frazer, Renan, Smith, and ethnography from New Caledonia).

What I want to examine, therefore, is Lagrange's exploration of the extent to which ancient Israel can be considered monotheistic,[4] which remains a complex question, only in part related to the Old Testament's presentation of God and other gods. The term monolatry was not coined until 1928 (by Friedrich Schleiermacher), but Lagrange rightly found "henotheism" (from Max Müller, 1860) to be of as little help as monotheism or polytheism (*RS*, 21).[5] Lagrange suggested "Kathenotheism," a phenomenon he claimed to find in Babylonian penitential psalms and Egyptian hymns and that he believed Tertullian had also found in pagan religion (*RS*, 21; Tertullian, *De testimonio animae* 100.2). I want to try anew to find a way to describe ancient Israelite religion as we now know it, and I will do so in dialogue with both Lagrange and present-day scholars. I propose a new lens for viewing ancient Israel's faith, African Traditional Religion, and I will conclude by suggesting ways that using this lens for Israel contributes to contemporary interreligious dialogue.

On the surface, abundant archaeological evidence suggests Israelites believed in more gods than just Yahweh, the God of Abraham. Nor is such a conclusion at odds with the biblical tradition, which affirms across multiple genres and multiple centuries that many Israelites worshiped "other gods." A simplistic scenario would envision a polytheistic society, attested by both

3. Angelo Tosato, *The Catholic Statute of Biblical Interpretation*, ed. Monica Lugato (Rome: Gregorian and Biblical Press, 2021), 37.

4. Mark S. Smith, *God in Translation: Deities in Cross-Cultural Discourse in the Biblical World*, FAT 57 (Tübingen: Mohr Siebeck, 2008), 164–65, provides a succinct discussion.

5. Smith, *God in Translation*, 165; Christian Frevel, "Beyond Monotheism? Some Remarks and Questions on Conceptualising 'Monotheism' in Biblical Studies," *Verbum et Ecclesia* 34, no. 2 (2013): 3; Nathan MacDonald, "The Origin of 'Monotheism,'" in *Early Jewish and Christian Monotheism*, ed. Loren T. Stuckenbruck, JSNTSup 263 (London: T&T Clark, 2004), 213. Originally, neither term had any evolutionary connotations (MacDonald, "Origin of 'Monotheism,'" 214).

texts (e.g., 2 Kgs 16:4; 17:11–12, 16–17; 21:6–7; 23:8–14; Isa 30:22; Jer 2:23) and artifacts, and condemned by a monotheistic tradition responsible for the biblical text.[6] Often, the polytheism is attributed to "syncretism," adoption by Israelites of "Canaanite" practices fundamentally foreign to Israel, usually portrayed as "fertility cults."[7] A slightly more sophisticated version would attribute the monotheism to agents of political and intellectual power and polytheism to "popular religion," a label we shall return to shortly.

The reality is much more complicated. The biblical traditions give, on the one hand, "an abundance of disparate representations of this God, who, though assumed to be the same deity before and throughout Israel's existence, is identified by different names, . . . described as having multiple bodies of varying size."[8] On the other hand, the Hebrew Bible preserves evidence of a plurality of divinities, of which Yahweh might be merely one.[9] Deuteronomy 32:8–9 presents Yahweh as one of many gods, although the greatest.[10] Yahweh also acquires attributes or becomes equated with other West Semitic deities, especially El and Baal, whose characteristics are assimilated to Yahweh both separately (Pss 20; 29:1–2; 48:2; 82:1; 89:5–10; Isa 6:1–8; 14:13; Hos 2) and jointly (Ps 18).[11] For archaeological evidence, on the one hand, inscriptions call upon the blessing of "Yahweh and his Asherah," although only from the ninth century onward is the name "Yahweh," rather than El(ohim), even attested. On the other hand, while personal names make reference to Baal, the only clear uses of the divine name Baal on its own are from one site, Kuntillet Ajrud, and the name Asherah only from Kuntillet Ajrud and Khirbet el-Qom.[12]

6. Examples cited in Smith, *God in Translation*, 191.

7. E.g., Athalaya Brenner, "The Hebrew God and His Female Complements," in *The Feminist Companion to Mythology*, ed. Carolyne Larrington (London: Pandora, 1992), 54.

8. Eric Trinka, *Cultures of Mobility, Migration, and Religion in Ancient Israel and Its World*, Routledge Studies in the Biblical World (New York: Routledge, 2022), 249.

9. Bob Becking, "The Boundaries of Israelite Monotheism," in *The Boundaries of Monotheism*, ed. Anne-Marie Korte and Maaike de Haardt, Studies in Theology and Religion 13 (Leiden: Brill, 2008), 13.

10. Psalm 82 seems to describe Yahweh's removal of the other gods from the pantheon. In Ps 58:12(11), the last verbal phrase, "God who judges the earth," has Elohim *shofetim* using the plural שֹׁפְטִים, where Elohim ordinarily takes a *singular* verb; this may show some vestige of a pantheon.

11. Trinka, *Cultures of Mobility*; Robert D. Miller II, *The Dragon, the Mountain, and the Nations: An Old Testament Myth, Its Origins, and Its Afterlives*, EANEC 6 (Winona Lake, IN: Eisenbrauns, 2018).

12. Johannes Renz, *Die althebräischen Inschriften*, vol. 2, pt. 1 of Handbuch der althebräischen Epigraphik (Darmstadt: Wissenschaftliche Buchgesellschaft, 1995), 91–93.

Since Lagrange, much has been made of the divine names found in Hebrew personal names, both those from the Bible and those found epigraphically (*RS*, 110–11, 121). Lagrange also studied divine names found in Palestinian place-names of the Iron Age. This evidence needs to be weighed carefully. Seth Sanders warns that studies of large numbers of names need to take account of diachronic changes and also of regional differences.[13] And our "naïve tendency to prefer statistically friendly quantity over archaeological and epigraphic quality" should make us very wary of material from the antiquities market.[14] Moreover, only 21 percent of Aramaic names involve epithets of the chief god Baal Hadad, so deducing religious preference from name choice is not straightforward.[15] Ammonite names only show the name of the dynastic god Milcom in 1 percent of names, while 82 percent of names derive from El.[16] Mitka Golub has undertaken extensive study of both biblical and epigraphic names. Golub's larger study included all names found in Judah and Cisjordanian Israel up to the end of 2012.[17] The distribution differed between the Northern and Southern Kingdoms.[18] In Judah, 74 percent of the names were Yahwistic (Yahu), 13 percent Elohistic, and the rest divine appellatives. In Israel, while 57 percent of the names drew on Yo, 19 percent had the divine name Baal; 15 percent were Elohistic and 7 percent divine appellatives. Golub notes that names in Kings and Chronicles match the Judahite distribution,[19] although the biblical text makes no distinction in the onomastica of the two kingdoms.[20] Viewed diachronically in Judah, the use of names with Yaho increased substantially from the start of the eighth to the end of the seventh century.[21] In comparison with the biblical tradition, this onomastic evidence suggests *more* monotheism than Jeremiah (e.g., 32:29), Zephaniah (e.g., 1:4–5), Hosea (e.g., 2:19), or Ezekiel (e.g., 6:13)

13. Seth L. Sanders, "'The Mutation Peculiar to Hebrew Religion': Monotheism, Pantheon Reduction, or Royal Adoption of Family Religion?," *JANER* 14, no. 2 (2014): 222.

14. Sanders, "Mutation," 222.

15. Sanders, "Mutation," 223.

16. Sanders, "Mutation," 224; Seth L. Sanders, "When the Personal Became Political: An Onomastic Perspective on the Rise of Yahwism," *HBAI* 4, no. 1 (2015): 99.

17. Mitka R. Golub, "Israelite and Judean Theophoric Personal Names in the Hebrew Bible in the Light of the Archaeological Evidence," *ANES* 54 (2017): 37.

18. Golub, "Israelite and Judean Theophoric Personal Names," 39.

19. Golub, "Israelite and Judean Theophoric Personal Names," 40.

20. Golub, "Israelite and Judean Theophoric Personal Names," 42.

21. Golub, "Israelite and Judean Theophoric Personal Names," 43. Smith, *God in Translation*, 160–61, suggests that, to a certain degree, this may have been in response to Assyrian imperial power.

would lead us to believe.[22] Perhaps naming customs cannot be the primary evidence for religious practice.

Like Lagrange before him, Ziony Zevit also appeals to place-names, noting the many mentions of Beth Anat and Ashtoreth and Beth Dagon (Josh 19:27) both in the Bible and in Egyptian texts (*RS*, 114).[23] He assumes that names like Baal Hazor, Beth Shemesh (to which 1 Sam 6:9–11 gives a supernatural role), and so on indicate the presence of shrines at those locations, and he then divides by the biblical tribal boundaries. If this is accurate, he finds shrines of Baal (1 Chr 14:11; Jdt 8:3), Resheph, Mot, Shemesh (cf. Execration Text E60), Rephaim (Isa 17:5; 1 Chr 14:9), Gad, and Dagon, ranging from a single shrine in Levi (to Mot) to eight in Judah.[24] To this we might add Horon (Josh 21:22; Tel Qasile Ostracon 2),[25] Lahamu (Gen 35:19), and the Moon/Yarih (Josh 6:1),[26] with worship of the latter noted in Deut 4:19; 17:3–5. Zevit also believes he can date the presence of many of these: the oldest being Beth Shemesh in Dan, the only example of a shrine continuing from the Late Bronze Age into the Iron Age; the latest, two eighth-century shrines of Baal in Reuben.[27]

Much of this is rather speculative, but what is clear is that new Israelite towns were founded with non-Yahwistic names.[28] Combining the place-name information with the personal names—especially noting that some non-Yahweh names appear for children of Yahweh-named individuals and vice-versa—we have something not very monotheistic but unlike the polytheism of Mesopotamia and Egypt. Zevit is probably correct that in the eighth century, for example, there were "no more than a few hun-

22. Smith, *God in Translation*, 192.

23. Ziony Zevit, *The Religions of Ancient Israel: A Synthesis of Parallactic Approaches* (London: Continuum, 2001), 597. Such inquiry was already undertaken by David R. Hunsberger, "Theophoric Names in the Old Testament and Their Theological Significance" (PhD diss., Temple University, 1969), 348–49. Ashtar[o]t[h]s are mentioned in texts of Thutmose III, Amenhotep III, EA 197 and 256, and Ptolemaic texts; Beth Anat in texts of Seti I and Ramesses II. See Shmuel Aḥituv, *Canaanite Toponyms in Ancient Egyptian Documents* (Jerusalem: Magnes, 1984), 72–73, 75–76.

24. Zevit, *Religions of Ancient Israel*, 603–4.

25. "Gold of Ophir to Beth Horon: 30 shekels." See André Lemaire, *Les ostraca: Introduction, traduction, commentaire*, vol. 1 of *Inscriptions hébraïques* (Paris: Éditions du Cerf, 1977), 253–55; J. Van Dijk, "Canaanite God Horon and His Cult in Egypt," *Göttinger Miszellen* 107 (1989): 60–63.

26. Hunsberger, "Theophoric Names," 349.

27. Zevit, *Religions of Ancient Israel*, 598, 603–4.

28. Zevit, *Religions of Ancient Israel*, 603.

dred . . . hard-core, trusted, exclusive 'Baal-only' partisans,"[29] while, as Jeremiah would also suggest, "Israelites adored certainly one, but most likely a few—not many—goddesses."[30]

Popular, Folk, and Family Religion

The distinction of "popular," "folk," or "family and household" religion from some more orthodox "established" religion is not helpful for ancient Israel any more than it is anywhere else.[31] Common, "lay" people innovate religion in established shrines and engage in religious reflection.[32] Communication between clergy and "laity" takes place in both directions.[33] Moreover, emotions are encouraged or suppressed, meaning given to lives, disasters coped with, and order maintained in city and country alike.[34]

Certainly, there was "religion-internal pluralism," but it cannot be easily compartmentalized.[35] There can be as much religious pluralism among

29. Zevit, *Religions of Ancient Israel*, 650.

30. Zevit, *Religions of Ancient Israel*, 651.

31. Becking, "Boundaries of Israelite Monotheism," 17–25, maintains such a dichotomy. Thus, "At the state level [only?] religion is connected with symbols of power" (18). "Birth and dying, illness and fear, crop failure and abundance are pivotal to . . . religion at the family level" (22). So, too, Rainer Albertz, "Welche Art von Individualität förderte die altisraelitische Familienreligion?," in *Religionspraxis und Individualität: Die Bedeutung von persönlicher Frömmigkeit und Family Religion für das Personkonzept in der Antike*, ed. Alexandra Grund-Wittenberg (Leiden: Brill, 2021), 133. On the history of "popular" traditions valorized as ancient, oral, and true, see Michel de Certeau, *Heterologies: Discourse on the Other*, Theory and History of Literature 17 (Minneapolis: University of Minnesota Press, 1986), 124–27.

32. Natalie Zemon Davis, "Some Tasks and Themes in the Study of Popular Religion," in *The Pursuit of Holiness in Late Medieval and Renaissance Religion*, ed. Charles Edward Trinkaus and Heiko Augustinus Oberman, Studies in Medieval and Reformation Thought 10 (Leiden: Brill, 1974), 308–9; Natalie Zemon Davis, "From 'Popular Religion' to Religious Cultures," pp. 321–41 in *Reformation Europe: A Guide to Research*, ed. Steven Ozment (St. Louis: Center for Reformation Research, 1982), 324, 326.

33. Davis, "Some Tasks and Themes," 313; Davis, "From 'Popular Religion' to Religious Cultures," 330.

34. Davis, "Some Tasks and Themes," 312.

35. Bob Becking, "More Than One God?," in *Divine Doppelgängers: YHWH's Ancient Look-Alikes*, ed. Collin Cornell (Winona Lake, IN: Eisenbrauns, 2020), 68; Davis, "From 'Popular Religion' to Religious Cultures," 330. Note also Denis Baly, "The Geography of Monotheism," in *Translating and Understanding the Old Testament: Essays in Honor of Herbert Gordon May*, ed. Harry T. Frank and William L. Reed (Nashville: Abingdon,

peasants as between peasants and ruling classes.[36] Both archaeology and text point to "an unfathomably complex religious environment."[37] However, "this is not to say that Judah was not in some sense Yahwistic, but rather that Yahwism was understood and practiced in ways that were very diverse."[38]

Monotheism, Monolatry, Henotheism, One-God Theism, and Pantheon Reduction

So what are we to call Israelite religion? Most scholars of the nineteenth century spoke confidently of Israelite monotheism and ancient Near Eastern polytheism,[39] although it was already clear to others that pure monotheism arose only gradually in preexilic Israel and Judah.[40] Monotheism's clearest definition is a mathematical one: "For the category or set called deity, there is only one member."[41] Twentieth-century scholars debated degrees of monolatry and henotheism.[42] In the former, one worships only one god regardless of how many are held to exist.[43] Henotheism is the trickiest to define. Machinist distinguishes it from monolatry by saying that, in henotheism, one god "has absorbed or embodied within itself other deities and

1970), 256: "One is driven to wonder . . . whether pluralism is not something of a polite and noncommittal word for polytheism."

36. Davis, "From 'Popular Religion' to Religious Cultures," 323.

37. Jeremy M. Hutton, "Southern, Northern and Transjordanian Perspectives," in *Religious Diversity in Ancient Israel and Judah*, ed. Francesca Stavrakopoulou and John Barton (London: T&T Clark, 2010), 167.

38. Christopher B. Hays, "How Many Histories of Death Does the Hebrew Bible Contain?," *CBQ* 81, no. 4 (2019): 687.

39. Frevel, "Beyond Monotheism," 2.

40. George A. Barton, "Native Israelitish Deities," in *Oriental Studies: A Selection of the Papers Read before the Oriental Club of Philadelphia, 1888–1894* (Boston: Ginn & Company), 86. William Robertson Smith, *Lectures on the Religion of the Semites: Second and Third Series*, ed. John Day, JSOTSup 183 (Sheffield: Sheffield Academic Press, 1995), 59, already in 1891 considered henotheism to be a wishful projection of modern scholars on a polytheistic ancient Israel.

41. Peter B. Machinist, "Once More: Monotheism in Biblical Israel," *JISMOR* 1 (2005): 26.

42. Oskar Goldberg, *Die Wirklichkeit der Hebräer*, rev. ed., ed. Manfred Voigts, Jüdische Kultur 14 (Wiesbaden: Harrassowitz, 2005), 15.

43. Benjamin Uffenheimer, "Myth and Reality in Ancient Israel," in *The Origins and Diversity of Axial Age Civilizations*, ed. Shmuel N. Eisenstadt (New York: State University of New York Press, 1986), 145.

their powers and functions [without] eras[ing] all traces, or even worship, of these others."[44]

For Machinist, the stages of this process remain visible in the Hebrew Bible, although he warns against reading a logical progression.[45] Texts like Gen 31:53; Exod 20:1–2; Deut 4:19; 6:4–5; 32:8–9; and Judg 11:24 show one Yahweh being worshiped while existing alongside an indeterminate number of other gods, "a wonderfully monolatrous statement."[46] In Psalm 82 (and 1 Kgs 18), those other gods are demoted to mortality by their failure to care for the poor. Only in texts like Isa 41:21–24; 43:10–13; and Deut 32:39, all from the exilic period, do no other gods exist.[47]

For the past century, this discussion of Israelite monotheism and its rise has revolved around "Yahweh and the Gods of Canaan."[48] The identity of the "sons of god(s)" or "divine council" in the Old Testament was subsumed under this discussion, despite the observation already made by Yehezkel Kaufmann that this "council" is nowhere connected with the "other gods" mentioned in the Bible, like Baal or Asherah.[49] Kaufmann noted that belief in the "sons of god(s)," along with *seirim*, Lilith, sons of Resheph, and so on, is nowhere condemned.[50] Yet Kaufmann also held that these beings were powerless mortal creatures of Yahweh,[51] which

44. Machinist, "Once More," 26.

45. Machinist, "Once More," 35. See the similar caution in MacDonald, "Origin of 'Monotheism,'" 215.

46. Machinist, "Once More," 33. Compare Konrad Schmid, "Gibt es 'Reste hebräischen Heidentums' im Alten Testament? Methodische Überlegungen anhand von Dtn 32,8f und Ps 82," in *Primäre und sekundäre Religion als Kategorie der Religionsgeschichte des Alten Testaments*, ed. Andreas Wagner (Berlin: de Gruyter, 2012), 2–3; Becking, "More Than One God," 68.

47. Machinist, "Once More," 36; Erhard S. Gerstenberger, "Weiblich von Gott Reden?," in *Christlicher Glaube und religiöse Bildung: Frau Prof. Dr. Friedel Kriechbaum zum 60. Geburtstag am 13. August 1995*, ed. Hermann Deuser and Gerhard Schmalenberg (Giessen: Fachbereich Evangelische Theologie und Katholische Theologie und deren Didaktik, 1995), 44; Becking, "More Than One God," 64–65.

48. W. F. Albright, *Yahweh and the Gods of Canaan* (Garden City: Doubleday, 1968); John Day, *Yahweh and the Gods and Goddesses of Canaan*, JSOTSup 265 (London: Sheffield Academic Press, 2002).

49. Yehezkel Kaufmann, "The Bible and Mythological Polytheism," *JBL* 70, no. 3 (1951): 181; Yehezkel Kaufmann, *The Religion of Israel: From Its Beginnings to the Babylonian Exile*, trans. Moshe Greenberg (Chicago: University of Chicago Press, 1960), 11.

50. Kaufmann, "The Bible and Mythological Polytheism," 181; Kaufmann, *The Religion of Israel*, 64.

51. Kaufmann, *The Religion of Israel*, 11, 62, 64.

we shall see is not even the biblical claim (Psalm 29; 58; 82:1–6; 89:6–8; Dan 3:25).[52]

We have missed the importance of these beings in narrow debates of monotheism versus polytheism. As Freedman writes, "There are other gods, that is clear. . . . There are too many active and articulate beings in and around the heavenly court to make a contrary claim."[53] The "terror of the night," the "arrow that flies by day," the "pestilence that walks in darkness," and the "noonday devil" of Ps 91:5–6 are a supernatural horde, for example.[54]

We need a heuristic model other than [number of gods] + "theism" to describe this system. We need to revisit the basic question of *what is a god.*[55] In Mesopotamia, for example, gods were always transcendent with respect to humanity but not with respect to the world, although they may be anthropomorphic, "elemental" (e.g., wind, sun), and astral at the same time.[56] Yet a *dingir* can also be attached to diseases, rivers, divine chariots or crowns, temples, or offices.[57] We need to envision monotheism and polytheism as not entirely incompatible.[58] As Lagrange insisted, we need to scrap any tele-

52. Margaret Barker, *The Great Angel: A Study of Israel's Second God* (Louisville: Westminster John Knox, 1992), 7; Becking, "Boundaries of Israelite Monotheism," 12; Annette Yoshiko Reed, *Demons, Angels, and Writing in Ancient Judaism* (Cambridge: Cambridge University Press, 2020), 41. For a fuller critique of Kaufmann, see Robert D. Miller II, "Lineamenta for an Understanding of Israelite Monotheism," *Bible Bhashyam* 32 (2006): 125, 127–29.

53. David Noel Freedman, "'Who Is Like Thee among the Gods?' The Religion of Early Israel," in *History and Religion*, ed. John R. Huddlestun, vol. 1 of *Divine Commitment and Human Obligation: Selected Writings of David Noel Freedman* (Grand Rapids: Eerdmans, 1997), 396; Yoshiko Reed, *Demons, Angels*, 43.

54. Becking, "More Than One God," 61; Becking, "Boundaries of Israelite Monotheism," 23.

55. Hays, "Histories of Death," 690; Yoshiko Reed, *Demons, Angels*, 71.

56. Ivan Hrůša, *Ancient Mesopotamian Religion: A Descriptive Introduction* (Münster: Ugarit-Verlag, 2015), 23.

57. Hrůša, *Ancient Mesopotamian Religion*, 25.

58. Frevel, "Beyond Monotheism," 4; Corinne Bonnet, "Que fait le genre aux dénominations divines, entre mondes grecs et sémitiques?," *Archimede* 8 (2021): 6. This is true at least for antiquity; I do not deny that contemporary monotheism envisions deity in a very different way than does polytheism, not as a sum total of numerable fragments but as a mode of reality that does not admit numeration. Compare Giorgio Buccellati, "Yahweh, the Trinity: The Old Testament Catechumenate (Part 1)," *Communio* 34 (2007): 44–45; Nicolas Wyatt, "The Rumpelstiltskin Factor: Explorations in the Arithmetic of Pantheons," in *Some Wine and Honey for Simon: Biblical and Ugaritic Aperitifs in Memory of Simon B. Parker*, ed. A. Joseph Ferrara and Herbert B. Huffmon (Eugene, OR: Pickwick, 2020), 25.

ological evolutionary schemas (*RS*, 24).[59] Even "pantheon reduction" misses the fact that the elevation of a single deity in the ancient Near East often accompanied a proliferation of minor divinities and demigods.[60]

African Traditional Religions

Scholars who have looked to contemporary religious conceptions like Hinduism to understand ancient Israel are not mistaken. Although a tendency to conform what we see vestiges of from archaeology and text to a clearer model before us warrants caution, models taken from actual human practice are preferable to theoretical constructs. To try to move beyond the monotheism/polytheism dichotomy in a new way, the comparand I would suggest is instead African Traditional Religions (ATR)—a comparison that to my knowledge has only otherwise been proposed (independently) by Dirk Human in 2021.[61]

"There is a general or universal consensus among Africans of the existence of God."[62] One supreme God is ubiquitous across the continent,[63]

59. Cf. Frevel, "Beyond Monotheism," 4; Yoshiko Reed, *Demons, Angels*, 43.

60. Note, for instance, new traditions about Amun-Re's many messengers that appeared just as he achieved supremacy in the mid-second millennium (Reed, *Demons, Angels*, 52).

61. Dirk J. Human, "Portraits of 'Angels': Some Ancient Near Eastern and Old Testament Perspectives in Relation to ATR Belief System(s)," *Pharos Journal of Theology* 102, Special Edition 1 (2021): 1–11. There were some slight comparisons made by Jean-Claude Bajeux, "Mentalité noire et mentalité biblique," in *Des prêtres noirs s'interrogent*, ed. Présence Africain with Msgr. Lefebvre (Paris: Éditions du Cerf, 1956), 64. Olena P. Ogiozee, "The Value of the Continuity between African and Old Testament Worldviews" (MA Thesis, Regent University, 2009), compares ATR with the Old Testament but not with ancient Israel as known by any other evidence. Klaus Nürnberger, *The Living Dead and the Living God: Christ and the Ancestors in a Changing Africa* (Pretoria: C. B. Powell Bible Centre, 2007), 64–70, makes the comparison for pastoral reasons, without using it to understand ancient Israel. I am also using ATR in a deliberate move to reverse intellectual colonization and bring into the discourse what has been largely silenced. See Tsenay Serequeberhan, *The Hermeneutics of African Philosophy: Horizon and Discourse* (London: Routledge, 1994), 119. On the history of terminology for African religion, see Aloysius Muzzanganda Lugira, *African Religion: A Prolegomenal Essay on the Emergence and Meaning of African Autochthonous Religions* (Nyangwe: Omenana, 1981), 24–27.

62. Wolor Topor, "The Concept of God in the African Philosophy," *Journal of African Religion and Philosophy* 1, no. 2 (1990): 2.

63. T. Tshibangu, *Le propos d'une théologie africaine* (Kinshasa: Presses Universitaires du Zaire, 1974), 29; Jacob Mapara, *Shona Sentential Names* (Mankon: Langaa, 2013),

a feature noted already by Muslim explorers of the eleventh century.[64] For as much as Christian missionaries may have imagined one high God in a culture where there in fact was none, it is certain that Europeans also *over*-emphasized spirits and ancestors, obscuring proper deities.[65] The Kavango (Namibia) supreme deity Nyambo or Shakandanga is "above all creatures and things . . . neither created nor was he born."[66] All-powerful, he created all things *except* for large river monsters that formed from worms emerging from souls of the dead.[67] Baila of the Bemba people is creator of all.[68] So also, for the Congo Nyanga, Ongo has created all things good, although humanity often rejects his gifts.[69] For the West African Akan, the creator God is eternal, without physical representation or gender.[70] The Fon people, however, symbolize their one creator God by the dawn.[71] For pre-Islamic Fula, Dogon, Mossi, and Songhai peoples, the supreme God was female.[72] Sometimes this deity is seen as very remote, having little to do with people—according to the Nyakyusa, for example, as well as some Igbo.[73] In some cases, this God has

92. For the Shona people, see François-Marie Lufuluabo, *Valeur des religions africaines selon la Bible et selon Vatican II* (Kinshasa: Éditions St. Paul Afrique, 1967), 79–80.

64. Mesmin-Noël Soumaho, *Éléments de méthodologie pour une lecture critique*, Recherches gabonaises (Libreville: CERGEP, 2002), 213–15.

65. Adolf E. Jensen, *Myth and Cult among Primitive Peoples* (Chicago: University of Chicago Press, 1963), 89; Lugira, *African Religion*, 16. See, for example, John Beattie, *Bunyoro: An African Kingdom*, Case Studies in Cultural Anthropology 3 (New York: Holt, Rinehart and Winston, 1960), 77.

66. Thomas J. Larson, "Nyambi, the High God of the Hambukushu," *South African Journal of Ethnology* 7, no. 1 (1984): 9.

67. Larson, "Nyambi," 10.

68. Aloysius Muzzanganda Lugira, *African Religion*, World Religions (New York: Facts on File, 1999), 38.

69. Daniel Biebuyck and Kahombo C. Mateene, eds. and trans., *The Mwindo Epic from the Banyanga* (Berkeley: University of California Press, 1971), 125.

70. Kofi Asare Opoku, "African Traditional Religion: An Enduring Heritage," in *Religious Plurality in Africa: Essays in Honour of John S. Mbiti*, ed. Jacob K. Olupona and Sulayman S. Nyang, Religion and Society 32 (Berlin: de Gruyter, 1993), 71.

71. Paul Hazoumé, "L'âme du Dahoméen animiste révélée par sa religion," *Présence Africaine* 14–15, nos. 3–4 (1957): 234.

72. Amadou Hampate Ba, "Présentation des religions traditionnelles africaines," in *Les religions africaines comme source de valeurs de civilisation*, ed. Alioune Diop (Paris: Présence Africaine, 1972), 66.

73. Kingsley Nyirenda, *Mbande Hill Sacredness*, Mzuni Documents 186 (Mzuzu: Mzuni, 2018), 11; Stephen N. Ezeanya, "God, Spirits and the Spirit World," in *Biblical Revelation and African Beliefs*, ed. Kwesi A. Dickson and Paul Ellingworth (Maryknoll, NY: Orbis, 1969), 36–39.

become what Adolf Jensen called a "dema-deity," having had a great impact on the primal past but no longer present and active, therefore making it "senseless to address prayers to it."[74] In other societies, as in the myths about Banyankore in Uganda and among the Akan people of West Africa, he is the beneficent provider.[75] Among the Grebo, Kpelle, Bassa, and Vai peoples of West Africa, all traditional sacrifices first invoke the supreme deity.[76]

Yet among the latter peoples, as well as the Igbo, sacrifices are offered to God through intermediary spirits as well.[77] "Spirits" is not quite the best term; as Lowie wrote long ago, "if we insist on the notion of completely incorporeal beings there are probably no examples to be found."[78] Corporeality need not involve solid matter; alterations of air or even of light can constitute a spirit that is by no means imaginary or "intellectual."[79] "Spirits" is the accepted terminology among Africanists, however, for these beings who "belong to a different order of existence from that of men, beasts, and rocks."[80] These are not worshiped directly but venerated for their mediating roles, which are often particular to each community or each family.[81] Among the Akan and Igbo, God is held to have used such spirits as agents to carry out some aspects of creation.[82] Thus, lesser spirits may be named individually, or they may merely be lumped into genera by their domain of power.[83] Yet for the Igbo, "they, unlike the Supreme God, can sometimes disappoint man."[84] It is rare that they have personalities to the extent that ancestors

74. Jensen, *Myth and Cult*, 91–92.

75. Lugira, *African Religion*, 43; J. O. Kayode, *Understanding African Traditional Religion* (Ile-Ife: University of Ife Press, 1984), 26–27; Mulago gwa Cikala M., *La religion traditionnelle des Bantu et leur vision du monde*, Bibliothèque du centre d'études des religions africaines 5 (Kinshasa: Faculté de Théologie Catholique, 1980), 129–30; Lufuluabo, *Valeur des religions africaines*, 80–82.

76. Topor, "Concept of God," 4.

77. Ezeanya, "God, Spirits and the Spirit World," 37; Topor, "Concept of God," 4.

78. Robert H. Lowie, *Primitive Religion* (New York: Liveright, 1948), 99.

79. Cf. Antonio Royo, OP, and Jordan Aumann, OP, *Theology of Christian Perfection* (Dubuque: Priory, 1962), 655.

80. Lowie, *Primitive Religion*, 99.

81. Topor, "Concept of God," 4.

82. Opoku, "African Traditional Religion," 72; Ezeanya, "God, Spirits and the Spirit World," 41; Soumaho, *Eléments de méthodologie*, 216.

83. P. T. Mtuze, *The Essence of Xhosa Spirituality and the Nuisance of Cultural Imperialism: Hidden Presences in the Spirituality of the AmaXhosa of the Eastern Cape and the Impact of Christianity on Them* (Florida Hills: Vivlia, 2003), 55–57.

84. Ezeanya, "God, Spirits and the Spirit World," 42.

do (see below).[85] There are some African traditions that lack "spirits," such as the Lobedu of South Africa, but those are the exception in sub-Saharan Africa.[86]

Animals may also have a spiritual nature of this sort, as among the Yoruba, Phla-Pherá-speakers, Fon, and Kavango.[87] Among the Venda, Mpondomise Xhosa, Zulu, and Swazi peoples, rivers, lakes, and groves are inhabited by such spirits.[88] A spirit in the form of a snake inhabits the Nyakyusa sacred hill of Mbande in Malawi.[89] A variant of this belief removes the intermediary level of "inhabitants" and vests the mountain, stone, tree, or lake with its own spirit, as with the Manyika Shona of Zimbabwe, Nyanga of the Congo, and Mende of Sierra Leone.[90] Life, therefore, is often seen as a quality that people, animals, plants, and objects all partake of, and that is fullest in God.[91] The San "Bushmen," however, have no nature spirits, and all "spirits" other than God are astral.[92]

The Yoruba and Igbo share several "non-good" spirits, although for the Igbo, these are always evil, while the Yoruba believe they can be employed for good as well.[93] The Kavango "devil," Shadipinyi, while an evil tempter, is nevertheless a creature of Nyambi, who alone knows why he created him.[94] Such malevolent spirits may be the agents of disease or rather perceived as

85. Nürnberger, *Living Dead*, 29–31.

86. W. D. Hammond-Tooke, "World View I: A System of Beliefs," in *The Bantu-Speaking Peoples of Southern Africa*, ed. W. D. Hammond-Tooke (London: Routledge & Kegan Paul, 1974), 321.

87. Hazoumé, "L'âme du Dahoméen," 237; Larson, "Nyambi," 12.

88. Hammond-Tooke, "World View," 321–22, 324; Godfrey Anyumba and Mkateko Nkuna, "Lake Fundudzi: A Sacred Lake in South Africa That Is Not Open for Tourism Development," *African Journal of Hospitality, Tourism and Leisure* 6, no. 4 (2017): 13; Penny S. Bernard, "Ecological Implications of Water Spirit Beliefs in Southern Africa," *USDA Forest Service Proceedings* 27 (2003): 149.

89. Nyirenda, *Mbande Hill Sacredness*, 3.

90. Tendai R. Mwanaka, *Language, Thought, Art and Existence: Creative Nonfictions* (Mankon: Langaa, 2017), 5; Kayode, *Understanding African Traditional Religion*, 20–22; Biebuyck and Mateene, *The Mwindo Epic*, 19.

91. Basile-Juléat Fouda, *La philosophie négro-africaine de l'existence: Herméneutique des traditions orales africaines*, Pensée africaine (Paris: L'Harmattan, 2013), 87; Ogiozee, "The Value," 63.

92. David Westerlund, "Spiritual Beings as Agents of Illness," in *African Spirituality: Forms, Meanings, and Expressions*, ed. Jacob Obafẹmi Kẹhinde Olupọna, World Spirituality 3 (New York: Crossroad, 2000), 154.

93. Ezeanya, "God, Spirits and the Spirit World," 44.

94. Larson, "Nyambi," 12.

partial agents alongside nefarious magic undertaken by other human beings.[95] Malevolent San astral spirits cause disease, and the greatest malevolent spirit is Gauwa—although Gauwa may also be seen as merely God's angry side, with the presence of disease ultimately being owed to one inscrutable God.[96]

The ancestors play a role similar to those contingent spiritual beings, also operating as intercessors between the living and God or between the living and the spirits.[97] Across Africa, the dead perpetuate a bond with their living family, still dependent on God for their new existence, at least for a time.[98] For these, the term "living dead" is regularly used (e.g., among the Chagga of Tanzania).[99] For the West African Akan, Konkomba, and Mende, the dead ancestors have their own abode apart from the living, but between the two, "there is constant traffic."[100] Among the Fon, the dead are fed as simply other members of the family by offerings made at tombs.[101] In the main, this close commerce only applies to the recently deceased, the remembered dead. Except for cultural heroes remembered by the entire community, when the memory of the deceased wanes, their interaction with the living does as well.[102]

There are some examples, however (e.g., the Congo Nyanga people), where at least some of the dead are very much *not* spirits but rather corporeal zombies, beings to be feared.[103] For the Venda, such a fate can befall some

95. Mtuze, *Essence of Xhosa Spirituality*, 27–29.

96. Westerlund, "Spiritual Beings," 157–59.

97. Topor, "Concept of God," 4; Tshiamalenga Ntumba, "Mythe et religion en Afrique," *Cahiers des religions africaines* 18, no. 36 (1984): 186; Lugira, *African Religion*, 48; Mtuze, *Essence of Xhosa Spirituality*, 49; Nürnberger, *Living Dead*, 32–33.

98. Hazoumé, "L'âme du Dahoméen," 244; Ezeanya, "God, Spirits and the Spirit World," 43; Cikala M., *La religion traditionnelle des Bantu*, 93; Lufuluabo, *Valeur des religions africaines*, 91; Marcel G. Kessy, "Death Rituals among the Chagga of Tanzania" (BA Thesis, Tangaza College/Catholic University of Eastern Africa, 2002), 25.

99. Opoku, "African Traditional Religion," 75; Mtuze, *Essence of Xhosa Spirituality*, 48; Nürnberger, *Living Dead*, 32; Aloo Osotsi Mojola, "The Chagga Scapegoat Purification Ritual and Another Re-Reading of the Goat of Azazel in Leviticus 16," *Melita Theologica* 50, no. 1 (1999): 57–83.

100. Opoku, "African Traditional Religion," 76; Hampate Ba, "Présentation des religions traditionnelles africaines," 66; Mtuze, *Essence of Xhosa Spirituality*, 25.

101. Hazoumé, "L'âme du Dahoméen," 245; Pierre-Dominique Coco, "Notes sur la place des morts et des ancêtres dans la société traditionnelle," in Diop, *Les religions africaines*, 233.

102. Jensen, *Myth and Cult*, 288.

103. Ntumba, "Mythe et religion en Afrique," 186.

deceased—in catastrophic punishments befalling whole villages, for instance (the Zwididwana zombies, former villagers of a settlement now flooded by Lake Fundudzi).[104] Thus, the dead who are not ancestors (or cultural heroes, who are treated much the same) may be viewed quite distinctly.[105] Only a few African cultures lack ancestor veneration (e.g., the Maasai).[106] And yet "ancestor veneration" is hardly the correct term, as "the ancestors themselves are not the objects of cultic reverence but enjoy their distinction in consequence of an over-all religious conception which centers about the relationship between deity and man . . . receiving from the deity a spiritual quality which constitutes his true 'life substance.'"[107]

Thus, three levels—supreme God, spirits, and ancestors—constitute a phenomenon widespread across Africa.[108] The middle layer shows the most variety: nature spirits and clan totems, malevolent monsters and intercessory psychopomps (*RS*, 112; Lagrange considered totemism certain for the ancient Levant).

Application to Ancient Israel

The value of ATR for understanding ancient Israelite religion is that the question whether it is "fundamentally monotheistic or polytheistic" is "an oversimplification of the problem."[109] We move beyond a "monotheism [that] leaves little room for other deities."[110] God remains "a singular entity," but the diversity of supernatural life—conceived "not . . . as necessary emanations or evolutions or even imitations of the Absolute"[111]—relieves us of rummaging for terms like monolatry and henotheism.[112] God "is the prime cause . . . remotely responsible for all occurrences experienced in our universe."[113] Yet that by no means debilitates other named spiritual beings,

104. Anyumba and Nkuna, "Lake Fundudzi," 14.
105. Lugira, *African Religion*, 49.
106. Westerlund, "Spiritual Beings," 160.
107. Jensen, *Myth and Cult*, 291.
108. Ezeanya, "God, Spirits and the Spirit World," 35.
109. Topor, "Concept of God," 2; Lugira, *African Religion*, 35–36.
110. Smith, *God in Translation*, 165.
111. Topor, "Concept of God," 3.
112. Nyirenda, *Mbande Hill Sacredness*, 6 (fig. 1), says ATR "compares favourably with henotheism."
113. Topor, "Concept of God," 3.

tree spirits (Judg 9:37; Gen 13:18; 21:33; 1 Sam 14:2; 22:6; 2 Sam 5:24), flying snakes (Isa 14:29), or anonymous river wrestlers (Gen 32:24–30; compare *RS*, 174). We shall also see the status of the dead in ancient Israel holds many parallels to ATR.

We have already seen how the onomastic data suggest a strong preference for one God, at first generally called El(ohim) and, increasingly, Yahweh. As for the higher spirits, those that have personal names in the Hebrew onomasticon, we must remember this is the level at which the biblical presentation and what is observable in the archaeological record most differ.

For the female demigoddesses, Astarte is considered an abomination (assuming she is intended by "Ashtoreth": 1 Kgs 11:5, 33; 2 Kgs 23:13).[114] However, the phrase *ashterôt ṣōnekā* in Deut 7:13; 28:4, 18, 51, usually translated "young of your flock," "is clearly a hangover from an early stage of belief in which the goddess Astarte was thought to be responsible for the fertility of the flocks of sheep."[115] If the "Queen of Heaven" of Jeremiah 44 is Astarte, then the biblical text at least claims that her worship was "deep-seated among both the ordinary people and rulers of Judah and Jerusalem and had gone back several generations."[116]

Asherah seems to have been understood both as a proper name (1 Kgs 11:33) and a cult image, either a tree or a symbolic tree in the form of a pole (2 Kgs 18:4; 23:14), and, as Lagrange stated, ancient Israelites would have made little differentiation between the two meanings (*RS*, 120).[117] On the one hand, Asherah or the Asherahs are repeatedly condemned (1 Kgs 15:13; 2 Kgs 18:4; 23:4–7, 15). On the other hand, these very condemnations indicate the presence of Asherah in the Jerusalem temple and the Northern temple at Bethel.[118] When the prophets of Baal and Asherah assemble at Mount Carmel in 1 Kings 18, Elijah calls for the slaughter only of

114. Day, *Yahweh and the Gods*, 128–30.

115. Day, *Yahweh and the Gods*, 131–32. Cf. *KTU* 1.148.18.

116. Day, *Yahweh and the Gods*, 148–49; cf. Susan Ackerman, "At Home with the Goddess," in *Symbiosis, Symbolism, and the Power of the Past: Canaan, Ancient Israel, and Their Neighbors, from the Late Bronze Age through Roman Palaestina: Proceedings of the Centennial Symposium, W. F. Albright Institute of Archaeological Research and American Schools of Oriental Research, Jerusalem, May 29/31, 2000*, ed. W. G. Dever and S. Gitin (Winona Lake, IN: Eisenbrauns, 2003), 461. On other possible identifications of the Queen of Heaven, see Tally Ornan, "Ištar as Depicted on Finds from Israel," in *Studies in the Archaeology of the Iron Age in Israel and Jordan*, ed. Amihai Mazar, JSOTSup 331 (Sheffield: Sheffield Academic Press, 2001), 251.

117. Ackerman, "At Home with the Goddess," 457.

118. Ackerman, "At Home with the Goddess," 458.

the prophets of Baal, while Asherah's prophets seem to escape unharmed. The biblical polemic against the Queen of Heaven, Asherah, and other goddesses indicates a vital cult until the exile.[119]

Archaeological evidence confirms this, although it is usually unclear which goddess is intended.[120] What needs to be emphasized, however, is that aside from the so-called Judean pillar figurines,[121] the majority of archaeological appearances of goddesses pair them with a major male deity, and in almost all of these cases, there is nothing that prevents us from seeing him as Yahweh. In fact, this is often explicit, as in the case of Sellin's cult stands from Taanach,[122] an incised potsherd from eighth-century Jerusalem, and perhaps the two *massevoth* in the ninth-century shrine of Arad.[123] Goddesses seem to have no *roles* attributed to them apart from Yahweh, even in the inscriptions from Kuntillet Ajrud and Khirbet el-Qom.[124]

The situation for named male divinities is somewhat murkier. Perhaps these were more likely to be seen as rivals to Yahweh. Halpern, for example, sees "the Baals" as a biblical blanket term for all of God's male underlings,

119. Silvia Schroer, "Gender and Iconography from the Viewpoint of a Feminist Biblical Scholar," *Lectio Difficilior* 2 (2008): 2; Scott B. Noegel, "The Women of Asherah: Weaving Wickedness in 2 Kings 23:7," *CBQ* 83, no. 2 (2021): 217–18; Judith M. Hadley, *The Cult of Asherah in Ancient Israel and Judah: Evidence for a Hebrew Goddess*, University of Cambridge Oriental Publications 57 (Cambridge: Cambridge University Press, 2000), 77; Ackerman, "At Home with the Goddess," 465; Baruch Halpern, *From Gods to God: The Dynamics of Iron Age Cosmologies*, FAT 63 (Tübingen: Mohr Siebeck, 2009), 60.

120. Note the tenth-century Pella cult stand and the tenth-century Taanach cult stand. See Hadley, *Cult of Asherah*, 167–76; Joanna Töyräänvuori, "An Iconographic Allusion to the Northwest Semitic Sea Deity Yamm from 8th Century BC Jerusalem?," in *"My Spirit at Rest in the North Country" (Zechariah 6.8): Collected Communications to the XXth Congress of the International Organization for the Study of the Old Testament, Helsinki 2010*, ed. Hermann Michael Miemann and Matthias Augustin, BEATAJ 57 (New York: Peter Lang, 2011), 193–202.

121. These may be Asherah, or they may not be deities at all but fecundity votive objects. See Ackerman, "At Home with the Goddess," 463; Karel Van der Toorn, "Goddesses in Early Israelite Religion," in *Ancient Goddesses: The Myths and the Evidence*, ed. Lucy Goodison and Christine Morris (Madison: University of Wisconsin Press, 1998), 92.

122. Hadley, *Cult of Asherah*, 179.

123. See Garth Gilmour, "Iconism and Aniconism in the Period of the Monarchy: Was There an Image of the Deity in the Jerusalem Temple?," in *Visualizing Jews through the Ages: Literary and Material Representations of Jewishness and Judaism*, ed. Hannah Ewence and Helen Spurling (London: Routledge, 2015), 91–103.

124. Van der Toorn, "Goddesses in Early Israelite Religion," 91; for the texts, see Renz, *Die althebräischen Inschriften*, 175–77.

the veneration of which was wholly condemned.[125] The horse-and-rider figures common to eighth- and seventh-century Judah have been identified with Shamash, whose worship is noted critically in 2 Kgs 23:11 and Ezek 8:16.[126] Worship of Gad and Manat is decried in Isa 65:11, but both personal and place-names suggest Gad had a role, albeit minor, in Israelite life.[127] Resheph is clearly an independent spirit in the Levant, known from late second-millennium Egypt and Ugarit through late first-millennium Phoenicia and associated, among other things, with "arrows of plague."[128] In the Hebrew Bible, he is in many places a spirit in service of Yahweh, delivering arrows of plague (Hab 3:5; Ps 76:4).[129] Even where Resheph or "sons of Resheph" seems to indicate sparks (Song 8:6; Job 5:7; Ps 78:48; cf. Exod 9:24), the meaning of pestilence is not excluded,[130] and the mythological personification is never lost (thus, even in the Song of Songs, Resheph appears alongside Mot).[131] Here, however, lies a distinction from ATR: only God uses spirits in the Bible, while in ATR humans can regularly employ them.[132] Nevertheless, what practice in ancient Israel may have been—and how it may have differed from the biblical account—remains unclear. Personal names also suggest Shahar[133] and Shalem.[134]

125. Halpern, *From Gods to God*, 57–58, 61–62.

126. See Gilmour, "Iconism and Aniconism."

127. Gaetano Di Palma, "'Lia disse: "Per fortuna!" E lo chiamó Gad' (Gen 30,11)," *Aisthema* 1, no. 2 (2014): 48–50; Nahman Avigad and Benjamin Sass, *Corpus of West Semitic Stamp Seals*, Publications of the Israel Academy of Sciences and Humanities, Section of Humanities (Jerusalem: Israel Academy of Sciences and Humanities, 1997), figs. 105, 454, 627, 628, 629, 1134, 1135.

128. John H. Choi, "Resheph and Yhwh Ṣĕbāʾôt," *VT* 54, no. 1 (2004): 17–28; Maciej M. Münnich, *The God Resheph in the Ancient Near East*, Orientalische Religionen in der Antike 11 (Tübingen: Mohr Siebeck, 2013), 265–66. See *KTU* 1.82.2; 1.14 i.16–20.

129. Shaul Bar, "Resheph in the Hebrew Bible," *JBQ* 45, no. 2 (2017): 120–21; Münnich, *The God Resheph*, 218, 222; Petra Schmidtkunz, *Das Moselied des Deuteronomiums: Untersuchungen zu Text und Theologie von Dtn 32,1–43*, FAT 2/124 (Tübingen: Mohr Siebeck, 2020), 191.

130. Bar, "Resheph in the Hebrew Bible," 122; Münnich, *The God Resheph*, 219.

131. Münnich, *The God Resheph*, 233; C. L. Seow, *Job 1–21: Interpretation and Commentary*, Illumination Commentaries Series (Grand Rapids: Eerdmans, 2013), 437–38.

132. Ogiozee, "The Value," 65.

133. Avigad and Sass, *Corpus of West Semitic Stamp Seals*, figs. 108, 454, 548, 562, 627, 629, 672, 673, 701; Graham I. Davies, ed., *Ancient Hebrew Inscriptions: Corpus and Concordance* (Cambridge: Cambridge University Press, 1991), 1:123.

134. Avigad and Sass, *Corpus of West Semitic Stamp Seals*, 172, 508; Davies, *Ancient Hebrew Inscriptions*, 1:29; Tobshalom from Lachish and from En Gedi; Lemaire, *Les ostraca*, 50, 95.

For the lesser spirits, the parallels with ATR are substantial. Some of these are malevolent—"demons" in many Bible translations, although substantially different from both the demons of the New Testament and from those of later Judaism.[135] The *seirim*, or so-called goat demons of Lev 17:7; 2 Kgs 23:8; Isa 13:21; 34:14; 2 Chr 11:15, may correspond to the winged goat on an eighth- or seventh-century seal from Dor or a human-headed, winged goat on a seventh-century Hebrew seal belonging to Baqqashat, daughter of Ebed-Jerah.[136] The *qeteb* of Hos 6:2; 13:14–15; Deut 32:24; Isa 28:2; Ps 91:6 appear to be a phylum of malevolent being, as in postbiblical tradition.[137] These are, however, agents of God's angry will, not forces opposed to him, as the term "demon" comes to mean (Hab 3:5; Ps 91:6).[138]

Other genera of spirits tend to operate more favorably toward humanity. Judges 5:20 says, "The stars fought from heaven" on behalf of Deborah, and Job 38:31–32 alludes to myths about the stars and constellations known to the Israelite author. Like many African cultures, it is unlikely that ancient Israelites "distinguish[ed] between mythical and real animals."[139] Isaiah 30:6 lists animals and mythical creatures indiscriminately: lion and lioness, viper and fiery flying seraph. If the seraphim of Isaiah 6 are meant to be the same creatures, "fiery" envisions smoke bellowing from the mouth and nostrils as they speak.[140] What cherubim are seems to have been a developing concept, often

135. Such demons appear already in Tobit and potentially in Psalm 95. Why the Septuagint chose to translate many of these earlier creatures as *daemonia* is a larger question, on which see Michael J. Morris, *Warding off Evil: Apotropaic Tradition in the Dead Sea Scrolls and Synoptic Gospels*, WUNT 2/451 (Tübingen: Mohr Siebeck, 2017).

136. Maciej J. Münnich, "What Did the Biblical Goat-Demons Look Like?," *UF* 38 (2006): 526.

137. Johannes C. De Moor, "'O Death, Where Is Thy Sting?'," in *Ascribe to the Lord: Biblical and Other Studies in Memory of Peter C. Craigie*, ed. Lyle Eslinger and Glen Taylor, JSOTSup 67 (Sheffield: Sheffield Academic Press, 1988), 100–104; André Caquot, "Sur quelque démons de l'Ancien Testament (Reseph, Qeteb, Deber)," *Sem* 6 (1956): 65–66.

138. Schmidtkunz, *Moselied*, 192.

139. Allan Dyssel, "Behemoth, Beast of the Negev? A Fusion of Animals, Mythical Beasts and Monsters in Isaiah 30:6," *Pharos Journal of Theology* 99 (2018): 1.

140. Dyssel, "Behemoth," 2. I do not think seraphim were simply Egyptian uraeuses; they have six wings, breathe fire, "brandish" (עפף), and fly—only in Numbers 21 and Deuteronomy 8 are they equated with serpents. See Nicolas Wyatt, "Grasping the Griffin: Identifying and Characterizing the Griffin in Egyptian and West Semitic Tradition," *Journal of Ancient Egyptian Interconnections* 1, no. 1 (2009): 31–32; Isaiah Horowitz, *Bereshit*, vol. 1 of *Shney Luchot Habrit*, 2nd ed., trans. Eliyahu Munk (Jerusalem: Lambda, 1999), 56. For the uraeus view, see K. Jaroš, "Seraf(im)," *NBL* 2:574.

depicted curiously due to the nature of prophetic visions.[141] Winged quadrupeds, perhaps human- or eagle-headed lions seem most likely (2 Sam 22:11).[142] The *ṣip'oni* of Prov 23:32 may be an Ottoman viper or European cat snake, or it may be a basilisk (as the NJPS has it). The *ziz* of Psalms 50 and 80 may be some sort of beetle or leafhopper,[143] or it may be a fearsome mythological bird like the Mesopotamian Anzu, since Ps 50:10–12 pairs it with Behemoth.[144]

And then there are the giants, variously "semi-divine, as anti-law and anti-king, as elite adversary and elite animal, as unruly vegetation, and as the defeated past."[145] Genesis 6:1–4 (and, seemingly, Sir 16:7) makes them semidivine, and other texts connect them with the Rephaim, who are either living beings (Gen 14:5; 15:20; Deut 2:11, 20; 3:11, 13; Josh 12:4; 13:12; 17:15) or spirits of the dead (Isa 14:9; 26:14, 19; Ps 88:11; Prov 2:18; 9:18; 21:16; *RS*, 273). As living ogres, they function as paradigmatic foes for heroes (Num 13; Deut 1:28, 1:46–2:1, 14; Josh 11–15; 1 Sam 17; Amos 2:9). Joshua 17:14–18 "draws the confrontation with the giant into a floral narrative of clearing out unruly vegetation" to be "cut out" and "cleared."[146] Perhaps some of them were rather like Ents—after all, 2 Sam 18:8 says, "The forest devoured more people that day than the sword."

What of the dead? As we have seen in ATR, the distinction between dead ancestors as objects of worship and prayers and rituals designed to assist the dead is a spectrum, with the dead's ability to help the living (albeit

141. Stéphanie Anthonioz, "Chérubins / *keruvim*: Évolutions et mutation," in *Les chérubins /* keruvim *dans l'antiquité: Approche historique et comparée*, Kasion 6, ed. Philippe Abrahami and Stéphanie Anthonioz (Münster: Zaphon, 2021), 95; Alice Wood, *Of Wings and Wheels: A Synthetic Study of the Biblical Cherubim*, BZAW 385 (Berlin: de Gruyter, 2008), 117, 140.

142. Wood, *Of Wings and Wheels*, 200–203; Wyatt, "Grasping the Griffin," 29–31, 33–34.

143. Richard Whitekettle, "Bugs, Bunny, or Boar? Identifying the *Zîz* Animals of Psalms 50 and 80," *CBQ* 67, no. 2 (2005): 262.

144. Nili Wazana, "Anzu and Ziz: Great Mythical Birds in Ancient Near Eastern, Biblical, and Rabbinic Traditions," *JANES* 31, no. 1 (2009): 119, 129, 131–32; Alexander Mitarev and Leonid Kogan, *Animal Names*, vol. 2 of *Semitic Etymological Dictionary*, AOAT 278 (Münster: Ugarit-Verlag, 2005), 324, item no. 255.

145. Brian R. Doak, "The Giant in a Thousand Years: Tracing Narratives of Gigantism in the Hebrew Bible and Beyond," in *Ancient Tales of Giants from Qumran and Turfan: Contexts, Traditions, and Influences*, ed. Matthew Goff, Loren T. Stuckenbruck, and Enrico Morano, WUNT 360 (Tübingen: Mohr Siebeck, 2016), 15. See further Brian R. Doak, *The Last of the Rephaim: Conquest and Cataclysm in the Heroic Ages of Ancient Israel*, Ilex Foundation Series 8 (Washington, DC: Harvard University Center for Hellenic Studies, 2012).

146. Doak, "The Giant in a Thousand Years," 25.

never on the level of major deities) somewhere in between.[147] That the dead might be in need of food and drink in no way jeopardizes their efficacious power on the one hand or their potential danger on the other.[148] As Lagrange points out, bringing food to the tomb can mean either feeding the hungry dead or offering to the powerful dead (*RS*, 286–87). The same variability of veneration obtains for ancient Israel (Deut 18:9–14; 26:14; 1 Samuel 28; 2 Sam 18:18; Isa 8:19–20; 29:3; 29:4; 57:6–9; Jer 16:7; Ps 89:6–9; 106:28).[149] Although there are biblical texts that object to some versions of ancestor veneration (Isa 8:19; Sir 30:18–19), the prohibition in Deut 26:14 on offering tithed firstfruits to the dead implies that presenting food to the dead is otherwise permissible (also Jer 16:5–8).[150] Tobit 4:17 advises one to "place your bread on the grave of the righteous." An inscribed bowl from Beth Shemesh may have served in this capacity.[151] And graves at Samaria have holes in the floor, possibly for drink offerings.[152]

Interreligious Implications

The Belgian Franciscan Placide Tempels, whose 1945 book *Bantu Philosophy* pioneered the positive treatment of ATR by Western Christian theologians, drew a connection from ATR not to ancient Israelite religion but to Catholic theology. "What Catholic theology teaches concerning, in particular, the supernatural realities of grace," he writes, "that it is a supernal reinforcement of our being, that it is able to grow and to be strengthened in itself, is an idea similar to what the Bantu accept in the natural order as true of all being, of all

147. Hays, "Histories of Death," 690.

148. Hays, "Histories of Death," 685; Jacob Milgrom, *Leviticus 17–22*, AB 3A (New Haven: Yale University Press, 2007), 1774; contra Matthew Suriano, *A History of Death in the Hebrew Bible* (Oxford: Oxford University Press, 2018), 176; and Brian B. Schmidt, *Israel's Beneficent Dead: Ancestor Cult and Necromancy in Ancient Israelite Religion and Tradition* (Winona Lake, IN: Eisenbrauns, 1996).

149. Justin E. Gillespie, *The Development of the Belief in the Resurrection within the Old Testament*, Pontificia Università della Santa Croce Dissertationes Series Theologica 26 (Rome: Edizioni Santa Croce, 2009), 147n36; Milgrom, *Leviticus 17–22*, 1777.

150. Doak, *The Last of the Rephaim*, 173; André Chouraqui, *Paroles: Deutéronome* (Paris: J.-C. Lattès, 1993), 269.

151. Suriano, *History of Death*, 161. Most funerary remains from ancient Israel and Judah suggest supplies for an ongoing daily life.

152. Milgrom, *Leviticus 17–22*, 1772–73.

force."[153] There, he focuses on a notion supposedly in the Bantu worldview that we have not explored for ancient Israel. Nevertheless, there are several other valid elements of comparison.

In recent years, I have tried to move from discussing *how* we can bring biblical scholarship to theological relevance to actually trying to do it.[154] Now, if we are able to view ancient Israelite religion through the lens of ATR—and not merely those parts of ancient Israelite practice the prophets deem pagan or heterodox but elements of the faith the Old Testament itself promotes—then we can reverse the equation. We can view ATR through the lens of the Old Testament. I am not here talking about enculturation of text, though I agree that the text is always actualized through cultures (see Laurie Brink's essay in this volume). Rather, I am talking about using my insights into text for theology of culture. My argument is that reading ATR as, in many ways, the same faith as that of Samuel, Elijah, and Hezekiah has great value for how we approach those faiths from a Catholic perspective, both in terms of missiology and in interreligious dialogue.

In making such moves, we build on Cardinal Arinze's exhortation (which draws on John Paul II) to "appreciate the African soul which searches for God through traditional religion . . . not without some errors here and there, but with a clear idea that there is one God and that there are good and evil spirits and that there are ancestors to be honored."[155] John Paul II had written earlier: "Adherents of African traditional religion should therefore be treated with great respect and esteem, and all inaccurate and disrespectful language should be avoided."[156] The 1994 Synod for Africa invited schol-

153. Placide Tempels, *Bantu Philosophy*, trans. Margaret Read, Collection Présence Africaine (Orlando: HBC, 2010), 56.

154. See my *Many Roads Lead Eastward: Overtures to Catholic Biblical Theology* (Eugene, OR: Cascade, 2016); Robert D. Miller II, OFS, "Iron Age Medicine Men and Old Testament Theology," in *Between Israelite Religion and Biblical Theology: Essays on Archaeology, History, and Hermeneutics*, ed. Robert D. Miller II, CBET 80 (Leuven: Peeters, 2016), 87–128. See also Hans Urs von Balthasar, *Martin Buber & Christianity: A Dialogue between Israel and the Church*, trans. Alexander Dru (New York: Macmillan, 1961), 101.

155. Quoted in Jean-Baptiste Sourou, "African Traditional Religion and the Catholic Church in the Light of the Synods for Africa: 1994 and 2009," *African Human Rights Law Journal* 14, no. 1 (2014): 146.

156. John Paul II, Post-Synodal Apostolic Exhortation *Ecclesia in Africa* (September 14, 1995) §67 (quoted in Sourou, "African Traditional Religion," 147). The terms "respect" and "esteem" had already been used in the 1984 Secretariat for Non-Christians document *The Attitude of the Church towards the Followers of Other Religions: Reflections*

arly work on approaches to ATR, "especially for matters concerning . . . the veneration of ancestors, and the spirit world."[157] The 1993 letter of the Pontifical Council for Interreligious Dialogue, *Pastoral Attention to Traditional Religions*, singled out "the irreplaceable role of the Bible" in "the necessary framework within which the riches of the Traditional Religions can attain their fulfillment."[158]

Consider, then, the ancestors, which the South African theologian Klaus Nürnberger begs us to stop calling "demons."[159] Wolor Topor writes, "The Ancestors constitute in a real sense of the word an objective community with the living—a sort of 'communio sanctorum' of Christianity."[160] As Nürnberger writes, death is disruptive, and ancestor veneration does not downplay the horrible finality of death. Yet it keeps departed loved ones in the communion of the saints rather than conceiving of them as homeless spirits.[161] The Spiritan Father Marcel Kessy precisely compares Tanzanian Chagga views of the dead with those in the Bible.[162] Nürnberger acknowledges that the range of action available to the living dead in ATR exceeds that ascribed to the Christian dead in Rom 8:38–39; 1 Cor 15:22–23; 1 Thess 4:13–18; Phil 1:21–24; and even Hebrews 12[163]—even if they seem much more prone to action in the Old Testament (1 Sam 18:13; 2 Kgs 13:21; Isa 29:4; Sir 48:13–14), as Kessy notes.[164] Rabbinic literature includes several examples of requesting the deceased patriarchs to pray on one's behalf (Midr. Tann. 179; b. Bava Met-

and Orientations on Dialogue and Mission §§1.3; 2.4, 26, https://www.dicasteryinterreligious.va/dialogue-and-mission-1984.

157. Sourou, "African Traditional Religion," 147. Quite the contrary is the work of Ludovic Lado, "The Roman Catholic Church and African Religions: A Problematic Encounter," *The Way* 45, no. 3 (2006): 7–21. Lado denies monotheism in Africa (12–13) and concludes that "dialogue is not realistic" (16) and that any "fashionable talk of inculturation and still more any idea that there can be successful inculturation rather obscures [the] central reality of Christian witness" (21).

158. Pontifical Council for Interreligious Dialogue, *Pastoral Attention to Traditional Religions* (November 21, 1993) §11.

159. Nürnberger, *Living Dead*, 14.

160. Topor, "Concept of God," 4.

161. Nürnberger, *Living Dead*, 24–25.

162. Kessy, "Death Rituals," 37–39. See also Emmanuel Chinedu Anagwo, "Cult of the Ancestors and Saints from the Igbo (Nigerian) Experience: A Liturgical Evaluation," *Grace & Truth* 35, no. 2 (2018): 14–18. Anagwo also makes this comparison but while critiquing ancestor cults that exclude women, the childless, and those who do not die a "good death."

163. Nürnberger, *Living Dead*, 85, 88.

164. Kessy, "Death Rituals," 39.

zi'a 85b), especially at their tombs (Gen. Rab. 82.10; b. Sotah 34b; b. Ta'anit 16a).[165] The Rite Zaïros, approved by the Congregation for Divine Worship in 1988, opens with an invocation to the ancestors—including those from before Christian contact—and repeats acknowledgment of the ancestors throughout the Mass.[166]

Or consider the spirits. The *Celestial Hierarchy* of Pseudo-Dionysius preserved the cherubim and seraphim; the *ophanim* (Ezek 10:9) and *seirim* gave way to Pauline thrones, dominions, and powers. Clement of Alexandria still debated the relationship between angels and the stars over which they were set and governed, including the sun (*Ecl.* 55–56).[167] Yet the development of angelology over the course of Christian history moved angels further from what they are in both ATR and in ancient Israel: "Mediaeval man robs the angels of their bodies; renaissance man robs them of their functions; modern man robs them of their existence."[168] Jean-Claude Bajeux insists there is a difference: the God of Genesis creates directly without secondary causes, whereas the spirits regularly intervene in ATR.[169] Yet Genesis 1 has God repeatedly say, "Let the earth bring forth," delegating the act of creation, albeit not to spirits. Peter Lombard draws an analogy between the way God bestows the power to forgive sins upon the ordained and the power of creating that God is able to permit his creatures (*Sententiae in IV libris distinctae* 4.5.3), although Thomas Aquinas subsequently said God not only does not but cannot use secondary agents in creating (*Summa theologiae* I, q. 44, art. 2).[170] Nürnberger notes that spirits in ATR have no personalities;

165. Uri Ehrlich, "The Ancestors' Prayers for the Salvation of Israel in Early Rabbinic Thought," in *Jewish and Christian Liturgy and Worship: New Insights into Its History and Interaction*, ed. Albert Gerhards and Clemens Leonhard, Jewish and Christian Perspectives 15 (Leiden: Brill, 2007), 251–55.

166. Anagwo, "Cult of the Ancestors," 19–20.

167. See Clement of Alexandria, *Excerpts of Theodotus*, trans. William Wilson (Waterford, Ireland: CrossReach, 2019), 34, 36.

168. D. E. Harding, *The Hierarchy of Heaven and Earth: A New Diagram of Man in the Universe* (Gainesville: University of Florida Press, 1979), 231. This aphorism ignores the supernatural's resurgence in the Baroque era. See Thornton Wilder and Joseph Cermatori, "The Barock; or, How to Recognize a Miracle in the Daily Life," *Proceedings of the Modern Language Association of America* 136, no. 2 (2021): 249–50.

169. Bajeux, "Mentalité noire et mentalité biblique," 63; cf. Jonathan S. McIntosh, *The Flame Imperishable: Tolkien, St. Thomas, and the Metaphysics of Faërie* (Kettering, Ohio: Angelico, 2017), 157.

170. McIntosh, *The Flame Imperishable*, 160–61. Interestingly, Shaykhi Shi'a Muslims interpret Qur'an 23:14 ("God is the best of creators") to mean that other spirits also cre-

"though part of the mythological canopy," they are not "existentially relevant like ancestors."[171] In most ATR, they cannot be communicated with even to the degree that the living dead can.[172] As Lagrange writes, "Primitive simple monotheism is perfectly reconcilable with the existence of a number of spirits and even with the philosophical error of animism" (*RS*, 36–37).

When we get to the named demigods, of course, it would be difficult to sustain a Christian place for them (unless their names are Gabriel or Michael). Shamash, Gad, Astarte, and Asherah are as problematic as Jeremiah and Ezekiel made them. I do note, however, that ATR has very few such figures; its spirits are largely well situated below God and under his control. And even the Old Testament is lenient here. Note the perspective in Wis 13:2: "Either fire, or wind, or the swift air, or the circuit of the stars, or the mighty water, or the luminaries of heaven, the governors of the world"—and I wonder who they are—"they considered gods." Wisdom continues:

> Now if, charmed by their beauty, they have taken these for gods, let them know how far more excellent is the Lord than these; for the original source of beauty fashioned them. Or if they were struck by their might and energy, let them realize from these things how much more powerful is the one who made them. For from the greatness and the beauty of created things their original author, by analogy, is seen. But yet, little blame attaches to them; for they have gone astray perhaps, though they seek God and wish to find him. Familiar with his works, they investigate them and fall victim to appearances, seeing so much beauty [ὅτι καλὰ τὰ βλεπόμενα]. (Wis 13:3–7)[173]

And lest we think that the biblical giants, flying snakes, and phoenix—like their African counterparts, the dragon-like Ninki Nanka of Gambia, the giant

ate. See Muhammad Iqbal, *The Development of Metaphysics in Persia* (Lahore: Bazm-i-Iqbal, 1954), 144.

171. Nürnberger, *Living Dead*, 30–31.

172. Nürnberger, *Living Dead*, 32.

173. NABR, altered with corrections from Jean-Louis Chrétien, *The Ark of Speech*, trans. Andrew Brown (London: Routledge, 2004), 81. Also consider: "Christianity is monotheistic only because it asserts that the absolute has but one constituent Life." Michel Henry, "Speech and Religion: The Word of God," in *The Michel Henry Reader*, ed. Scott Davidson and Frédéric Seyler, trans. Leonard Lawlor et al., Northwestern University Studies in Phenomenology and Existential Philosophy (Evanston, IL: Northwestern University Press, 2019), 219.

Owuo of Togo, and various river monsters (e.g., the Songhai Hira, Sengwer Dingonek, Lozi Ilomba)—are beyond the range of consideration, Christian writers had little doubt such creatures existed. First Clement 25 discusses the phoenix. Isidore of Seville defined the basilisk as king of snakes because of its killing glare and poisonous breath (*Etymologies*). Albert the Great wrote about its killing gaze, citing Hermetic literature as his source, but dismissed all other legends. Albert also discussed winged dragons in his commentary on Aristotle's *History of Animals*, listing their various breeds, their methods of killing, and their traditional enmity with elephants (*De animalibus* 2.367r, 409v, 416v–420v). Thomas Aquinas's celestial and terrestrial hierarchies left open gaps and distinct theoretical possibilities that such creatures might realize.[174] Only with Hobbes and his century were lesser spirits, from angels to satyrs, dismissed as merely fancy.[175]

Magic, a common feature of ATR, is at times condemned in the Old Testament, though never condemned when performed by Gideon, Elijah, Elisha, the high priest with Urim and Thummim, and so on. Psalm 58:6 and Eccl 10:11 assume snake charming works. Not everything that one might call magical in ATR is equally prohibited in the Old Testament. If one looks at the history of Christianity, we find two opposite responses toward magic, both negative. Either magic was all fake and therefore wrong, or it was very real and also wrong.[176] The Council of Elvira in 305 took the latter stance, in Canon 9: "If someone kills another by sorcery or magic, that person shall not receive communion, even at the time of death, for this action is a form of idolatry."

Premodern Christian writers were quite willing to extend the range of divine action beyond the domain of Israel and the church and to allow for human capacity for interacting with that action outside those bounds. Titus 1:12 refers to Epimenides of Cnossos as a prophet. Augustine listed Ver-

174. McIntosh, *The Flame Imperishable*, 158. The "totemism" of ATR (and ancient Israel) bears consideration in light of persistent animal-saint linkages in Christian history. See Emma Grover, "The Saint and the Swan: Animal Interactions in the Hagiography of Hugh of Avalon," *Quidditas* 41 (2020): 7–16. What is notable for Hugh of Avalon's swan is the hagiography's insistence that their connection, probably historical, was not miraculous (Grover, "The Saint and the Swan," 11, 13).

175. M. H. Abrams, *The Mirror and the Lamp: Romantic Theory and the Critical Tradition* (Oxford: Oxford University Press, 1971), 265. Joseph Glanville and William Temple tried to salvage witchcraft while discarding the fairies, elves, and goblins, with only a century's success (Abrams, *Mirror*, 266).

176. Charles Williams, *Witchcraft* (Cleveland: World, 1959), 28.

gil as an authentic prophet of God, specifically in his *Fourth Eclogue* (lines 13–14).[177] Innocent III quoted Vergil as prophecy in a Christmas homily.[178] Cyril of Alexandria, Jacob of Edessa, Gregory Nazianzus, Didymus the Blind, Quodvultdeus of Carthage, and Albert the Great all stated that Hermes Trismegistus—probably not a real person—was an inspired prophet.[179] As Eugen Rosenstock-Huessy writes, "Theologians can only distinguish between true and false prophets, between Moses and the magicians of the pharaoh, between Paul and Simon the magician, or between Swedenborg and Hamman, if they can and may pre-suppose the general faculty of prophecy within the realm of the soul."[180]

Lagrange concludes that Israelites and their neighbors venerated things like stones (Gen 28:18; 35:14; 1 Kgs 1:9) because they "wanted to make God more present and sensible" (*RS*, 187). This is true of ATR as well. And it remains a desideratum for Christianity. As William Law writes, "A religion that is not founded in nature is all fiction and falsity, and as mere a nothing as an idol."[181]

Second Peter 2:11 criticizes those who "show no respect for the glorious beings above [and] insult things they do not understand." The same is said in Jude 8–10. In light of such passages, my final argument is that while ATR can help us understand ancient Israel, and ancient Israel help us dialogue with ATR, this two-way conversation can also help us resist a kind of demythologization Pope Francis describes in *Fratelli tutti* as "new forms of cultural colonization."[182] This new demythologization is not that of Baur and others critiqued by Lagrange,[183] one which just removes the miracles. It is rather

177. Augustine, *Ep.* 137 to Volusian. See Domenico Comparetti, *Vergil in the Middle Ages* (Hamden, CT: Archon, 1966), 101n16.

178. Christmas Sermon 2 (Comparetti, *Vergil in the Middle Ages*, 102).

179. M. David Litwa, *Hermetica II: The Excerpts of Stobaeus, Papyrus Fragments, and Ancient Testimonies in an English Translation with Notes and Introductions* (Cambridge: Cambridge University Press, 2018), 205, 221, 250. Cf. Cyril of Alexandria, *Adv. Julian* 1.4.8.14–1.4.9.7; 1.46.9; Jacob of Edessa, *Hexameron* 149b11–150a17; Gregory Nazianzus, *Or.* 28.4; Didymus the Blind, *Comm. Ps.* 22–26.10; 88.8–18; Quodvultdeus, *Against Five Heresies* 3.4.

180. Eugen Rosenstock-Huessy, *Practical Knowledge of the Soul* (Eugene, OR: Wipf & Stock, 2015), 13.

181. William Law, *Liberal and Mystical Writings of William Law*, ed. Williams Scott Palmer (London: Longmans, Green, 1908), 33.

182. Francis, Encyclical Letter *Fratelli tutti* (October 3, 2020) §§13–14.

183. Marie-Joseph Lagrange, OP, *Historical Criticism and the Old Testament*, trans. Edward Myers (London: Catholic Truth Society, 1905), 43–45.

a Yehezkel Kaufmann form of neocolonialism, demystifying the world, demanding the removal of an eldritch, faërie world—anachronistically on ancient Israel and contemporarily on ATR.[184] Moreover, and perhaps more damaging to our full reception of God's revelation, the "symbolic character of reality"[185] is lost, an *analogy of culture* has been raised to the level of the *analogy of faith*, and we are all at risk of its homogenizing swathe, limiting the creator of "all things visible and *invisible*."[186]

184. This process had already "purified" Europe after the Council of Trent.

185. Kurt Stalder, *Sprache und Erkenntnis der Wirklichkeit Gottes: Texte zu einigen wissenschaftstheoretischen und systematischen Voraussetzungen für die exegetische und homiletische Arbeit*, ed. Urs von Arx, Ökumenische Beihefte zur Freiburger Zeitschrift für Philosophie und Theologie 38 (Freiburg: Universitätsverlag, 2000), 47.

186. That is not to say that the enchanting, the eldritch, might not also be terrifying. See Charles Williams, *The English Poetic Mind* (New York: Russell & Russell, 1963), 14 (on Wordsworth). From a secular perspective, Marina Warner, *Signs and Wonders: Essays on Literature and Culture* (London: Chatto & Windus, 2003), 445, notes the modern loss of an enchanted worldview, the marvelous now being "purely literary rather than spiritual."

Foreshadowings of the Kingdom

An Essay in Biblical Theology

Nina Sophie Heereman

In 1950, Fr. Henri de Lubac received fan mail from the most unexpected quarters. Fr. R. P. Hugues Vincent, Fr. Marie-Joseph Lagrange's long-time coworker, disciple, friend, and confidant, had just finished reading de Lubac's *History and Spirit: The Understanding of Scripture according to Origen* and could not contain his excitement.[1] Anyone only slightly acquainted with the heated debates over the correct interpretation of Scripture in the nineteenth and twentieth centuries, and with the trenches dividing those who embraced the historical-critical method and those who denied it any merit, might be astonished to learn of the letter's content. According to Fr. Vincent, Fr. de Lubac's principles in retrieving the exegesis of the church fathers were *exactly the same* as those that he, Fr. Vincent, had learned from Fr. Lagrange.[2] He even went so far as to suggest that "*History and Spirit* might become the manual of scriptural hermeneutics both for today's generation and for tomorrow's."[3]

Although he would not live to fully witness it, Fr. Vincent's desire proved to be prophetic. A mere fifteen years later, the church made the principles laid down by both Lagrange and de Lubac her own and synthesized them in the now famous §12 of the dogmatic constitution *Dei Verbum*. They have been reiterated by the magisterium ever since, not least, in recent years,

1. Henri de Lubac, *History and Spirit: The Understanding of Scripture according to Origen*, trans. Anne Englund Nash (San Francisco: Ignatius, 2007).

2. "During the years 1891–1900, when Père Lagrange absolutely pulverized my entire attitude towards Holy Scripture, its basic theological notion, its character, and its interpretation, he drilled into me principles which are amazingly identical to those on which the masterly treatment of Père de Lubac rests." Henri de Lubac, *Scripture in the Tradition*, Milestones in Catholic Theology, trans. Luke O'Neill (New York: Crossroad, 2000), 231.

3. De Lubac, *Scripture in the Tradition*, 234.

by Pope Benedict XVI, who in his apostolic letter *Verbum Domini* gave a powerful reminder of the basic elements that any exegesis faithful to the Council should observe:

> Only where both methodological levels, the historical-critical and the theological, are respected, can one speak of a theological exegesis, an exegesis worthy of this book. . . . While today's academic exegesis, including that of Catholic scholars, is highly competent in the field of historical-critical methodology and its latest developments, it must be said that comparable attention needs to be paid to the theological dimension of the biblical texts, so that they can be more deeply understood in accordance with the three elements indicated by the Dogmatic Constitution *Dei Verbum*.[4]

Here the former pontiff himself points to—what seems to me—the greatest challenge for Catholic exegetes today: to recuperate the theological dimension of the text without losing any of the rigor that the great Fr. Lagrange and his disciples dedicated to the historical dimension of the sacred page.

It would be presumptuous to attempt the realization of this much-desired exegesis in the space of this essay. Instead, I would like to apply just one of de Lubac's principles, the benefit of theological hindsight on religious historical data, to reap some theological fruits from Lagrange's foundational work in the study of Semitic religions and the historical-critical method.

According to de Lubac, "we can study the history of religion—including the religion of Israel—like any other collection of facts, but we cannot do it in any serious fashion without carefully educing, by means of an effort which goes further than mere critical erudition, the religious meaning of the texts which express it."[5] In order to do so, the historian must "not deny himself the advantages which are his by reason of his having been born in a later generation and of his ability to encompass a long series of events in a single glance."[6] For the Christian exegete, in particular, this means consciously appropriating the enormous advantage gained in hindsight by the fullness of revelation in Jesus Christ. While the Old Testament has a unity of its own and an eschatological thrust toward its fulfillment, "it stops at the

4. Benedict XVI, Post-Synodal Apostolic Exhortation *Verbum Domini* (September 30, 2010) §34.

5. De Lubac, *Scripture in the Tradition*, 25.

6. De Lubac, *Scripture in the Tradition*, 25.

threshold of Christian reality, whose flowering results from the appearance of a new principle."[7] This new principle is the gift of the Spirit, which simply had not been given before (see John 7:39). Though the Spirit of Christ was at work from the beginning of history, the *spiritual meaning* of the Old Testament could not be obtained from the biblical facts until the Spirit was actually given through the Lord's paschal mystery. It is the core conviction of the New Testament authors and the church fathers that "all the ancient Scriptures 'reveal the mystery of the Cross,' but they in turn are revealed by it, and by it alone. It [Christ's Passover] is the only key which can make us grasp their meaning. From then on they are bathed in its light. The Old Testament is definitively recaptured, reread, and reinterpreted *in the spirit* of the New."[8] It thus happens that events that are seemingly unrelated within the Old Testament appear as the unfolding of a divine plan when read in light of the New Testament's revelation.

It is this remarkable continuity of the divine plan on which I want to focus in the following reflection on the foreshadowing of the *Kingdom of God*, not only in the Old Testament but even, as through a broken mirror, in the "Semitic religions," to use Fr. Lagrange's term for the belief of those peoples in whose midst the divine revelation first occurred.[9] In what follows, then, I hope to show how much we owe to Fr. Lagrange's discovery that "it is impossible ever to understand documents without knowing the society from which they sprang."[10] At the same time, I also hope to suggest how this discovery can be used to establish a foundational historical-critical infrastructure for the spiritual exegesis advocated by de Lubac—an exegesis that itself ties the "spiritual" to the historical unfolding of revelation. In this way, I seek to show how much the knowledge gained by Lagrange's rigorous dedication to the historical method and the history of the ancient Near East helps us to better understand the mystery of the Word incarnate and the kingdom he proclaimed, specifically by considering "kingship" and the kingdom of God.

In Fr. Lagrange's day, the kingdom of God was already a subject of much discussion, owing to the publication of Alfred Loisy's *L'Évangile et l'Église*, in which he coined the now famous phrase, "Jesus foretold the kingdom,

7. De Lubac, *Scripture in the Tradition*, 34.

8. De Lubac, *Scripture in the Tradition*, 35–36 (italics original).

9. See Marie-Joseph Lagrange, OP, *Études sur les religions sémitiques*, EBib (Paris: Lecoffre, 1903).

10. Marie-Joseph Lagrange, OP, *Historical Criticism and the Old Testament*, trans. Edward Myers (London: Catholic Truth Society, 1905), 50.

and it is the Church that came."[11] Though Loisy himself, as noted by Joseph Ratzinger, did not intend to pit church and kingdom against each other in the way his statement was later received,[12] it still caused Fr. Lagrange to respond: "The kingdom of God has come, it is the Church."[13] Nonetheless, he closed an open letter discussing the Loisy controversy with the following paragraph:

> There yet remains to be made a closer study of the idea of the Kingdom of God and of the Messias. It has yet to be shown that the idea of the Messias was as narrow as it is now maintained to have been, and whether Jesus Christ was not Himself conscious that His mission and His person went beyond the general expectation of His time. Criticism and history will again come to our assistance in the study of this difficult problem, for we still contend that they are in nowise compromised, nor yet have we lost our trust in them.[14]

While this paper in no way pretends to provide this still-needed deeper study, I hope to show how vital it is to understand the notion of kingship in the ancient Near East and the Old Testament for a correct understanding of the kingdom of God in the New Testament. For, in the words of de Lubac, "Before we can undertake any spiritual interpretation of the Old Testament through the New, we must first have historically understood the New Testament through the Old."[15]

The arrival of God's kingdom stands at the very core of Jesus's proclamation and is powerfully summed up in his first words to the world: "The time is fulfilled, the kingdom of God is at hand, repent and believe in the εὐαγ-

11. Alfred Loisy, *The Gospel and the Church*, trans. Christopher Home (New York: Charles Scribner's Sons, 1904), 166.

12. See Joseph Ratzinger, *Called to Communion: Understanding the Church Today*, trans. Adrian Walker (San Francisco: Ignatius, 1996), 21.

13. Marie-Joseph Lagrange, OP, *M. Loisy et le modernisme: A propos des "Mémoires"* (Paris: Éditions du Cerf, 1932), 244.

14. Lagrange, *Historical Criticism and the Old Testament*, 243.

15. De Lubac, *Scripture in the Tradition*, 28. It is interesting that de Lubac himself quotes Lagrange on this principle, pointing out that the latter "suggested an analogous distinction, which stemmed from the same concern, when he distinguished in prophecy a 'literal meaning considered under its religious aspect' from a 'spiritual meaning'" (de Lubac, *Scripture in the Tradition*, 28n48). He references Marie-Joseph Lagrange, OP, "Pascal et les prophéties messianiques," *RB* 3, no. 4 (1906): 533–60.

γελιον" (Mark 1:15).[16] The εὐαγγέλιον τοῦ θεοῦ—"gospel" or "glad tidings of God"—that Jesus has come to announce (Mark 1:14) consists precisely in the fact that the kingdom of God has arrived and that repentance and faith in the εὐαγγελιον are necessary for entering into it.[17] Should we not think that God would have prepared his people beforehand to have a minimal grasp of this proclamation? True, Jesus uses mainly parables to describe and define the kingdom, which may be an indication of the fact that a first-century Jewish understanding alone was insufficient for its full comprehension. And yet, we would fall into a Marcionite trap if we thought that we could dispense with the Old Testament's prefiguration of the kingdom of God and still get it right.

Skimming through several books on the kingdom of God, I was surprised to find that few take the time to first establish in what way the Old Testament prepared Jesus's contemporary audience to grasp this central aspect of his preaching.[18] This is a serious lacuna, one that the present article does not so much fill as suggest outlines for how it might be filled. In order to properly understand its Old Testament prefiguration, however, as Fr. Lagrange has taught us, one needs to reach even further back, namely to the cultural context in which revelation first occurred and the metaphors that it borrowed, cleansed, and elevated in order to communicate. These myths were, so to speak, the human alphabet the divine author adopted in order to reveal himself. As we will see, they contain an astounding primordial knowledge about God's plan of salvation.[19]

I will proceed as follows: (1) I will first provide an outline of the ancient Near Eastern understanding of kingship, then (2) show how this plays out in the Old Testament, (3) flesh out how this finds its fulfillment in Jesus's paschal mystery, and (4) finally close with a brief reflection on how this casts

16. The above is my translation. Elsewhere in this essay, unless otherwise noted, Bible translations are from the NABR.

17. With regard to Jesus proclaiming the arrival of the kingdom versus its "mere" nearness, see the excellent summary in G. R. Beasley-Murray, *Jesus and the Kingdom of God* (Grand Rapids: Eerdmans, 1986), 71–72.

18. Commendable and very insightful, on the other hand, are Beasley-Murray, *Jesus and the Kingdom of God*; Dale C. Allison Jr., *Constructing Jesus: Memory, Imagination, and History* (Grand Rapids: Baker Academic, 2010).

19. "There is a surprising commonality . . . even between civilisations that could have never been in touch with one another. In this commonality we can get a good grasp of the profound and never altogether lost contact that human beings had with God's truth." Benedict XVI, *In the Beginning: A Catholic Understanding of Creation and Fall*, trans. Boniface Ramsey, OP, Ressourcement (Grand Rapids: Eerdmans, 1995), 10.

light on the question to what extent the kingdom of God is already among us and to what extent we are still praying for its coming.

The Understanding of Kingship in the Ancient Near East

Everywhere in the ancient Near East (ANE), the understanding of kingship, be it divine or human, was rooted in creation mythology. Divine kingship as such was self-evident. The only questions were, Which god is king? How did he come to be king? And how is his kingship realized on earth?

According to the pervasive mythic view, attested in key texts spanning the Levant from twenty-second-century BCE Sumer to eighth-century BCE Neo-Assyria, creation was the result of a primordial battle between a divinity and the cosmic forces of chaos. Following his victory, the divinity established his kingship and, in so doing, set up order in the cosmos. The god's decisive supremacy over chaos was then symbolized in his enthronement. This entailed the establishment of an earthly throne and dwelling place, that is, a temple.[20] The divinity's taking possession of his earthly abode was celebrated in the dedication of the temple, which was often understood as the realization of a sacred marriage by which the union of the heavenly and earthly realms came about.[21]

The two most famous witnesses to this ANE creation mythology with the most prominent influence on the Bible were, arguably, the Canaanite Baal Cycle and the Babylonian creation epic Enuma Elish.[22] Both reflect a similar pattern and are equally important. In the limited scope of this paper, however, it will suffice to summarize the Enuma Elish, as its *Sitz im Leben* is slightly better attested. It was probably composed in the eighteenth century BCE and read during the liturgy of the New Year festival well into

20. See Moshe Weinfeld, "Sabbath, Temple and the Enthronement of the Lord: The Problem of the Sitz im Leben of Genesis 1:1–2:3," in *Mélanges bibliques et orientaux en l'honneur de M. Henri Cazelles*, ed. André Caquot and Matthias Delcor, AOAT 212 (Kevelaer: Butzon & Bercker, 1981), 501–12.

21. See Jerrold Cooper, "Sacred Marriage and Popular Cult in Early Mesopotamia," in *Papers of the First Colloquium on the Ancient Near East – The City and Its Life Held at the Middle Eastern Culture Center in Japan (Mitaka, Tokyo)*, ed. Eiko Matsushima (Heidelberg: Winter, 1993), 81–96.

22. See Mark S. Smith, *The Ugaritic Baal Cycle: Introduction with Text, Translation & Commentary of KTU I.1–I.2*, VTSup 55 (Leiden: Brill, 1994); the Enuma Elish translation by Benjamin R. Foster in *COS* 1:390–402.

the Seleucid period of the first millennium. It is the myth of the establishment of Marduk's kingship, the creation of his city (Babylon) and his central temple, the Esagila. It recounts the creation of the world as the result of a cosmic battle and the victory of the god Marduk over the monster Tiamat, the symbol of chaos, from whose carcass Marduk created heaven and earth (IV.138–139). As a result of his victory, supreme kingship among the gods was awarded to Marduk, and the gods built his temple, the Esagila, in Babylon as a counterpart to the heavenly temple.[23] In it, Marduk and the gods were to find their rest (VI.54).

The Enuma Elish was *the* foundational myth of Assyrian and later Babylonian kingship. In classical Mesopotamian royal ideology—as also in preexilic Jerusalem—the structure of the earth was understood to imitate that of heaven; thus, the institutions of kingship and the temple below reflected the heavenly kingship and the temple above.[24] This meant that the king was to reflect on earth what Marduk did in heaven: he was responsible for maintaining the cosmic order by fighting the enemy—understood as an earthly, historicized version of the forces of cosmic chaos—and for completing the act of creation by building a palace/temple for his god patterned after the heavenly template. "Establishing the divine legitimacy of his rule was deeply bound up with this service."[25] Thus Enuma Elish VI.112 reads: "He shall make on earth the counterpart of what he brought to pass in heaven." As a result, the Esagila, the Babylonian temple of Marduk, was seen as "the image of heaven and earth,"[26] "the mirror (*maṭṭalātu*) of the *Apsu*, the image (*tamšil*) of *Ešarra*, the counterpart (*mehret*) of Ea's dwelling, 'the image of the Iku constellation.'"[27]

Every year during the autumn or the spring equinox (or both; this varied over the centuries), the Babylonians would celebrate the Akitu festival,

23. See Enuma Elish VI.112, where it states about Marduk's ziggurat temple in Babylon: "He shall make on earth the counterpart of what he brought to pass in heaven."

24. See Benjamin D. Sommer, "The Babylonian Akitu Festival: Rectifying the King or Renewing the Cosmos?," *JANES* 27, no. 1 (2000): 83–84: "Thus, the *narām Marduk* ('Marduk's beloved one') had sat on the throne in Babylon, just as the *bekôr* of YHWH ('YHWH's first-born,' to use Ps 89's term) or the *ṣemaḥ ṣedeq* ('the righteous shoot,' as several Northwest Semitic writers called the ruler) had reigned in Jerusalem and elsewhere."

25. See Nina Sophie Heereman, "'Where Is Wisdom to Be Found?' Rethinking the Song of Songs' Solomonic Setting," *ZAW* 130, no. 3 (2018): 6.

26. *ANET*, 332, line 276.

27. Rylke Borger, *Die Inschriften Asarhaddons,* Königs von Assyrien, Archiv für Orientforschung 9 (Graz: Ernst F. Weidner, 1956), 21.47–48. See also Enuma Elish VI.61–66: "They raised up Esagila, the counterpart to Apsu, They built the high ziggurat of (counterpart-) Apsu, For Anu-Enlil-Ea they founded his . . . and dwelling."

during which the Enuma Elish was recited. The Akitu was "a cosmogonic New Year's festival." That is, "through its rites, the Esagila temple, and hence the world, were symbolically razed, purified, and re-created; kingship, and hence cosmic order, were abolished and renewed. Thus the Akitu festival also effects a return to the time of creation, which culminated in the enthronement of Marduk and the construction by the gods of Marduk's temple in Babylon, the Esagila."[28] Its celebration signified the ritual reenactment of the chief god's original entry into his city and temple.[29]

In most places, the New Year festival included some form of a sacred marriage rite.[30] These celebrations were the ritual enactment of the supreme deity's marriage with his consort upon his entry into the temple (theogamy), a public feast in which the faithful participated with joyful celebration. Other versions of sacred marriage were the ritual enactment of the king's union to a goddess (hierogamy), who would mediate to him the divine knowledge necessary for right governance. In either case, the belief was that "life on earth depended on an ever-renewed union with the realm of the gods, brought about by actual or symbolic *theogamies* or *hierogamies* celebrated in the temple."[31]

In summary, the following elements were constitutive of the pattern: a divinity's victory over forces of evil and the institution of peace/order on earth; the construction of the divinity's palace on earth—that is, a temple—and his enthronement therein, which was often accompanied by the celebration of a sacred marriage symbolizing the union of heaven and earth that came about through the divinity's enthronement.

The Kingdom of God in the Old Testament

Divine Kingship through Victory

The ANE tradition of the god's enthronement after triumphing over his enemies is also reflected in the Bible,[32] namely in the very old Song of the Sea

28. Sommer, "The Babylonian Akitu Festival," 85.

29. See Mark E. Cohen, *The Cultic Calendars of the Ancient Near East* (Bethesda, MD: CDL, 1993), 406.

30. Though the evidence is scant for the later Babylonian period, it is beyond doubt that in earlier periods and in Mesopotamian locations other than Babylon the New Year festival contained sacred marriage rites. See Cohen, *Cultic Calendars*, 439; cf. also 235, 311–12, 324, 337.

31. Heereman, "Wisdom," 422.

32. On this whole section see Weinfeld, "Sabbath," 501–8. See also Francolino J.

in Exodus 15. In it, the Lord is praised for having overcome Pharaoh, who now takes the mythological place of the chaos monster, with the following words:

> I will sing to the Lord, for he is gloriously triumphant. . . .
> Pharaoh's chariots and army he hurled into the sea. . . .
> your right hand, O LORD, shattered the enemy.
> In your great majesty you overthrew your adversaries;
> you loosed your wrath to consume them like stubble.
> (Exod 15:1, 4, 6–7)

Just as Marduk had redeemed the minor gods from the tyranny of Tiamat (or, in the Canaanite version, redeemed Baal from the tyranny of Yam), so God now redeems and thereby "creates" a people for himself, whom he then guides to Mount Sinai, which the song calls God's "holy dwelling" and which corresponds to God's sanctuary: "In your love you led the people you redeemed; in your strength you guided them to your *holy dwelling*" (Exod 15:13, emphasis added). The victory over Pharaoh and the redemption of the people are subsequently—just as in the ANE myth—followed by God's enthronement as king and the construction of his sanctuary, the "throne" of his kingship, as expressed in the poetic climax of the song:

> You brought them in, you planted them
> on the mountain that is your own—
> The place you made the *base of your throne*, LORD,
> *the sanctuary*, LORD, your hands established.
> May the Lord *reign* forever and ever.
> (Exod 15:17–18, emphasis added)

The ancient mythological pattern is easily discernible: victory over God's enemies; redemption of his people; ascent of Mt. Sinai, which is called God's "dwelling," the "base" of God's "throne," "the sanctuary" that God established with his own hands in order to reign for ever and ever. Thus is God's divine kingship established on earth.

Another striking example that connects victory and enthronement, cre-

Gonçalves, "Deux systèmes religieux dans l'Ancien Testament: De la concurrence à la convergence," *Annuaire EPHE, Sciences religieuses* 115 (2007): 117–22.

ation and temple, in a way echoing the Mesopotamian epic, is Psalm 93.[33] In it, the Lord is praised for having overcome the mighty waters, a reminiscence of the mythical chaos monster, whose function in the Bible is assumed by the primordial death-bringing waters (cf. Gen 1:2; 6–9). Here, too, the Lord is praised for having established his kingship (Ps 93:1). The Lord's acclamation as "king" follows the creation of the world. His "throne" is now firmly established (Ps 93:2), and his house, the temple, is praised.[34]

In Psalm 89, we again find the idea of creation as God's victory over the raging sea and swelling waves. We even find mention of the mythical sea dragon Rahab, another personification of the primeval chaos (cf. Ps 89:12–13; Isa 51:9–10; Job 26:12). Most importantly, however, we find here a reflection of the Mesopotamian understanding of kingship, namely, that the earthly king has been chosen by God and is to be God's earthly reflection and lieutenant. Everything that God has previously done himself, David is now empowered to do through the "holy oil" with which God himself has anointed him. In this Psalm, the voice of the Lord declares:

> I have set a leader over the warriors;
>   I have raised up a chosen one from the people.
> I have chosen David, my servant;
>   with my holy oil I have anointed him.
> My hand will be with him;
>   my arm will make him strong.
>
> . . .
>
> *I will set his hand upon the sea,*
>   *his right hand upon the rivers.*
> He shall cry to me, "You are my Father,
>   my God, the Rock of my salvation!"
> I myself make him *the firstborn,*
>   Most High over the kings of the earth.
> Forever I will maintain my mercy for him;
>   my covenant with him stands firm.
> I will establish his dynasty forever,
>   *his throne as the days of the heavens.*
>
> . . .

33. See Weinfeld, "Sabbath," 508.

34. This pattern of the Lord's victory over the mighty waters and the enthronement of the Lord in "his temple" is also found in Psalm 29.

> By my holiness I swore once for all:
> I will never be false to David.
> His dynasty will continue forever,
> his throne, like the sun before me.
> Like the moon it will stand eternal,
> forever firm like the sky!
> (Ps 89:20–22, 26–30, 36–38; emphasis added)

Because God is the king of the universe forever, the dynasty granted to his chosen one must endure forever as well. By divine anointing, the king (hence the term Messiah, "the anointed") is adopted as "Son of God" and empowered with the same divine dominion over the forces of evil. He is to be (in the language of Col 1:15) "the visible reflection of the invisible God" in his way of governing God's people.

Royal Ideology in Israel

The same "royal ideology," or rather "royal theology," also undergirds the Bible's narrative account of Israel's kingship.[35] In order to reflect the actions of God, who created the people of Israel by overthrowing Pharaoh and leading them to his holy mountain, the king is anointed primarily in order to "save" the people from the enemy (1 Sam 9:16) and re-create paradise on earth.[36] This entails fighting the enemy, restoring peace to the country, and promulgating divinely given laws as well as the construction of a temple. That is why David's first act after having been anointed as a child was to go out and slay the head of the enemy's army, Goliath (see 1 Sam 16–17). Later, he gathered a mercenary army around him and delivered all the land from Philistine occupation (1 Sam 21–2 Sam 5).

35. For a more exhaustive treatment of this topic, see Nina Sophie Heereman, *Behold King Solomon on the Day of His Wedding: A Symbolic Diachronic Reading of Song 3,6–11 and 4,12–5,1*, BETL 321 (Leuven: Peeters, 2021), 300–312, 790–808.

36. According to the royal ideology of the ancient Near East, attested to in many royal inscriptions, the king's subjugation of the enemies is followed by domestic achievements that symbolize the re-creation of paradise on earth, "a sort of Eden." See Douglas J. Green, *"I Undertook Great Works": The Ideology of Domestic Achievements in West Semitic Royal Inscriptions*, FAT 2/41 (Tübingen, Mohr Siebeck, 2010). The same royal ideology undergirds the Persian Achaemenid Empire. See Bruce Lincoln, "À la recherche du Paradis Perdu," *HR* 43, no. 2 (2003): 139–54.

When "the LORD had given him rest from his enemies on every side" (2 Sam 7:1), David rightly discerned the propitious moment to construct a temple for the Lord in order to establish God's kingdom in Israel and thereby his own (cf. Deut 12:10).[37] At this point, the Bible introduces a massive deviation from the ANE pattern: God promises an everlasting dynasty to David despite not permitting him to build a temple for the Lord. In the ANE, the promise of an everlasting dynasty was typically given as a reward for temple building.[38] At the same time, however, God promises David a son who will build a house for the Lord's name and whose throne will be established forever (2 Sam 7:11–16). Seen from a historical perspective, this promise was fulfilled in Solomon, who built the Lord a glorious temple and thereby accomplished what any ANE king needed to do in order to achieve an everlasting kingship (1 Kgs 8). The pair of David and Solomon, the warrior king and the king of peace, together mirrored the divine action of re-creating Israel in the image of paradise restored.

What about the sacred marriage motif? According to the Mesopotamian pattern, the temple dedication would have been followed by a sacred marriage of the gods in the temple.[39] In many cases, this would have been ritually enacted on earth, with the king playing a key role in the ritual. Such a ritual was obviously out of the question for ancient Israel, whose rejection of polytheism had also consistently led to the rejection of goddess worship and the fertility rites (like sacred marriage) that went along with it. Nevertheless, the notion of sacred marriage, which was to bring about the union of heaven and earth, was not abandoned altogether. Instead, it was transformed.

While any self-respecting Mesopotamian god had at least one wife—Ea had Damkina, Marduk had Sarpanitu, Nabu had Tashmetu, etc.—the God of Israel did not have an "Asherah," the name of the mother goddess in Canaan, whose worship was a constant temptation for the Israelites, as the biblical lit-

37. See Gerhard von Rad, "Es ist noch eine Ruhe vorhanden dem Volke Gottes," in *Gesammelte Studien zum Alten Testament*, TB 8 (Munich: Kaiser, 1958), 102.

38. See Jacob Klein, "Building and Dedication Hymns in Sumerian Literature," *ASJ* 11 (1989): 27–67; Victor Avigdor Hurowitz, "'Solomon Built the Temple and Completed It': Building the First Temple according to the Book of Kings," in *From the Foundations to the Crenellations: Essays on Temple Building in the Ancient Near East and Hebrew Bible*, ed. Mark J. Boda and Jamie Novotny, AOAT 366 (Münster: Ugarit-Verlag, 2010), 281–302; Heereman, *Behold King Solomon*, 680–88.

39. See Victor Avigdor Hurowitz, *I Have Built You an Exalted House: Temple Building in the Bible in Light of Mesopotamian and Northwest Semitic Writings*, JSOTSup 115 (Sheffield: JSOT Press, 1992), 45, 58, 60.

erature amply attests (cf. 1 Kgs 15:13; 16:33; 18:19; 2 Kgs 13:6; 23:4; Jer 44:17). Instead—and this is unique in the history of religion—God revealed to Israel that *she* was to be his "Asherah"; she was to be his wife. The prophet Hosea was the first to proclaim this truth. God's covenant with Israel was, in fact, a marriage covenant. The Canadian scholar Ehud Ben Zvi synthesizes Hosea's transformation of the ancient goddess worship well:

> The text contains no reference to Asherah, or to any other goddess, but it develops a metaphorical world in which YHWH has a spouse. . . . The text adapts and revises common ancient Near Eastern mythological constructions, with *one most substantial* change: Israel (/land) now stands in the mythological slot of a goddess. The text thus conveys an ideological frame of mind that not only removes the place of the/any goddess as the spouse of the deity of heavens, but also elevates Israel (and, indirectly, its land; see also Hos 9:3; cf. Ps 9:3; cf. Ps 85:2) well above the level of that which may be considered worldly.[40]

At Mount Sinai, God had betrothed Israel to himself: the marriage contract was the Torah, the marriage gift was to be the Promised Land, and the temple was the marriage canopy. There, in the temple, God and Israel were to become forever one. The king was to be the mediator of this marriage in constructing the temple and in representing God to the people (Hos 1–3; Ps 45).[41] The consummation of the marriage thus took place on the day when Solomon dedicated the temple and God came to take possession of it, which was the embodiment of the people of Israel (cf. 1 Kgs 8).

According to the depiction in 1 Kings 5–9, Solomon's reign was the epitome of the kingdom of God in Old Testament terms. All the promises given to the patriarchs seemed to have been fulfilled. The borders of the land corresponded to the promise received by Abraham (cf. Gen 15; 1 Kgs 4:20–5:1). Israel lived in security, "everyone under their own vine and fig tree" (1 Kgs 5:5)—a proverbial indicator of messianic peace (cf. Mic 4:4). Everything was made of gold, "for in Solomon's time silver was reckoned as nothing" (1 Kgs 10:21). The king of Israel governed over the entire known world, and "the whole world sought audience with Solomon, to hear the

40. Ehud Ben Zvi, *Hosea*, FOTL 1/21A (Grand Rapids: Eerdmans, 2005), 75 (italics added).

41. I must drastically oversimplify the concept on account of the limited space of this article. For more, see Heereman, *Behold King Solomon*, 45, 58, 60.

wisdom God had put into his heart" (1 Kgs 10:24). God had once again taken his dwelling with man and was audible through Solomon's mouth. Solomon, indeed, resembled a new Adam with his new Eve, the people of Israel, living in the paradisial garden land in the presence of and in perfect communion with God in the temple.[42] The kingdom of Solomon thus represents the only fleeting moment of the realization of God's kingdom in Israel.

While 1 Kings will also depict Solomon as Adam in a more negative sense—a second "old Adam" who repeats the sin of the first by allowing himself to be seduced by women into the worship of foreign divinities (1 Kings 11) and thereby commits *the* "original sin" of the kings that will eventually cause Israel to lose "paradise" again—the Chronicler leaves no doubt that Solomon's reign was the epitome of God's kingdom on earth. Not only are Solomon's moral stains whitewashed, the Chronicler also insists that Solomon inherited YHWH's own throne: "Then Solomon *sat on the throne of* YHWH as king in place of David his father; and he prospered, and all Israel obeyed him" (1 Chr 29:23; my translation and emphasis). As Isaac Kalimi observes correctly: "Solomon's kingship symbolizes the union of theocracy and monarchy: he is the representative of God on earth, as well as the king of the people and their representative in front of God."[43] It is here that we find for the first time the concept of the "kingdom of YHWH" that was to become so central to both Jewish and Christian thought. In the theology of the Chronicler, "Israel's kingdom and the kingship of YHWH are identical, and, at the same time, Israel's kingdom is established through David's sons. These two facets of kingship in Israel limit each other: the Davidic monarchy is still 'the kingdom of the Lord,' and YHWH's kingship is only realized by means of David's dynasty."[44]

In the kingdom of Solomon as depicted by the Chronicler, we have the perfect prefiguration of Christ's kingdom, the reign of the true Solomon, whose kingship realizes in truth what had been promised regarding Solomon: "He shall be a man of peace [*shalom*]. I [God] will give him peace [*shalom*] from all his enemies on every side; for his name shall be Solomon

42. See Jean-Pierre Sonnet, "Côté cour, côté jardin: Salomon, l'Adam royal," in *Le roi Salomon, un héritage en question: Hommage à Jacques Vermeylen*, ed. Claude Lichert and Dany Nocquet, Le Livre et le Rouleau 33 (Brussels: Lessius, 2008), 247–60.

43. Isaac Kalimi, "The Rise of Solomon in the Ancient Israelite Historiography," in *The Figure of Solomon in Jewish, Christian and Islamic Tradition: King, Sage and Architect*, ed. Joseph Verheyden, TBN 16 (Leiden: Brill, 2013), 40.

44. Sarah Japhet, *The Ideology of the Book of Chronicles and Its Place in Biblical Thought*, BEATAJ 9 (Frankfurt: Lang, 1989), 397.

[*shlomoh*], and I will give peace [*shalom*] and quiet to Israel in his days. He shall build a house for my name. He shall be a son to me, and I will be a father to him, and I will establish his royal throne in Israel forever" (1 Chr 22:9–10; my translation). But here I am getting ahead of myself.

Kingdom Expectations after the Exile

We have to return to the Solomon of old and to the consequences of his fall. As is well known, the peace of the kingdom was soon disturbed on account of the idolatry of its kings and people. By the end of 2 Kings, or else by the year 587 BCE, Israel finds herself once more "east of Eden." King and people are taken to Babylon, the temple is destroyed, and the kingdom is no more.

It is in the aftermath of this catastrophe that the concept of the coming of God's kingdom gained momentum. Looking back upon its past, Israel discerns a pattern that now informs her future hopes and increasingly "eschatologizes" them. The same God who had led them out of Egypt and planted them on his holy mountain will also rescue them from Babylon and bring them back to Zion. Again, it is the ANE combat myth of the dragon slayer that gives expression to their hope in another act of divine redemption understood as an act of re-creation.[45] Thus, Isaiah prays and promises at the height of the Babylonian exile:

> Was it not you who crushed Rahab,
> you who pierced the dragon?
> Was it not you who dried up the sea,
> the waters of the great deep,
> You who made the depths of the sea into a way
> for the redeemed to pass through?
> Those whom the LORD ransomed will return
> and enter Zion singing,
> crowned with everlasting joy. (Isa 51:9–11)

In the same way that the Lord had once crushed Rahab and pierced the dragon—metaphors for the death-bringing waters of the Reed Sea and Pha-

45. So-called Deutero-Isaiah in particular, standing toward the end of the exile, proclaims the "consolation of Israel" in a kingdom that comes through God's new creative activity (see, e.g., Isa 40:1–11; 41:17–20; 43:1–7; 44:24–28; 48:6–13).

raoh[46]—Isaiah promises that God will ransom Israel by crushing Babylon and bringing his people back to Mount Zion, God's "holy mountain" and "the city of the great king" (Ps 48:2–3). Throughout the book of Isaiah, the redeeming savior of Israel is depicted as a divine warrior who will overcome Israel's enemies and thereby restore Israel to God's kingship (see also Isa 59:15–20; 63:1–6). So instead of creation and kingship through *Chaoskampf* as in the ancient myth, we now have re-creation and kingship through salvation understood as a divine victory over the enemy. Noteworthy in this respect is the Greek rendition of Deutero-Isaiah's famous oracle of salvation: "My people shall know *my name* in that day, because *I am* [ἐγὼ εἰμι] the one who speaks: I am here . . . like the feet of one evangelizing/bringing glad tidings [εὐαγγελιζομένου] of a report of peace, like one evangelizing/bringing glad tidings [εὐαγγελιζόμενος] of good things, because I will make your salvation [τὴν σωτηρίαν σου] heard, saying to Sion, 'Your God shall reign' [Βασιλεύσει σου ὁ θεός]"[47] (Isa 52:6–7 LXX; my translation and emphasis). Indeed, the final pronouncement comes across even more powerfully in the Masoretic Hebrew: "Your God is King." We have here the perfect summary of what the gospel announced by Jesus will be: the *euangelion* of salvation will be that *God is King*, implying that Israel has been wrested from the enemy's dominion and transferred into the kingdom of God![48]

While most of the prophetic oracles portray the features of this kingdom entirely in this-worldly terms, a progressive "eschatologization" of Israel's hope in the coming of God's kingdom clearly takes place. The kingdom of God will bring about a restoration of the primordial paradise on Mount Zion, radiating outward into the kingdom of Israel (Isa 11:6–9; 65:25; Ezek 47; Joel 4(3):17–21; Zech 14:6–11). Isaiah 65–66 even speaks of a kingdom that

46. Note the commentary on Isa 51:9–11 in John L. McKenzie, *Second Isaiah*, AB 20 (Garden City, NY: Doubleday, 1968), 123: "An allusion to the cosmological myth in which the creative deity slays the monster of chaos. *Rahab* is a mythological name found only in the OT; see Ps 89:11; Job 9:13, 26:12. The *Dragon* appears in Job 7:12; Isa 27:1; Ezek 29:3; Ps 74:13. Compare the Ugaritic myth of Baal's defeat of Yamm (Sea) and Nahar (River) in ANET, pp. 130–31. . . . The passage of the sea in the Exodus is represented as a reenactment of the cosmological myth of Yahweh's victory over the monster of the sea."

47. Compare also Obad 17–21.

48. It is noteworthy in this respect that in the LXX, the verb εὐαγγελίζω (*euangelizō*)—from which our English "to evangelize" derives—is, with one exception (Jer 20:15), consistently used to designate a victory in battle. God's salvation and his kingship will be the result of his victory over the enemies of his people. As we will see, the Gospel of Mark announces just that.

will involve the creation of a new heaven and a new earth (Isa 65:17–25; 66:22–23).

The Lord's return as king to Zion and the reconstruction of his earthly palace, the temple, will of course effect a covenant renewal (Jer 31–33; Ezek 34; 37; cf. Isa 52:10; 55:3). The latter, as one would expect from the ANE pattern, is again announced under the symbol of a marriage. Famous in this respect are passages from Isaiah such as these: "For your Maker is your husband, the LORD of hosts is his name; the Holy One of Israel is your Redeemer, the God of the whole earth he is called" (Isa 54:5 NRSV); "as the bridegroom rejoices over the bride, so shall your God rejoice over you" (Isa 62:5 NRSV). Less famous is Psalm 45, but this text, too, views the return from exile under the symbol of a marriage between God and Israel in which the Messiah acts as God's lieutenant.[49] This leads us to the last missing element: What role will the King of Israel play in the coming of God's kingdom? Has the catastrophe of the exile, which is mainly blamed on Israel's dysfunctional monarchy, put an end to the promise bestowed upon David? Though this seems to be the case from an earthly perspective, well expressed in Ps 89:40, it is not so for those who see with the eyes of the Spirit, the prophets.

The Role of the Messiah

Along with the promise of a new exodus, the hope in the birth of a new Davidic king who would repeat the saving actions of David and Solomon increasingly informs the prophetic oracles. The famous child-king promised by Isaiah fulfills all the canonical requirements of an ANE king whose actions are to mirror those of his God: he will smash "the yoke that burdened them, the pole on their shoulder," and the "rod of their taskmaster"; he will be a "Prince of Peace," with a dominion "vast and forever peaceful"; he will sit on "David's throne, and over his kingdom" and confirm that kingdom with "judgment and justice" (Isa 9:3, 5–6), the two pillars of God's throne (Ps 89:15). In other words, just as Solomon did in the past, the future son of David will bring about the kingdom of God in the kingdom of Israel. The son of David promised by Micah, Jeremiah, Ezekiel, and Zechariah has es-

49. See Konrad Kremser, *Die Hochzeit des Königs: Exegetisch theologische Untersuchungen zu Psalm 45*, Österreichische Bibel Studien 51 (Berlin: Peter Lang, 2019); Frank-Lothar Hossfeld and Erich Zenger, *Die Psalmen: Psalm 1–50*, NechtB 29 (Würzburg: Echter, 1993), 278–84.

sentially the same traits. He shall be a shepherd by the strength of the Lord (Mic 5:3[4]). He "shall reign and govern wisely. . . . In his days Judah shall be saved, Israel shall dwell in security. This is the name to be given him: 'The Lord our justice'" (Jer 23:6; cf. 33:15–16). "He shall banish the chariot from Ephraim, and the horse from Jerusalem; The warrior's bow will be banished, and he will proclaim peace to the nations. His dominion will be from sea to sea, and from the River to the ends of the earth" (Zech 9:10). Under his reign, the Lord will make an "everlasting covenant" with Israel; he will multiply them and—most importantly—"put [his] sanctuary among them forever. My dwelling shall be with them; I will be their God, and they will be my people. Then the nations shall know that I, the Lord, make Israel holy, by putting my sanctuary among them forever" (Ezek 37:26–28).

While all these hopes were modeled on the re-creation of another Solomonic kingdom, probably in the confines of this world, we observe a clear "eschatologization" in the famous vision of Daniel 7. Once again, we witness the adaptation of the ancient myth to the Bible's revelation. "In Daniel it is combined with the concept of a series of world ages and four empires of world history."[50] The last empire appears to represent Antiochus Epiphanes who—in the words of Beasley-Murray—"is represented as manifesting the characteristics of the chaos monster beyond his predecessors. . . . As the chaos monster was conquered by a champion of heaven [in the myth], so also the tyrant faces an annihilating judgment from the ruler of the universe."[51] The ruler coming with the clouds of heaven (symbolizing a theophany) is

> One like a son of man.
> When he reached the Ancient of Days
>   and was presented before him,
> He received dominion, splendor, and kingship;
>   all nations, peoples, and tongues will serve him.
> His dominion is an everlasting dominion
>   that shall not pass away,
> his kingship, one that shall not be destroyed. (Dan 7:13–14)

The vision differs from the myth in that it does not allude to any battle. However, "since the sovereignty that belonged to the monster is handed over to the cloud-rider, it is natural to deduce that the latter is the one who kills the

50. Beasley-Murray, *Kingdom*, 26.
51. Beasley-Murray, *Kingdom*, 26.

monster and receives the dominion as his reward."[52] With this vision, we are on the threshold of the New Testament.

The Kingdom of God in the New Testament

How, then, do the ANE creation myth and its reworking as a drama of historical redemption in the Old Testament play out in the New Testament's account of the world's re-creation? It is in the person of Jesus Christ that the "job description" of an ANE king is uniquely realized. In him, the eternal Son of the Father becomes incarnate as a descendant of the divinely chosen royal house of David so as to accomplish the true mission of an ANE king. Let us recall the elements of this mission: (1) to deliver the country from the enemy and thereby (2) to restore peace to the kingdom, (3) to establish both his and God's throne on earth by erecting a temple for God, and (4) to consummate the divine-human marriage that brings about the (re-)unification of heaven and earth.

The Slaying of the Dragon

While the Old Testament demythologized the ancient myth and replaced the chaos monster with Israel's historical enemies, the New Testament takes yet a further step and reveals the true name and nature of the "huge dragon, the ancient serpent, who is called the Devil and Satan, who deceived the whole world" (Rev 12:9). The dragon is not coeternal with God but rather only a creature. It, too, had originally been created as a good angel, but in its rebellious desire to be like God rather than to serve God, it had fallen from its rank among the angels and become the one we now know as Satan (cf. Rev 12:7–18). As the entire New Testament makes clear, it is this enemy that the son of David came to fight and overcome in order to deliver us from "the power of darkness" and bring us into his "kingdom" (Col 1:13).

It is true, the kingdom of God and the person of Jesus cannot be separated, because—to borrow an expression from Origen that was very dear to Pope Benedict XVI—Jesus is the *autobasileia*. He himself is the kingdom. In the incarnation, heaven and earth have been united, God has pitched his tent among us (John 1:14), and the kingdom has come into our midst

52. Beasley-Murray, *Kingdom*, 26.

(Luke 7:21).[53] Even the sacred marriage has already been consummated, first in the union of Christ's divine and human natures but also—and importantly so—in the fact that the king of Israel has made his dwelling in Daughter Zion, Mary.

And yet the New Testament depicts the coming of the kingdom as a work in progress. Even though Jesus is one with the Father and the Holy Spirit from the moment of his conception, there is still a moment in his life when he receives *in his humanity* the messianic anointing from the Father that makes him *the Christ, the Messiah.* Jesus's public mission as Messiah-King of Israel begins on the day of his baptism in the Jordan, when the heavens open, the Holy Spirit descends on him, and the Father's voice declares: "This is my beloved Son, with whom I am well pleased" (Matt 3:17)—a clear echo of the ancient enthronement psalm prayed on the day of the king's royal anointing: "You are my son; today I have begotten you" (Ps 2:7). The anointing in the Jordan marks the beginning of Christ's public messianic mission, which he alone of all human beings could fulfill. This is the mission of being truly in essence what the ANE kings were only figuratively by office: *the visible image of the invisible God* (Col 1:15). As such, we now see him do and speak only what he has seen and hears the Father do and say (cf. John 5:19).

The king's first task, as we have seen, is to overcome the chaos monster, the archenemy of humanity. Thus, just as with David, who set out to slay Goliath right after his messianic anointing, Jesus's own anointing is—in all the Synoptic Gospels—immediately followed by his being driven by the Holy Spirit to confront and overcome Satan in the desert. He returns victorious, "proclaiming the gospel of God [εὐαγγέλιον τοῦ θεοῦ]. . . . The kingdom of God is at hand. Repent, and believe in the gospel [εὐαγγέλιον]" (Mark 1:14–15). What is this εὐαγγέλιον? According to the above-mentioned prophecy in Isa 52:7 (cf. 40:9; 61:1) it is the good news that deliverance has come and that God is king. Jesus himself makes this connection in Matt 12:28, where he says, "If it is by the Spirit of God that I drive out demons, then the kingdom of God has come upon you." In the power of the Spirit, he first ties up "the strong man" before he plunders his house through his public ministry (cf. Matt 12:29; Mark 3:27). And so, also like David, he sets out for the outskirts

53. "In ihm, dem Menschen Jesus—der selbst das Reich Gottes ist, weil in ihm 'Gott alles in allem' ist (vgl. 1 Kor 15:28), so dass er wahrhaft Gott und wahrhaft Mensch ist—ist das Ziel bereits anfanghaft verwirklicht, zu dem die Geschichte des Menschengeschlechtes hinstrebt." Joseph Ratzinger, *Zur Lehre des Zweiten Vatikanischen Konzils: Formulierung, Vermittlung, Deutung*, Gesammelte Schriften 7/2 (Freiburg: Herder, 2012), 180.

of his kingdom and delivers it from enemy occupation by "doing good and healing those oppressed by the devil" (Acts 10:38).

The enemy, however, does not relinquish his property easily. Jesus's entire life is one prolonged single combat with the enemy, culminating on the cross, where through his own death he definitively destroyed "the one who has the power of death, that is, the devil" and freed "those who through fear of death had been subject to slavery all their life" (Heb 2:14–15). It is here, on the cross, that the ancient myth has become a bittersweet reality: Christ slays the dragon through the cross and then descends into his territory to break the supremacy of hell. In his resurrection, he destroys the "last enemy," which is death (1 Cor 15:26), ascends triumphant "far above all the heavens, that he might fill all things" (Eph 4:10), and inherits an eternal kingdom.

The cross, of course, is also Christ's throne, as the Gospel of John so powerfully displays. It is both Jesus's throne and the iron rod with which he rules all nations (cf. Ps 2:9; Rev 12:5). This throne has its glorious counterpart in heaven, where he sits at the right hand of the Father and from where he now begins to expand his kingdom, the church, over all the earth.

The Construction of the Temple and the Sacred Marriage

Slaying the primordial enemy, as we have seen, is not an end in itself but an act of re-creation that is to result—according to the mythic and Old Testament pattern—in the establishment of God's reign on earth as it is realized in the king's own realm. The outstanding characteristic of this kingdom will be peace. It is therefore no coincidence that, in John, the very first words of the victorious and risen Lord to the frightened disciples after the resurrection are a twice-repeated "Peace be with you" (John 20:19, 21). The messianic peace is now available to all who acknowledge Jesus as Lord and God.

A reign calls for a palace and, thus, for the construction of a temple. The temple, again, will be the place of the sacred marriage, uniting heaven and earth. "Destroy this temple and in three days I will raise it up," Jesus proclaims in John 2:19. By "this temple," as John explains, he means the temple of his body (John 2:21; cf. 1:14). The juxtaposition of the wedding of Cana and the purification of the temple in John 2:1–22 renders an important key to the paschal mystery: what had been vaguely intuited by the pagan New Year festival, that the re-creation of the world would demand the purification of the temple and lead to a divine-human marriage, becomes a reality. The cross is the hour of Christ, the hour of his wedding to his people in which the new covenant is established, *and* it is the moment of the purification of the temple, the living temple of his body, upon which he had gathered up the sins of the world. It is torn down, that is, purified, and rebuilt; it is undefiled and indestructible in his resurrection. His crucified and yet glorified body is this temple from which flows the source of purification for the entire world, as prophesied in Ezek 47:1–12 and in Zech 14:8: "On that day, fresh water will flow from Jerusalem. . . . The LORD will be king over the whole earth; on that day the LORD will be the only one, and the LORD's name the only one." John sees all this accomplished on the cross.

Luke-Acts has a more narrative approach that fleshes things out a bit more. In Luke, the dedication of the temple, and therefore the sacred marriage between God and his people, quintessentially takes place on the day of Pentecost. On this day, the presence of the Lord descends onto the nascent church in the person of the Holy Spirit and makes her his dwelling among humanity (Acts 2:1–36). The kingdom of God has been established on earth. It subsists in the church, who is at once the body and bride of the Son of God and the temple of the Trinity (cf. 1 Cor 6:19; 12:12–26; 2 Cor 11:2; Eph 5:27–27).

Thy Kingdom Come

Why, then, did Jesus ordain his followers to continue praying for the coming of the Father's kingdom? While the New Testament makes it clear that the kingdom has already come and is present in this world, it also leaves no doubt that it is still coming. It does not yet encompass all of creation. Creation's ongoing groaning is an expression of the famous "already and not yet" (cf. Rom 8:19–23). By virtue of their baptism and confirmation, Christians become "citizens" and "members of the household of God" (Eph 2:19–20), which is another way of saying that they become citizens of the kingdom. Christians are the temple in whom the Holy Spirit dwells (1 Cor 6:19), both individually and corporately. In every Eucharist, the wedding feast of the Lamb is anticipated as a present reality, and *yet* the words of 1 John 5:19 are also true: "We know that we belong to God, and the whole world is under the power of the evil one."

The reality of this "already and not yet" is powerfully expressed in Jesus's parables of the kingdom (Matt 13; Mark 4). There are those to whom knowledge of the "mystery of the kingdom of God" has been granted, and there are those to whom "everything comes in parables" (Mark 4:11). These groups are mixed and cannot be distinguished by the naked eye, as exemplified by the parable of the weeds; only the end of the ages will tell (Matt 13:24–30). The kingdom of God is, indeed, like the yeast, almost invisible and yet leavening the dough of all humanity (Matt 13:33). And the kingdom is like a wedding feast that a king gave for his son. The guests are still being summoned (Matt 22:3).

God, in his mysterious plan of salvation, has decreed that the victory won by his Son on the cross is yet to be applied by his people, both in themselves and in the world. Like Israel of old, the church is implicated in the ongoing battle against the forces of evil, "not with flesh and blood but with the principalities, with the powers, with the rulers of this present darkness, with the evil spirits in the heavens" (Eph 6:12). The book of Revelation says it clearly: "The dragon was angry with the woman, and *went off to make war on the rest of her children*, those who keep the commandments of God and hold the testimony of Jesus" (Rev 12:17 NRSV; emphasis added). In the words of the *Catechism*: "Ever since Pentecost, a decisive battle has been joined between 'the flesh' and the Spirit."[54]

The final victory, however, belongs to our God (cf. Rev 19:1). It is only when Christ returns that the victory will be complete, the Lord will establish his reign, and the New Jerusalem will come down from heaven, prepared as a bride adorned for her husband (Rev 21–22). Only then will the wedding feast of the lamb be celebrated in a temple that will encompass a new heaven and a new earth. Until then, the mystery is anticipated in sacrament. That is why we pray with the Spirit and the Bride, *Maranatha*, come Lord Jesus (Rev 22:17, 20). Or, in the words of our Lord's Prayer: "Thy kingdom come!"

54. *CCC* §2818.

Eucharistic Hermeneutics

The Gospel of Mark

Kelly Anderson

Among the many possible paths of future Catholic biblical scholarship, one path may be to consider that the *Sitz im Leben* of the Scriptures is a liturgical, worshiping community. Such a provenance has already been suggested for the Synoptic Gospels, and this was accomplished by implementing the techniques of the historical-critical movement. According to Joseph A. Fitzmyer, SJ, the historical-critical method "borrows its techniques from both historical and literary criticism. . . . Since the Bible narrates events that affected the lives of ancient Jews and early Christians, its various accounts have to be read, compared, and analyzed in their original languages, against their proper human and historical backgrounds, and within their contemporary contexts."[1] Denis Farkasfalvy, OCist, in his 2010 book *Interpretation and Inspiration: A Theological Introduction to Sacred Scripture*, demonstrates that the "proper human and historical backgrounds" and "contemporary contexts" of the Synoptic Gospels—in Fitzmyer's words—were liturgical, worshiping communities engaged in eucharistic celebrations. "It was therefore in a Eucharistic cradle provided by early Christian worship that the narrative tradition which stands behind the Synoptics was formed and shaped in a live exchange with an audience assembled for hearing about Jesus."[2] Thomas Esposito, following Farkasfalvy, shows how the early form critics of the twentieth century also considered the *Sitz im Leben* of the Synoptics to be a liturgical, worshiping community: "It is one thing to say that the Last Supper influences the liturgical life of the early believers, and

1. Joseph A. Fitzmyer, SJ, *Scripture, the Soul of Theology* (New York: Paulist, 1994), 19.
2. Denis Farkasfalvy, OCist, *Interpretation and Inspiration: A Theological Introduction to Sacred Scripture* (Washington, DC: Catholic University of America Press, 2010), 72; see 67–75.

that the meals portrayed in the Synoptic Gospels reflect this liturgical life; it is another thing entirely to affirm that the Gospel pericopes themselves are born as a result of the liturgical life of the early community. Yet that is precisely the point made by several influential form critics nearly a century ago."[3] Given this, Esposito reads the meal scenes in the Gospels as having been developed in a living, liturgical tradition.[4]

This study will presuppose Farkasfalvy's and Esposito's findings and apply them to the Gospel of Mark while employing a narrative-critical reading of the Gospel. Narrative critics of Mark's Gospel have shown that it is a composite text in which one episode mutually interprets the other. According to Joel F. Williams,

> The experience of reading a narrative (or listening to it, for that matter) involves a combination of memory and anticipation. At any point in the narrative, our understanding of the story is shaped by our memory of what has come before and our anticipation of what is to come. . . . Mark's Gospel normally controls memory and anticipation through foreshadowing and echoes. . . . Mark uses foreshadowing and echoes in order to

3. See Thomas Esposito, *Jesus' Meals with Pharisees and Their Liturgical Roots*, AnBib 209 (Rome: Gregorian and Biblical Press, 2015). Esposito (*Jesus' Meals*, 28–31) points to K. L. Schmidt ("the formation of the early Christian Scriptures must be understood to emerge from the cult"), M. Dibelius ("the *Kultus* in the life of the Church ultimately gives rise to the pericopal form of the Gospel"), and R. Bultmann (who acknowledged "the liturgical role in the formation of the Synoptic material"). The liturgical background in Mark is seen most clearly in the passion narrative, which unfolds in three-hour intervals that appear to span a twenty-four hour framework (Mark 14:17, 72; 15:1, 25, 33, 34, 42). The Last Supper could take place at 6 p.m. ("When it was evening"; 14:17), Jesus and the disciples go to Gethsemane at 9 p.m., where he thrice chastises them for not keeping watch one hour. He is therefore arrested at midnight, and Peter denies Jesus during the Jewish trial at 3 a.m., when the cock crows (14:72). Jesus is brought to Pilate at dawn (πρωΐ; 15:1), and Jesus is crucified at 9 a.m. (15:25). At noon, darkness covers the land until 3 p.m. (15:33), the hour Jesus dies (15:34). See Mark Goodacre, "Scripturalization in Mark's Crucifixion Narrative," in *The Trial and Death of Jesus: Essays on the Passion Narrative in Mark*, ed. Geert Van Oyen and Tom Shepherd, CBET 45 (Peeters: Leuven, 2006), 44. For further studies on the backdrop of the passion narrative being formed in a liturgical milieu, see Gottfried Schille, "Das Leiden des Herrn: Die evangelische Passionstradition und ihr 'Sitz im Leben,'" *ZTK* 52, no. 2 (1955): 161–205; Raymond E. Brown, *The Death of the Messiah: From Gethsemane to the Grave; A Commentary on the Passion Narratives in the Four Gospels*, ABRL (New York: Doubleday, 1994), 1:51. See also Judith H. Newman, *Before the Bible: The Liturgical Body and the Formation of Scriptures in Early Judaism* (Oxford: Oxford University Press, 2018), 1–19.

4. Esposito, *Jesus' Meals*, 31–32.

move the narrative toward his account of the death of Jesus and in order to allow the passion narrative to reflect back on the earlier parts of the story.[5]

Williams's observation has been noted by other narrative-critical scholars.[6] Note in particular Joanna Dewey's analysis: "The Gospel of Mark does not have a single structure made up of discrete sequential units but rather is an interwoven tapestry or fugue made up of multiple overlapping structures and sequences, forecasts of what is to come and echoes of what has already been said."[7] Given this narrative structure, I propose to combine the results of form criticism, which states that the provenance of Mark's Gospel was a liturgical, eucharistic community, with the results of narrative critics, who see the episodes of the Gospel as mutually interpretive.

I will examine Mark 6:34–8:21, where the word ἄρτος (bread) is present sixteen times.[8] The two miracles of the loaves that are found in this section (6:34–44; 8:1–9) are connected to the Last Supper (14:22–24), where the word ἄρτος appears in a strikingly similar phrase to that of the two feeding miracles:

εὐλόγησεν καὶ **κατέκλασεν** τοὺς **ἄρτους** καὶ **ἐδίδου** τοῖς **μαθηταῖς**. (6:41)
He blessed and broke the bread(s) and gave them to his disciples.

λαβὼν τοὺς ἑπτὰ **ἄρτους**, εὐχαριστήσας **ἔκλασεν** καὶ **ἐδίδου** τοῖς **μαθηταῖς** αὐτου. (8:6)
Taking the seven breads, after giving thanks, he broke them and gave them to his disciples.

λαβὼν ἄρτον εὐλογήσας ἔκλασεν καὶ **ἔδωκεν** αὐτοῖς. (14:22)
Taking the bread, after blessing it, he broke it, and gave it to them.

5. Joel F. Williams, "Foreshadowing, Echoes, and the Blasphemy at the Cross (Mark 15:29)," *JBL* 132, no. 4 (2013): 916–18.

6. See Elizabeth Struthers Malbon, "Echoes and Foreshadowings in Mark 4–8: Reading and Rereading," *JBL* 112, no. 2 (1993): 211–30; Dean B. Deppe, *The Theological Intentions of Mark's Literary Devices: Markan Intercalations, Frames, Allusionary Repetitions, Narrative Surprises, and Three Types of Mirroring* (Eugene, OR: Wipf & Stock, 2015); Sun Wook Kim, "An Investigation of a Cyclic Pattern in Mark 4:35–8:21 and Its Theological Significance," *BTB* 47, no. 4 (2017): 205–15.

7. Joanna Dewey, "Mark as Interwoven Tapestry: Forecasts and Echoes for a Listening Audience," *CBQ* 53, no. 2 (1991): 221–36, at 225.

8. **Ἄρτος** is used sixteen times in Mark 6:34–8:21 (6:37, 38, 41 [2x], 44, 52; 7:2, 5, 27; 8:4, 5, 6, 14 [2x], 16, 17, 19). Outside these, ἄρτος is found only in 2:26; 3:20; 14:22.

The two miracle stories are preceded by "hearing" episodes, indicating a liturgical context (6:34; 7:31–37), since "hearing the word/receiving the bread" is the basic liturgical structure. The Last Supper is preceded by the whole of Jesus's ministry, which functions as the "hearing of the word" prior to that final, climactic gift of bread. Thus, the whole Gospel is crafted as a liturgical sequence (hearing the word/receiving the bread).[9] Beyond that, the two miracles of loaves are each followed by a boat scene (the Last Supper narrative's apparent but significant lack of a boat scene will be addressed below). Thus, the paradigmatic structure for the liturgical cycles is the following:

	Hearing the Word	**Receiving the Bread**	**Navigating the Boat**
6:34–56	6:34	6:35–44	6:45–52
7:1–8:21	7:31–37	8:1–9	8:14–20
14:22–24	1:1–14:20	14:22–24	—

Finally, the fact that there are *three* episodes with ἄρτος in nearly the same phrasing is evocative. The number three indicates geographical/spatial completion, particularly regarding sacred space.[10] There are three realms of

9. The Gospel has a lengthy section of Jesus's teachings, miracles, and interactions communicated in episodic fashion (1:1–14:11), followed by the Last Supper, crucifixion, death, and aftermath, which is presented as one continuous episode (14:12–16:20). The first, episodic section corresponds to the "hearing" that precedes any ritual of the breaking of the bread, and this is followed by the gift of Jesus's body/bread, "receiving the bread."

10. "Numbers in the ancient world communicated both measure *and* meaning. They did not merely function as mathematic figures designating quantities or sums, but as signs pointing to other realities, whether historical or metaphysical." Jonathan Morgan, "Number Symbolism in Cyril of Alexandria's Interpretation of Scripture," *Phronema* 34, no. 1 (2019): 88. The number three indicates wholeness or completeness. "There are three major pilgrimage feasts for Israelite males (Exod. 23:14–19); three standard times for Jewish prayers (Dan. 6:10; Ps. 55:17 [MT 18]); three sections to the universe (Phil. 2:10); three sections in the sanctuary (1 Kgs. 6:2–22); and special efficacy of three-year-old sacrifices (Gen. 15:9; 1 Sam. 1:24). Jonah was in the sea creature's belly three days and three nights (Jonah 1:17), and Jesus was in the tomb three days (Matt. 12:40)." Keith A. Burton, "Numbers," *EDB*, 973. See also Mark Verman, "The Power of Threes," *JBQ* 36, no. 3 (2008): 171–81.

God's creation (earth, heaven, highest heaven), three places in the tabernacle/temple (court, holy place, holy of holies), three groups in the priesthood (Levites, priests, high priest), three entities in the desert encampment (tribes, priests, ark). It is difficult to find a depiction of sacred space without the number three. The fact that there are three nearly identical phrases regarding Jesus's actions during the bread ritual, while the final one, the Last Supper, frames the entirety of the Gospel as a liturgical sequence, means the Gospel itself is presented as sacred space; it is crafted as a *liturgical icon*. Each episode penetrates deeper into the divine, and so the final ἄρτος episode, the Last Supper, corresponds to the realm of God. Thus, the Gospel not only reflects or is born in a liturgical setting; it explicates it, penetrates it, presents it, and ultimately draws the audience into it.

To summarize, I will analyze the ἄρτος sections as two liturgical cycles, each of which finishes with a boat scene. Then I will examine the Last Supper. I will assume that the episodes are formed in and for a worshiping community in a eucharistic, liturgical setting and that the Gospel is a composite wherein the episodes mutually interpret one another.

Three Liturgical Cycles

First Liturgical Cycle: Mark 6:34–56

Mark 6:34–56 is composed of two major pericopes: the multiplication of the bread (vv. 34–44) preceded by Jesus's teaching and the boat scene and its aftermath (vv. 45–56). The word ἄρτος occurs five times, four in the miracle of the bread (vv. 37, 38, 41, 44) and once at the end of the boat scene (v. 52), thus connecting the episode at sea with the miracle of the bread.

Mark 6:34–44 recounts the first miracle of the loaves. Jesus sees the hapless crowd, feels compassion (σπλαγχνίζομαι), and teaches them.[11] As it becomes late, the disciples advise Jesus to dismiss the crowd so they can get something to eat. But Jesus commands them to give the crowd something to eat, and they protest that they do not have money to buy enough food (ἄρτους) to feed the crowd (6:37). Jesus then commands them to go and gather

11. The verb σπλαγχνίζομαι describes pity that moves one to act in a beneficial and self-sacrificing way toward the other. This type of pity, which linguistically suggests a movement of the viscera (from the root σπλαγχ- meaning "innards"), can best be described as something close to "gut-wrenching" pity.

what loaves (ἄρτους) they have (6:38). They produce five loaves, often seen as being symbolic of the Torah, and two fish, thus making seven, a number that represents the eschatological gathering of humanity.[12] Jesus orders the people to be seated in groups of hundreds and fifties to be fed upon the green grass, recalling the camp of the Israelites in the wilderness (6:39; cf. Exod 18:21, 25).[13] He takes the five loaves, looks up to heaven, blesses and breaks them, and gives them to his disciples, who distribute them.[14] The disciples are rendered capable of obeying his first command (6:37) by obeying his second command (6:38), and they give the people the broken and blessed bread (6:41). After the crowd eats, they are "satisfied" (ἐχορτάσθησαν; 6:42)—an allusion to Ps 145:16, which depicts God as satisfying his people. Finally, the fragments (κλάσματα) are gathered in twelve baskets, a number corresponding to the twelve tribes, a reminder that Jesus is gathering around himself a new Israel (cf. 3:13–19).[15]

Mark 6:45–52 recounts a miracle at sea (cf. 4:35–41).[16] Jesus compels (ἠνάγκασεν) his disciples to get into the boat, a symbol of the church, and go before him to Bethsaida, and then Jesus goes to the mountain and prays.[17] Jesus is testing his disciples to see if they can navigate the boat in the wind without him.[18] Whereas in Matthew, the *boat* is buffeted (Matt 14:24), in Mark the *disciples* are in distress.[19] The verb βασανιζομένους, depicting them as "straining" in their rowing, illustrates their torment. Mark uses this verb one other time, to describe how the demons perceive Jesus's action of driv-

12. See Charles A. Bobertz, *The Gospel of Mark: A Liturgical Reading* (Grand Rapids: Baker Academic, 2016), 67.

13. Given that there are no natural grassy plains in Palestine, Mark 6:39 is likely a reference to Ps 23:2, depicting Jesus as the good shepherd who prepares a banquet.

14. The verb "gave" is imperfect (ἐδίδου), while the verbs "blessed" (εὐλόγησεν) and "broke" (κατέκλασεν) are aorist. The imperfect tense signifies that Jesus's action of giving bread is a continuous one.

15. Κλάσμα (fragment) is the word used in the Didache explicitly for the eucharistic species (Did. 9.3–4; cf. also 9.1 and 9.5).

16. For similarities between the two episodes, see Joel Marcus, *Mark: A New Translation with Introduction and Commentary*, AB 27–27A (New Haven: Yale University Press, 2000–2009), 2:428.

17. For the boat as a symbol of the church, cf. Eph 4:14. See Tim Woodroof, "The Church as Boat in Mark: Building a Seaworthy Church," *ResQ* 39, no. 4 (1997): 231–49.

18. Origen says, "The Savior then compels the disciples to enter into the boat of temptations and to go before Him to the other side" (Origen, *Commentary on Matthew* 11.5; in *ANF* 9.435; noted in Deppe, *Theological Intentions*, 316).

19. John Paul Heil, *Jesus Walking on the Sea: Meaning and Gospel Functions of Matt 14:22–33, Mark 6:45–52 and John 6:15b–21*, AnBib 87 (Rome: Biblical Institute Press, 1981), 68.

ing them out (5:7). The book of Revelation employs the verb to describe cataclysmic destruction (Rev 9:5; 11:10; 14:10; 20:10), and in the second century, the word was deployed to describe martyrdom.[20] All this means that the disciples are passing through the trial of their lives.

Jesus comes to them in the "fourth watch" of the night, indicating that the struggle has been going on for some time. Jesus walks on the waves of the sea wanting to "pass by" them (παρελθεῖν). In the Old Testament, God "passes by" (παρέρχομαι) before Moses (Exod 34:6; cf. Exod 33:19, 22) and Elijah (1 Kgs 19:11), and thus the appearance of Jesus can be likened to an epiphany of God.[21] Given this, Jesus wants to pass them by to give them strength and courage to succeed in their mission.[22] But he is thwarted by their lack of recognition and fear, and immediately he reveals himself using the name of God (ἐγώ εἰμι; Mark 6:50), he gets into the boat, and the winds cease.[23] The trial is over, and the disciples fail in their mission to bring the boat to shore, specifically because they do not recognize Jesus when he comes. The narrator solemnly explains why they failed: they did not understand about the loaves (ἐπὶ τοῖς ἄρτοις), and their hearts were hardened (6:52), an expression in the New Testament indicating those who cannot or will not perceive the truth (see 3:5).[24]

Why is the failure linked to the bread? Only in the prior episode are the disciples directly involved in any miracle. They were given the impossible command to feed the people, but then their subsequent obedience to Jesus

20. Deppe, *Theological Intentions*, 316.

21. Heil, *Jesus Walking on the Sea*, 69–72. In Job 9:8, God "walks upon the sea as on ground" (περιπατῶν ὡς ἐπ' ἐδάφους ἐπὶ θαλάσσης), and in Job 9:11, "he passes by me" (παρέλθῃ με).

22. Suzanne Watts Henderson notes, "In the case of both Moses and Elijah, God orchestrates a 'passing by' precisely at the point of the character's deepest desperation: Moses has just weathered the golden calf episode, and Elijah has reached a point of despondency when he cries, 'I alone am left, and they are seeking my life, to take it away.'" "'Concerning the Loaves': Comprehending Incomprehension in Mark 6:45–52," *JSNT* 24, no. 83 (2001): 4, 20–21. Harry Fleddermann concludes that the phrase "pass by" means "to rescue from disaster" and "to save." "'And He Wanted to Pass by Them' (Mark 6:48c)," *CBQ* 45, no. 3 (1983): 391.

23. While it is possible that the phrase can mean "Here I am" or "It is I," the divine epiphany context leads to the conclusion that Jesus is using the divine name to reveal himself. For the use of the absolute ἐγώ εἰμι, see Joel Marcus, *Mark*, 1:427. For absolutes of ἐγώ εἰμι, compare LXX Deut 32:39; Isa 41:4; 43:10, 25; 45:18; 46:4; 51:12.

24. The phrase is used most with reference to Israel's failure to recognize Jesus as their Messiah (Rom 11:7, 25; 2 Cor 3:14; John 12:40). See R. T. France, *The Gospel of Mark: A Commentary on the Greek Text*, NIGTC (Grand Rapids: Eerdmans, 2002), 150–51.

enabled them to obey that command. Similarly, the disciples are now compelled to get in the boat and row to Bethsaida, an equally impossible command because of the winds. Given the prior sequence, the disciples should have expected Jesus to render them capable of fulfilling that command. And, in fact, that is what Jesus was doing, but the disciples fail to recognize him because they do not understand the bread.

Presumably, if the disciples had understood about the bread, that is, the authority the presence of Jesus gives them to overcome their human limitations (cf. 3:15), they would have recognized Jesus's presence and divinity and could have successfully navigated the waters. The word "understand" (συνίημι; 6:52) has been used thus far in Mark only in 4:12 to describe those who see and hear superficially. The disciples have not done the hard work of listening and pondering who Jesus is (4:3, 9, 23); thus they do not understand the bread or recognize him, and they cannot successfully navigate the boat.

In this first liturgical sequence, Jesus is depicted as the shepherd who teaches and feeds his people as God did in the Old Testament. Recognizing Jesus and understanding the bread are interwoven realities that are necessary for navigating the boat and bringing it to shore.

Second Liturgical Cycle: Mark 7:1–8:21

1. Mark 7:1–8:10. There are four pericopes in Mark 7:1–8:10. A controversy about eating bread (ἄρτος) with unwashed hands (7:1–23) is followed by three stories involving unclean people in an unclean land (7:24–8:9): the Syrophoenician woman (7:25–30), the healing of the man who was deaf and mute (7:31–37), and the feeding of the four thousand (8:1–10). Each of these is marked with the word ἄρτος (7:2, 5, 27; 8:4, 5, 6) except the episode of the deaf man, but Mark connects this passage to the feeding of the four thousand by the phrase ἀναβλέψας εἰς τὸν οὐρανόν (6:41; 7:34), the only two times anyone in the Gospel "looks up" to heaven.

In 7:1–23, the Pharisees question why the disciples eat ἄρτος with unclean hands, against the tradition of the elders. This elicits a strong rebuke from Jesus, who accuses them of being more concerned with their traditions than the commands of God (7:7–13) and teaches that nothing that enters a person can defile (7:14–15). But Jesus also rebukes the disciples for being without understanding in this matter (ἀσύνετοί ἐστε; 7:18), and then he "cleanses all the food" (καθαρίζων πάντα τὰ βρώματα; 7:19),[25] indicating that the gentiles

25. The participle καθαρίζων can mean either "make clean" or "declare clean." "'Make

are not defiled by what they eat and allowing them to partake of the gift of the ἄρτος, which is given them in 8:1–9.[26]

In Mark 7:24–30, Jesus enters the pagan region of Tyre, where he wants to remain unknown to further instruct his disciples on the significance of the bread. Despite this, a Syrophoenician woman finds Jesus and begs him to cast a demon from her daughter. Jesus's reply that the children be "filled" (χορτασθῆναι) first recalls the feeding miracle, the only other place this verb has been used (ἐχορτάσθησαν; 6:42). Jesus continues his act of feeding/ instructing his disciples/children, who have not yet understood about the loaves (ἄρτον τῶν τέκνων; 7:27; cf. 6:52; 7:18); until they do, Jesus does not intend to engage in further public ministry.[27]

But the woman, while agreeing with Jesus that the children be filled first, changes the dog metaphor from a scavenger to a house pet who receives food from the table, inviting Jesus to consider the gentiles as invited guests who partake in the crumbs of the children (ἀπὸ τῶν ψιχίων τῶν παιδίων).[28] By reconfiguring the bread as crumbs, she suggests that she is asking for little from Jesus; it is entirely within his power to give her and would not deprive the children of what is rightfully theirs. In other words, Jesus can continue to instruct his disciples *and* grant her request.

Because of her *word*, Jesus acquiesces (7:29), unlike in Matthew, where Jesus marvels because of her *faith* (Matt 15:28). The woman has demonstrated that, unlike the disciples, she has understood the abundance of the ἄρτος and Jesus's capacity to give it. She is thus granted a favor Jesus was reluctant to give, effectively changing his ministry from one in which the

---

clean' is a causative, 'to cause to be clean,' not in the sense of manufacturing or cleansing, but in the meaning 'declaring clean' or 'establishing as clean.'" The masculine participle modifies Jesus (λέγει; 7:18), and it is a participle of manner; thus, Jesus cleanses the food by means of his word (Robert G. Bratcher and Eugene A. Nida, *A Handbook on the Gospel of Mark*, UBS Handbook Series [New York: United Bible Societies, 1961], 232). Jesus has already demonstrated that his words are performative and effective (cf. Mark 2:5–12).

26. Scholars debate whether Jesus abrogated the Torah's dietary laws in Mark 7:19. Throughout the Gospel, Jesus cleanses defilement: He touches the leper (1:41), the hemorrhaging woman touches his clothes and is healed (5:28–29), and he raises a girl from the dead (5:41), yet he remains undefiled because purity and healing power annihilate and overcome the defilement. Mark presents food situations analogously: *His word renders all food clean*, thus rendering the dietary laws unnecessary. See Acts 10:15, which states that God has cleansed the food, implying that there was a time when it was not clean.

27. John Paul Heil, *The Gospel of Mark as Model for Action: A Reader-Response Commentary* (Eugene, OR: Wipf & Stock, 2001), 161.

28. John R. Donahue, SJ, and Daniel J. Harrington, SJ, *The Gospel of Mark*, SP 2 (Collegeville, MN: Liturgical Press, 2002), 234.

"dogs" would have to wait for bread until the children were filled to one where the "dogs" will now be given "crumbs." And in fact, her word and understanding set off two pericopes in gentile territory, culminating in a situation wherein the gentiles receive bread (8:1–9).

In Mark 7:31–37, Jesus enters the Decapolis. The people bring to him a deaf man with a speech impediment and beg Jesus to lay hands on him. Jesus places his fingers into the man's ears and uses his spittle to touch the man and so "to make his tongue alive with his own life."[29] Jesus then looks up to heaven, groans, and commands that the man's ears be opened. The man immediately hears properly, the chains of his tongue are loosened, and he speaks correctly. The capacity to hear the voice of God (Deut 6:4) and to proclaim his glory among the nations (Deut 32:3; Ps 145:6) are the defining acts that constitute the identity and mission of the people of God.[30] The deaf and mute man is symbolically representative of all gentiles who have never heard the word of God, and thus have been deprived of its life-giving force and vitality, but who now are rendered capable of hearing God's word and proclaiming his glory.[31] Though Jesus puts his fingers in the man's ears (τὰ ὦτα; 7:33), Mark does not say that the man's ears are opened but rather that the *man's capacity for hearing* (αἱ ἀκοαί; 7:35) is opened, thus enabling the man to give testimony (7:37).[32] The crowd responds by exclaiming that Jesus does all things well, recalling Gen 1:31.

Mark weaves into the text several commonalities to the raising of the dead girl (5:37–43). These are the only miracles up to this point deliberately done in private, and only in these two episodes has Mark employed the verb διαστέλλομαι (5:43; 7:36 [2x]). Only Jairus and the people who bring the deaf and mute man beg Jesus to lay his hand(s) upon the person needing the miracle (ἐπιθῇς τὰς χεῖρας αὐτῇ; 5:23; ἐπιθῇ αὐτῷ τὴν χεῖρα; 7:32).

29. William L. Lane, *Commentary on the Gospel of Mark*, NICNT (Grand Rapids: Eerdmans, 1975), 267.

30. Juan Alberto Casas Ramírez, "*Effatha*: Aproximación exegética al relato de curación del tartamudo sordo en Mc 7,31–37," *Fran* 58, no. 166 (2016): 149–50.

31. It is generally agreed that the healing is symbolic. Compare Karl Kertelge, *Die Wunder Jesu im Markusevangelium: Ein redaktionsgeschichtliche Untersuchung* (Munich: Kösel, 1970), 160; Heil, *Gospel of Mark*, 165; France, *Gospel of Mark*, 301; Mary Healy, *The Gospel of Mark*, Catholic Commentary on Sacred Scripture (Grand Rapids: Baker Academic, 2008), 148.

32. Reinhard von Bendemann, "Auditus et Testamentum: Die Heilung des Tauben/Stummen in der Dekapolis (Mk 7,31–37)," in *Systematisch Praktisch: Festschrift für Reiner Preul zum 65. Geburtstag*, ed. Wilfried Härle et al., ThSt 80 (Marburg: N. G. Elwert, 2005), 67.

Only in these two episodes has Mark deployed a non-Greek phrase in the healing followed by a translation—"*Talitha koum*, which means 'little girl,' I say to you, get up" (5:41); "*Ephphatha*, which means 'be opened'" (7:34).[33] Finally, after healing her, Jesus commands that she be given something to eat (5:43), and after the healing of the deaf man, the crowds partake in the bread (8:1–9). Mark is showing how Jesus's action vis-à-vis the deaf man symbolically makes him a new creation, a symbolic return to life, specifically by spitting, that is, with his own physical being.[34] The reference to Gen 1:31 also points to the act of creation, precisely that of humankind on the sixth day (Gen 1:26–27).[35]

But while the narrative looks back to the dead girl, it also looks ahead to the sacrifice of Jesus on the cross, where he will speak again using non-Greek, translated words—"'*Eloi, Eloi, lema sabachthani*?' which means 'My God, my God, why have you forsaken me?'" (15:34; cf. 5:41; 7:34)—and give his body for salvation. And this is the same body whose spittle and hands healed the man, that is given to the disciples as bread (14:22), and that is crucified for the ransom of many (10:45). By pointing to the cross, where Jesus will bring life by giving his own life, the narrative mysteriously suggests how the deaf-mute returns to life.

When the healing of the deaf-mute is read considering these two other passages and as part of a liturgical sequence, it can be reasonably concluded that Jesus's "groan" (ἐστέναξεν) when healing reflects the pain of his sacrificial death memorialized in the liturgy (7:34). The term "groan" indicates a vocal expression of inner grief or suffering.[36] Only this miracle elicits a

33. Ἐφφαθά probably represents the Aramaic imperative of פתח and could be translated "Open up!" (Donahue and Harrington, *Gospel of Mark*, 240). Some scholars have argued that the term is Hebrew, and according to France the problem appears intractable (*Gospel of Mark*, 304).

34. Elisa Estévez López notes that a deaf man has never heard God's creating word (*palabra creadora*); thus, the man is condemned to remain on the sidelines of God's creative activity ("'Y todos los que lo tocaban quedaban sanados': El cuerpo como espacio de gracia," *Sal Terrae* 100 [1997]: 329).

35. Daniel Frayer-Griggs points to three texts from Qumran that state that God created the world with spittle and clay, buttressing the idea that Mark intended the healing to be seen as a new creation: 4Q264, 8–10, 1QH^{a} XX, 24–27, 31–32, 4Q511 28–29, 3–4. See Daniel Frayer-Griggs, "Spittle, Clay, and Creation in John 9:6 and Some Dead Sea Scrolls," *JBL* 132, no. 3 (2013): 659–70.

36. The term στενάζω is a vocal expression of inner grief in situations of oppression (Isa 21:2; 1 Macc 1:26), dying and destruction (Job 24:12; Isa 24:7; Nah 3:7), torture (2 Macc 9:21), hunger (Isa 19:8), unrealized desires (Sir 30:20), and shame and

cry of pain from Jesus, and it expresses the sacrificial, ransoming aspect of this healing, which can be seen in tandem with his suffering on the cross, wherein he becomes a ransom for many (10:45).[37] Jesus takes the suffering and "death" of the deaf and mute man into himself and, through his spittle, gives the man new life born from his own life. "Jesus, as the representative of the sick person and for his sake, presents that person's suffering to God with extraordinary personal empathy," for Jesus's own life and vitality bring this potency to another.[38]

Mark 8:1–10 recounts a second feeding miracle in the desert with many similarities to the feeding miracle of 6:32–44, indicating that the two should be read as mutually interpretive.[39] The second miracle illustrates how the gentiles are now recipients of the bread (cf. 7:24–30) while continuing to underscore the incomprehension of the disciples.

Jesus shares in his inner life by disclosing his compassion for the crowd to his disciples. Previously, Jesus felt compassion for the leper and immediately healed him (1:41), and when he saw the hapless crowd, he likewise took immediate action and taught them (6:34). In this case, Jesus discloses his compassion, but instead of taking immediate action, he invites the disciples to ame-

---

death (Lam 1:8, 21; Ezek 21:11). Στενάζω translates שׁמם (Job 18:20; Ezek 26:16), שׁוע (Job 24:12), עגם (Job 30:25), זעק (Job 31:38), נוד (Nah 3:7), אבל (Isa 19:8), אנח (Isa 24:7; Lam 1:8, 21; Ezek 21:11), אנק (Ezek 26:15), and other terms. In the New Testament, the term is an oral elicitation or manifestation of one's inner life due to an oppressed state, specifically that of sin (Rom 8:23; 2 Cor 5:2, 4). "Sighing takes place by reason of a condition of oppression under which man suffers and from which he longs to be free because it is not in accord with his nature, expectations, or hopes." John Schneider, "στενάζω, κτλ," *TDNT* 7:601.

37. Scholars show wide disagreement concerning the intentionality of the emotion. Some postulate that Jesus groans out of compassion for the suffering man (Vincent Taylor, *The Gospel according to Saint Mark* [New York: St. Martin's, 1963], 355; Lane, *Gospel of Mark*, 267). Stephen Voorwinde agrees that the groan expresses Jesus's empathy for the man's plight but says it also expresses his hope for the new age that is still to come, foreshadowed by the miracle he is about to perform (*Jesus' Emotions in the Gospels* [London: T&T Clark, 2011], 100). Some say the groan expresses the difficulty of effecting the miracle (Robert H. Gundry, *Mark: A Commentary on His Apology for the Cross* [Grand Rapids: Eerdmans, 1993], 389; Heil, *Gospel of Mark*, 164), while others say it is an expression of prayer (Donahue and Harrington, *Gospel of Mark*, 242; Robert H. Stein, *Mark*, BECNT [Grand Rapids: Baker Academic, 2008], 360).

38. H. Balz, "στενάζω," *EDNT* 3:272.

39. See Marcus for a detailed list of similarities between the two accounts (*Mark*, 2:494–95).

liorate the suffering. Jesus is testing them to see if they, too, will be moved by compassion to act and if they will trust in Jesus's ability to feed the crowd.

The numbers recounted are symbolic of a gentile setting. Instead of the five (books of the law) and twelve (tribes of Israel), here the use of the numbers four (corners of the earth) and seven (completeness) point to a worldwide dimension of Jesus's mission.[40] Σπυρίς (8:8) is a general term for basket, in contrast to the more specific Jewish term κόφινος (6:43).[41] Also, there are no judicial groupings that reflect Exod 18:25, no grassy plains that recall Ps 23:2, nor has Jesus just acted as the shepherd by teaching his flock and fulfilling the prophecies of Ezek 34:23 and Zech 13:7. But the locale of the desert remains (ἐρημία; 8:4), and it becomes the basis of the disciples' unwillingness to try to feed the people.

The disciples consider the task of feeding herculean specifically because of the locale: *where* can anyone satisfy them with bread *here, in a desert* (πόθεν . . . ὧδε . . . ἐπ' ἐρημίας; 8:4)? Their question also indicates that nobody, not even Jesus, who had already fed the multitude (δυνήσεταί τις . . . χορτάσαι), could satisfy them in this place of desolation and abandonment. Mark has exclusively used ἔρημος to indicate the locale of the wilderness, but here he uses the much less common word ἐρημία, a hapax in the Gospel. In the LXX, ἔρημος translates נֶגֶב, מִדְבָּר, חָרְבָּה, and יְשִׁימוֹן ("Negev," "wilderness," "ruin," and "wasteland," respectively), while ἐρημία only translates Hebrew words meaning desolation or waste (חָרְבָּה, חֹרֶב, and שְׁמָמָה). They are not just in a deserted place but, metaphorically, a place of destruction or abandonment, reflecting a gentile context.[42] But Jesus's miracle indicates that they do have enough bread; in fact, they have a complete amount (seven loaves). Jesus can provide for all with the bread supplied by the disciples, even in the darkest places.

2. Mark 8:11–21. There are two pericopes in 8:11–8:21: the confrontation with the Pharisees (8:11–13) and the discussion between Jesus and the disciples in the boat (8:14–21). The word ἄρτος appears five times in the last pericope (8:14 [2x], 16, 17, 19), connecting it back to the prior ἄρτος episodes.

As Jesus reenters Jewish territory, the hostile Pharisees demand a sign from heaven, that is, a sign from God to confirm that God stands behind

40. France, *Gospel of Mark*, 306. For further symbolic meanings of the numbers, see Gundry, *Mark*, 396–97.

41. France, *Gospel of Mark*, 309.

42. "Ἐρημία denotes an uninhabited (Mark 8:4 par. Matt 15:33), therefore dangerous (2 Cor 11:26), inhospitable, and hostile (Heb 11:38) land." W. Radl, "ἔρημος," *EDNT* 2:51.

Jesus's words and deeds.[43] The Pharisees remain unconvinced that Jesus is impelled by divine power, and thus they expect no forthcoming sign. The lack of a sign would demonstrate that Jesus's potency does not derive from God. Jesus interprets the Pharisees' request as a wicked and evil one that should and will never be fulfilled.[44]

Mark 8:14–21 recounts the final episode with Jesus and his disciples in a boat. Mark reveals that the disciples forgot to bring bread (literally "breads"; ἄρτους) and have only one bread in the boat (ἄρτος; 8:14). Jesus then warns his disciples of the leaven of the Pharisees and Herod. Leaven/yeast is essential to fermentation and baking, but it can also make the bread stale or moldy, rendering it a symbol of corruption (Exod 12:15, 19; 13:3, 7).[45] Jesus warns his disciples about the Pharisees' refusal to ascribe to him divine ability and their conclusion that he is colluding with evil powers, while Herod's "leaven" is the murder of John the Baptist, an act that prefigures the death of Jesus and his disciples.

The disciples discuss this and conclude that they have no bread (ἄρτους οὐκ ἔχουσιν; 8:16). But actually, they have one bread (8:14), which they seem not to know about or have forgotten. Their discussion elicits a strong rebuke from Jesus, specifically because they think they have no bread (ἄρτους οὐκ ἔχετε; 8:17). Jesus excoriates them for not hearing, seeing, or remembering (8:17–18), verbs that ominously evoke Mark 4:12. But instead of showing them the one bread, he reminds them of the overwhelming abundance of the bread he gave when he fed the crowds, *thus identifying himself as the one bread they do indeed have*.[46] The disciples think they are without bread because they have not recognized the one "bread," that is, Jesus. Instead, they have more than they could possibly fathom: they have Jesus, who can feed thousands and have plenty left over. As the disciples were hard-hearted after the first miracle of the loaves (6:52), so do they remain (8:17). Once again,

43. Stein, *Mark*, 375; Jeffrey B. Gibson, "Jesus' Refusal to Produce a Sign (Mk. 8:11–13)," *JSNT* 12, no. 38 (1990): 37; cf. also K. H. Rengstorf, "σημεῖον, κτλ," *TDNT* 7:234–36; Olaf Linton, "The Demand for a Sign from Heaven (Mark 8.11–12 and par.)," *ST* 19, nos. 1–2 (1965): 112–29.

44. Jesus makes a solemn oath, appearing to use an elliptical form of a Hebrew oath formula that would roughly mean "If a sign is given, may I die" or "May God's judgment fall upon me if a sign is given."

45. Donahue and Harrington, *Gospel of Mark*, 252.

46. Healy, *Gospel of Mark*, 15. See also Heil, *Gospel of Mark*, 171; Deppe, *Theological Intentions*, 68.

understanding the presence of Jesus is interwoven with recognizing and understanding the bread.

In this liturgical sequence, the paradigmatic structure of hearing the word/receiving the bread is present but in a much more complex fashion. The basic idea is that the gentiles are not defiled by what they eat. Then, because the Syrophoenician woman understands the powerful capacities of Jesus to give superabundant bread, Jesus changes his mission. He first enables the deaf man to hear, a symbol of all the gentiles, and then gives bread in a wasteland where life seems impossible. The Pharisees remain hostile entities whose corrupting influence can distort the identity of Jesus. The disciples do not seem to know of the one bread in the boat (8:14), which Jesus identifies as himself, who is capable of feeding thousands with plenty remaining (8:19–20). Finally, the liturgical actions, that is, the gift of hearing and the bread, spring from the empathy and compassion of Jesus, which he allows his disciples to see and experience.

The term bread (ἄρτος) has appeared sixteen times in 6:34–8:21 and has been a major theme. It will be used only once more, in the Last Supper narrative (14:22).

Third Liturgical Cycle: Mark 14:22–24

In the Last Supper, the word ἄρτος appears for the final time, when Jesus identifies his body, which will soon be given on the cross, with the bread (14:22).[47] As Jesus celebrates the Passover, he diverges from the usual rites and gives the traditional elements of the Passover liturgy a new meaning.[48] Jesus takes the bread (ἄρτος), identifies it as his body, the same body that had recently been anointed for burial (14:8), and then gives this body to his

47. "In the Torah, the meaning of the unleavened bread is always explained with reference to the redemption of Israel from slavery, the haste with which they departed, and/or the suffering they endured in the exodus." Brant Pitre, *Jesus and the Last Supper* (Grand Rapids: Eerdmans, 2015), 407. For the argument that Jesus is also identifying his body as the unleavened bread *and* the Passover lamb, see Pitre, *Jesus and the Last Supper*, 405–11.

48. Timothy Gray, *The Temple in the Gospel of Mark: A Study in Its Narrative Role*, WUNT 2/242 (Tübingen: Mohr Siebeck, 2008), 159. Gustavo Martín-Asensio points out that the words τοῦτό ἐστιν τὸ σῶμά μου (v. 22) and τοῦτό ἐστιν τὸ αἷμά μου (v. 24) are performative and effective (cf. 2:5; 7:19). Just as Moses's words in Exod 24:8 establish or ratify that covenant, so do Jesus's words now renew it. See Gustavo Martín-Asensio, "Dicho y hecho: Las palabras de institución como acto de habla en Marcos 14," *EstBib* 73, no. 1 (2015): 40.

disciples, who take it. Jesus likewise identifies the contents of the cup as his blood, which is to be poured out for many (ὑπὲρ πολλῶν; v. 24). Jesus already said his death was a ransom (λύτρον; 10:45), and therefore his death is more than martyrdom; it is a sacrifice. Jesus thus reconfigures the Passover meal, showing that the ransom will no longer come from animal sacrifices in the temple but rather from his sacrificial death.[49]

Jesus interprets his sacrificial, ransoming death as being for the benefit of others, specifically in that it will be for the atonement of sins. Just as the priest poured out (ἐκχέω) the blood of the sacrificed animals on the altar to atone for the sins of the people (Lev 4:7, 18, 25, 30, 34), so Jesus offers his own blood to be poured out (ἐκχυννόμενον; 14:24) at his death for the atonement of sins.[50] Finally, the acts of taking the bread/body and drinking from the cup of wine/blood bring the disciples into union with Jesus and draw them into his future atoning death and resurrection.

When all three pericopes are examined together as mutually interpreting one another, it becomes clear that *Jesus is the miraculous bread that is to be given in the future, reconfigured Passover liturgy.* He is the "one bread" in the boat who fed the prior crowds, who can even nourish in any dark wasteland, and who atones for their sins. Further, the two miraculous meals concluded with the disciples distributing the bread to the crowds. The pattern within the meals implies that when the disciples take this bread that is identified as Jesus's body, they are to distribute it to people in future celebrations of this reconfigured Passover meal.[51] Thus, the communion Jesus now has with his disciples through the mutual eating of the bread/body of Jesus will continue through them to others after his death.

49. Gray, *Temple*, 161. Heil explains it as such: "The bread and wine Jesus gives his disciples (14:22–24) constitute a new sacrificial meal surpassing the sacrificial system (11:15–17; 12:33) of the damned temple. In contrast to the dead bodies of animals sacrificed in the temple and later eaten in meals of communion with God, and especially in contrast to the body of the sacrificed lamb eaten in the Passover meal (14:12), the bread Jesus designates as 'my body' (τὸ σῶμά μου), already anointed for burial (14:22; cf. 14:8), becomes a sacrificial victim to be eaten by his disciples, that it may unite them with his salvific death." John Paul Heil, "The Narrative Strategy and Pragmatics of the Temple Theme in Mark," *CBQ* 59, no. 1 (1997): 94–95.

50. Heil, "Narrative Strategy," 95.

51. Heil, *Gospel of Mark*, 290.

Scripture as a Liturgical Icon

This exposition has shown five things. First, the two episodes of the miraculous loaves ought to be seen as liturgical sequences in tandem with the Last Supper episode, also a liturgical sequence. When all three are considered together, it can be concluded that Jesus's body is the miraculous bread given to the disciples.

Second, it is necessary for Jesus's followers to understand the significance of the bread, for such understanding impacts one's future activities or requests. After each bread miracle, there is a boat scene wherein the disciples do not understand the bread because their hearts are hardened (6:52; 8:17). In the first case, their lack of understanding results in fear, nonrecognition of Jesus, and the incapacity to bring the boat to shore. In the second case, they are unable to recognize the wiles of Herod and the Pharisees or recognize Jesus as the one bread in the boat with them (8:14). Contrary to this is the Syrophoenician woman (7:24–30), who understands the superabundance of the bread and recognizes Jesus's capacity to give it, and thus the miracle she receives is in conjunction with her understanding of the bread. Further, her grasp of the significance of the bread changes the ministry of Jesus, resulting in the gentiles participating in the miraculous bread.

Third, "hearing the word and receiving the bread" is the basic liturgical structure. In the first miracle, Jesus sees the crowds, who are described as sheep without a shepherd, and from his wellspring of compassion he teaches them (6:34). They listen to him at length and receive the gift of the miraculous bread. The liturgical paradigm is much more dramatic in the second bread miracle. Jesus takes a deaf and mute man who has never heard the word of God and enables him to hear and give testimony (7:31–37). After that, the gentiles receive the gift of the bread in an inhospitable wasteland. Each of these basic paradigms is followed by a boat scene. The "hearing the word" that precedes the Last Supper Passover meal is Mark 1:1–14:21, that is, all that comes prior to the passion and death of the Lord. When the Gospel in its entirety is seen as patterned after a liturgical sequence, and when the symbolism of the boat is seen as the church, it can be concluded that the audience is now in the boat, and it will successfully navigate the boat inasmuch as it sees, hears, and remembers the bread (cf. 8:14), which is identified with Jesus.[52]

52. Woodroof examines the boat scenes in the Gospel and concludes, "Mark's boat acts as a complex setting in which numerous and important events unfold. It functions to define a unique lifestyle, as a boundary between disciples and the crowds, as a teaching

Fourth, the disciples are involved in the two bread miracles in a way in which they are not in Jesus's other miracles. Jesus not only commands them to feed the crowds but takes from what they have and accomplishes for them what he commands. They can feed the crowds when they are obedient to his subsequent commands, even when they do not understand the significance of the bread. Given the connection between the bread miracles and the Passover meal, it can be concluded that in the future Passover meals, the disciples will give the bread, even if the disciples do not understand the bread, provided they follow Jesus's subsequent commands. This reading of the miracles of the loaves correlates well with the Catholic understanding of the sacraments being confected *ex opere operato*; for it is Jesus himself who, as in the bread miracles, is the primary celebrant of the new Passover liturgy of the Eucharist.[53]

Fifth, Jesus is emotionally vulnerable to his disciples, whom he allows to gaze upon his interiority and see his anguish and his compassion. Thus, the whole of the liturgy wherein Jesus gives himself in word and sacrifice issues forth from his empathy and compassion for the misery of human suffering, which he invites his disciples to share in and experience.

Considering the Scriptures as shaped in a liturgical milieu for a worshiping community could have wide implications for the future of Catholic biblical scholarship. I attempted to show one such result through the examination of the cluster of the word ἄρτος: the Gospel of Mark is shaped as a liturgical icon with an exposition on the Eucharist presented in its heart (6:34–8:21). By connecting the ἄρτος section to the Last Supper, I demonstrated how the reconfigured Passover meal is meant to be seen as eucharistic banquet, where Jesus gives his body and blood for atonement, thus showing how the church's teaching on the Eucharist is valid. Future studies could continue to show the intrinsic nexus between Scripture and liturgy, Scripture and tradition, which could further buttress and demonstrate the church's teaching on sacraments, the priestly life, and ecclesiology.

---

platform, as a spiritual battleground, as a place to experience the presence of Jesus, as a means to further ministry, and as a gathering of people noted more for commitment than for competence. In each of these ways, the church offers an analogous function, leading the reader to wonder whether Mark might be talking about the church as he describes what Jesus and his disciples did in the boat." Woodroof, "Church as Boat in Mark," 245–49.

53. The phrase *ex opere operato* is translated "by the very fact of the action's being performed" (*CCC* §1128). According to the Council of Trent, grace is "conferred by the sacraments of the new law through the sacramental action itself [*ex opere operato*]." See "First Decree on the Sacraments, Canon 8," in *Decrees of the Ecumenical Councils*, ed. Norman P. Tanner, SJ (London: Sheed and Ward, 1990), 2:685.

Memory and the Human Dimension of Inspiration

Rethinking Historical Jesus Research

Michael Patrick Barber

In September 2019, Pope Francis declared the Third Sunday of Ordinary Time as "Word of God Sunday." In establishing this celebration, the Holy Father appealed to Vatican II, which he says "gave great impulse to the rediscovery of the word of God." Specifically, Francis invokes *Dei Verbum*, one of the major documents of the Council, explaining that it "deserves to be read and appropriated ever anew."[1] This paper seeks to respond to this invitation to reappropriate the Council's teaching by focusing on one of *Dei Verbum*'s core emphases: the human dimension of biblical inspiration.

Dei Verbum insists that the human writers of the biblical books wrote as "true authors" who "made full use of their powers and faculties."[2] Although this aspect of the document's teaching hardly seems controversial today, Catholic exegetes should not forget that this was not always the case. In his own day, the pioneering Catholic biblical scholar Marie-Joseph Lagrange was viewed with suspicion for emphasizing the human dimension of biblical inspiration. I will therefore begin with a discussion of Lagrange's account of inspiration, which ultimately received magisterial approval in *Dei Verbum*'s formulation. Second, I will look at recent developments in memory research, which have important implications for thinking through *Dei Verbum*'s insistence that the biblical writers employed their own "powers and faculties." I will demonstrate how these developments have important

1. Pope Francis, Apostolic Letter issued "motu proprio" *Aperuit illis* (September 30, 2019) §2.

2. Vatican Council II, Dogmatic Constitution *Dei Verbum* (November 18, 1965) §11. Hereafter, references to this source will be placed in the text as *DV*. English translations of the documents of Vatican II are taken from Austin Flannery, OP, ed., *Vatican Council II: The Basic Sixteen Documents*, rev. ed. (Northport, NY: Costello, 1996). The Latin reads, "Quos facultatibus ac viribus suis utentes."

implications for historical Jesus research. In particular, I will explore the implications advances in memory studies have for thinking through Matthew's role in historical Jesus scholarship.

Lagrange and the Human Dimension of Biblical Authorship

Lagrange in Context

It is important to set Lagrange's project of biblical studies in its historical context. Lagrange was a teenager in 1870, when the First Vatican Council issued the dogmatic constitution *Dei Filius*. This document emphasizes that the church recognizes the biblical books as "sacred and canonical" because of the doctrine of biblical inspiration: the biblical books are recognized by the church "because, being written under the inspiration of the holy Spirit, they have God as their author, and were as such committed to the church."[3] What the Council left unsaid, however, was the precise role the human writers had in producing the biblical texts. It affirmed God as "author" but, notably, did not use that term for the humans involved in the writing of Scripture.

The same year *Dei Filius* was promulgated, Cardinal Johann Baptist Franzelin published his explanation of the dynamics of inspiration.[4] Since Franzelin had been intimately involved with the drafting of *Dei Filius*,[5] his interpretation was given special weight by theologians. Franzelin sought to make a distinction between the formal and material aspects of inspiration. He argued that God supplied the biblical writers with the essential ideas found in their writings and that the human writers merely provided the words that gave expression to these ideas. As Joseph Chaine explains, "This results in something close to dictation, for God communicates the book already made, at least as regards the thoughts, to the author charged with its wording."[6]

3. Vatican Council I, Dogmatic Constitution *Dei Filius* (April 24, 1870) §2. Translation in Norman P. Tanner, SJ, *Decrees of the Ecumenical Councils* (London: Sheed and Ward, 1990), 2:806.

4. J. B. Franzelin, *Tractatus de divina Traditione et Scriptura* (Rome: Typographia Polyglotta, S. C. de Propaganda Fide, 1870).

5. For a fuller account of his involvement, see Bernhard Knorn, SJ, "Johann Baptist Franzelin (1816–86): A Jesuit Cardinal Shaping the Official Teaching of the Church at the Time of the First Vatican Council," *Journal of Jesuit Studies* 7, no. 4 (2020): 592–615.

6. Joseph Chaine, "The Old Testament – Semitism," in *Père Lagrange and the Scriptures*, trans. Richard T. A. Murphy, OP (Milwaukee: Bruce, 1946), 12.

Lagrange's Doctrine of Inspiration

Lagrange argued that Franzelin's explanation was faulty. It ignored what source critics had come to emphasize, namely, that biblical writers likely did not produce all of their works *ex nihilo*. Lagrange shows that *the biblical text itself* reveals that the sacred writers drew on other sources. For instance, he points out that the book of Proverbs introduces a series of sayings with the statement "These things also come from the wise men" (Prov 24:23). He writes:

> Who was inspired? The sages, or the compiler? . . . It is enough for us to know that the work we read is canonical, and is therefore inspired. And yet one occasionally meets men who are indignant and scandalized if you suggest that Moses alone did not write the Pentateuch.[7]

Indeed, Lagrange believed that attributing the whole of the Pentateuch to Moses alone overlooks important data. On the one hand, the text of the Pentateuch *itself* bears witness to its use of earlier materials. Within the book of Numbers, we find a quotation from "the Book of the Wars of the LORD" (Num 21:14). He observes that no passage suggests that Moses had to have written all of the Torah. Deuteronomy also ends by speaking of the death of Moses, adding, "no man knows the place of his burial to this day" (Deut 34:6). This indicates the final form of the book dates to a period after Moses's death. Moreover, he argues that details in the biblical texts indicate the use of earlier sources. Why the differing details in the two creation accounts in Genesis 1–2? Lagrange argues that the most natural explanation is that the biblical writer drew from different sources.[8]

Furthermore, Lagrange pointed out that a widespread patristic tradition held that Ezra had a hand in restoring the Scriptures after they had been corrupted (or lost altogether) at the time of the Babylonian exile. He cites statements from Irenaeus, Origen, Clement of Alexandria, Tertullian, John Chrysostom, Isidore of Seville, and Jerome to this effect.[9] It would appear

7. Marie-Joseph Lagrange, OP, *Historical Criticism and the Old Testament*, trans. Edward Myers (London: Catholic Truth Society, 1905), 97.

8. Marie-Joseph Lagrange, "L'innocence et le péché (Gen. II,4–III)," *RB* 6, no. 3 (1897): 370–71.

9. See Irenaeus, *Haer.* 3.21.2; Origen, *Sel. Jes. Nav.* (PG 12:824); Clement of Alexandria, *Strom.* 1.22 (149.3); Tertullian, *Cult. fem.* 1.3; John Chrysostom, *Hom. Heb.* 8; Isidore of Seville, *Origines* 6.3.1–2; and Jerome, *Helv.* 7.

that traditionalists like Franzelin were themselves ignorant of tradition. In short, nothing would seem to prohibit a Catholic from affirming that the Pentateuch was edited after the exile.

Lagrange therefore offered his own account of inspiration. Influenced by Thomas Aquinas's view that the human authors were "instruments" of the divine author, Lagrange was quick to point out that God moved the biblical authors in a way consistent with their nature, such that they should be thought of as employing all their natural powers and senses.[10] Inspiration did not simply need to involve God introducing fully formed ideas into the biblical writers' minds. Rather, it could be understood as divine illumination of the intellect, through which the human writers were able to make judgments of their own about knowledge they gained in various ways. This explanation of inspiration better accounts for the biblical writers' use of preexisting materials and their redactional activity.

The following passage from Lagrange is worth quoting at length, for here we see the seeds of the Second Vatican Council's teaching. Speaking of the analogy of the human authors as instruments, Lagrange writes:

> Some theorists had thought to make this notion clearer by comparing the sacred writers to musical instruments played by the Holy Spirit; to Him alone would belong the melody and the accord. This comparison, like most comparisons, may suggest untrue ideas. One who imagines God using the inspired person as a fluteplayer his flute, is apt to think of an Isaias or Paul as a sort of phonograph. The main current of the Church's tradition has always preserved the personality of the inspired writer and assigned to him functions of a real author, who exercises his faculties in full liberty under the enlightening and guiding action of God. To know what God teaches, we must determine the thought of the human teacher.[11]

Lagrange thus rejects notions that ignore the distinct personalities and traits of the human writers of Scripture. The biblical writers must be recognized as "real" authors. He emphasizes that in order to understand the divine author's

10. Lagrange, *Historical Criticism and the Old Testament*, 83–116. See also Marie-Joseph Lagrange, OP, "L'inspiration et les exigences de la critique," *RB* 5, no. 4 (1896): 496–518; "Inspiration des Livres Saints," *RB* 5, no. 2 (1896): 199–220; "Une pensée de saint Thomas sur l'inspiration scripturaire," *RB* 4, no. 4 (1895): 563–71; "A propos de l'encyclique 'Providentissimus,'" *RB* 4, no. 1 (1895): 48–64.

11. Marie-Joseph Lagrange, OP, *The Meaning of Christianity according to Luther and His Followers in Germany*, trans. W. S. Reilly, SS (New York: Longmans, Green, 1920), 96.

intended meaning, one must pay special attention to what the human writer wanted to communicate.

Dei Verbum*'s Magisterial Confirmation of Lagrange*

The similarities between Lagrange's teaching about inspiration and *Dei Verbum* are striking. Not only does Lagrange anticipate the Second Vatican Council's teaching that the human authors used their own "powers and faculties"; he also lays the groundwork for its teaching that to determine the meaning of the divine author, the exegete must focus attention on the intention of the human author.

> Seeing that, in sacred Scripture, God speaks through men in human fashion, it follows that the interpreter of sacred Scriptures, if he is to ascertain what God has wished to communicate to us, should carefully search out the meaning which the sacred writers really had in mind, that meaning which God had thought well to manifest through the medium of their words. (*DV* §12)

After these words, *Dei Verbum* goes on to talk about how the exegete must explain the meaning intended by the human authors by examining the "literary forms" they used and the circumstances in which they wrote. Here we have yet another parallel with Lagrange. Just after emphasizing the need to recognize Scripture's human writers as "real" authors (in the passage cited above), he goes on to state that exegetes must pay attention to the writers' historical context because "the human individual is born in a social group and depends on it."[12]

Dei Verbum's definition of inspiration and its approval of historical-critical methods are thus widely seen as giving magisterial approval to Lagrange's approach. Philip Moller writes, "The model that has shaped the course of the Catholic theology of inspiration over the past century has been the Thomist synthesis of Marie-Joseph Lagrange."[13] This was a needed corrective to approaches such as Franzelin's, which downplayed the human dimension of the Scriptures. Comparing the word inspired in Scripture to the Word incarnate, *Dei Verbum* declares that just as Christ became man, "the words of

12. Lagrange, *Meaning of Christianity*, 102.

13. Philip Moller, SJ, "What Should They Be Saying about Biblical Inspiration? A Note on the State of the Question," *Theological Studies* 74, no. 3 (2013): 619.

God, expressed in human language, have been made like human discourse" (*DV* §13). Lagrange's emphasis on the human aspect of biblical authorship guards against what we might call a biblical Docetism, that is, a view that regards Scripture as only divine and as merely appearing to involve real human authorship. By describing the biblical writers as "true authors," *Dei Verbum* gives a full-throated affirmation to Lagrange's emphasis on the human dimension of inspiration. The future of Catholic biblical scholarship will certainly not involve a course reversal in this regard. In the rest of this paper, I will contend that the future of Catholic biblical studies should carry forward this recognition of the human aspect of biblical authorship by availing itself of advances in memory research.

Memory Research and Jesus Studies

Memory and Historiography

As we have seen, *Dei Verbum* gives special emphasis to the way the biblical authors employ all their "powers and faculties" in producing the biblical texts. These human powers would obviously include the faculty of *memory*. In recent years, historians have paid increasing attention to the fruits of memory research. It is now recognized that the work of historical analysis entails wrestling with the social and cognitive factors associated with remembrance. Above all, researchers have emphasized that mnemonic activity is not simply a matter of retrieving perceptions of the past stored in a mental recording bank. Memory also necessarily entails a constructive property.

In his application of social memory theory to historical Jesus research, Anthony Le Donne[14] has highlighted the work of Michael Schudson, who identifies different types of "distortion" that are inherent in remembrance:

- *Distanciation:* memories become fuzzy on details, emotional associations lessen in intensity, and broader perspectives on past events are gained.
- *Narrativization:* memories are structured into a recognizable plot.
- *Cognitivization and conventionalization:* memories of the past conform to familiar experiences and stereotypes.[15]

14. Anthony Le Donne, *The Historiographical Jesus: Memory, Typology, and the Son of David* (Waco, TX: Baylor University Press, 2009), 52.

15. See Michael Schudson, "Dynamics of Distortion in Collective Memory," in *Mem-*

To these, Le Donne adds another:

- *Articulation:* memories "conform to language conventions."[16]

Recognizing all of this, Le Donne writes, "*All memory is distortion.*"[17]

Moreover, it is important to stress that the different forms of memory distortion are connected to one another. Memories become fuzzy over time (distanciation) precisely because elements are lost that do not conform to familiar plots (narrativization). In other words, structuring memories into story form involves a selection process that either retains or eliminates details.[18] This feature of memory is a necessary part of remembrance; every element cannot be retained. Furthermore, what is retained remains because it is somehow deemed more "significant" or "relevant" than other impressions. *Memory is thus unavoidably interpretive.*

This constructive quality of memory has an important communal dimension. The "schemas" to which memories conform involve scripts that are usually socially and culturally defined.[19] Recognizing these dynamics, social memory theorists speak of the way memories are "keyed" to archetypes and familiar scripts.[20]

These developments in memory research have led some to despair of accurate knowledge of the past. Some hold that all perceptions of the past are wholly determined by the needs of the present. This perspective is often identified as the "presentist" model.[21] Yet this approach is not without its critics. A number of researchers insist that the historian must account for the way the past and present mutually influence one another. As Barry Schwartz writes, "To focus solely on memory's constructed side is to deny

ory Distortion: How Minds, Brains, and Societies Reconstruct the Past, ed. D. L. Schachter (Cambridge: Harvard University Press, 1995), 346–64.

16. Le Donne, *Historiographical Jesus*, 52.

17. Le Donne, *Historiographical Jesus*, 51.

18. Alan Kirk, *Memory and the Jesus Tradition*, RJFTC (London: Bloomsbury T&T Clark, 2018), 216.

19. See the discussion of scripts in Jocelyn Penny Small, *Wax Tablets of the Mind: Cognitive Studies of Memory and Literacy in Classical Antiquity* (London: Routledge, 1997), 196–97; David C. Rubin, *Memory in Oral Traditions: The Cognitive Psychology of Epic Ballads, and Counting-out Rhymes* (Oxford: Oxford University Press, 1995), 21–28.

20. See, e.g., Eric Eve, *Behind the Gospels: Understanding the Oral Tradition* (Minneapolis: Fortress, 2014), 95; Kirk, *Memory and the Jesus Tradition*, 28.

21. See, e.g., John Bodnar, *Remaking America: Public Memory, Commemoration, and Patriotism in the Twentieth Century* (Princeton: Princeton University Press, 1992), 15.

the past's significance as a model for coming to terms with the present."[22] Schwartz and others maintain that the presentist model ignores an important dynamic: uncomfortable and painful memories are preserved despite concerted attempts to blot them out.[23] One can easily see, for example, how the presentist approach might play dangerously into the hands of those who wish to erase the past, such as Shoah deniers.

Le Donne insists that the implications of memory distortion can be harnessed by the historian. He prefers to speak of "refraction" rather than "distortion" because "the term *distortion* carries too many negative associations."[24] In his view, the historian should not seek to "dig for an unrefracted memory"—which is impossible—but "to account for the earliest mnemonic refractions of a memory-story."[25] By charting out various trajectories in our sources, Le Donne argues that the historian can engage in "historical triangulation."[26]

Given that memory registers new perceptions by means of established archetypes and scripts, Le Donne believes the historian can apply this to thinking about the historical Jesus. As an example, Jesus researchers have long viewed intertextual biblical echoes in the Gospels as the result of later redaction. In Matthew and John, Jesus's arrival at Jerusalem is explicitly linked to Zech 9:9: "Shout aloud, O daughter Jerusalem! Behold, your king comes to you; he is righteous and victorious, humble and riding on a donkey, on a colt, the foal of a donkey" (cf. Matt 21:4; John 12:14). Yet Mark's and Luke's depictions of the scene also seem shaped by Zechariah's oracle (cf. Mark 11:1–11; Luke 19:28–40). Recognizing that the presentation of Jesus's entrance into the city is likely colored by Zechariah's oracle, one might suppose that the story of Jesus's entrance into the city was fabricated altogether. Yet Le Donne cautions against assuming that such typological allusions were only the result of the Gospel writers' creativity.[27] He cites E. P. Sanders, who writes: "There

22. Barry Schwartz, *Abraham Lincoln and the Forge of National Memory* (Chicago: University of Chicago Press, 2000), ix–x.

23. Schwartz, *Abraham Lincoln*, 6, 204. Schwartz is regularly cited by New Testament scholars on this point. See Alan Kirk, "Social and Cultural Memory," in *Memory, Tradition, and Text: Uses of the Past in Early Christianity*, ed. Alan Kirk and Tom Thatcher, SemeiaSt 52 (Atlanta: Society of Biblical Literature, 2005), 14; Rafael Rodríguez, *Structuring Early Christian Memory: Jesus in Tradition, Performance and Text*, LNTS 407 (London: T&T Clark, 2010), 62–64.

24. Le Donne, *Historiographical Jesus*, 51.

25. Le Donne, *Historiographical Jesus*, 87.

26. Le Donne, *Historiographical Jesus*, 81–86.

27. On the specifics of the so-called triumphal entry, see Le Donne, *Historiographi-*

are no absolutely certain signs that tell us when a passage in the gospels has been invented as a parallel to an earlier stage of the history of salvation, when it has been recast to emphasize an actual parallel, and when Jesus himself (or John the Baptist) intentionally created a reminiscence."[28] Sanders goes on to acknowledge that some of these parallels may very well be later inventions. Nevertheless, Sanders insists that one must grant the possibility of "Jesus's own conscious imitation of scriptural types."[29] Le Donne, therefore, writes, "If it can be granted . . . that Jesus did evoke scriptural types during his life, such typologies might have been further developed by those who remembered him and told stories about him."[30]

Memory Research and Rethinking "Authenticity"

As others have noted, the recognition that all memory is in some way interpretive has important methodological implications for Jesus studies. Conventionally, historical Jesus research has operated on the principle that the researcher's aim is to sort the material in the Gospels into two piles: the "authentic" and the "inauthentic." The "authentic" represents the historical kernel, while the "inauthentic" involves the subsequent "layers" of later material that accrued to the Jesus tradition. Drawing on insights from memory studies, Chris Keith has offered a trenchant critique of this conception of the quest. Keith writes, "The authentic/inauthentic dichotomy is false precisely because, in memory, the past is always packaged in interpretive frameworks borrowed from the present."[31] He concludes, "If there is no such thing as past-without-interpretation in gospel tradition, there is no such thing as 'au-

cal Jesus, 52–59 and 191–220. Interestingly, Le Donne argues that the connections could have been recognized by those present at the event, but he insists that we cannot know if Jesus intentionally evoked such echoes. I have argued, however, that it is unlikely that the crowd made the connection while Jesus was merely oblivious to this. See Michael Patrick Barber, *The Historical Jesus and the Temple: Memory, Methodology, and the Gospel of Matthew* (Cambridge: Cambridge University Press, 2023), 115–56.

28. E. P. Sanders, *The Historical Figure of Jesus* (New York: Penguin, 1993), 85.

29. Sanders, *Historical Figure of Jesus*, 85.

30. Le Donne, *Historiographical Jesus*, 5.

31. Chris Keith, "The Indebtedness of the Criteria Approach to Form Criticism and Recent Attempts to Rehabilitate the Search for an Authentic Jesus," in *Jesus, Criteria, and the Demise of Authenticity*, ed. Chris Keith and Anthony Le Donne (London: T&T Clark, 2012), 40. This book's importance is emphasized by Rodríguez, *Structuring Early Christian Memory*, 156–58, 178–79, 224–25.

thentic tradition' as the criteria approach defines it, and therefore nothing for the criteria of authenticity to extricate."[32] His point, then, is not simply that the standard criteria of authenticity have limitations that fail to produce conclusions about what is historically "certain." Keith is not advancing historical naivete. He recognizes that historical work does not seek certainties but probabilities. Rather, his argument is that the criteria are inadequate because they depend on a conviction that the researcher can ultimately reach an uninterpreted Jesus.

Indeed, leading scholars are now dispensing with the standard criteria of authenticity, including Dale Allison, who once used them himself.[33] Rather than trying to test each saying or episode's "authenticity," these scholars advocate beginning with the broader shape of the Jesus tradition. Acknowledging the limits of our historical tools, Allison maintains that "the historicity of most—not all—of the sayings attributed to [Jesus]"[34] cannot be determined. Yet Allison does not therefore insist that the quest should be abandoned altogether. Drawing on recent research, Allison shows that memory tends to be most reliable when it relates the "gist" of previous experiences.[35] Eyewitnesses may forget the color and make of the cars involved in an accident, but *that* an accident occurred is not disputed. The fog of war causes details to become hazy, but *that* there was a war and the identity of the major powers involved are details that are not easily lost.

Allison makes an additional point that is worth considering: even false

32. Keith, "Indebtedness of the Criteria Approach," 40. See also Chris Keith, "Social Memory Theory and Gospels Research: The First Decade (Part Two)," *Early Christianity* 6, no. 4 (2015): 526–27.

33. See, e.g., Dale C. Allison Jr., "How to Marginalize the Traditional Criteria of Authenticity," in *How to Study the Historical Jesus*, vol. 1 of *The Handbook for the Study of the Historical Jesus*, ed. Tom Holmén and Stanley E. Porter (Leiden: Brill, 2010), 3–30. See also other treatments by Dale C. Allison Jr.: "It Don't Come Easy: A History of Disillusionment," in Keith and Le Donne, *Jesus, Criteria, and the Demise*, 186–99; Dale C. Allison Jr., *The Historical Christ and the Theological Jesus* (Grand Rapids: Eerdmans 2009), 53–60; Dale C. Allison Jr., *Jesus of Nazareth: Millenarian Prophet* (Minneapolis: Fortress, 1998), 1–78. See further Chris Keith, *Jesus' Literacy: Scribal Culture and the Teacher from Galilee*, LNTS 413 (London: T&T Clark, 2011), 44–47; Rafael Rodríguez, "Authenticating Criteria: The Use and Misuse of a Critical Method," *JSHJ* 7, no. 2 (2009): 152–67; the essays by Chris Keith, Morna Hooker, and Rafael Rodríguez in Keith and Le Donne, *Jesus, Criteria, and the Demise*.

34. Dale C. Allison Jr., *Constructing Jesus: Memory, Imagination, and History* (Grand Rapids: Baker Academic, 2010), 22.

35. See especially Allison, *Constructing Jesus*, 10–15. Allison touched on this topic in his earlier book on Jesus. See Allison, *Jesus of Nazareth*, 45.

memories can provide important information about the past. Students may remember a teacher as an "absent-minded professor." The specific episodes recalled that reinforce this memory may not all reflect the actual past. Yet where there is smoke, there is often fire. The memories—even ones that fail to have verisimilitude in different ways to the past—nonetheless do tell us something about that past. So, too, Allison explains, material deemed "inauthentic" can preserve important impressions made by Jesus. For example, Allison discusses the Synoptic narrative of Jesus being tempted by Satan in the desert (Matt 4:1–11). Allison views these accounts as "haggadic fiction."[36] Nevertheless, he insists that they are not irrelevant to the historian. The episode emphasizes the idea that Jesus understood himself to be engaged in a conflict with demonic forces. In fact, as Allison shows, this idea appears throughout the Gospel tradition.[37] Instead of setting it aside as irrelevant, Allison insists that the historian should ask a key question about such traditions: why was Jesus remembered in *this* way? He suggests the temptation scene preserves impressions made by Jesus himself, that is, the perception that he was engaged in a spiritual struggle with evil powers. Allison writes, "Fiction need not be pure fiction . . . fiction can indeed preserve the past."[38]

Keith writes, "One must quest for the historical Jesus by accounting for the interpretations of the Gospels, not by dismissing them and certainly not by fragmenting them."[39] Elsewhere, I have argued that we should apply this insight to the broader narrative and interpretive framework of the Gospel of Matthew.[40] In his magisterial commentary on Matthew, Ulrich Luz raises a fascinating question. Highlighting the Jewish character of the Gospel, Luz asks, "Could it be that some of the Matthean 'systematizations' (or 'nonsystematizations') of Jesus might be very close to Jesus himself, just because they are constructions of a Jew who was temporally and culturally

36. See Allison, "It Don't Come Easy," 191. Allison's fuller argument is found in "Behind the Temptations of Jesus: Q 4:1–13 and Mark 1:12–13," in *Authenticating the Activities of Jesus*, ed. Bruce Chilton and Craig A. Evans, NTTS 28/2 (Leiden: Brill, 1999), 195–214.

37. Allison, *Constructing Jesus*, 18.

38. Allison, "It Don't Come Easy," 191. Along similar lines, see the discussion of the charge that Jesus is in league with Beelzebul in Mark 3:22 in Rodríguez, *Structuring Early Christian Memory*, 178–79.

39. Keith, *Jesus' Literacy*, 66.

40. For the fuller form of the argument given here, see Barber, *The Historical Jesus and the Temple*.

close to him?"[41] It seems to me that Luz is onto something here. Given that Jesus should be recognized as a Jewish teacher, it makes sense to think that Matthew's particular emphases and configurations of the Jesus tradition may provide a window into the kinds of concerns and priorities Jesus himself would have had. In short, I believe the value of the Gospel of Matthew for Jesus research should be rethought. Rather than trying to "authenticate" specific traditions, I argue that it is important to look at the Gospel's overall presentation of Jesus, a portrait that is especially characterized by a Jewish perspective.[42] Instead of seeking to bypass Matthew's narrative framework and special interests, there are good reasons to believe that they can help us think through the way Jewish concerns would have shaped Jesus's ministry. It may also help us understand how these concerns could be coordinated with one another.

Rethinking the Gospel of Matthew's Role in Jesus Research

Matthew's Jewish Concerns

It is often assumed that Mark, the earliest canonical gospel, must be more reliable than Matthew. However, to quote John Kloppenborg, we should recall that "tradition-history is not convertible with *literary history*."[43] As any historian will know, it is not always the case that earlier sources are more reliable than later ones. While Matthew appears to have been dependent upon Mark, it is not always the case that Mark's account of episodes is more plausible than Matthew's. When it comes to Jewish matters, this is especially the case.

Take, for instance, the episode involving Jesus's controversy with the Pharisees over handwashing. In Mark, we read: "For the Pharisees, and

41. Ulrich Luz, "Matthew's Interpretive 'Tendencies' and the 'Historical' Jesus," in *Jesus Research: New Methodologies and Perceptions; The Second Princeton-Prague Symposium on Jesus Research*, ed. James H. Charlesworth with Brian Rhea and Petr Pokorný (Grand Rapids: Eerdmans, 2014), 597.

42. For important recent studies on Matthew's Jewish perspective, see Anders Runesson and Daniel M. Gurtner, eds., *Matthew within Judaism: Israel and the Nations*, ECL (Atlanta: Society of Biblical Literature, 2019); John Kampen, *Matthew within Sectarian Judaism*, AYBRL (New Haven: Yale University Press, 2019).

43. John S. Kloppenborg, *The Formation of Q: Trajectories in Ancient Wisdom Collections*, 2nd ed., SAC (Harrisburg, PA: Trinity Press International, 2000), 244.

all the Jews [πάντες οἱ Ἰουδαῖοι], do not eat unless they wash their hands, holding the tradition of the elders" (Mark 7:3; emphasis added). Yet Mark's statement that "all Jews" washed their hands before meals is probably exaggerated. The Sadducees did not observe all the traditions Pharisees maintained (see Josephus, *Ant.* 13.297). As Matthew Thiessen shows, handwashing was likely a practice observed by the latter and not the former.[44] Notably, then, in his version of the story, Matthew omits Mark's line about what "all Jews" did.

In Mark's account, Jesus goes on to say, "Do you not understand that whatever goes into a person from outside is not able to defile because it enters not the heart but the stomach, and goes out into the sewer?" (Mark 7:18). Mark offers an interpretation of Jesus's teaching here: "Thus he declared all foods clean [καθαρίζων πάντα τὰ βρώματα]" (Mark 7:19).[45] Traditionally, it has been assumed that this statement depicts Jesus as abolishing the kosher laws.[46] More recent work is calling this view into question.[47] Regardless of that interpretive debate, however, that the line is not repeated by Matthew is surely no accident. It is easy to see how Mark's interpretive aside could undermine a crucial aspect of Jesus's teaching in Matthew, namely, that he has come to uphold the Torah's teaching. Most strikingly, Jesus proclaims, "Whoever then relaxes *one of the least of these commandments* and teaches men so, shall be called least in the kingdom of heaven" (Matt 5:19; emphasis added). Scholars routinely explain that Matthew, therefore, leaves out Mark's interpretation of Jesus's statement about handwashing on the

44. Matthew Thiessen, *Jesus and the Forces of Death: The Gospels' Portrayal of Ritual Impurity within First-Century Judaism* (Grand Rapids: Baker Academic, 2020), 190–91. Among other pieces of evidence, Num. Rab. 20.21 reveals that such differences continued well after the destruction of the temple.

45. Joel Marcus claims that the line is a later interpolation based on the awkwardness of the grammar (*Mark: A New Translation with Introduction and Commentary*, AB 27–27A [New Haven: Yale University Press, 2000–2009], 1:455). Yet this line of reasoning is unpersuasive, since Mark's grammar is often far from smooth.

46. See, e.g., David C. Sim, "Matthew and Jesus of Nazareth," in *Matthew and His Christian Contemporaries*, ed. David C. Sim and Boris Repschinski, LNTS 333 (New York: T&T Clark, 2008), 160.

47. For alternate takes, see the discussions in Thiessen, *Jesus and the Forces of Death*, 187–95; James G. Crossley, *The Date of Mark's Gospel: Insight from the Law in Earliest Christianity*, JSNTSup 266 (London: T&T Clark, 2004), 183–205; Jesper Svartvik, *Mark and Mission: Mk 7:1–23 in Its Narrative and Historical Contexts*, ConBNT 32 (Stockholm: Almqvist and Wiksell, 2000), 109–204. See also Logan Williams, "The Stomach Purifies All Foods: Jesus' Anatomical Argument in Mark 7.18–19," *NTS* (forthcoming).

grounds that it would conflict with his portrait of Jesus's insistence on the validity of the law.[48]

David Sim points out that Matthew's stress on the importance of Torah observance also coheres well with what we know about the early Jesus movement in Jerusalem.[49] It would seem that the Jesus movement in Jerusalem gave special emphasis to the need for Torah observance (cf. Gal 2:12; Acts 21:17–26). Sim argues that Matthew's narrative provides insight into the kinds of interests that shaped the first followers of Jesus.[50] For example, he looks at the way Matthew handles Mark's descriptions of Jesus's activity in gentile regions (cf. Mark 8:1–10; Matt 8:34).[51] In Mark, we are told that Jesus came into the region of Tyre, healing a gentile woman's daughter after he "entered a house [εἰσελθὼν εἰς οἰκίαν]" (Mark 7:24). Matthew, however, tells us only that the Canaanite woman who sought Jesus's help "*came out* [ἐξελθοῦσα] *from that region*" (Matt 15:22; emphasis added). In other words, Matthew avoids the impression that Jesus entered a non-Israelite's house.[52] From this, Sim argues that Matthew might help us to better think through the kinds of issues that Jesus would have had to deal with during his ministry.

Other areas where Matthew seems to offer a more historically plausible account than Mark could be mentioned here. Due to limited space, we will name just one more: the soldiers' mocking of Jesus during the passion narrative. In Mark's account, the Roman soldiers clothe Jesus in "purple" (πορφύραν; Mark 15:17). Matthew, however, relates that it was a "scarlet cloak" (χλαμύδα κοκκίνην; Matt 27:28).[53] As commentators point out, Matthew's report is more historically probable since the color he describes better describes the color the Roman troops would have worn.[54]

48. See, e.g., Matthias Konradt, *The Gospel according to Matthew: A Commentary*, trans. M. Eugene Boring (Waco, TX: Baylor University Press, 2020), 237; Ulrich Luz, *Matthew*, Hermeneia (Minneapolis: Fortress, 2001–2007), 2:332.

49. Sim, "Matthew and Jesus," 163–67.

50. See, e.g., Donald Senior, CP, "Viewing the Jewish Jesus of History through the Lens of Matthew," in *Soundings in the Religion of Jesus: Perspectives and Methods in Jewish and Christian Scholarship* (Minneapolis: Fortress, 2012), 88; Craig S. Keener, *A Commentary on the Gospel of Matthew* (Grand Rapids: Eerdmans, 1998), 18–19.

51. See Sim, "Matthew and Jesus," 156–59.

52. See Anders Runesson, *Divine Wrath and Salvation in Matthew: The Narrative World of the First Gospel* (Minneapolis: Fortress, 2016), 75n77.

53. A variant (D it sy^{s}) of Matt 27:28 mentions a ἱμάτιον πορφύρουν, yet this is most likely the result of influence from Mark.

54. W. D. Davies and Dale C. Allison Jr., *The Gospel according to St. Matthew*, ICC (Edinburgh: T&T Clark, 1988–1997), 3:602.

Matthew's Coordination of Jesus Traditions

Matthew's overall narrative allows us to see how apparently contradictory material can work together. Take, for instance, Jesus's attitude toward the temple. Throughout our sources, Jesus frequently endorses the temple cult. In Matthew, we find episodes such as Jesus's cleansing of the leper, a scene that involves a command from Jesus that the man offer sacrifice in the temple (Matt 8:1–4). This episode is found in the other Synoptics (cf. Mark 1:40–45; Luke 5:12–16). Yet we also encounter scenes in Matthew unique to this Gospel that further reinforce Jesus's respect for the temple—for example, his instructions on offering sacrifice in Matt 5:21–26 and his teaching on the holiness of the temple in Matt 23:16–22.

On the other hand, Matthew contains certain traditions that many have viewed as downplaying or even rejecting the temple's validity. Again, while some of these stories appear in other sources, such as his predictions of the temple's destruction (Matt 24:2; cf. Mark 13:2; Luke 21:6), others are found only in Matthew—such as Jesus's quotation from Hos 6:6, "I desire mercy, not sacrifice" (cf. Matt 9:13; 12:7). How can these traditions fit comfortably within the same Gospel?

First, I would insist with others that none of the "anti-temple" interpretations of these episodes is convincing. Jesus's quotation from Hosea illustrates some of the problems into which certain interpreters have fallen. What is overlooked by those who view the passage as proof for an anti-cultic agenda in Jesus's teaching is that the verse employs a Hebraic idiom that conveys the sense of a comparative contrast, not a strict negation. Its meaning is best taken as "I desire mercy *more* than sacrifice."[55] This reading is confirmed by Luz, who shows that this is how the Targum and other Jewish sources understand the Hosea passage.[56] The point is that God rejects the sacrifices of those who do not show mercy to others, a lesson that ties in with other Matthean texts (Matt 5:23–24; 6:12). Indeed, Matthew's overall framework makes it impossible to think he is opposing sacrifice, since elsewhere in Matthew Jesus tells people to make such offerings.

55. See, e.g., Luz, *Matthew*, 2:34; Eyal Regev, *The Temple in Early Christianity: Experiencing the Sacred*, AYBRL (New Haven: Yale University Press, 2019), 136–37; Daniel M. Gurtner, *The Torn Veil: Matthew's Exposition of the Death of Jesus*, SNTSMS 139 (Cambridge: Cambridge University Press, 2007), 105–6.

56. Luz, *Matthew*, 2:34.

Others take a more nuanced approach: Jesus upheld the temple's holiness until he was rejected by the Jerusalem authorities.[57] A crucial passage cited in support of this theory is found in Matt 23:38: "Behold, your house is left to you desolate [ἰδοὺ ἀφίεται ὑμῖν ὁ οἶκος ὑμῶν ἔρημος]." On the narrative level, Anders Runesson makes the case that it is here that Matthew indicates a shift in Jesus's view: "Jesus accepts the temple and the sacrificial cult, at least until 23:38."[58] Yet Matthew goes on to depict Jesus warning those who live in Judea to take flight when they behold "the abomination of desolation spoken about by the prophet Daniel" (Matt 24:15). For Jesus, then, the desolation of the temple is a *future* event. Notably, in Daniel this language is repeatedly connected to the cessation of sacrifice (cf. Dan 9:26–27; 11:31; 12:11).[59] It is also worth noting that the saying about the coming "desolation" of the sanctuary in Luke is linked to the days when gentile armies will surround Jerusalem (cf. Luke 21:20). It would seem, then, that at least one other Gospel writer connected this saying to the events of 70 CE and not to Jesus's death.

Some may point to Matthew's account of the rending of the temple veil at Jesus's death (Matt 27:51) as evidence of God's departure from the temple. This is unpersuasive. A close reading of the whole of Matthew's Gospel makes it a difficult sell. In Matt 24, Jesus speaks of "the abomination of desolation" in connection *not with his death* but rather with the temple's coming destruction (cf. Matt 24:15). The most natural reading of Matthew, then, is that the temple remains sacred up until this future event. If the temple was already "desolate" at Jesus's death, how could a future event effect "desolation"? Furthermore, the evangelist continues to refer to Jerusalem as "the holy city" (Matt 27:53). If the temple is desolate—and recall that in Matthew it is the *altar* and the *temple* that make things holy (Matt 23:16–22)—why continue to refer to Jerusalem as "holy"? It is also worth mentioning that Luke appears to be under the impression that the temple remains holy after Jesus's death. Though he too mentions the tearing of the temple veil (Luke 23:45), he indicates that the disciples returned there after Jesus's ascension to praise God (Luke 24:52). All of this makes it difficult to insist that the rending of the temple veil in Matthew is indicative of the sanctuary's loss of sacral status.[60]

57. Simon J. Joseph, *Jesus and the Temple: Crucifixion in Its Jewish Context*, SNTSMS 165 (Cambridge: Cambridge University Press, 2016), 105.

58. Runesson, *Divine Wrath*, 58.

59. See Brant Pitre, *Jesus, the Tribulation, and the End of the Exile: Restoration Eschatology and the Origin of the Atonement*, WUNT 2/204 (Tübingen: Mohr Siebeck, 2005), 303–9.

60. For the fuller argument on this point see Barber, *Historical Jesus and the Temple*, 81–114.

Why does Jesus then speak in the present tense in Matt 23 when he says the temple is "left to you desolate"? Here again it is helpful to read our Gospel within its Jewish context. Jewish sources indicate that the future is already seen by God (cf. Jub. 1:4). As Morna Hooker puts it, prophetic words of future judgment were understood to reveal a "reality that lies beyond time and place, disclosing not simply events which will one day take place on earth, but the truth as it already exists in heaven."[61] When Jesus refers to the temple as "desolate," he can therefore be understood to be speaking in the "prophetic present." In fact, we have evidence for this kind of approach elsewhere in the Gospel. In Matt 26, before the feast of Passover, Jesus speaks of the future as if it is already present, saying, "*The Son of Man is handed over* to be crucified [ὁ υἱὸς τοῦ ἀνθρώπου παραδίδοται εἰς τὸ σταυρωθῆναι]" (Matt 26:2).[62] The upshot of all of this is that Jesus's statement in Matt 23:38 is hardly proof that he believed the temple of his day had been vacated by God. What further speaks against such a reading is the Last Supper narrative.

In Matt 26, Jesus is portrayed as eating the Passover meal with his disciples. Although scholars debate how to interpret the apparent conflicts between the Synoptic and Johannine chronologies, in Matthew it is clear that Jesus's Last Supper is a Passover meal.[63] We are explicitly told that, following Jesus's instructions, the disciples "prepared the Passover [ἡτοίμασαν τὸ πάσχα]" (Matt 26:19). The Greek term πάσχα can be rendered "Passover meal." However, the noun can also refer to the Passover lamb *itself*. Thus, when Matthew reports that the disciples "prepared the πάσχα," it is entirely probable that the evangelist is referring to the disciples preparing the Passover lamb.[64] Of course, for Jesus to eat a Passover meal without a ritually slaughtered lamb would have constituted a major break with Jewish practice.[65] It seems more probable than not, then, that Matt 26 implies that Jesus ate a Passover lamb that had been sacrificed in the temple. As Paula Fredriksen explains, the episode indicates that "at least one of Jesus's circle of

61. Morna D. Hooker, *The Signs of a Prophet: The Prophetic Actions of Jesus* (Harrisburg, PA: Trinity Press International, 1997), 4. See also R. B. Y. Scott, *The Relevance of the Prophets* (New York: Macmillan Company, 1960), 98.

62. See the discussion in Janice Capel Anderson, *Matthew's Narrative Web: Over, and Over, and Over Again*, JSNTSup 91 (Sheffield: JSOT Press, 1994), 167.

63. For the most recent comprehensive discussion, see Brant Pitre, *Jesus and the Last Supper* (Grand Rapids: Eerdmans, 2015), 251–373.

64. See Pitre, *Jesus and the Last Supper*, 352–56.

65. See, e.g., Evans, *Matthew*, 428–29. For the paschal character of the Last Supper in the Synoptics, see the discussion in Pitre, *Jesus and the Last Supper*, 315–24.

disciples had been up to the temple to offer the lamb during the afternoon of the day of 14 Nisan."[66] Since Matthew likely portrays Jesus and his disciples participating in the temple's sacrificial role in the Passover celebration, it seems highly implausible that Jesus's earlier saying about the temple being desolate (Matt 23:38) should be read as a statement offering definitive repudiation of the temple cult's validity.

In sum, Matthew never presents Jesus as rejecting the holiness of the temple itself. His final act, in fact, is to celebrate a meal consisting of a lamb that has been sacrificed there. To quote Daniel Gurtner: "Matthew is positive towards the temple in general, affirming the validity of its sacrifices and the presence of God within it."[67]

The "Problem" of Jesus's Prediction of the Temple's Destruction

But if Matthew portrays Jesus as positively disposed toward the temple, what are we to make of his predictions of the temple's destruction? The majority view among scholars is that the historical Jesus himself made statements that gave rise to these impressions. James Dunn speaks for many when he writes, "According to the tradition, the key charge brought against Jesus was that he had threatened to destroy the Temple (Mark 14.58 pars.).... The core of the tradition is clear, as also its diverse elaboration in the different versions: Jesus's talk of destroying (*katalysai*) the temple. The case for recognizing historical memory enshrined here is surprisingly strong."[68] Not only are such traditions recurrently attested, but they are also consistent with the view—now widespread[69]—that Jesus's teaching was influenced by Jewish apocalyptic traditions.

The apocalyptic visions in Daniel repeatedly mention the interruption of the temple's cultic life (cf. Dan 8:13–14; 9:26–27; 11:3). Significantly, Je-

66. Paula Fredriksen, *When Christians Were Jews: The First Generation* (New Haven: Yale University Press, 2018), 38.

67. Gurtner, *Torn Veil*, 99.

68. James D. G. Dunn, *Jesus Remembered*, vol. 1 of *Christianity in the Making* (Grand Rapids: Eerdmans, 2003), 631–32.

69. See, e.g., Helen K. Bond, *The Historical Jesus: A Guide for the Perplexed* (London: T&T Clark, 2012), 9: "The dominant position is still to acknowledge a strongly future apocalyptic dimension to Jesus' teaching." See Allison, *Constructing Jesus*, 32–43. For greater clarity on what Allison means by "apocalyptic," see his *Jesus of Nazareth*, 154–57; Dale C. Allison Jr., "Jesus and the Victory of Apocalyptic," in *Jesus and the Restoration of Israel: A Critical Assessment of N. T. Wright's "Jesus and the Victory of God,"* ed. Carey C. Newman (Downers Grove, IL: InterVarsity Press, 1999), 126–41.

sus's announcements of the temple's future destruction employ the language of "the abomination of desolation [τὸ βδέλυγμα τῆς ἐρημώσεως]" (Matt 24:15//Mark 13:14; cf. Luke 21:20), an obvious use of Danielic imagery (Dan 9:27; 11:31; 12:11).[70] Matthew makes the connection explicit: Jesus refers to "the abomination of desolation *spoken of by the prophet Daniel*" (Matt 24:15). The nod to Daniel should not be dismissed as mere coincidence. Other aspects of Jesus's teaching about the apocalyptic future draw from Danielic motifs, including

- "tribulation" (θλῖψις; Matt 24:9, 21, 29//Mark 13:19, 24; Dan 12:1)
- nations in conflict who "rise up" (ἐγείρω; Matt 24:7//Mark 13:8//Luke 21:10; cf. Dan 7:3 [ἀναβαίνω], 17 [ἀνίστημι])
- the "handing over" (παραδίδωμι) of God's people to the persecution of rulers (Matt 24:9; Mark 13:9; Dan 7:25)
- the falling of the stars (Matt 24:29; Mark 13:25; Dan 8:10)
- and, most prominently, the coming of the "son of man" figure (Matt 24:30–31; Mark 13:26; Dan 7:13).

That Jesus himself was responsible for making such impressions of himself and of his apocalyptic teaching seems more probable than not.[71] In sum, given that Jesus's apocalyptic message was likely influenced by Daniel, it would not only make sense that part of his message would include judgment; it would also seem likely that a cessation of the temple's activity would be part of his future outlook.

If Jesus did foretell a coming judgment, it makes sense that this would be coupled with another broadly attested theme in our sources: a call to repentance. E. P. Sanders famously doubted that this latter element played a role in Jesus's message.[72] However, as Helen Bond writes, "This is perhaps the aspect of Sanders's work which has been most criticized by other scholars."[73] As James Crossley points out, "The *theme* of repentance is found across the Synoptic tradition, even if the precise words are not."[74] A brief overview of

70. The Danielic reference is caught by commentators of all three Synoptic reports. See, e.g., Luz, *Matthew*, 3:195–96; Marcus, *Mark*, 2:889; Joseph A. Fitzmyer, *The Gospel according to Luke*, AB 28–28A (New York: Doubleday, 1981–1985), 2:1345.

71. For a comprehensive argument, see Pitre, *Jesus, the Tribulation*, 219–379.

72. E. P. Sanders, *Jesus and Judaism* (Philadelphia: Fortress, 1985), 115.

73. Bond, *Historical Jesus*, 129.

74. James G. Crossley, *Jesus and the Chaos of History: Redirecting the Life of the Historical Jesus* (Oxford: Oxford University Press, 2015), 109.

these passages in which repentance and judgment are highlighted in Jesus's teaching might be helpful:

1. Woe upon Chorazin and Bethsaida for not repenting (Matt 11:21// Luke 10:13 [Q?])
2. Failure to repent like Nineveh leads to judgment (Matt 12:41// Luke 11:32 [Q?])
3. Repentance is needed because "the kingdom of heaven/God is at hand" (Matt 4:17//Mark 1:15)
4. Whoever rejects Jesus's disciples' message faces judgment (Mark 6:11)
5. Jesus sends the disciples out to proclaim repentance (Mark 6:12)
6. Unless one turns and becomes childlike, one will not enter the kingdom (Matt 18:3–4)
7. Jesus has come to call sinners to repentance (Luke 5:32)
8. "Unless you repent, you will all likewise perish" (Luke 13:3, 5)
9. "There will be more joy in heaven over one sinner who repents than over ninety-nine righteous persons" (Luke 15:7)
10. "There is joy before the angels of God over one sinner who repents" (Luke 15:10)
11. The rich man pleads to be allowed to warn his brothers to repent (Luke 16:30)
12. "Pay attention. . . . if [your brother] repents, forgive him" (Luke 17:3–4)
13. The Christ had to suffer "that repentance for the forgiveness of sins should be proclaimed in his name to all the nations" (Luke 24:47)
14. "Whoever hears my word and believes . . . has eternal life" and "does not come under judgment" (John 5:24)
15. "For judgment I came into this world, that those who do not see may see, and those who see may become blind" (John 9:39)
16. "Whoever hears my words and does not keep them . . . the word that I have spoken will be his judge" (John 12:47–48)
17. "They would not have sin, but now they have seen and hated both me and my Father" (John 15:24)

Not only is the theme of repentance recurrently attested, but it also fits comfortably within Jesus's first-century Jewish context. Highlighting numerous sources, Davies and Allison show that repentance from sin was "a central concept" in Jewish works.[75] Finally, judgment and repentance were appar-

75. Davies and Allison, *Matthew*, 1:306, citing, among other things, CD-A 4:2; 6:4–5;

ently linked in the early Jesus movement (e.g., Rom 2:4–5; 1 Cor 10:1–22; 11:27–34; 2 Cor 7:9–10; 1 Thess 1:9–10). All of this makes it difficult to insist that such elements were not a part of Jesus's message.[76]

I would submit that Matthew interprets Jesus's teaching through an apocalyptic Jewish outlook. Since Jesus's own preaching was shaped by such traditions, this can be instructive. When Matthew depicts Jesus's essential mission as saving his people from sin (Matt 1:21), this likely reflects impressions made by Jesus himself, who preached the need for repentance in view of coming judgment.

It is not surprising, then, that Matthew's portrait can combine both the traditions that Jesus endorsed the temple cult and participated in its ritual life *and* the recollection that he anticipated the temple's coming downfall. Within a Jewish context, both emphases can work together. This is especially on display in Matt 23, where Jesus issues a condemnation of scribes and Pharisees.

At one point, Jesus is remembered in Matt 23 as endorsing the holiness of the temple's sacrifices. He asks, "Which is greater, the gift or *the altar that makes the gift holy* [τὸ θυσιαστήριον τὸ ἁγιάζον τὸ δῶρον]? Therefore, whoever swears by the altar [ἐν τῷ θυσιαστηρίῳ] swears by it and by everything that is on it. And whoever swears by the temple [ἐν τῷ ναῷ] swears by it and by *the one who dwells in it*" (Matt 23:19–21; emphasis added). Here the evangelist not only portrays Jesus as affirming God's presence in the temple; Jesus states, in a strikingly Jewish way, that the sacrificial altar *itself* "makes the gift holy" (cf. Exod 29:37). Yet Jesus then goes on to announce the coming downfall of Jerusalem, which implies the coming destruction of the temple:

> Woe to you, scribes and Pharisees, hypocrites! For you build the tombs of the prophets and decorate the graves of the righteous. And you say: "If we had lived in the days of our fathers, we would not have been *sharers in the blood of the prophets* [κοινωνοὶ ἐν τῷ αἵματι τῶν προφητῶν]." Therefore, you witness against yourselves that you are the sons of those who murdered the prophets. *Fill up* [πληρώσατε], then, the measure of your fathers. You serpents, you brood of vipers, how will you escape the

---

8:16; 19:16; 20:17; 1QS 10:20; 1QH[a] 2:9; 14:24; 4Q171 3:1–3. See also the texts and discussion in Crossley, *Jesus and the Chaos of History*, 106–8.

76. Bond, *Historical Jesus*, 95. *Pace* Sanders, *Jesus and Judaism*, 117. See the critiques of Sanders in Bond, *Historical Jesus*, 129; Crossley, *Jesus and the Chaos of History*, 109–11; Craig S. Keener, *The Historical Jesus of the Gospels: Jesus in Historical Context* (Grand Rapids: Eerdmans, 2009), 44–45.

> judgment of Gehenna? For this reason, behold, I send to you prophets and wise men and scribes: and some of them you will kill and crucify, and some of them you will scourge in your synagogues and pursue from city to city, so that upon you will come all *the righteous blood poured out on the earth* [πᾶν αἷμα δίκαιον ἐκχυννόμενον], from *the blood of righteous Abel* [τοῦ αἵματος Ἅβελ τοῦ δικαίου] to *the blood of Zechariah* son of Barachiah, whom you murdered between the temple and the altar. Amen I say to you, all these things shall come upon this generation. O Jerusalem, Jerusalem, who kills the prophets and stones those who are sent to her! How often I wanted to gather your children together, as a hen gathers her young under her wings, and you were not willing! Behold, your house is left to you desolate. For I say to you, you will not see me from now on, until you say, "Blessed is he that comes in the name of the Lord" [Ps 118:26]. (Matt 23:29–39; emphasis added)

Here the religious elite are viewed as participating in the wicked deeds of previous generations. Because of their actions, the fate of the city is sealed. The spilling of Jesus's righteous blood, along with all those from Abel to Zechariah, is therefore portrayed as part of this; within the overall Gospel story, it serves as a sort of climax to the history of sin described. Within Matt 23 specifically, however, the culmination of the evil deeds committed has its locus *in the sanctuary*. Jesus identifies the spilling of righteous blood in the sanctuary as the capstone of wickedness, indicating his own outrage at the defilement of the temple.

Here is the key: none of what we have seen above supports the idea that Jesus taught that the temple cult was *invalid*. At no point have we found a passage that portrays Jesus as condemning cultic worship per se. Rather, Matthew's overall point is that the spilling of Jesus's righteous blood will ultimately trigger judgment for the sins that have been piling up for a long while. Here, however, is the crucial point for our analysis: in Matthew, *the announcement of the temple's coming destruction is not an expression of an anti-temple agenda*. The temple's holiness is affirmed even though its coming demise is anticipated.

Looking at Jesus *with* Matthew Instead of Looking at Jesus *through* Matthew

Applying the insights of memory research carries on Lagrange's project of reviving a focus on human authorship. What memory studies are revealing is that the conventional approach to Jesus research asks too much from our tools. Lagrange once wrote that "the first condition of sound historical criticism is, that we should not seek from history more than history can give."[77] I would submit that the criteria of authenticity seek to do more than is possible. To try to pry the uninterpreted "authentic" material from later "inauthentic" layers of interpretation ignores the fact that there is no uninterpreted past. Yet all is not lost. Rather than trying to look *through* Matthew's Jewish interpretations of Jesus's message, we should consider that Matthew's Jewish outlook can tell us much about the kinds of concerns that would have shaped Jesus's own teaching. Above all, Matthew shows us how, within an apocalyptic Jewish matrix, reverence for the temple can sit alongside oracles of a coming judgment in which the sanctuary is destroyed. If we think like Lagrange and take seriously Matthew's Jewish personality, we recognize how he can help us think about the kinds of priorities Jesus himself likely had, since he was also a Jew and his message was couched within an apocalyptic Jewish outlook. As Allison suggests, focusing on the details of the memories of Jesus in the Gospels may be less helpful than looking at what their broader shape can tell us. But I think that general shape can indeed tell us much.

77. Lagrange, *Historical Criticism and the Old Testament*, 13.

Jesus as God and Man in the Gospels

Père Lagrange on Mauriac's Vie de Jesus

Anthony Giambrone, OP

Who is the *homo unius libri*, the "one-book man," reputedly spoken of by Thomas Aquinas?[1] Whether this figure was originally conceived to model the wise man's exclusive focus on Scripture, or whether he was invented instead to characterize the narrow idiot savant whom one should abhor (*hominem unius libri timeo*), the label implies a forceful examination of scholarly conscience. In either case, we can easily imagine that Père Marie-Joseph Lagrange would have pleased his confrere Thomas, for Lagrange had the gift to be powerfully focused and yet exceptionally broad, to order immense learning to his all-consuming passion for Scripture.

An interesting index of this aspect of Lagrange's work appears in an often-overlooked set of opuscula. Among the 1,786 titles listed in the monumental bibliography of the founder of the École biblique, a staggering number of book reviews appears.[2] He produced thirty-nine in the year 1896, for example, with another twenty-five appearing in the following year, and thirty-four in the year thereafter. For more than four decades, Lagrange maintained this pace, digesting and discussing enormous deposits of technical literature alongside the publication of his own numerous articles, monographs, and commentaries. He canvassed titles in five modern languages, ranging imposingly over an extraordinary spectrum of challenging subjects. Hardly a branch of recondite

1. The sentence "Beware of a man of one book" appears in a celebrated American anthology of quotations, where the Latin version and attribution to St. Thomas are included in an entry under Robert Southey's name in John Bartlett, *Bartlett's Familiar Quotations*, 9th ed. (Boston: Little, Brown, and Co., 1909), 853. I am unaware of any sources prior to the seventeenth century that credit Thomas with the quote.

2. For a complete, enumerated, year-by-year listing of Lagrange's published works, see F.-M. Braun, *L'oeuvre du Père Lagrange: Étude et bibliographie* (Fribourg en Suisse: St. Paul, 1943), 191–286.

research linked to the cultural context and study of the Bible is missing. Whole domains today sequestered off as proper fields of specialization fell within his ample purview: from Semitic inscriptions and editions of Mesopotamian texts to pointed historical and exegetical studies to pertinent theological treatises and at times even belles lettres, if occasion arose. The scale of Lagrange's *studiositas* naturally appears beyond the reviews as well; his articles and private journal reveal a still greater depth of reading. From Vergil and Dante to Goethe and Herder right down to the latest novels, Lagrange mastered far more than the secondary scholarship of the day. Yet he always had the Scriptures foremost in his mind, turning his learning to exegetical profit. The father of modern Catholic biblical study understood well that to read the Bible rightly, one had to be a good reader *tout simple.*

One of the most enduring of his numerous reviews came near the very end of Lagrange's productive life and career. In 1936, less than two years before his death, the veteran scholar wrote a substantial twenty-four page response to the recently published *Vie de Jésus* of his younger contemporary François Mauriac.[3] For multiple reasons, it is instructive today to revisit the seasoned exegete's reply to the bold novelistic foray of Mauriac, a confessing Catholic, *académicien*, and future Nobel laureate in literature. Mauriac's effort to capture by his art the christological mystery of Jesus was coupled with an open reproach aimed at the failures of "the exegetes" on all sides. The very first sentence of the book openly throws down the gauntlet: "Of all the historians, the exegete is the most disappointing" (*De tous les historiens, l'exégète est le plus décevant*).[4] What follows is not more generous to the guild. In this sense, despite mentioning Lagrange by name as a sort of rare exception, Mauriac put the priest's profession directly on trial. The confrontation of these two great but very different French Christian voices thus takes on a special interest, and Lagrange's response was not without force. The review ultimately helped Mauriac quietly rethink his own position and release a revised second edition of the book. If the exegete thus finally prevailed over the artist as a superior reader of the Gospels, the problem at stake in this short episode was above all how to discern and describe the role of grace and the two natures of Christ.

In what follows, after first positioning the *Vie de Jésus* within Mauriac's life and oeuvre, I will discuss the review written by Lagrange. This will open the

3. Marie-Joseph Lagrange, OP, "La *Vie de Jésus* par M. François Mauriac," *RB* 45, no.3 (1936): 321–45. See François Mauriac, *Vie de Jésus* (Paris: Flammarion, 1936).

4. Mauriac, *Vie de Jésus*, vii.

way for a concluding reflection on the question of theological hermeneutics raised by this interesting but forgotten exchange.

Mauriac's *Vie de Jesus*

Mauriac's *Vie de Jesus* is a biography of Jesus with a strong autobiographical color. At the time of its publication in 1936, one critic even snickered that the book was more a life of Mauriac channeled through Jesus than a biography of Jesus authored by Mauriac: "Ce n'est pas une *Vie de Jésus* par François Mauriac mais une *Vie de François Mauriac* par Jésus."[5]

The book appeared on the far side of a serious moral crisis in the author's own life, which lasted for approximately three years, from 1925 to 1928, and ended with what the lifelong Catholic afterward called his "conversion."[6] At root was the father of four's intense temptation to commit adultery,[7] a harrowing interior trial that he ultimately overcame through the concerned intervention of Jacques Maritain.[8] Moreover, the faith itself, and not only morals, was at stake in the matter, for just as Mauriac was fighting this thorn in the flesh, he confronted what he saw as a forced choice between the authenticity of his art and an equally honest belief. He could not see how to remain at once both a sincere believer and a real artist. Mauriac's account of what then happened is intentionally sparse on detail, but his life was changed, he said, for putting up no resistance: "I was miraculously cured, literally, without doing anything except not to say no."[9] Whatever transpired, what emerged in the end was not merely a deepened Christian conviction on Mauriac's part but a powerful new insight into the psychology and theology of sin. This fueled, in turn, a new preoccupation with the workings of grace and a new stage of expression in the novelist's craft. Indeed, in the view of

5. Cited in François Mauriac, *Les paroles restent* (Paris: Grasset, 1985), 108.

6. See Claude Escallier, "La spiritualité de François Mauriac," *Etudes de langue et littérature françaises* 60 (1992): 108–23.

7. A recent, controversial two-volume biography suggests that Mauriac had multiple homosexual affairs. See Jean-Luc Barré, *François Mauriac – Biographie intime* (Paris: Fayard, 2009–2010).

8. Maritain introduced Mauriac to a certain Abbé Altermann, a priest with a special touch for reaching intellectuals and artists (for example, Jean Cocteau).

9. "C'est bien simple, je suis converti. . . . N'en parlez pas. J'ai été miraculé, à la lettre, sans rien faire que de ne pas dire non." Letter to Henri Guillemin, cited in Barré, *Mauriac*, 1:423.

Claude Escallier, this personal experience of conversion and the *Vie de Jésus* that soon followed represent a fundamental pivot and central phenomenon in Mauriac's artistic career.[10]

Notwithstanding the importance of this pivot, the arc taken by Mauriac's career shows that he retained his attention to the phenomenon of human sin. Established as an acclaimed author since the early 1920s, Mauriac had a fixed thematic interest in what Pascal called "l'usage criminal et delicieux du monde," the doomed and sordid pleasure of fallen fleshly passions: "le misère de l'homme sans Dieu" (the wretchedness of man without God). A gloomy atmosphere envelops his unsympathetic characters, for whom the power of religion and respectability has no salvific force and whose downward trajectories lead them consistently to end up more miserable than they began. This is clear from the time of his breakthrough novel, *Le baiser au lépreux*, in 1922. But the best example comes in Mauriac's most famous work, *Thérèse Desqueyroux*, published in 1927, at the height of his personal crisis, a work later mentioned in his 1952 Nobel citation. The story concerns the tragically unhappy marriage of a melancholic woman who tries to poison her husband, fails, is falsely acquitted, and must then continue living with him in an impossible fate of intense hypocrisy, suffering, and aversion. Mauriac often remarked that whatever he tried, he could not convert Thérèse (he wrote three more novels about her). More revealing still (with a wink at Flaubert), he also confessed that the character was a figure of himself: "Thérèse Desqueyroux, c'est moi!" It is little surprise if Mauriac's reputation as a Catholic author was cause for laughter in 1928.[11] To this day, there are those who reckon him to be "an insidious sensualist posing as a Catholic."[12]

Despite Mauriac's lifelong preoccupation with the workings of sin, and despite those who have doubted the authenticity of his turn to God, the string of novels that commences after Mauriac's "conversion" is immediately marked by a notable new plot trajectory. In contrast to doomed figures like Madame Desqueyroux, his later characters, though still gripped by perverse desires, begin to manifest late-life changes of course. After a false start with

10. See Claude Escallier, *Mauriac et l'évangile* (Paris: Beauchesne, 1993). See also Jason Lewallen, "Interpreting Conversion: Hermeneutic Training in François Mauriac's *Le noeud de vipères*," *Christianity & Literature* 68, no. 2 (2019): 213–32.

11. A letter to Mauriac from Roger Martin du Gard exposes this perception: "Je rigole, mon cher Mauriac, je rigole quand on fait de vous un écrivain du catholicisme! Il n'y a pas une oeuvre d'incrédule ou d'athee ou le péché soit plus exaltée." Cited in Lewallen, "Interpreting Conversion," 214.

12. Lewallen, "Interpreting Conversion," 213.

his first effort to articulate his new vision (in the book *Ce qui était perdu*, 1930), Mauriac's revised Christian plotline attained a structural brilliance in *Le noeud de vipères* (1932). Here the wretched and hateful protagonist's final turn to religion at the end of his life is left open-ended in the narration, and the reader is left with two contesting interpretations: that of the man's son, who doubts the sincerity of his father's conversion, and that of his granddaughter, who contends that her grandfather's final faith was real. The ingenious effect of this open ending not only avoids an overwrought deus ex machina and final moralizing thrust at edification; it also casts the readers themselves within the story, observing and judging the action's final outcome, thus positioning the interpretation of the novel within the novel's own frame. It thereby directly confronts those doubting the sincerity of Mauriac's own conversion. For contemporary critics, such as Jason Lewallen, *Le noeud de vipères* is accordingly not to be dismissed as a moralistic *roman à these* but to be appreciated instead as a type of "formative fiction," a text that trains its readers to adopt a particular worldview rather than coercively preaching or protesting too much.[13]

It is not incidental that this exceedingly light touch, which Mauriac gave to the grace of conversion in *Le noeud de vipères*, recalls the story of Thérèse of Lisieux and the repentance of the murderer Pranzini, famously recounted in chapter 11 of Thérèse's *The Story of a Soul*. Did the wicked criminal really convert, or did he not? Versions differ, while Thérèse herself was from the start prepared to go without any obvious sign to confirm her trust in the criminal's last-minute conversion. Mauriac's own personal discovery of grace owed much to St. Thérèse and this form of a hope in divine mercy that is more buoyant than all the heavy sludge and overwhelming evidence of sin. One was never forced to deny even suffocating sinful darkness; grace itself might remain entirely unseen. In Thérèse's conception of an "all is grace" sort of mercy, Mauriac found his way back to an alternative spiritual childhood modeled on the Little Flower: an open antithesis to the pessimistic austerity of his own Jansenism-tinged youth, a sweet *folie de confiance*—an audacious, almost foolish trust—that he linked to the folly of the cross in a letter to Maritain.[14] In simple trust, Mauriac defied the most grievous mortal sins and discovered the gracious mercy of a God who was not repulsed even by the worst of humankind's sinful passions ("qu'aucune de nos passions les plus tristes ne rebute").

13. Lewallen, "Interpreting Conversion," 219.
14. François Mauriac, *Nouvelles lettres d'une vie 1906–1970* (Paris: Grasset, 1989), 137.

It is precisely in the wake of this forceful encounter with a new vision of grace and divine mercy that the *Vie de Jésus* must be understood. Literarily, of course, undertaking to write a life of Jesus represented a very bold step beyond the artistic solution Mauriac had found in *Le noeud de vipères*. An entirely different order of narrative possibilities emerged here for advancing his theology of the victory of God's grace over sin.[15] But formidable new challenges also faced him.

Mauriac had already penned two biographies: *La vie de Jean Racine* (1928) and *Blaise Pascal et sa sœur Jacqueline* (1931). He had likewise increasingly become an essayist on religious themes.[16] The task of rewriting the Gospels' account of Jesus's singular triumph of grace from the perspective of an author of novelistic fiction nonetheless presented Mauriac with the new and exceptionally delicate problem of affirming the story's forceful reality—the actual victory of God's mercy—while adventurously probing the psychology not only of sinners but even of the sinless Jesus himself.

In his *Vie de Jésus*, the dialectic of sin and grace as it had taken shape in Mauriac's new way of thinking became, at one level, the daring exposure of a certain impotence of Jesus, a specific incapacity to overcome the tenacious hold of sin upon fallen humankind. "For Mauriac, Christ seems powerless before hearts subject to the reign of concupiscence or of wealth. The battlements raised are such that the Son of Man cannot enter in without the surrender of these cities that defy his rule. 'Neither the wind nor the sea can resist him,' writes Mauriac, 'but hearts torn apart by love and the flesh roused by desire possess a fanatical power to refuse.'"[17] The unplumbable depths of human vileness and evil somehow overwhelm the reach and resources even of Jesus's own powers, which might thus be shrouded in a sort

15. "Le Christ de Mauriac est celui qui s'avance vers l'homme abandonné à sa chair, à ses turpitudes. Et de cette rencontre peut naître l'inimaginable: le triomphe de la Grâce sur le déchaînement des passions." Philippe Dazet-Brun, "Mauriac et sa *Vie de Jésus*: Le romancier devenu biographe," *Anabasis* 28 (2018): 245.

16. The following titles reveal Mauriac's religious turn of mind: *Supplément au Traité de la concupiscence de Bossuet* (1928); *Souffrances du chrétien* (1928), *Bonheur du chrétien* (1929), and *Souffrances et bonheur du chrétien* (1931); *Petits essais de psychologie religieuse* (1933).

17. Dazet-Brun, "Mauriac," 242–43. "Pour Mauriac, le Christ semble impuissant devant les cœurs soumis à l'empire de la concupiscence ou à celui du lucre. Les remparts dressés sont tels que le Fils de l'homme ne peut y pénétrer sans une capitulation de ces cités rétives à son règne. 'Ni le vent ni la mer ne lui résistent,' écrit Mauriac, 'mais les cœurs déchirés par l'amour, mais la chair soulevée par le désir ont une puissance forcenée de refus.'"

of destitute darkness. Mauriac was determined to expose this weakness and so to offer a rendering of the gospel in which the dark drama of Jesus's mortal struggle with sin was not betrayed through pious platitudes or moralizing misdirection.

Naturally, this aspect of the crushing human failure of Jesus before the weight of sin and even unto his own death on the cross does not encompass the entirety of Mauriac's message. As true Son of God, infinite divine love—infinite mercy—is also at work in the person of Jesus; and the conquering, prevenient power of his supernatural love is obviously no less central to the Gospel than the countering strength of human sin in the flesh. The critical challenge for Mauriac as an author was to balance and properly portray the theological and psychological tension of these two forces in a Jesus at once fully divine and fully human.

In the *Vie de Jésus*, the dialectic of sin and grace has thus assumed new shape as the more stark dialectic of man and God in Christ. Thirty years later, in his *Bloc-notes*, Mauriac says quite plainly: "At the time when I dared to write a *Life of Jesus*, during most of my labor, I ran up against this contradiction of the two natures, against the impossibility of this cohabitation, in one living being, of a fisherman from Nazareth and the Son of God."[18] The christological shape of the dialectics of grace additionally maps onto another dichotomy, an exegetical division already clearly announced in the preface to the *Vie de Jésus*. Here Mauriac sets modern biblical scholars as a foil, splitting the world of exegetes neatly into two groups: believers and unbelievers. There are "those types" who reject the supernatural straightaway and never discern the divine nature of Jesus; and there is the more pious Christian exegete, who instead submerges the manhood of Jesus in the "blinding light" of the second person of the Godhead—"la fulguration de la deuxième Personne divine."[19]

The simplicity of this latter division clearly owes something to Mauriac's own history of reading the Gospels; for, with an entire generation, he had been profoundly troubled by the raging Modernist crisis, to the point that for years he could no longer read or trust the Gospel of John. A certain facile type of pious reaction obviously also did not content him. When Mauriac

18. François Mauriac, *1968–1970*, vol. 5 of *Bloc-notes*, ed. Jean Touzot (Paris: Seuil, 1993), 327. "À l'époque où j'ai osé écrire une Vie de Jésus, je me suis heurté, durant la plus grande partie de mon travail, à cette contradiction des deux natures, à l'impossibilité de cette cohabitation, dans un être vivant, de ce pêcheur nazaréen et du Fils de Dieu."

19. Mauriac, *Vie de Jésus*, vii.

accordingly seeks with his *Vie de Jésus* to accommodate both the divine and the human in Jesus, he is, in his fashion, attempting what Lagrange also, in a very different manner, set as his own committed life's work: to provide a compelling, orthodox answer to modernism. Mauriac's effort at a truly Chalcedonian balance in this way vaunts his particular literary solution as accomplishing what professional exegesis somehow failed to secure: an authentic Catholic reading of the Gospels.

Lagrange's Review

In the copy of the first edition of Mauriac's text held in the library of the École biblique, page ix of the preface is marked in pencil by an unmistakable hand. Twice in the margin, in the tight script of Père Lagrange, the word "Non" is written and demonstratively underlined. Once it contests Mauriac's claim that Jesus issued from the lower class, and once it disputes Mauriac's still bolder description of Jesus as "angry, impatient, sometimes furious" (*irrité, impatient, quelquefois furieux*). It was the latter of these points that tested Lagrange's own patience the most.

The impact made by Mauriac's *Vie de Jésus* was predictable: it was, Lagrange says, an unprecedented success.[20] Since 1933, the author had been a member of the *Académie française*, and such stature drew inevitable attention to this peculiar and highly confessional work. For some, the book promised to reawaken a complacent Christian faith, degraded into pious convention and grown insensitive to the raw force of the gospel message. One reviewer hailed the book as a sign of enormous hope.[21] Jules Lebreton, a Jesuit to whom Mauriac had shown the unfinished manuscript, lauded the intensity and genuineness of the author's Christian witness.[22] Other reactions were also to be heard, however. Édouard Dujardin, for instance, saw the work confirming his own skeptical views, undermining a naive faith in Jesus's very existence: "With his *Vie de Jésus*, M. Mauriac has not written his best novel; but he has doubtless brought grist to the mill for the many people who are beginning to doubt the historicity of his hero."[23]

20. Lagrange, "*Vie de Jésus*," 21.

21. Max-Pol Fouchet, "François Mauriac: Vie de Jésus," *Esprit* 44 (1936): 228–29.

22. "C'est un chrétien qui rend témoignage à son Maitre; le témoignage est véritable, beaucoup l'entendront, et le Maitre l'agréera." Jules Lebreton, "La Vie de Jésus de F. Mauriac: Le témoignage d'un chrétien," *Études* 227 (April, 1936): 57.

23. Édouard Dujardin, "Le Jésus de M. Mauriac," *Europe* (June 15, 1936), 204.

Against this excited background buzz, Lagrange's intervention was helpfully nuanced and focused. He begins by offering an echo of the high-flown reactions and the questions being asked about Mauriac's book. Did it truly mark a "new era" in the history of the study of Jesus? Without ever offering a simple reply to this question, Lagrange's implicit answer tempers the enthusiasm in notable ways while paying Mauriac the respect he deserves. Above all, however, Lagrange redirects the discussion to put the focus where he always prefers to place it: How can this new work help us better understand the person of Jesus?[24]

Promptly plotting the text against the grid of previous *Leben-Jesu-Forschung*, Lagrange briefly highlights the contrasting German and French strains of Jesus research. He recalls in succinct fashion facts that were well-known to his readers: the two editions of Strauss's skeptical *Life of Jesus* and the fact that liberal German Protestantism, exemplified by Harnack, though dispensing with Jesus's divinity, was determined nevertheless to retain his person and doctrine. On the French side, several landmarks are also mentioned, which help to situate Mauriac's book.

Of first importance, of course, was Ernest Renan, whose own *Vie de Jésus* remained a cultural point of reference. Renan had rejected not only the church's Christ but the Germans' approach as well, supplying France with its own sickeningly sweet "charmer," a "Jesus douceatre." Lagrange collects a small catalog of citations illustrating Renan's distastefully sugary Jesus; and Lagrange is clearly of one mind with Mauriac that this is all too much to stomach. Yet, as Lagrange recounts, Loisy had already long since dispensed with Renan, for Loisy recognized that the Germans took Jesus more seriously as a real historical figure. Loisy thus dropped Renan's gentle Jesus and turned French scholarship in a more solid scholarly direction, co-opting the apocalyptic Jew presented by Johannes Weiss. Loisy ostensibly deployed this prophetic, Jewish Jesus against Harnack's own compromised liberal project—tacking on a nominal admission of Jesus's divinity.[25]

Lagrange makes mention of one additional author and his extreme position, fitted to the French taste for "straightforward solutions, no matter how radical" (*solutions franches, fussent-elles radicales*): Paul-Louis Couchoud,

"M. Mauriac n'a pas, avec sa Vie de Jésus, écrit son meilleur roman; mais sans doute a-t-il apporté de l'eau au moulin des nombreuses personnes qui commencent à douter de l'historicité de son héros."

24. Lagrange, "La *Vie de Jésus,*" 321.

25. On Loisy's reply to Harnack see Anthony Giambrone, OP, "Aux sources du petit livre rouge de Loisy," *Codex* 23 (April 2022).

who held that Jesus never existed. The traction this excessive position enjoyed is evident from Dujardin's review, cited above. Lagrange credited the two men with at least this one real insight: one does not raise a cult around the figure of a vulgar criminal or make a God from a mere notice in the evening news. Despite the conclusion that the radical critics drew from this premise, there is an honesty in the way they posed the problem. *Everything* is somehow simultaneously at stake in giving an account of Jesus's life: his humanity and his divinity hang together or fall together. It is characteristic of Lagrange to discern in this way the integral historical and theological importance even of a wild position.[26]

How does Mauriac fit within this range of perspectives, in Lagrange's opinion? The novelist's contribution is most certainly not that it set Jesus within his true historical context; on this point Lagrange is clear.[27] Others, like Loisy, had already made greater strides toward a historically accurate presentation, and Renan himself had at least taken the trouble to travel through Galilee. Mauriac, by contrast, admitted to having done no research beyond simply reading the Gospels.[28] However much this was calculated to avoid what earlier lives of Jesus had simply invented, a manifest lack of learning inevitably shows. The new *Vie de Jésus* scores poorly on the historical-critical report card. Neglecting many worthy studies that might have informed his work leaves Mauriac's text open to any number of evident errors—for instance, a number of geographical howlers (e.g., Jesus finds Nathanael at Bethany instead of Bethsaida). They are minor points perhaps, but without belaboring the issue, the old exegete begs the "wicked little pleasure" of showing the pertinence of his ignored lifetime of diligent labor.

> Put yourself in the place of an old commentator. He has taken great pains to fix the smallest details of the text. If he lived in the Holy Land, he measured the distances, counted the steps, had the names spelled out, ascertained traditional habits and customs. Let us therefore give this veteran that wicked little pleasure, as a consolation for his inferiority as a writer,

26. See Marie-Joseph Lagrange, OP, *Le sens du christiansime d'après l'exégèse allemande*, EBib 5 (Paris: Gabalda, 1918); and Anthony Giambrone, OP, *A Quest for the Historical Christ: Scientia Christi and the Modern Study of Jesus* (Washington, DC: Catholic University of America Press, 2022), 51–71.

27. Lagrange, "La *Vie de Jésus*," 324.

28. See the source cited in Lagrange, "La *Vie de Jésus*," 328.

> of pointing out certain matters of negligence in the geographical data of the land, which cannot be solicited or moved about like the texts.[29]

Still, after noting this sloppiness on the topographical plane, it would be a mistake, Lagrange says, to try to catch Mauriac on such trifles. These material details hold no interest for this author's higher project, which aims to penetrate to a deeper order of knowledge, into the psyche itself.[30]

In allowing the work to be judged on its own terms and stepping with Mauriac beyond a strict historical discussion of Jesus, Lagrange makes a revealing concession. Having indulged his "wicked little pleasure," Lagrange is not a petty exegete unable to transcend the order of historical analysis and his own expert field of research. He is content even to follow Mauriac's bold exploration of the psychological workings of Jesus—an undertaking that risks naive impertinence. In permitting this, Lagrange manifests a characteristic extension of sympathetic good will. Still, as we shall see, he never wavers in theological rigor. He likewise shows no interest at all in Mauriac's wider depictions of the psychology of sinners in the Gospels but remains exclusively interested in the book's specific depiction of Jesus. "The entire interest of the book is in the value of this psychological probe—a supreme interest indeed, for Jesus is the very essence of Christianity."[31] How successful is the work, then, on this decisive score?

Lagrange is very gracious to Mauriac's Christian intention, even touched by the great man's simple faith.[32] Nonetheless, he is unambiguous and stringent in his exegetical and theological judgment. The novelist has embraced a streak of illogicality as the marker of the inner life of Jesus's person. Indeed, for Mauriac, Jesus is "the least logical because he is the most alive" (*le moins logique parce qu'il est le plus vivant*).[33] For Lagrange, this dubious formulation is at once inaccurate and a riddle. Must life be illogical? Jesus in his

29. Lagrange, "La *Vie de Jésus*," 325. "Mettez-vous à la place d'un vieux commentateur. Il s'est donné beaucoup de mal pour fixer les moindres détails du texte. S'il a vécu en Terre Sainte, il a mesuré les distances, compté les pas, fait épeler les noms, s'est informé des us et coutumes héréditaires. Donnons donc à ce vétéran cette petite satisfaction maligne, pour le consoler d'être si inférieur comme écrivain, de relever quelques négligences dans les données géographiques du sol, qui ne se laisse pas solliciter ni déplacer comme les textes."

30. "Son oeuvre ressortit à la psychologie pure." Lagrange, "La *Vie de Jésus*," 324.

31. Lagrange, "La *Vie de Jésus*," 326. "Tout l'intérêt du livre est dans la valeur de cet examen psychologique, un intérêt suprême, car Jésus, c'est l'essence même du christianisme."

32. Lagrange, "La *Vie de Jésus*," 326.

33. Mauriac, *Vie de Jésus*, viii.

manhood seems, in the view of Lagrange, to have been entirely dominated by his mission as messenger of the kingdom and to have been, in this way, quite impressively logically consistent.[34] Mauriac's Jesus, by contrast, is an often inscrutable and capricious force. He appears tossed between fits of frustrated humanity and serene divine affection, simultaneously outmatched and in sovereign, loving control.

Lagrange registers here his obvious displeasure, especially at the way Mauriac has handled Jesus's anger—a sensitive issue for Lagrange, as noted above. Mauriac, he says, has "greatly exaggerated" (*fort exagéré*) the anger of Jesus.[35] The distortion is condemned by Lagrange in the first place for its infidelity to the Gospel sources. Whatever the novelistic and theological intention, Mauriac introduces Christ's anger into situations where no indication exists for it in the texts themselves. Mauriac's contention that a reservoir of profound peace lies beneath this irritable surface ("violence apparente et calme dans la profondeur"[36]) does little to assuage Lagrange's acute concern. Is this appearance of anger merely a docetic show, he wonders. This would hardly serve to highlight the humanity that Mauriac is at pains to expose.

A second and closely allied exaggeration concerning Christ's humanity is also astutely flagged by Lagrange. Once the voluble anger of Mauriac's Jesus finally subsides, he sinks into a sort of malaise of battered resignation—"nothing can irritate or even surprise him anymore" (*rien ne peut plus l'irriter ni même l'étonner*).[37] He has no more energy except to submit and endure. By Passion Week, Christ is thus already defeated and "out of steam" (*à bout de soufflé*). "All that remains of Jesus's strength is to cope and suffer."[38] This again, in Lagrange's estimation, simply does not accord with the texts. As the Gospels recount it, Jesus mounts an energetic entrance into Jerusalem and asserts himself in the temple with dazzling force, enthralling the crowd and thrusting his enemies back on their heels, provoking *them* to react—not simply slumping fatigued and beaten into their hands (e.g., Luke 22:41–44; Mark 12:35–37; Matt 21:42–46).

It is not, in the end, that Lagrange wants to say that exhaustion and anger have no place in the story of Jesus. He simply calls for greater moderation in depicting the humanity of Christ and greater care, ultimately, in attending to what the Gospels actually reveal.

34. Lagrange, "La *Vie de Jésus*," 329.

35. Lagrange, "La *Vie de Jésus*," 331.

36. Mauriac, *Vie de Jésus*, x.

37. Mauriac, *Vie de Jésus*, 189.

38. Mauriac, *Vie de Jésus*, 212. "Seule reste à Jésus la force de supporter et de souffrir."

> That Jesus may have shown a more ardent character, that he may have suffered more at seeing those perish whom he had come to save, that these powerful emotions may have manifested themselves in irritation and painful dejection, is often alleged as a proof that he possessed a truly human nature, more human in its depths than some frigid affectation, a stoicism which would not go without disdain. But one should not exaggerate, and it seemed to us, on rereading the texts, that Mr. Mauriac did not avoid this pitfall.[39]

The adjunct to Mauriac's overdrawn image of the ragged limitations of Jesus's humanity is at first more amenable to Lagrange's spiritual taste. In dialectical tandem with Jesus's created nature, enmeshed in its death struggle with a fallen world, appears the radiant divine pole of Jesus's persona. It is above all here, in Mauriac's expressions of the mercy of Jesus, that one senses the sincere genius of the author. But even here, Lagrange's theological eye remains uncompromisingly sharp.

If the exegete openly chastened Mauriac's vision of the human Jesus, the Dominican theologian has still more to offer concerning the *académicien*'s Jesus as God. Mauriac promises us something other than an excessively saccharine Jesus, but what doctrine has the novelist presumed in casting God's love and Jesus's godly nature as he does? It is a merciful love that reaches so far beyond any interest in the good works of man to be called by Mauriac a sort of loving "injustice." By that same token, however, this very excess of love becomes a predilection that can look ruthlessly arbitrary. He writes: "And such is the injustice of love: on that day, of two women occupied at the same task, the one will be taken and saved, the other abandoned."[40] Can divine love be the cause not only of being saved but also of being abandoned, Lagrange poignantly wonders. Jesus's illogical streak encroaches on his divine nature here in a way that leaves the exegete increasingly uneasy. Without naming it, an extreme conception of efficacious grace—and its

39. Lagrange, "La *Vie de Jésus*," 334. "Que Jésus ait montré un caractère plus ardent, qu'il ait souffert davantage de voir se perdre ceux qu'il était venu sauver, que ces émotions puissantes se soient manifestées par de l'irritation et un abattement douloureux, c'est une preuve souvent alléguée qu'il possédait une nature vraiment humaine, plus humaine dans ses profondeurs qu'une affectation de froideur, stoïcisme qui n'irait pas sans dédain. Mais il ne fallait pas exagérer, et il nous a paru, à relire les textes, que M. Mauriac n'a pas évité cet écueil."

40. Mauriac, *Vie de Jésus*, 191. "Et telle est l'injustice de l'amour: en ce jour-là, de deux femmes occupées à la même besogne, l'une sera prise et sauvée, l'autre abandonné."

shadow of reprobation—has taken hold of Mauriac's Jesus, a theology that Lagrange clearly finds repellent, but deliciously calls a "blunt" and "a tad outdated" Thomism (*franc thomisme . . . quelque peu dépassé*).[41] Even allowing for paradoxical formulations, Mauriac has embraced another dangerous exaggeration, Lagrange contends.

The story of the rich young man serves as a significant illustration. It is one of the Gospels' most subtle and moving revelations of Jesus's love. Yet Mauriac takes the occasion to articulate a theology rather worrisome for Lagrange. Filling the moment between Jesus's invitation to follow him and the young man's saddened response, the novelist supplies the following: "Had Jesus not loved him with a special love, he would doubtless have given this young man the power to leave just as others had done. He had subjected him to an all-powerful grace. But love wants to obtain nothing from the beloved that is not given freely. This stranger was too well loved to be forcibly ravished. The Son of Man was awaiting a spontaneous movement of the heart, some impulse, from him."[42] This appears to Lagrange a tad too abstract ("un peu quintessencié"), even for human love; but for divine love, he finds it strange and downright concerning. Does not God's love always suppose the consent of the beloved? And if a fitting consent does not have its source in God's own all-powerful grace, whence shall it spontaneously arise? Lagrange diagnoses a confused theological tangle, mixed up somewhere between Calvinist and semi-Pelagian commitments: on the one hand, a grace that requires no consent; on the other, an anterior, spontaneous consent. "We are oscillating," Lagrange writes, "or rather Mr. Mauriac puts himself outside the extreme oscillations of the Catholic pendulum."[43]

Lest this appear to be a fussy theological digression, Lagrange brings home the critical point. The story of the young rich man is in fact, for Lagrange, one of the Gospels' most exceptional revelations of Jesus's *human* love. It is not, as Mauriac insists, a depiction of some "brutal" intervention

41. Lagrange mentions no specific Thomists by name, but he may have earlier rigorists like Tomás de Lemos and Diego Alvarez in mind. Billuart corrected these authors' positions, and his corrections were later embraced by Garrigou-Lagrange.

42. Mauriac, *Vie de Jésus*, 196. "Si Jésus ne l'avait pas aimé d'une dilection particulière, sans doute eût-il donné à ce jeune homme la force de quitter tout comme d'autres l'avaient fait. Il l'eut soumis à une grâce toute-puissante. Mais l'amour ne veut rien obtenir de qu'il aime, qui ne soit librement consenti. Pour être ravi de force, cet inconnu était trop aimé. Le Fils de l'homme attendait de lui un mouvement spontané du cœur, un élan."

43. Lagrange, "La *Vie de Jésus*," 336. "Nous oscillons, ou plutôt M. Mauriac se place en dehors des oscillations extrêmes du pendule catholique."

of an all-powerful divine mode of loving.[44] With wonderful irony, Lagrange then adds as a parenthetical postscript a little riposte with reference to Mauriac's preface: "And here is a case, surely very notable, where the perspective of the exegete—for sometimes one is an exegete in spite of oneself—could well have been obscured by the blinding light of the second divine Person [la fulguration de la second Personne divine]."[45] It is the Christian novelist, in other words, who has fallen prey to that very same trap from which he high-mindedly sought to set the Christian exegete free. This is in fact the most sensitive point ("le point le plus délicat") that Lagrange, in the end, felt compelled to make: Mauriac has consistently confused Jesus's (unconfused) divine and human natures.[46]

Mauriac's explanation of the purpose of the parables provides an additional case where Lagrange, on the same point, must again put the novelist back in his place—gently, but also with mounting verve. Mauriac supposed himself to have easily solved an issue that had long stumped biblical scholars, whom he disparaged for their stupid lack of insight. The parables, he claims, are designed both to give light to the simple and from others to positively hide the doctrine that Jesus reveals, recalling Jesus's explanation for his use of parables by citing Isaiah's words that the people will "see and not see" (cf. Mark 4:12; Isa 6:9). Lagrange concedes that for a Jansenist of Port Royal, this double operation, with its active work of blinding, might well be an attrac-

44. "L'auteur a exprimé la fraicheur de cette affection avec son charme coutumier: 'Jésus l'ayant regardé, l'aima.' 'Après l'avoir regardé . . . Une certaine expression touchait le Fils de l'homme, — cette grâce d'un jeune être: cette lumière des yeux qui vient de l'âme' (p. 195). Mais de quel droit ajouter: 'Il l'aima donc et comme un Dieu à qui tout est soumis, sans aucune préparation, presque brutalement.' — Si la nature divine était intervenue, à qui tout est soumis, la grâce eût eu raison de ce jeune homme, et il n'y aurait point à imaginer une démarche préliminaire de sa part. *Jésus l'a aimé comme homme, et c'est comme homme qu'il a exprimé sa tristesse, abandonnant le riche découragé a la grâce de Dieu et a son libre arbitre.*" Lagrange, "La *Vie de Jésus*," 337 (italics added).

45. Lagrange, "La *Vie de Jésus*," 337. "Et voilà un cas, assurément très notable, ou le regard de l'exégète—car on l'est parfois malgré soi,—pourrait bien avoir été obscurci par la fulguration de la second Personne divine."

46. "Voici le point le plus délicat. M. Mauriac a voulu nous rendre l'humanité de Jésus tout entière, telle qu'elle est fixée par les évangélistes, humanité qu'on avait trop souvent atténuée, sacrifice a la manifestation du Verbe. Avant lui, les exégètes catholiques en majorité ont eu leur regard obscurci par la fulguration de la deuxième Personne divine: c'est la formule que nous ramenons toujours. Et je me vois contraint d'avancer que lui-même a fait apparaître la divinité dans des actions ou nos anciens auteurs voyait simplement l'humanité de Jésus, enrichie, cela va sans dire, de cette grâce suprême qui convenait à l'union de nature avec une personne divine." Lagrange, "La *Vie de Jésus*," 339.

tive idea.[47] Still, he meekly protests, one may excuse the exegetes for having searched in Isaiah's original citation in order to find an understanding that was perhaps a bit less horrific ("moins terrible"). That the parables give light to the simple is true; it is explained by the rustic Galilean upbringing and the native pedagogical skill of Jesus's human nature. The rather perverse theory of an active work of blinding, by contrast, is again the false view of one blinded by a false apparition of "la fulguration d'une Personne divine."[48]

The problem here becomes a recurring embarrassment when it comes to Jesus's supernatural gifts. It thus arises with Jesus's prophecy of the destruction of the temple; for again Lagrange finds Mauriac overtly displacing Jesus's humanity with his divine nature.[49] Yes, it is beautifully audacious, but is it a proof of divinity to defy time by the light of prophetic knowledge? What of the miracles? Is it Jesus's divinity that blazes forth ("fulgurates") in the calming of the storm at sea? This is not, Lagrange notes, what Matt 8:27 implies. What about the miracle of the loaves? None of Jesus's mighty works, in fact, surpasses what Moses or Elijah accomplished, as the Jews of Jesus's day could rightly protest.

The ultimate sign, for Lagrange, of Mauriac's serious christological misstep—Mauriac who desired to portray the Son of Man without sacrificing anything of his humanity to his divine nature—is that the devout novelist has misrepresented the love between Jesus and his mother. And this is a matter of "souveraine importance" for Christian piety, the exegete says.[50] Without ever denying Mary's firm faith in the divinity of Jesus, Mauriac erects a barrier in the connection and intimacy of mother and son. This appears in multiple passages: twice Mauriac says that Jesus wishes to drive her away ("repousser"); at another point he pretends that they spoke only the most necessary, practical words ("aucun colloque entre eut n'est imaginable"); and so on. All told, Lagrange finds a profoundly disturbing lack of Christian feeling.

> Mr. Mauriac insists, with a logic that one would not have believed of his taste. In at least one place, he comes quite close to envisioning the divine maternity as a matter of necessity that involved no intimacy, no

47. "Le texte serait en effet limpide dans l'hypothèse des jansénistes; quant à la terreur, on sait que Port-Royal trouvait une sorte de délectation sacrée dans le jugement divin d'endurcissement." Lagrange, "La *Vie de Jésus*," 337.

48. Lagrange, "La *Vie de Jésus*," 338.

49. Lagrange, "La *Vie de Jésus*," 340.

50. Lagrange, "La *Vie de Jésus*," 341.

> exchange of thought through kind words, for fear of compromising the independence of God: "None of Christ's words to his mother, as told in the Gospels (excepting the last), fail to manifest harshly his independence with regard to the woman: as if he had used her to become incarnate, had come out of that flesh, and beyond that there was nothing in common between her and him."[51]

Opposite exaggerations, Lagrange freely admits, are possible in excessively pious forms of Marian devotion; but one discerns the sure sign here of a theologian who has lost his way—and the way taken by the whole tradition—to the full humanity of Jesus.

With this characteristic turn to the mother of Jesus, Lagrange is content to close his review. In the final assessment, two things emerge.

On the one hand, Lagrange is unafraid to voice his opinion that Mauriac's book is an unskilled work. "Dare we express our entire opinion? Let us say, bravely, that he lacked critical sense."[52] The prolific novelist looks like the "one-book man" in the less flattering sense; indeed, he resembles Samuel Johnson's man who writes more books than he reads (whereas Lagrange recalls another of Dr. Johnson's quips: "A man will turn over half a library to make one book").[53] With deftly muted humor, Lagrange makes his own harsh judgment an excuse for Mauriac's aversion to exegetes.[54] Still, the novelist's open disrespect for those biblical scholars who carefully studied the Gospels before him leads him into some notable, lamentable errors. And Mauriac's tendency toward excess (including an excessive dismissal of exegetical know-how) ends by undermining his own stated purpose.

On the other hand, Lagrange is alert to the very personal, even autobi-

51. "M. Mauriac insiste avec une logique qu'on n'eut pas crue de son goût. Dans un endroit du moins, il est bien près d'envisager la maternité divine comme un fait nécessaire, qui ne comportait aucun épanchement, aucun échange de la pensée par des paroles affables, de peur de compromettre l'independence du Dieu: 'Aucune des paroles du Christ à sa mère, relatées dans les évangiles (sauf la dernière), qui ne manifeste durement son indépendance à l'égard de la femme: comme s'il était servi d'elle pour s'incarner, et il était sorti de cette chair, et il n'y avait plus rien de commun entre elle et lui.'" Lagrange, "La *Vie de Jésus*," 342.

52. Lagrange, "La *Vie de Jésus*," 338. "Oserons-nous dire toute notre pensée? Disons bravement qu'il a manqué de critique."

53. See Bartlett, *Familiar Quotations*, 365.

54. "J'ai fini. M. Mauriac n'a pas été très indulgent pour ses devanciers, car lui-même a fait, a commis de l'exégèse. Et on les accuse volontiers d'avoir mauvais caractère. Je viens de faire la preuve surabondamment." Lagrange, "La *Vie de Jésus*," 344.

ographical, aspects of Mauriac's book. If this implies the danger of introducing certain confusions into this complicated artist's very personal version of the gospel story—Lagrange conjures the analogy of Goethe's *Dichtung und Wahrheit*—it also carries one great and obvious advantage. It is precisely the autobiographical context of the author's account of Jesus that confers upon it the bracing force of genuine witness. Given that *Vie de Jésus* was the work of an extremely prominent and deeply convicted and converted Christian man of letters, Lagrange was not foolish in his readiness to share Mauriac's personal hope: that this little book would (in spite of its shortcomings) lead many to see Jesus Christ as true God and true man.

Jesus as God and Man in the Gospels

The interest aroused by Mauriac's *Vie de Jésus* was a brief and localized episode in the end. In the half-century that has passed since his death, Mauriac's status and influence, even as a writer of fiction, have enormously waned. (His fame, in fact, reached its acme through his later work as a midcentury political commentator—an inevitably ephemeral occupation.) Mauriac's cultural role is thus confined today to that place where he did not wish to go as an artist: the canon of twentieth-century "Catholic authors." If his fate is accordingly to play a bit part in the intellectual history of the post-modernist church, the experiment of his *Vie de Jésus* holds a lasting significance for the way it staged a theological problem of enduring importance. How shall the two natures of Jesus be properly recognized in the Gospels?

It is difficult to deny that Mauriac knew something real of the tenacity and dark power of sin. His attempt to bring this knowledge to bear in his reading of the Gospels is promising and commendable as such. Newman once highlighted something much to the point: "The doctrines of the *forgiveness* of sins, and of a new birth from sin, cannot be understood without some right knowledge of the *nature* of sin, that is, of our own heart."[55] We are free to wonder if Lagrange has not proven insensible to this dimension of Mauriac's work, ignoring his treatment of Mary Magdalene and Judas, for instance, or his remarkably stark and generally successful portrayal of the hour in Gethsemane (where the kiss of Judas is provocative but open to question). At the same time, however, we are free to wonder if Mauriac has not also

55. John Henry Newman, "Secret Faults," in *Parochial and Plain Sermons* (San Francisco: Ignatius, 1997), 31.

skewed something in the shape of Jesus's own struggle. The fact that the book jumps from the baptism by John straight to Jesus's call of the first disciples, skipping entirely the temptation in the desert, suggests not only an inability to engage the principal revealed form of Jesus's personal conflict with the dark power but also a failure to register the swift and sovereign victory of his graced humanity in the face of this terrible trial. Whatever embarrassing problems the Gospels' temptation narrative presents, it is plotted as a major and early event, and its omission alters the proportions of the story. If this was a missed opportunity for the exercise of Mauriac's genius, it was also an invitation to overexert in sketching Jesus's interior life in alternate ways.

For all its potential insights, Mauriac's bold novelistic probing of the psychology of Jesus must clearly be acknowledged as a temerarious technique. It was not a complete novelty, however. In one way, even if the ahistorical and openly confessional effort broke with the line of nineteenth-century German *Leben Jesu* writing, it nevertheless represented in France an odd reflux of the antiquated project of Renan.[56] Lacking entirely Renan's imposing rhetoric and (often genuine) demonstrations of learning—the numerous footnotes, ancient source citations, and the confident and factual-sounding, succinctly declarative prose style—Mauriac's echo of the work still clearly intended to be a reply to the professor of the Collège de France and his epigones: above all, as a reversal of his rejection of the divinity of Christ. That Renan's volume, despite its scientific trappings, was and remains qualified as a novel means that Mauriac had not simply miscalculated the order of discourse.[57] Yet, in adopting this precise literary form, properly adapted to fiction, he should have anticipated a trap that had already snagged his predecessor; for, despite everything, "a novelist who lends thoughts to Christ ends up as a theologian."[58] The interior life of Jesus is not a place one should recklessly venture, certainly not as a creative artist lacking adequate theological equipment—whatever formidable imaginative powers as an armchair psychologist one may possess. Renan the historian had the distinct advantage of having no divine nature to try to expose; whereas the fiction writer Mauriac's project to discern Jesus's divinity somewhere in his human psyche looks like a foolhardy attempt that is doomed to fail from the start. The aberrations

56. See the conference proceedings on the theme "VieS de Jésus" (*sic*) collected in *Oeuvres & Critiques* 26, no. 2 (2001).

57. See Pierre-Louis Rey, "Vie de Jésus, un roman idéaliste," *Oeuvres & Critiques* 26, no. 2 (2001): 48–58.

58. Rey, "Roman idéaliste," 51: "un romancier qui prête des pensées au Christ finit en théologien."

that might result have been noted above. Not only does the divine nature assert itself in problematic ways and in places it does not belong. Displacing humanity in this way from its proper position affects the portrayal of that same created nature: Jesus becomes an angry, rather than compassionate, man. The conclusion is clear. Using speculative psychology as the principal leverage to erect a Chalcedonian hermeneutic is at best well-minded christological malpractice.

This is not intended to set a moratorium on genuine questions about Christ's mysterious divine and human consciousness—however precarious even ontologically disciplined theological speculation in this domain must remain. Mention might be made, for instance, of Bernard Lonergan's impressive examination of the psychological constitution of Christ.[59] With a heavy apparatus of now out-of-fashion neoscholastic distinctions, Lonergan's firm insistence upon understanding the double consciousness of the incarnate Logos in terms of "experience" rather than "perception" attempts to safeguard the truth of the assumed humanity and the unity of the person in two natures.[60] Thus, not only can and must we affirm Christ's unstructured ("informis") experiential human knowledge of his own humanity and true human condition ("sub rationi experti Christus ut homo Christum ut hominem attinget").[61] For Lonergan, we can and must also affirm that in Christ, under the formality of an intellectual judgment about reality ("sub rationi entis"), a divine person is conscious of a divine person through a human consciousness ("per conscientiam vere et proprie humanam persona divina est personae divinae conscia").[62] Christ accordingly enjoys both an ontological and psychological unity located in his one, undivided divine person, a single subject subsisting in two distinct natures and conscious of this double consciousness.[63]

59. See Bernard Lonergan, *The Ontological and Psychological Constitution of Christ*, Collected Works of Bernard Lonergan 7 (Toronto: University of Toronto, 2014).

60. Lonergan's emphasis on "experience" rather than "perception" signals the subject delivered or present to itself through its operations rather than self-known in a subject-object relation.

61. Lonergan, *Ontological and Psychological Constitution of Christ*, 204.

62. Lonergan, *Ontological and Psychological Constitution of Christ*, 210.

63. "Si conscie conscientia humana personae divinae et consciae additur, sequitur ipsam personam divinam esse consciam duarum suarum conscientiarum." Lonergan, *Ontological and Psychological Constitution of Christ*, 244. The "I" of Christ is accordingly the "I" of the divine subject—in contrast to the views of authors like Paul Gautier, in whose double "I" Lonergan sees a Nestorian risk, or more recently Thomas Weinandy, who denies Jesus any divine "I" altogether.

What does all this mean for the much-discussed *self-consciousness* of Jesus? Might it be a subject of prime interest for the "future of Catholic biblical interpretation"? Or should that be considered forever off-limits? The lesson learned through Mauriac's adventure urges caution. An absolute abandonment of the category, although at times advanced and defended, nevertheless appears unwarranted and ill-advised. Lonergan's analysis indicates how modes of reflection that are metaphysically and doctrinally sound might support and defend a confident exegetical essay. And here Lagrange points the straight way forward. The logical coherence that he observed as characteristic of Jesus's self-conception—his unwaveringly focused identity as messenger of God's kingdom—is a historical datum that can and should be recognized and explored.[64] This may be done in a controlled fashion that resists undisciplined inventions, with respect for the sources and without any prurient speculation. It remains essentially an external, historical analysis of Jesus's words and deeds, his recorded acts of self-revelation, not a tentative exploration of his interior states or interpolation of more or less plausible feelings and thoughts in order to fill gaps in the Gospels' sparse narrative sequence. If Albert Schweitzer's epochal break with the whole *Lives of Jesus* tradition is indeed, as Loisy and Lagrange both firmly agreed, a major advance for honest and serious research, the advance is in the agreement with Johannes Weiss—not, however, on the hypothesis of an eschatologically deluded Jesus heralding the imminent end of the world (*pace* Loisy and Schweitzer). The key assent is to the deeper and more important historical insight: the robustly messianic self-understanding of Jesus.

Does Jesus's divinity then come to expression through his exteriorized self-conception? For Lagrange, as noted above, we catch surprisingly little glimpse of Jesus's blazing Godhead—much less than a devout reader like Mauriac was inclined to see. The fastidious exegete appears, in this way, like a stereotypical historical-critical scholar, pooh-poohing Jesus's divinity at every turn. Knowing the deep faith of Père Lagrange, however, this should give us pause and invite reflection.

The divine nature never simply eclipses the assumed instrument of Christ's human nature; the opposite is more truly the case (the "hidden"

64. "Tout en Jésus est dominé par ce qu'on nommerait dans un autre l'obsession de son message, la consécration absolue de tout lui-même a la mission qu'il tenait de Dieu, le devoir pressant de faire connaître aux hommes ce que Dieu l'avait chargé de dire. Déjà de cette manière, il est la parole de Dieu agissante." Marie-Joseph Lagrange, OP, *L'Évangile de Jésus Christ avec la synopse évangelique*, ed. Ceslas Lavergne, OP (Paris: Perpignan Artège Lethielleux, 2017), 655.

God, *Deus absconditus*).[65] The kenotic movement invests God with a servile human form, and it is this *forma servi*, this "form of a slave," that is constantly perceived in the Gospels. "God Visible" is manifest only in Jesus's human flesh.[66] Granting, therefore, that Jesus's humanity is the sensible organ of his invisible and eternal divine being, we must be careful to understand properly this incarnational *exegesis* of the God whom no one has seen (John 1:18).

Overstated forms of "partitive exegesis"—the neatly divided apportioning of Gospel passages to one or the other nature, human or divine[67]—can potentially go astray to the extent that they disrupt the "undivided" (ἀδιαιρέτως) and "unseparated" (ἀχωριστῶς) end of the Chalcedonian spectrum. Mauriac's procedure arguably runs this risk and makes especially clear the narrative strain of holding together, on the psychological plane, a single divine hypostasis in two distinct natures. This evidence of a breakdown on the narrative level of characterization, which looks like a juxtaposition of contrasting character traits, recalls the failure of the Nestorian vision of a moral union in Christ ("reciprocal presence")—though the attunement of the human to the divine in Mauriac's Jesus is sometimes unclear.[68] Classical conciliar hermeneutics, nevertheless, readily adopted the partitive practice in ways that were markedly less concerned with ensuring forms of narratival, psychological, or historical coherence.[69] The resulting partition of verses into things said and done respectively ὡς ἄνθρωπος or ὡς θεός—an adverbial echo of wider patristic discourse about the Word's economic modality—is an arrangement that serves at a minimum to highlight the conceptual power of the unique person of the Logos to secure a unity that the variegated and lacunary textual data otherwise resist. For Alexandrians like Cyril and his δογματικωτέρα ἐξήγησις (*Praef. In Jo.* 1.7), "one and the same Logos, equal

65. See Mateusz Przanowski, "Christ as *Deus Absconditus* in Thomas Aquinas's Theology," *Nova et Vetera* 16, no. 3 (2018): 881–98.

66. I allude here, of course, to Brian E. Daley, SJ, *God Visible: Patristic Christology Reconsidered*, Changing Paradigms in Historical and Systematic Theology (Oxford: Oxford University Press, 2018).

67. The earliest use of the terminology of "partitive exegesis" is, to my knowledge in Lars Koen, "Partitive Exegesis in Cyril of Alexandria's Commentary on the Gospel according to St. John," *StPatr* 25 (1993): 115–21.

68. On this language and precursors to the vision, see Joanne M. Dewart, "'Moral Union' in Christology before Nestorius," *Leval théologique et philosophique* 32 (1976): 283–99.

69. On the ultimate origins of this interpretative technique, see Lewis Ayres, *Nicaea and Its Legacy: An Approach to Fourth-Century Trinitarian Theology* (Oxford: Oxford University Press, 2004), 106.

and consubstantial with God the Father, utters human and divine words (αἱ ἀνθρώπιναι καὶ θεϊκαὶ φωναί)."[70]

With regard to this hypostatic resolution and method of exegesis by nature, it is noteworthy that for Gregory of Nazianzus, one of its most important practitioners, the long catena (perhaps an existing florilegium) of "great and sublime" texts that he provides in *Or.* 29.17 as revealing the Son's divinity includes no single citation from the Synoptic Gospels.[71] Instead, we find a high density of Johannine traditions and terms—often, though not always, predications *about* Jesus rather than his own reported words (John 1:1, 18; 14:6; 8:12; 6:27). By contrast, the companion catalogue supplied in *Or.* 29.18, illustrating the Son's true human flesh, alongside another ample round of texts from the Fourth Gospel (John 20:17; 14:28; 10:36; 18:9; 15:15; 10:18; 9:4; 5:19; 12:49; 8:15; 1:14; 4:6; 11:35), this time includes (always allusively) a healthy number of Synoptic traditions as well (Mark 10:40; Matt 26:39; 24:36; Luke 2:51; 6:12; 2:46; 2:52; Matt 8:24; 4:2; Mark 14:33). In this latter column of the created nature, the emphasis obviously falls upon Jesus's "humbler" traits (τὰ ταπεινότερα): his experiences of ignorance, hunger, fear, fatigue, and so on. What neither list contains, interestingly, despite the clear corporeal locus of the passions in Gregory's logic, is any mention of Jesus's higher passionate movements like anger, compassion, and love. Nor is his temptation by Satan—or his surmounting that temptation—ever mentioned (except perhaps implicitly to help prove that Jesus hungered). No place is given for Jesus's mighty demonstrations of power, and no mention is made of his prophetic knowledge. In fact, in Gregory's anti-Eunomian and highly polemical purpose, there is no interest at all in making a comprehensive attempt to sift through every Gospel tradition about Jesus's words and deeds and classify them as human or divine, or even to consider the Gospel material in its original context and on its own terms. The same could be said for this whole patristic partitive tradition, which was unabashedly in the business of focused proof-texting (not noted here as a facile judgment).

The interpretative pattern that emerges from the tradition, taken for what it is, displays not merely a dogmatic but also a highly schematic canonical form. Within the unified fourfold Gospel, the divinity of Jesus remains a theme exclusive to John. "No one ever spoke about the divinity like John,"

70. Koen, "Partitive Exegesis," 119.

71. Perhaps the most principled expression of partitive exegesis appears in a short explanatory passage in Gregory of Nazianzus, *Or.* 29.18. See John Behr, *The Nicene Faith* (Crestwood, NY: St. Vladimir's Seminary Press, 2004), 349.

Augustine says (*Tract. Ev. Jo.* 36.1). John speaks, we might immediately add, about both the divine nature and the divine persons. Matthew, Mark, and Luke intone more humbly, by contrast, Jesus's human nature. The broad classical consensus on this thematic or theological partition is strong. Accordingly, the orthodoxy of one like Lagrange, who insists on seeing Jesus's manhood revealed in key Synoptic traditions, is in full harmony with this patristic precedent and presents no cause for theological concern. By the same token, it is no sign of confessional weakness today if one should object, as many have done, to Simon Gathercole's academically "unorthodox" theory about the Son's preexistence in the Synoptics.[72] The theory might be calmly resisted as overzealous maximalism, if better arguments are found. Accepting the theory is also an option, of course, with all due deference to the stylized patristic motif of John as the "spiritual" Gospel. I note only that Gathercole's more contemporary and contextualized form of proof-texting has the merit of concentrating the proof upon Jesus's own words in ways that we might helpfully collate with a (short) list of additional "Johannine thunderbolts."[73] In that way, something of the distinctive Johannine (or better Jesuanic) voice is preserved as a consistent marker of those "great and sublime" revelations of Jesus as God.

Aside from John's Prologue (and let us not forget Hebrews), explicit thematization of the divine nature is rare in New Testament writings. Jesus's humanity, by contrast, is permanently on display. Deductive reasoning from the one to the other must be very cautiously approached. As Lagrange notes, the Scriptures did not clearly prophesy that the messiah would be God, nor were Jesus's miracles adequate to demonstrate his divinity.[74] What evidence, then, convinced the disciples that Jesus was in reality God? For Lagrange it is the *words* of Jesus to which we must turn to apprehend what they grasped when they beheld the glory of the Father's only Son. We must regard these words of the Word, moreover, to be confirmed by Jesus's miracles and conformed to what the Scriptures foretold. This precise shape of Jesus's self-attestation, alone fitting for the witness of God's self-revelation and open equally to faith and disbelief, is uniquely evident in both John 5 and Luke 11. There is mat-

72. Simon J. Gathercole, *The Preexistent Son: Recovering the Christologies of Matthew, Mark, and Luke* (Grand Rapids: Eerdmans, 2006).

73. See Giambrone, *Quest for the Historical Christ*, 286–300.

74. "Les miracles de Jésus n'auraient pas suffi. Les prophètes avaient fait des miracles et même ressuscité des morts. . . . Les prophéties n'étaient pas tout à fait claires sur ce point que le Messie serait Dieu, et de fait les Juifs ne les comprenaient pas ainsi, du moins les docteurs les plus autorisées." Lagrange, *L'Évangile de Jésus Christ*, 663.

ter here (in my opinion) for elaborating the foundations of a christological vision that is at once robustly conciliar and biblical.[75]

This is obviously only a single gesture to a key point of leverage for thinking of Jesus as God and man. One thing further may be said before closing. By the logic of the incarnation and the doctrine of the Second Council of Nicaea, the instrumentality of Jesus's manhood permits an "undivided" act of theological perception, strictly analogous to the veneration of an icon of Christ: a vision that passes through the image of his human nature to attain to the subsistent person of the Father's only Son as the one true God.[76] This access, on the hypostatic plane, to the divine nature of Jesus extends beyond those select sayings where Christ makes himself unambiguously known. Particular circumscribed acts in the Gospels, therefore, though proper to the historical circumstances of some set time and place, can be fittingly read in a spiritual sense as theandric deeds that reveal a deeper meaning. Accordingly, there is no reason why Jesus's eruptions of human anger when confronted with bullheaded sin—an anger that impressed Mauriac (too) much—might not indeed present a true parable and image of God's wrath and of divine justice revealed. Likewise, the stirrings of love that moved Mauriac so, though bound to the created compassion of Christ's human heart, are not void of real power thereby to reveal God's infinite riches of mercy.

The Final Word

Marie-Joseph Lagrange's review of François Mauriac's *Vie de Jésus* is modest but a miniature masterpiece of theological exegesis and critique. It is also a wonderful introduction to the person and work of Père Lagrange. It exposes the humor and gentle sarcasm, the gracious deference yet serene self-assertion, the patience, the rigorous and even ruthless precision, but also the extreme delicacy of judgment and resolute fairness of the father of modern Catholic biblical studies. One meets his culture and learning, penetrating intelligence, and his acute theological mind, but above all the tender yet

75. I have attempted to sketch the outlines of such a Christology in my *Quest for the Historical Christ*, especially chapters 4, 6, and 12.

76. Beyond the Studite theology and Nicaea II, one is reminded here of Balthasar's "fountainhead of all Christian aesthetics": "Er [Jesus] ist was er ausdrückt, nämlich Gott, aber er ist nicht der, den er ausdrückt, nämlich der Vater." Hans Urs von Balthasar, *Schau und Gestalt*, vol. 1 of *Herrlichkeit: Eine theologische Ästhetik* (Freiburg: Johannes, 2019), 27.

purely matter-of-fact piety, the firm faith, and the manifest love of Lagrange for the person of Jesus and his mother. This love was naturally a love of the truth and the truth about Jesus's person—a love that led the Dominican friar to risk writing severely, even against one who similarly loved Jesus and who was, finally, an ecclesial friend.

For Lagrange it is obvious: the Gospels themselves are the only lives of Jesus that can be written.[77] Despite this, and despite Mauriac's own later retractions, the old genre of the *Life*, nevertheless, lived happily on. It might be credited to Lagrange's theological instincts, however, that the next French *Vie de Jésus* to make a sensation (Jean Steinmann's in 1959) would do so with the distinction of being the last book ever placed on the *Index*.[78] Ready though Lagrange was to read all, even errant theological novels, for his own work he preferred as a principle to carve as close to the Gospel texts as he possibly could. His tendency to restate what he read has at times appeared disappointing to his own readers, but it issues from his cleaving tightly to the one book that he loved above all—precisely because *the gospel* is so much more than a book.[79] It is a living reality and a divine indwelling: "an invasion of things divine . . . the insertion of divinity into humanity, human nature participating in the divine nature by grace."[80] It is no accident, in any case, that Lagrange's own great personal effort to offer a comprehensive theological and exegetical statement on Jesus takes the self-effacing, canonical shape of a commentary on the fourfold Gospel. Entitled not the *Vie* but *L'Évangile de Jesus Christ*, it is an ecclesial vision normed by the tradition and

77. "Les évangiles sont la seule vie de Jésus Christ qu'on puisse écrire. Il n'est que de les comprendre le mieux possible." Lagrange, *L'Évangile de Jésus Christ*, 26.

78. Steinmann himself recognized the project of hazarding a *Life of Jesus* to be outmoded: "Il semble paradoxal d'oser écrire en 1959 une Vie de Jésus. L'obstacle qu'on estime insurmontable vient, dit-on, du genre littéraire des évangiles." Jean Steinmann, *La Vie de Jésus* (Paris: Les Libraires Associés, 1959), 247. For the Pontifical Biblical Commission's condemnation, which came two years after the publication, see *In generali consessu*, *AAS* 54 (1961): 507–8, and also the short notice published in *Le Monde* on June 29, 1961.

79. "L'évangile n'est pas seulement un livre, car il serait ainsi l'apanage d'une catégoire savante, et il a été donné à tous. Il n'est pas seulement une doctrine, car la doctrine suppose encore des recherches et un privilège des lettres, et il a été donné aux petits et aux simples. Il faut donc que nous le considérions tel que saint Paul l'a défini: La vertu de Dieu pour le salut de quiconque croit." Lagrange, *L'Évangile de Jésus Christ*, 674.

80. Lagrange, *L'Évangile de Jésus Christ*, 675: "un envahissement des choses divines . . . la insertion de la divinité dans l'humanité, la nature humaine participant par la grâce à la nature divine." He continues and concludes: "On est tenté de dire que c'est trop beau!"

informed by Lagrange's own minute philological labor and Gospel synopsis. The one surprise and obvious disruption of the established Gospel sequence is the place allotted to Christ's nature as God. John's Prologue—which like Jesus's temptation somehow found no spot in Mauriac's version—serves as Lagrange's *epilogue* and final word.

A Postcolonial Latino/a Catholic Biblical Interpretation in the Americas

Reading Scripture from a Historical Context

J. L. Manzo

The common heritage of all Christians is the Bible, the word of God, written in human language through the inspiration of the Holy Spirit to give witness to Jesus Christ as Lord and Savior. Scripture has been subjected to different translations and interpretations continually over the centuries. The church fathers of the Alexandrian schools interpreted the Bible allegorically, while those of the Antiochian school stressed its literal interpretation. By the end of the nineteenth century, the historical-critical method was popularized for biblical studies and has dominated much of biblical research undertaken in the twentieth century and in the present.

The historical-critical method's emphasis on the historical setting of the text and its author's intended meaning shifted to the relationship between the text and the reader in Latin America's biblical interpretation in the early 1960s. In this type of biblical interpretation, the reader plays an interpretative role from his or her historical setting. As Elisabeth Schüssler Fiorenza has said, "One's social location or rhetorical context is decisive on how one sees the world, constructs reality, or interprets biblical texts."[1] In this essay, I would like to address the postcolonial reading of the Bible in Latin America, focusing on the following four topics: (1) Catholicism and the Bible in Latin America; (2) the postcolonial context of Latin America in the 1960s; (3) the church's response to the historical setting of Latin America in the 1960s and the emergence of liberation theology; and (4) the future of Catholic liberation theology in the Americas.

1. Elisabeth Schüssler Fiorenza, "The Ethics of Biblical Interpretation: Decentering Biblical Scholarship," *JBL* 107, no. 1 (1988): 5.

Catholicism and the Bible in Latin America

Iberian Catholicism came to Latin America with the arrival of Christopher Columbus in 1492 and the subsequent colonization. This type of Catholicism, which has been present in Latin America for over five centuries, was motivated by two factors: The first was the military conquest of the America of the South to increase the territorial power and wealth of the Spanish and Portuguese monarchs. The other was theological—the conversion of the indigenous people to Christianity.[2] Iberian Catholicism espoused mysticism and a strong devotion to Mary as the Immaculate. Knowledge of the Bible remained with the elite conquistadores who proclaimed it among the newly conquered people. With the arrival of the first missionaries in Mexico (1522), the proliferation of the Bible grew on the continent. By the middle of the twentieth century, biblical scholarship from Argentina had a great impact throughout the America of the South. Fr. Johannes "Juan" Straubinger, a German professor of Scripture at La Plata Seminary, whose maxim was "The Bible to the people through the priest," founded *La Revista Bíblica* (1939), whose aim was to bring the word of God to the faithful through scientific interpretative principles and pastoral application.[3] *La Revista Bíblica*, the most prominent biblical journal in Latin America, celebrated eighty years of biblical exegesis in 2019. Straubinger also revised the Bible translation of Felix Torres Amat (1823–1825) according to the text of the Vulgate (1941) and two years later provided a critical update.[4] In 1942, Archbishop Chimento, Bishop of La Plata, Argentina, asked for a new edition of the New Testament for the Americas.[5] Straubinger responded by publishing "La Biblia Platense" (1951)—the first Catholic Bible in Spanish published in Latin America—based on the original languages.[6] The work incorporated philological, archaeological, geographical, and historical annotations; additionally, patristic interpretation was incorporated for readers' spiritual edification.

2. María Pilar Aquino, *Our Cry for Life: Feminist Theology from Latin America* (Maryknoll, NY: Orbis, 1992), 44.

3. Pablo Nazareno Pastrone, "Juan Straubinger, pionero del movimiento bíblico argentino," in *80 años de exégesis bíblica en América Latina: Actas del Congreso Internacional de Estudios Bíblicos organizado con ocasión del 80º aniversario de Revista Bíblica*, ed. Eleuterio R. Ruiz, RevistBSup 7 (Estella: Verbo Divino, 2019), 27–29.

4. Pastrone, "Juan Straubinger," 22–23. Fr. Johannes "Juan" Straubinger arrived in Argentina in 1938 after he was forced to flee Germany for translating and reading from the pulpit Pope Pius IX's encyclical *Mit brennender Sorge* on March 21, 1937.

5. Pastrone, "Juan Straubinger," 24.

6. Pastrone, "Juan Straubinger," 25–26.

Straubinger says of the latter: "Teniendo en cuanta el ambiente en que vivimos-decía-y para el cual escribimos, damos preferencia a la explicación práctica, destacando las ideas fundamentales de la Biblia y mostrando su aplicación en la vida."[7] Straubinger's legacy regarding the new historical-critical approaches and patristic spirituality contributes to a greater understanding of Scripture, and the maxim "The Bible to the people through the priest" resonated with the faithful and in the academy. By the 1960s, Latin America experienced political and economic upheavals that shifted the knowledge of Scripture through the mediation of the priest to the reader and gave new meaning to Straubinger's words "mostrando su aplicación en la vida" (showing its application to life).

The Postcolonial Setting of Latin America in the 1960s

After the Second World War, financial investment, technological innovations, and capitalism made the United States and Europe wealthy and powerful. Many economists felt that the lack of prosperity and development in Latin America was caused by a lack of investment and innovation. Consequently, the continent witnessed a campaign for modernization, urbanization, and globalization approved by the US government, the International Monetary Fund (IMF), the Catholic Church, and Christian democratic political parties. Capitalism did modernize certain sectors and regions, but it also dramatically increased social inequality among the population. Otto Maduro says, "Economic dependency, inflation, unemployment, malnutrition, illiteracy, concentration of capital in the hands of a few, the growing poverty of the majority, internal conflicts and massive emigration increased instead of decreasing, and frustration led to increasing protest by the oppressed against the 'solutions' put forward by various forms of Capitalism in Latin America."[8] By the 1950s, political secular unions and socialist parties gained the support of the marginal communities that were the most disproportionately affected.[9] The people's disillusion with the capitalist system that enriched a few through control of the production and distribution of goods

7. Pastrone, "Juan Straubinger," 26. My translation: "Considering the environment in which we lived—he said—and for which we write, we preferred the practical explanation, highlighting the fundamental ideas of the Bible and showing its application to real life."

8. O. Maduro, "Christian Democracy and the Liberating Option for the Oppressed in Latin American Catholicism," *Concilium* 193 (1987): 113.

9. Fernando Segovia, "Latin American Biblical Interpretation in the Diaspora: Latinx American Biblical Criticism," in Ruiz, *80 años de exégesis bíblica en América Latina*, 175.

and lands saw the Cuban revolution (1959) as the inspiration for overcoming the imperialistic policies of the ruling class that had oppressed minorities.[10] Latin America began to experience a period of social and political struggles instigated by popular movements either favoring or rejecting democratic governments and free-market systems. The latter were supported by communist-backed guerrilla groups that opposed colonization and capitalism in favor of a more Marxist system that, instead of founding a classless society and self-satisfying modes of labor, moved many countries deeper into poverty and oppression. Fernando Segovia summarizes as follows:

> Following upon the configuration of the Second World War (1939–1945), one finds the eruption of what would turn out to be a long Cold War between the East and the West (1945–1989). This would be a struggle for global supremacy involving two world visions and world-projects: on the one hand, a system of liberal-democratic government and capitalist-market economy, led by the United States; on the other hand, a system of authoritarian-people's government and central-planning economy, led by the Union of Soviet Socialist Republics. . . . The contenders had a fair share of social and cultural, political and economic, traits in common: both constituted imperial frameworks—the American Empire and the Soviet Empire; both embodied different variations of capitalism—market and state; and both engaged in broad violations of human rights as well as social rights—exploitation and repression, propaganda and destabilization.[11]

Thus, the democratic-capitalist system's promises of prosperity failed. So, too, failed the vision of a just society pledged by Marxist regimes. The urgent need to find a resolution to the oppression and violence suffered by so many prompted the church to speak on behalf of the poor.

The Church's Response and the Emergence of Liberation Theology

While most of Latin America struggled over the dominance of two opposing political ideologies, an important event was taking place in the religious sphere—the Second Vatican Council. The conciliar constitutions *Dei Verbum*

10. Néstor O. Míguez, "Latin American Reading of the Bible: Experiences, Challenges and Its Practice," *ExpTim* 118, no. 3 (2006): 121.

11. Segovia, "Latin American Biblical Interpretation," 175.

(1965) and *Gaudium et spes* (1965) promulgated, according to P. A. García Arenas and J. A. Casas Ramírez, a new hermeneutical method with the maxim "de la palabra de Dios escrita a la Palabra de Dios hecha vida y hecha pueblo" (from the written Word of God to the Word of God made life and people).[12] The reception and consequences of the conciliar statements on the word of God as action within the history of the faithful's life were formalized in the second plenary session of the Council of Latin American Bishops, known as CELAM, or the Consejo Episcopal Latinoamericano in Medellín, Colombia (1968). The session focused on the themes of revolution and class conflict. The Medellín documents state that Latin America was suffering a new "neocolonialism," both internal and external, under an international imperialism that profited from the world's marginalized people through unfair economic practices.[13] Such economic exploitation brought about a social inequality that, according to the church's teachings, constituted serious sin and an act of injustice (CELAM §§I.2; II.18–19). The bishops appealed to the conscience of businessmen, organizations, and political authorities to make an effort to conduct their business according to the guidelines supplied by the social teaching of the church, that the social and economic change in Latin America be channeled toward a truly human economy. According to the bishops, social change depended on the implementation of structures that facilitated the participation of individuals and businesses alike to drive progress at all levels of the society. The Medellín documents also rejected Marxism as a system that violates the dignity of the human person (CELAM §I.10).

The bishops called the church to a greater solidarity with and preferential treatment of the poor (CELAM §§II.22–23). They charged her to work for the liberation of the oppressed and to develop *comunidades de base* (base communities) to tend to their needs. Thousands of base communities were formed throughout Latin America in the wake of the conference. The Medellín document describes the base communities as follows:

12. Paula Andrea García Arenas and Juan Alberto Casas Ramírez, "Una visión panorámica sobre la hermenéutica bíblica latinoamericana," in Ruiz, *80 años de exégesis bíblica en América Latina*, 306.

13. CELAM (Consejo Episcopal Latinoamericano in Medellín), *Documentos finales de Medellín*, 1968 §§I.10; II.2–10. These documents can be found at http://www.celam.org/doc_conferencias/Documento_Conclusivo_Medellin.pdf. Hereafter, they will be cited in the text.

> The Christian ought to find the experience of communion to which he has been called, in his "base community," that is, to say, in the community, local or environmental, which corresponds to the reality of the homogeneous group and whose size allows for personal fraternal contact among its members. Consequently, the Church's pastoral efforts must be oriented toward the transformation of these communities into a "family of God," beginning by making itself present among them as leaven by means of a nucleus, although it be small, which creates a community of faith, hope and charity. Thus, the Christian base community is *the first and fundamental ecclesial nucleus,* which on its own level must make itself responsible for the richness and expansion of the faith, as well as of the cult which is its expression. She is, then, the initial cell of the ecclesiastical structures and the focus of evangelization, and it currently serves as the most important source of human advancement and development. The essential element for the existence of Christian base communities are their leaders or directors. These can be priests, deacons, men or women religious, or laymen. (CELAM §§XV.10–11)[14]

The base community's identification as "the first and fundamental ecclesial nucleus" makes it an integral part of the institutional church. Bishops and parish priests were responsible for ministerial formation and for appointing the base community leaders who not only introduced the Bible as the written word of God but also engaged in social justice movements promoting advancement and development (CELAM §§XV.11–12). Direct contact with Scripture allowed the communities to read it from their historical praxis—a liberating theology that challenges oppressive systems and authorities and

14. The above quotation is my translation of the original Spanish: "La vivencia de la comunión a que ha sido llamado, debe encontrarla el cristiano en su 'comunidad de base': es decir, una comunidad local o ambiental, que corresponda a la realidad de un grupo homogéneo, y que tenga una dimensión tal que permita el trato personal fraterno entre sus miembros. Por consiguiente, el esfuerzo pastoral de la Iglesia debe estar orientado a la transformación de esas comunidades en 'familia de Dios', comenzando por hacerse presente en ellas como fermento mediante un núcleo, aunque sea pequeño, que constituya una comunidad de fe, de esperanza y de caridad. La comunidad cristiana de base es así el primero y fundamental núcleo eclesial, que debe, en su propio nivel, responsabilizarse de la riqueza y expansión de la fe, como también del culto que es su expresión. Ella es, pues, célula inicial de estructuración eclesial, y foco de la evangelización, y actualmente factor primordial de promoción humana y desarrollo. Elemento capital para la existencia de comunidades cristianas de base son sus líderes y dirigentes. Estos pueden ser sacerdotes, diáconos, religiosos, religiosas o laicos."

works to establish institutions with new models of being church. Gustavo Gutiérrez, a Peruvian Dominican priest and founder of liberation theology, says:

> This is a theology which does not stop with reflecting on the world, but rather tries to be part of the process through which the world is transformed. It is a theology which is open—in the protest against trampled human dignity, in the struggle against the plunder of the vast majority of humankind, in liberating love, and in the building of a new, just, and comradely society—to the gift of the Kingdom of God.[15]

Further, he writes:

> The Christian community professes a "faith which works through charity." It is—at least ought to be—real charity, action, and commitment to the service of others. Theology is reflection, a critical attitude. Theology follows; it is the second step. . . . The pastoral activity of the Church does not flow as a conclusion from theological premises. Theology does not produce a pastoral activity; rather it reflects upon it. Theology must be able to find in pastoral activity the presence of the Spirit inspiring the action of the Christian community.[16]

Gutiérrez's methodology gives primacy to a Christian faith that commits to transform society by charity first. A theology that becomes solely an academic exercise or is spiritualized fails to live the gospel message of solidarity with the poor.[17] This mode of biblical interpretation, known as the popular reading of Scripture, seeks to relate Scripture to social realities.

15. Gustavo Gutiérrez, *A Theology of Liberation: History, Politics, and Salvation*, rev. ed., trans. and ed. Caridad Inda and John Eagleson (Maryknoll, NY: Orbis, 1988), 174.

16. Gutiérrez, *Theology of Liberation*, 9.

17. "Real poverty is, according to the Bible, an evil, a situation not intended by the God of life, an acceptance of means seeking to eliminate the injustices that causes the spoliation and mistreatment of the poor. This effort necessarily presupposes a solidarity with their hopes and interests, friendship with them, and a sharing both of their lives and of their struggle for justice. This commitment and quest manifest an acceptance of God's will, and this acceptance in turn is the core of spiritual poverty or spiritual childhood; in other words, is the essence of discipleship." Gustavo Gutiérrez, *The God of Life*, trans. Matthew J. O'Connell (Maryknoll, NY: Orbis, 1991), 122. For Gutiérrez, spirituality has a historical praxis. See Gustavo Gutiérrez, "Towards a Theology of Liberation," *Liberation Theology: A Documentary History*, ed. Alfred T. Hennelly (Maryknoll, NY: Orbis, 1990), 72–73.

The early 1970s witnessed a series of academic publications following Gutiérrez's work. José Luis Segundo, an Uruguayan Jesuit priest, authored *Liberación de la teología* (1973).[18] He is one of the most prominent scholars in the field. According to Alfred T. Hennelly, if Gutiérrez is the founder of liberation theology, Segundo is the "dean" of all liberation theologians.[19] Segundo built upon Gutiérrez's historical praxis in the light of the Scripture by offering a new theological approach based on Bultmann's hermeneutical circle. For Bultmann, a hermeneutical circle refers to the continuous circular motion in which existential questions either correspond or clash with an interpreter's previous understanding of texts and their current interpretations.[20] Bultmann excludes social praxis, an element Segundo deems essential for the correct interpretation of the hermeneutical circle: "[The hermeneutical circle] is the continuing change in our interpretation of the Bible which is dictated by the continuing changes in our present-day reality, both individual and societal. . . . And the circular nature of this interpretation stems from the fact that each new reality obligates us to interpret the word of God afresh, to change reality accordingly, and then to go back and reinterpret the word of God again, and so on" (*LT*, 8).

According to this definition, an interpretation of Scripture that merges systematic principles with social sciences fits better within the notions of a hermeneutical circle. This is because the biblical text is read in its original cultural, historical, and literary context along with present realities. According to Segundo, two preconditions are necessary for the hermeneutical circle (*LT*, 9). The first condition raises profound questions and suspicion about social realities; the second condition is a new interpretation of the Bible that explains the present. Four decisive steps flow from these preconditions: (1) The interpreter's social reality leads to ideological suspicion. (2) The interpreter applies the ideological suspicion to the ideological superstructure and theology. (3) The interpreter moves to a new experience of theological reality—that is, exegetical suspicion that has not considered in particular the

18. José Luis Segundo, SJ, *Liberación de la teología* (Buenos Aires: Carlos Lohlé, 1975). For the English version, see *The Liberation of Theology*, trans. John Drury (Maryknoll, NY: Orbis, 1976). Hereafter, the English translation will be cited in the text as *LT*.

19. Alfred T. Hennelly, SJ, *Liberation Theologies: The Global Pursuit of Justice* (Mystic, CT: Twenty-Third Publications, 1995), 26.

20. John Painter, *Theology as Hermeneutics: Rudolf Bultmann's Interpretation of the History of Jesus*, Historic Texts and Interpreters in Biblical Scholarship 4 (Sheffield: Almond, 1987), 56–66.

social reality of minorities. (4) The interpreter develops a new Scriptural interpretation with the new pieces of data (*LT*, 9).

Segundo presents the writings of Harvey Cox, Karl Marx, Max Weber, and James Cone as examples of the hermeneutical circle, but he concludes that only Cone's *A Black Theology of Liberation* completes it (*LT*, 25–34). In the first step, Cone formulates a definition of theology that arises out of his own experience of the reality of oppression in the Black community. In his understanding, theology "is a rational study of the being of God in the world in light of the existential situation of the oppressed community, relating the forces of liberation to the essence of the gospel, which is Jesus Christ. This means that its sole reason for existence is to put into ordered speech the meaning of God's activity in the world, so that the community of the oppressed will recognize that its inner thrust for liberation is not consistent with the gospel but is the gospel of Jesus Christ" (quoted in *LT*, 26).[21] Black theology is a commitment to a community that seeks to define its existential reality in view of *God's liberating work* in the world. In the second step, Cone has developed the ideological suspicion that Black oppression comes from a racial difference that is lodged in human psychology. He applies this suspicion to the role of classical interpretation, which ignores the cause of the oppressed, spiritualizing it or speaking of sin in the abstract, pushing aside liberation in concrete historical situations. In the third step, Cone applies exegetical suspicion, namely, that the teaching of the Bible tends to conceal the plight of the oppressed and that a new experience of theology must integrate the quest for social liberation with the revelation of God. In the final step, Cone reaches his new hermeneutic: to know the meaning of God's revelation in the Black community's present struggle for liberation. The application of the hermeneutical circle to Cone's work illustrates how Segundo challenges the classical biblical methodology that ignores human suffering and contributes to it. He offers instead a new theological methodology that connects the gospel message to the present historical reality of the poor.

Gutiérrez's and Segundo's work inspired many liberation interpretations of Scripture. The book of Exodus has been a favorite of liberation theologians. José Severino Croatto's work *Liberación y libertad: Pautás hermeneuticas* (1973) takes the experience of the Israelites' liberation from Egypt, mentioned in the introduction of the Medellín documents as a move "de condiciones de vida menos humanas, a condiciones más humanas" (from less than human conditions to truly human), as a political liberation based

21. James H. Cone, *A Black Theology of Liberation* (Philadelphia: Lippincott, 1970), 17.

for Latin America's own struggles.[22] Croatto proposes a reading in which the Israelites' memory of liberation becomes the first hermeneutical key (or eisegesis, which for him is concomitant with exegesis) for the dispossessed in Latin America, who experienced discrimination and oppression, first during the conquest and subsequently by neo-empires.

In addition to Exodus, the prophets' message about colonization by the great Assyrian and Babylonian Empires has been interpreted as capturing the present reality of oppressed people throughout the world. Among the New Testament writings, the Gospel of Luke has received the most attention. The Magnificat has been studied from the perspective of the social, political, and economic institutions of the time that marginalized the poor, particularly women.[23] The book of Revelation is read today mostly as an anti-imperialistic manifesto.[24] Liberation theologians seek to find meaning in the experiences of injustice, suffering, and marginalization through God's self-revelation in the history of the world.

The church's hierarchy expressed several concerns about the hermeneutics of the theologies of liberation.[25] First, it felt that liberation theologians

22. J. Severino Croatto, *Liberación y libertad: Pautas hermenéuticas* (Buenos Aires: Mundo Nuevo, 1973), 24: "*Mi* momento hermenéutico es distinto al de este o de aquel lector; para escribir estas páginas con una perspectiva hermenéutica y 'Latinoamérica' no debo practicar la exégesis de los pasajes bíblicos y *después* sintonizarla con los hechos de nuestro mundo o de nuestro continente oprimido. Más bien, éstos han de ser y son el *antes* de mi interpretación de la Palabra bíblica. Sólo así ésta es eisegética (literalmente, 'que conduce hacia adentro') y no puramente exegética ('que conduce hacia *afuera*, que saca'). El lector podrá ser orientado a la interpretación del mensaje sagrado a partir de este intento hermenéutico, pero el tendrá que 'decir su palabra' en prolongación a la mía, enfrentarse a la Palabra desde *su* situación." Compare CELAM, *Documentos finales*, Introducción §6: "Así como otrora Israel, el primer Pueblo, experimentaba la presencia salvífica de Dios cuando lo liberaba de la opresión de Egipto, cuando lo hacía pasar el mar y lo conducía hacia la tierra de la promesa, así también nosotros, nuevo Pueblo de Dios, no podemos dejar de sentir su paso que salva, cuando se da el verdadero desarrollo, que es el paso, para cada uno y para todos, de condiciones de vida menos humanas, a condiciones más humanas." CELAM cites here *Populorum progressio* §20–21 on the social injustice of individuals within industralized countries.

23. Arturo Paoli, *La perspectiva política de San Lucas* (Buenos Aires: Siglo XXI, 1973); Marcos Villamán, *Leyendo el evangelio de Lucas* (México: CAM, 1982); Gerd Theissen, *Sociología del movimiento de Jesús: El nacimiento del cristianismo primitivo*, trans. José Antonio Jauregui (Santander: Sal Terrae, 1979); René Krüger, *Dios o el Mamón: Análisis semiótico del proyecto económico y relacional del Evangelio de Lucas* (Buenos Aires: Lumen, 2009).

24. See the essays on Revelation in the themed issue of *RIBLA* 34 (1999).

25. Robert McAfee Brown, *Gustavo Gutiérrez: An Introduction to Liberation Theology* (New York: Orbis, 1990), 42–43.

had bridged the gap separating church and state.[26] Second, it worried that the political and liberationist reading given to texts like Exodus or the Magnificat led to a reductionist interpretation of the biblical text.[27] Third, it was concerned that permitting the uneducated to formulate theology would weaken orthodoxy and challenge the traditional church's hierarchy.[28]

Liberation theologians responded to the church's first two concerns by quoting from the Medellín documents, which advocated for preferential treatment for the poor in defense of their hermeneutics.[29] The third concern was addressed by assuring the ecclesial authorities that after the poor have found themselves in the Bible and have discovered in it the meaning of their lives, the reading of the base communities will be supplemented by means of biblical and exegetical courses. In this way, their reading of Scripture is brought together with exegetical knowledge.[30]

Today, liberation theology is one interpretive approach approved by the Catholic Church.[31] Despite its limitations and risks, the church has acknowledged its contribution to a deeper awareness of God's presence in the lives of the people, its communal aspect, its liberative praxis, and its emphasis on the word of God in the midst of people's struggles.[32] Liberation theology has proliferated throughout Latin America's faith-based communities, which meet today to study Scripture, and it is taught in institutions of higher learning as a scientific study of the Bible. We move now to consider the impact of liberation theology in North America.

26. See the Congregation for the Doctrine of the Faith, Instruction *Libertatis nuntius* (August 6, 1984), treating aspects of liberation theology. Text in J. Neuner, SJ, and J. Dupuis, SJ, *The Christian Faith: Doctrinal Documents of the Catholic Church* (New York: Alba House, 1990).

27. Congregation for the Doctrine of the Faith, *Libertatis nuntius*, 99.

28. Gustavo Gutiérrez, *The Density of the Present: Selected Writings* (Maryknoll, NY: Orbis, 1999), 173.

29. Gutiérrez, *Density of the Present*, 124–28, 168.

30. Gutiérrez, *Density of the Present*, 172–73; Carlos Mesters, *Defenseless Flower: A New Reading of the Bible* (Maryknoll, NY: Orbis, 1989), 19.

31. Pontifical Biblical Commission, *The Interpretation of the Bible in the Church* (Rome: Libreria Editrice Vaticana, 1993) §I. E.1.

32. Joseph A. Fitzmyer, SJ, *The Biblical Commission's Document "The Interpretation of the Bible in the Church": Text and Commentary*, SubBi 18 (Rome: Pontifical Biblical Institute, 1995), 95.

Latin Catholic Biblical Scholarship in the United States

Latino/a biblical scholars in the United States constitute a minority, despite their population being composed of more than sixty million Latin Americans from very diverse historical, cultural, and ethnic backgrounds.[33] Most Latin Americans in the United States identify as Christians and have had a great impact on different faith traditions. Latino/a biblical scholars' embrace of a hermeneutic of liberation has been more prolific among Protestant scholars. There are, however, a small number of Latino/a Catholic scholars prominent in this area. They are Fernando F. Segovia, Jean-Pierre Ruiz, and María Pilar Aquino. In what follows, I want to point out certain presuppositions in the work of these scholars.

As already suggested above, the most influential Latino liberation theologian in the United States is Fernando F. Segovia. His primary area of interest is postcolonial and non-Western minority methods of interpretation. Segovia's starting point for a theology of liberation is grounded in his own experience in the United States as a political refugee from Cuba in the 1960s. Segovia has brought sustained attention to resisting the oppression of migrants within this country because of their gender, race, class, or ethnicity with a "hermeneutics of the diaspora, of otherness and engagement."[34] Migration from Latin America to the United States has been commonly triggered by internal sociopolitical and class struggles and by external socioeconomic dominion of the region by Canada and the United States, which has created economic disparity among its citizens and among its countries based on trade, aid, and investment (THD, 60). This has resulted in a new form of colonialism and in the migration of millions of people to the north.[35] Segovia identifies these as diasporic communities—"the sum total of all those who presently live, for whatever reason, on a permanent basis in a country other than that of their birth." Migrants from Latin America have become "children of colonialism and neocolonialism" (THD, 60) who fled their colonized

33. Ahida Calderón Pilarski, "Los estudios de género: La investigación feminista y la perspectiva Latino/a/x en la hermenéutica bíblica en los Estados Unidos," in Ruiz, *80 Años de Exégesis Bíblica en América Latina*, 162.

34. Fernando Segovia, "Towards a Hermeneutics of Diaspora: A Hermeneutics of Otherness and Engagement," in *Social Location and Biblical Interpretation in the United States*, vol. 1 of *Readings from This Place*, ed. Fernando F. Segovia and Mary Ann Tolbert (Minneapolis: Fortress, 1995), 57–74. Hereafter, this source will be cited in the text as THD.

35. It is estimated that just in the last two years, approximately two million people have journeyed from Latin America to the United States seeking asylum.

world to dwell in the colonizers' world in a condition of "otherness." The status of "otherness" is imposed by the dominant culture's identification of all Latin American immigrants as a monolithic group—they are Hispanic, Hispanic Americans, or Latinos, when in reality the inhabitants of the America of the South are ethnically, geographically, linguistically, and culturally diverse—and by being disparaged as lazy, violent, and undisciplined (THD, 62–63). Segovia argues that the designation of "otherness" (despite its negative connotation) should be the focus of an identity through which liberation is proclaimed on their behalf: "I would argue . . . that our theological and hermeneutical voice must be grounded in and grow out of this identity of otherness" (THD, 65).

When applied to the interpretation of Scripture, a "hermeneutics of otherness and engagement" argues for the historical remoteness of the biblical text as an interpretative tool that arises from the bicultural reality of the Hispanic community as "other" (THD, 67–68). The aim is to first "understand the biblical text . . . as another to us, with its own words and visions, allowing it to speak on its own, to unravel its own narrative, and to define its own identity" (THD, 69). Second, the reader gives meaning to the text based on their own social and cultural reality. A reader-response approach permits reality to be presented from a diversity of voices. Finally, Segovia proposes that the biblical text's remote background as "other" allows readers to reconstruct their past by considering their social location and, in doing so, to anticipate a better tomorrow (THD, 70–71).

Like Segovia, Jean-Pierre Ruiz reads the Bible through the migrant movement currently facing the United States from South America. His book *Reading from the Edges: The Bible and People on the Move* proposes an interdisciplinary approach to ministry and theology—*pastoral de conjunto* and *teología de conjunto*—reading *with* people on the move to recognize the diversity of readers in the world *in front* and *behind* the text, instead of *about* people on the move and the root causes of their migration.[36]

Ruiz illustrates the flight of the migrant with an *en conjunto* (with, or a collaborative theological) reading of the biblical accounts. Here we focus on Abram's and Sarai's flight to Egypt (Gen 12:10–20) and the Syrophoenician woman (Mark 7:24–30; *RE*, 44–50, 64–68). In Gen 12:10–20, Abram and Sarai travel to Egypt to reside as temporary aliens to escape a famine. As a foreigner, Abram knows he runs the risk of being killed by the Egyptians on

36. Jean-Pierre Ruiz, *Reading from the Edges: The Bible and People on the Move* (Maryknoll, NY: Orbis, 2011), 6–7. Hereafter, this source is cited in the text as *RE*.

account of the beauty of Sarai, whom he passes off as his sister. For Abram, the fear of dying was real. A postcolonial interpretation of reading *as immigrants* and *with immigrants* would consider a migrant's fear of death as they cross the border to the United States and the subsequent fear of being deported by legal authorities (*RE*, 64–67).

Abram's description of Sarai as "my sister" draws special attention to the dangers faced by women. Had it not been for a divine intervention, Sarai would have been violated by Pharaoh (Gen 12:17). She first becomes a victim of her own husband, who denies her to protect his own life. She is subsequently victimized by Pharaoh, whose attendants negotiate with Abram for her release to Pharaoh's house in exchange for profit. According to Ruiz, the narrative betrays the dynamics of power and gender in which Sarai's voice is silenced in submission to male dominance (*RE*, 67–68). Thus, a reading *with* will see Sarai's silence reflected in the lives of migrant women who are silenced into submission by smugglers who rape them or sell them into prostitution or by ruthless employers seeking to take advantage of their labor (*RE*, 69). A reading "as immigrants and with immigrants" stresses the importance of reading the biblical texts in the context in which they were written and in terms of the everyday experiences of the reader (*RE*, 66).

In the Syrophoenician woman's narrative, Mark presents Jesus's reluctance to restore her daughter to health on the reasoning that the children of Israel must be fed first. Jesus even calls her a dog—a derogative term used by Jews to refer to gentiles. Her condition as a poor and unclean foreigner relegates her to the status of "other," one who must be excluded from the Jewish community. The woman, however, does not take offense at Jesus's treatment but claims through her action and faith that she, too, as a gentile has a right to God's blessings. Ruiz embraces Segovia's "hermeneutics of otherness and engagement" as a reading strategy to promote solidarity with the migrants on the shared Christian commitment to justice; he suggests that if interpretation "focuses on 'the immigrant' as the object of our attention, however noble our attentions and however on target our summons to justice might be, we are implicated in the systemic othering that perpetuates the very injustice we seek to correct" (*RE*, 6–7, 50).

Finally, we consider the work of María Pilar Aquino. She is internationally renowned for her pioneering work in Latina feminist theology of liberation in Latin America and the United States.[37]

37. María Pilar Aquino, "Latina Feminist Theology: Central Features," in *A Reader in*

Feminist theology originated in the 1840s. Its most significant contributions were made in the United States in the nineteenth century and again in the 1960s and '70s. For Aquino, Latina feminist theology branches off of liberation theology because it "shares in the liberation process of the poor but pays special attention to the liberation of women who are triply oppressed"[38] by different forms of colonialism, racism, classism, and other forms of oppression. Feminist theologians rely on the historical-critical method and integrate a hermeneutic of suspicion and sociological theories in their analysis of biblical texts to determine gender roles and attitudes toward women that presume their secondary status. Aquino has written numerous works using these principles of biblical interpretation to establish a relationship between God's word and women's reality in existing patriarchal cultures to construct new social models free of patriarchal, political, and social dominance.[39]

In light of this background, I would like to offer some observations on the future of liberation theology in Latin America and in the United States. Since its origin in the 1960s, many have predicted its death. Conservative Catholic scholars have attacked it as illegitimate and, thus, rejected it. Liberation theologians themselves believed that Latin America's transition in the 1990s to democratic governments that ended much of the violence of the 1970s and 1980s would render it obsolete. Liberation theology is, however, very much alive throughout the continent. Four regional conferences were held in 2011, in Guatemala, Chile, Mexico City, and Colombia, in anticipation of the continental meeting in Brazil commemorating the fortieth anniversary of Gutiérrez's *Theology of Liberation*.[40] The Mexico City conference alone gathered more than three hundred liberation theologians and pastoral workers to discuss the future of the movement in light of the people's present struggles. They expressed the need to develop a theology of sufficiency (rejection of the neocapitalist consumer mindset) and of solidarity with the poor.

An important milestone was also reached with the eightieth anniversary of the publication of the *Revista Bíblica*. More than four hundred Latin American biblical scholars from nineteen nations gathered at the Pontifical Catholic University of Argentina in 2019 to celebrate the pioneers of bib-

---

Latin Feminist Theology: Religion and Justice, ed. María Pilar Aquino, Daisy L. Machado, and Jeanette Rodriguez (Austin: University of Texas Press, 2002), 133–60.

38. María Pilar Aquino, *Our Cry for Life*, 109.

39. See Aquino, "Latina Feminist Theology," 145–46; María Pilar Aquino, "Latin American Feminist Theology," *JFSR* 14, no. 1 (1998): 89–107.

40. See the report by Raymond Plankey, "Conference Looks to Future of Liberation Theology," *National Catholic Reporter*, November 23, 2011.

lical exegesis in Latin America, to discuss the political and social worldview of the continent in the 1960s, and to discuss the future and benefits of Latin American contributions to Catholicism in regard to biblical work and scholarship.

The theology of liberation has been part of Latino/a Catholic biblical scholarship in the United States, but it has not proliferated. This is perhaps because the economic and political reality of most Americans is quite different from the common reality of the peoples of Latin America. Another factor may be that Latino/a Catholic biblical scholars constitute a very small percentage of the guild.[41] Currently, about 19.6 million Latinos identify as Catholics in the United States; with more Latinos pursuing higher levels of theological education, liberation theology has the potential to become more prominent in the future.

Liberation Theology in Latin America

It is not surprising that liberation theology rose to prominence in Latin America as the theological body of thought against colonialism and the neocolonialist politics of dominance. Beyond the circumstances created by imperial dominance, the language of the "preferential option for the poor" employed by the Second General Conference of the Episcopate in Latin America held in Medellín in 1968 captured the imagination of church leaders and theologians alike.

Liberation theology's starting point is a biblical hermeneutics that highlights the situation of oppression of the people, who seek in the word of God meaning for their present life struggles. It has inspired biblical scholars to become agents of social change by integrating systematic doctrines and social-cultural and political theories into their interpretation of the Bible. The movement has spread worldwide. As long as the poor are among us, there will always be room for the ideals of justice, equality, freedom, and solidarity expressed by liberation theologians in view of the Christian message. It is thus an important task of the future of Catholic biblical interpretation.

41. Pilarski, "Los estudios," 162, notes that in a membership profile conducted in 2019 by the Society of Biblical Literature, 96 members out of 8,324 identified themselves as Latinos/as. Out of the 96, only 5 were female biblical scholars.

Catholic Biblical Interpretation

Participating in the Sacred Cosmic Story of God's Unfinished Universe by Hearing "Both the Cry of the Earth and the Cry of the Poor"

Kathleen P. Rushton, RSM

This essay explores how Catholic biblical interpretation is called to respond to the signs of the times by plunging deeply into the ongoing sacred cosmic story of God's unfinished universe to enable the people of God to participate with Jesus in completing the works of God by hearing "*both the cry of the earth and the cry of the poor*."[1] My exploration addresses a central question: What is the role of Catholic biblical interpretation in fostering a new synthesis of Catholic spirituality with contemporary science and biblical hope to call the church to be forward-looking as God ahead calls us into a new, evolving future?

I propose that one possible way consists of entering into a process of moving through the ever-expanding concentric circles of our personal story, our family story, our Christian story, our human story, our Earth story, and our cosmic story.[2] These circles are interconnected and cannot be addressed singularly or even chronologically. My task is a broad, ongoing one that can only be sketched in this essay.

Our Cosmic Story of God's Unfinished and Evolving Universe

Catholicism, in general, is still trapped in a static worldview, as John Haught reminds us:

1. Pope Francis, Encyclical Letter *Laudato si'* (May 24, 2015) §49. https://www.vatican.va/content/francesco/en/encyclicals/documents/papa-francesco_20150524_enciclica-laudato-si.html. Hereafter cited in the text as *LS*.

2. I acknowledge Maureen Wild, SC, who introduced me to these concentric circles in February 2014.

> News that the universe is dramatic, however, has yet to penetrate deeply into Catholic sensibilities. Our devotional life still presupposes an essentially static cosmos. The Church continues to nurture nostalgia for a lost original perfection and longs for union with an eternal present untouched by time and history. Its ageless inclination to restore an idyllic past or take flight into eternity has bridled the spirit of Abrahamic adventure and dampened the sense of a new future for the whole of creation. . . . Science's fresh picture of nature-as-narrative invites theology to transplant the central biblical motif of divine promise into a cosmological terrain that can give new breadth, nourishment, and vitality to our spiritual and ethical lives. It makes room for a theology that frames our unfinished universe with Abrahamic hope.[3]

Our cosmic story is influenced, consciously or unconsciously, by our other interconnected stories. That the universe is expanding and unfinished and is still coming into being has yet to permeate deeply into Catholic understanding. Internally and outwardly, Catholicism is in crisis. For John Haught, "At the bottom . . . the problem is both cosmological and metaphysical" (*RF*, 12). The church is anchored in a "worldview that lacks sufficient hope for the world's future, it clings to a sense of being that has yet to face the fact of the world's becoming" (*RF*, 12). In the main, our devotional life, worship, biblical interpretation, and theology are still based on presuppositions of a static cosmos. The church continues to focus on longing for the perfection lost in the Garden of Eden and is weighed down by working toward salvation in an otherworldly heaven. Such a focus is at variance with biblical hope or what is called Abrahamic hope—the hope of living into a future that will come into being by God's grace and human participation.

The Second Vatican Council, especially in *Gaudium et spes* (1965) and *Dei Verbum* (1965), encourages Catholics "to become more evolutionary in the understanding of the world and more biblical in their spirituality" (*RF*, 15; I draw on his summary on pp. 46–50). A new synthesis of Catholic spirituality with contemporary science and biblical hope is needed to call the church to be forward-looking as God calls humanity into a new, evolving future. The Council specified several significant paths that would lead to reviving Catholic spiritual life through a closer encounter of theology with the natural sciences.

3. John F. Haught, *Resting on the Future: Catholic Theology for an Unfinished Universe* (New York: Bloomsbury Academic, 2015), 1, 2–3. Hereafter, this source is cited as *RF* in the text.

Gaudium et spes acknowledges: "This scientific spirit exerts a new kind of impact on the cultural sphere and on modes of thought."[4] This implies two claims. The first is that "the human race has passed from a rather static concept of reality to a more dynamic, evolutionary one. In consequence, there has arisen a new series of problems . . . calling for efforts of analysis and synthesis" (*GS* §5).[5] Arising from this is a second claim: "A hope related to the end of time does not diminish the importance of intervening duties, but undergirds the acquittal of them with fresh incentives" (*GS* §21). Christian hope must not lead to a withdrawal from the world but an immersion into it for the "betterment" (*GS* §21) and "building up" of it (*GS* §34). In his "Closing Messages of the Council," Pope Paul VI spoke directly to scientists:

> Continue your search. . . . Never, perhaps, thank God, has there been so clear a possibility as today of a deep understanding between real science and real faith, mutual servants of one another in the one truth. Do not stand in the way of this important meeting. Have confidence in faith, this great friend of intelligence. Enlighten yourselves with its light in order to take hold of the whole truth.[6]

In 1988, John Paul II wrote to George V. Coyne, SJ, director of the Vatican Observatory:

> Does an evolutionary perspective bring any light to bear upon theological anthropology, . . . the problem of Christology—and even the development of doctrine itself? . . . Questions of this kind . . . require the sort of intense dialogue with contemporary science that has, on the whole, been lacking among those engaged in theological research and teaching. . . . In this process of mutual learning, those members of the Church . . . provide a much-needed ministry to others struggling to integrate the worlds of science and religion in their own intellectual and spiritual lives.[7]

4. Vatican Council II, Pastoral Constitution *Gaudium et spes* (December 7, 1965) §5. Hereafter, this source will be cited in the text as *GS*. Also, here and elsewhere in this essay, quotations from the documents of Vatican II are taken from Walter Abbott, *The Documents of Vatican II* (London-Dublin: Geoffrey Chapman, 1966).

5. In a footnote, Abbott comments: "The reference to dynamic evolutionary forces is perhaps one reason why some critics early objected to the influence of the thought of Pierre Teilhard de Chardin on the document" (*Documents of Vatican II*, 204n11).

6. In Abbott, *Documents of Vatican II*, 731.

7. John Paul II, "Letter of His Holiness John Paul II to Reverend George V. Coyne, SJ

In summary, while Vatican II calls for the church "to become more evolutionary in the understanding of the world and more biblical in their spirituality," in Haught's words (*RF*, 15), there is still much to be done. The descriptions of the problem in the 1960s and 1980s, outlined above, are valid still for the twenty-first century (Haught's book was written in 2015). Catholics, in the main, are still influenced by a worldview of a static universe. In this situation, Catholic biblical interpretation can offer, in the words just quoted from John Paul II, "a much-needed ministry to others struggling to integrate the worlds of science and religion in their own intellectual and spiritual lives." In developing such a ministry, the concentric circles of our personal story and our family story impinge on our awareness and openness to our cosmic story.

My Personal Story and Family Story

I am a Pākehā (European heritage) woman of Aotearoa New Zealand, a nation of Oceania, shaped by the signing of Te Tiriti o Waitangi (Treaty of Waitangi) between indigenous Māori and the British Crown in 1840. My Irish and English forebears arrived here in the 1860s–1870s. As a fourth/fifth-generation Pākehā of mainly Irish ancestry, I am aware that the laws that drove my Irish ancestors off their land were adapted by the British colonial power to drive the Māori from theirs. A hill-country upbringing enriches my understanding of creation. My experience of the evolving universe throughout the 2010–2012 earthquakes and aftershocks in my Otautahi Christchurch region was life-changing.[8] I am influenced by belonging to a particular Christian tradition, the Catholic Church, and by my academic education.

In my region, we are Aotearoa New Zealanders *of* Oceania.[9] According to Luamanuvau Winnie Laban, "in" and "of" are small words that have deep

Director of the Vatican Observatory," June 1, 1988, https://www.vatican.va/content/john-paul-ii/en/letters/1988/documents/hf_jp-ii_let_19880601_padre-coyne.html.

8. See my "On the Crossroads between Life and Death: Reading Birth Imagery in John in the Earthquake Changed Regions of Otautahi Christchurch," in *Bible, Borders, Belonging(s): Engaging Readings from Oceania*, ed. Jione Havea, David Neville, and Elaine Wainwright, SemeiaSt 75 (Atlanta: Society of Biblical Literature, 2014), 57–59.

9. The Islanders of this region often call this sea of islands "Oceania" or "Moana" rather than the name "Pacific Ocean" (*Mar Pacifico*) given by Ferdinand Magellan, who crossed this ocean in the early sixteenth century and gave Europe an image of a new world waiting to be explored, conquered, and colonized.

and subtle meaning. One can be *in* Oceania and stand apart as an observer or outsider. Being "of" the Oceania "gives a much greater sense of participation, of ownership, accountability and responsibility for actions taken."[10] While awareness of Oceania is growing increasingly in my region,[11] elsewhere "world" maps, globes, and photographs taken from outer space center on Northern Hemisphere land masses. Obscured is the Pacific Ocean, which extends over one-third of the surface of the planet and is the largest geographical feature on earth. This "water continent"[12] and "sea of islands"[13] has more than twenty thousand islands, in which all inhabitants, humans, sea creatures, animals, birds, insects, trees, and all life forms, are integrally related to one another. Today, the ancestral homes of Islanders are among the most threatened by climate change.[14] The affirmation of the goals of the Paris Agreement of December 2015 was largely due to input from Oceania leaders such as Anote Tong, former president of the Republic of Kiribati, one of the most affected nations.

Why is an acknowledgment of such belonging and my own story important to biblical interpretation? If we are unaware of our context, we remove Jesus, a tribal Middle Easterner, from his. We spiritualize and colonize the materiality and particularity of the incarnated Jesus who walked in sandals (John 1:27) on the Earth in a particular time and place dominated by the Roman Empire as well as the contexts in which the biblical texts were written

10. Luamanuvau Winnie Laban, "Closing Remarks," in *Resilience in the Pacific: Addressing the Critical Issues*, ed. Brian Lynch and Graham Hassall (Wellington: New Institute of International Affairs, 2011), 191.

11. The Episcopal Conference of the Pacific (CEPAC) begins its *Synod Synthesis CEPAC Conference* document with, "We are conscious that the Pacific Ocean gives an identity to the various dioceses of CEPAC," continuing then with creation, ocean and land. Episcopal Conference of the Pacific, *Synod Synthesis CEPAC Conference*, August 14, 2022, https://synod.org.pl/pacific-region-episcopal-conference-of-the-pacific-c-e-pac.

12. Steven Roger Fischer, *A History of the Pacific Islands*, 2nd ed. (Basingstoke: Palgrave Macmillan, 2013), xvii. On the political status of these twenty-two countries and territories, see Jon Barnett and John Campbell, *Climate Change and Small Island States: Power, Knowledge and the South Pacific* (London: Earthscan, 2010), 106–9. On the environment, history, culture, population, and economy, see Moshe Rapaport, ed., *The Pacific Islands: Environment and Society*, rev. ed. (Honolulu: University of Hawaii Press, 2013).

13. Coined by Epeli Hau'ofa in his article, "Our Sea of Islands," *The Contemporary Pacific* 6, no. 1 (1994): 148–61.

14. See the State of the Environment for Oceania reports published annually since 2014 by Caritas Oceania (https://caritas.org.nz/state-environment). See my "Pacific Island Peoples: Resilience and Climate Change," *Concilium* 3 (2017): 105–12.

and circulated.[15] The notion that the early Christian tradition was confined to its Greek and Latin expressions is still commonly held in biblical studies. In a world becoming ever more aware of Western colonial domination, Scripture needs to be interpreted in the light of Middle Eastern culture.[16] The theology of inspiration and revelation is always embedded and embodied culturally and cannot just focus on the text formation of the Gospels without the whole cultural, oral, and presuppositional milieu in which it occurred. This will take us beyond the obligation to focus on the four stages through which our canonical Gospels emerged:

1. The *life and teaching* of Jesus of Nazareth in *Aramaic*
2. The Aramaic *eyewitness testimony* to that life and teaching
3. The *translation* of that into *Greek*
4. The selection, arrangement, and editing of those *Greek texts* into *Gospels*[17]

Kenneth Bailey indicates ways for biblical interpreters to embark on such a quest. First, there are ancient, medieval, and modern written resources. Second, today in the Middle East are Christian people "who live, breathe, think, act and participate in Middle Eastern culture," and "their voices, past and present, need to be heard in biblical studies."[18] Third, their voices and writings focus on culture and also on rhetoric, whereby "for millennia they have constructed poetry and some prose using parallelisms."[19] Fourth, in the West, while inspiration may be discussed in exegesis,[20] the process of biblical inspiration is rarely considered as part of biblical interpretation.[21] The inspi-

15. In Oceania, "Jesus has been cast as the colonizer, imposed upon the native peoples." Te Aroha Rountree, "Once Was Colonised: Jesus Christ," in *Theology as Threshold: Invitations from Aotearoa New Zealand*, ed. Jione Havea, Emily Colgan, and Nāsili Vaka'uta, Decolonizing Theology (Lanham, MD: Lexington Books/Fortress Academic 2022), 161. Among the questions she poses is "*What if Jesus was not the colonizer, but rather among the colonized?*"

16. Kenneth E. Bailey, *Jesus through Middle Eastern Eyes: Cultural Studies in the Gospels* (London: SPCK, 2008), 11–21.

17. Bailey, *Jesus through Middle Eastern Eyes*, 18.

18. Bailey, *Jesus through Middle Eastern Eyes*, 12. Bailey lived in the Middle East for sixty years.

19. Bailey, *Jesus through Middle Eastern Eyes*, 12–18, examining Isa 28:8–14.

20. See, recently, James B. Prothro, "Theories of Inspiration and Catholic Exegesis: Scripture and Criticism in Dialogue with Denis Farkasfalvy," *CBQ* 83, no. 2 (2021): 294–314.

21. Bailey, *Jesus through Middle Eastern Eyes*, 19.

ration of the Gospels needs to be seen as a *process* that evolved over thirty to fifty-plus years. The Jesus story is about living participation and heart involvement. Scripture texts, therefore, need to be examined "holistically."[22] Crucial to understanding God's new unfolding future is the understanding of revelation, which leads to the concentric circle of our Christian story.

Our Christian Story

Theology is "as strong or weak as its understanding of revelation" and the presuppositions on which it is grounded.[23] This is surely so in the practice of biblical interpretation. Most people associate the word "revelation" with some special revelation of God in the history of Judaism and Jesus Christ, as particular, historical, and specific revelation.[24] The Jewish strand of revelation centers on the self-communication of God in the history of Israel, in the covenant of Sinai, and in creation. The strand of Christian revelation understands that the crystallization of Jewish and general revelation is found in the life and death-resurrection of Jesus as the Christ.[25] The primary emphasis for a Christian is placed on the personal revelation of God that takes place in Jesus, the mediator between God and humanity who is Word made flesh. In biblical interpretation, this is surely "the world of the biblical text."

The backdrop against which particular, historical, and specific revelation take place in both the ancient world and today is universal, cosmic, and general revelation. Early church theologians taught that God's loving self-communication, or what is called revelation, is revealed through the book of Nature and the book of Scripture. God also reveals Godself in the "seeds of the Word"[26] in the arts, philosophy, and science; in the beauty of cosmos and order of creation; in the action and presence of the Spirit of God in the lives of individuals; in culture and other religions.[27] The cosmic dimensions of God's revelation are increasingly before us in light of new cosmologies

22. Bailey, *Jesus through Middle Eastern Eyes*, 19–20.

23. Dermott A. Lane, *The Experience of God: An Invitation to Do Theology* (New York: Paulist, 2003), 46–47.

24. Lane, *Experience of God*, 46–72.

25. I hyphenate death-resurrection. On this unity and its subsequent separate emphasis, see my *The Parable of the Woman in Childbirth of John 16:21: A Metaphor for the Death and Glorification of Jesus* (Lewiston NY: Mellen, 2011), 6.

26. Vatican Council II, Decree *Ad gentes* (December 7, 1965) §22.

27. See the diagram "Different Layers of Revelation" in Lane, *Experience of God*, 65.

and astrophysics. I have indicated above that, in the main, Catholicism is trapped in a static worldview. In the light of this, the role of Catholic biblical interpretation is to engage with Scripture to critique "a distorting tradition" and uncover new readings.[28]

The interpretation of Scripture has a back-and-forth relationship with church tradition, a dialectical relationship that is a long, complex matter and a tension within which we must stand. As Francis Moloney reminds us, "The difficult balance between the word of Scripture and the living tradition of the Church can only be preserved when full consideration and respect is given to each in its uniqueness, made evident in our respect for the importance of both, in their mutuality."[29]

Further, the mutual relationship between Scripture and tradition, essential to Catholic teaching, has never been easy to either define or practice, as seen in *Dei Verbum* §9:

> Hence there exists a close connection and communication between sacred tradition and Sacred Scripture. For both of them, flowing from the same divine wellspring, in a certain way merge into a unity [*in unum quodammodo coalescunt*, "come together in some fashion"] and move towards the same goal.[30]

The fact of the mutuality of Scripture and tradition is affirmed. However, the relationship remains vague in the formulation: they come together in some fashion ("in unum quodammodo coalescunt"). The questioning of traditional practices through a careful use of the Scriptures is a delicate but necessary task in a human institution that always runs the risk of "distorting" its tradition.[31] As "Scripture and Tradition flow from the same divine well-

28. See my "Rediscovering Forgotten Features: Scripture, Tradition and Whose Feet May Be Washed on Holy Thursday Night," in *Reinterpreting the Eucharist: Explorations in Feminist Theology and Ethics*, ed. Anne Elvey et al. (Sheffield: Equinox Publishing, 2013), 93–96.

29. Francis J. Moloney, *A Body Broken for a Broken People: Divorce, Remarriage, and the Eucharist*, 3rd ed. (Mulgrave: Garratt Publishing, 2015), 5. I draw now on his insights from pp. 25–32.

30. Vatican Council II, Dogmatic Constitution *Dei Verbum* (November 18, 1965) §9 (Abbott's translation).

31. On *Dei Verbum* §9, Joseph Ratzinger raises the urgency of the need to face these "distortions" with the correcting role of the Scripture: "We shall have to acknowledge the truth of the criticism that there is, in fact, no explicit mention of the possibility of a distorting tradition and of the place of Scripture as an element within the church that is

spring," it is essential to pursue the challenge to learn from the source that nourishes faith rather than focus on either Scripture or tradition or set up a conflict between them, as I shall now consider in the concentric circle of our human story in God's unfinished, evolving universe. The complexity of this aspect of our story leads me to approach it in three parts and at greater length than the other concentric circles.

Our Human Story

Religion as the Inside Story of the Universe

Preceding life on earth, which goes back about 3.7 billion years, is the expanding universe, which stretches back over about 13.4 billion years.[32] Modern humans probably emerged 200,000 years ago. Scientific awareness attempts to connect the relatively short span of our human existence with the larger cosmic epic. This is sometimes referred to as "Big History," which seeks "to tell the story of *everything* that has taken place in the past, including what was going on in the universe before Homo sapiens arrived."[33] According to John Haught, what is missing and unexplored is sustained reference to the inside story of the universe, which is about the drama of life's awakening to interiority and religious awareness, which cannot be measured by science or merely historical reporting (*NCS*, 2).[34]

A narrative is needed that tells how religion fits into the cosmic story. "We humans are latecomers in the cosmic story, and religion came with us" (*NCS*, 8). Those expounding the Big Story treat religion as part of the human story and resort to historical methods, the social sciences, psychology, and

also critical of tradition, which means that a most important side of the problem of the tradition, as shown by the history of the church—and perhaps the real crux of the *ecclesia semper reformanda*—has been overlooked. . . . That this opportunity has been missed can only be regarded as an unfortunate omission." Joseph Ratzinger, "Chapter II, The Transmission of Divine Revelation," in *Commentary on the Documents of Vatican II*, ed. Herbert Vorgrimler, trans. William Glen-Doepel et al. (New York: Herder and Herder, 1968), 3:192–93.

32. For a summary, see Denis Edwards, *How God Acts: Creation, Redemption, and Special Divine Action* (Hindmarsh: ATF Theology, 2010), 1–14.

33. John F. Haught, *The New Cosmic Story: Inside Our Awakening Universe* (New Haven: Yale University Press, 2017), 1. Hereafter, this source is cited in the text as *NCS*.

34. Writers who overlook this include Stephen Hawking, Stephen Jay Gould, and Richard Dawkins.

evolutionary biology. Even though the history of religion is ambiguous and sometimes barbarous, its role in the story of cosmic emergence and awakening must be taken into account (*NCS*, 13, 15; on "wrongness," see pp. 159–73). Although we cannot know for certain, religion—the most significant way in which humans have looked for meaning—probably arose indistinctly with the birth of human consciousness. Our ancestors began to develop a sense of a spiritual world and, through religious rituals, sought to enter it. Haught explains: "In the Dao de Jing in China, in the Upanishads and sermons of the Buddha in India, in the philosophical dialogues of Plato in Greece, and in the Abrahamic traditions of the Near East, a new turn was taking place in the story of the universe . . . it is not enough to view the extraordinary axial transformation of religious consciousness simply as a set of local geographical, historical, cultural, and terrestrial curiosities. It is also a whole new era in cosmic history" (*NCS*, 11).

In this new era, the term "religion" indicates an awakening to the dawn of "rightness" (*NCS*, 12). A new yet continuing movement of consciousness began making ever clearer distinctions between a right way and a wrong way to live, think, act, work, and pray. The "purpose" of religion is the realizing of rightness. In the particularity of each distinctive tradition are characteristics common to many religious perspectives. For Haught, "every aspect of religion gains new meaning and importance once we link it to the new scientific story of an unfinished universe" (*NCS*, 10). Religion, therefore, is an indispensable new epoch in a cosmic story. He contends that "biblical studies have corrected the extreme otherworldliness of traditional eschatological expectation" (*NCS*, 115). In my experience, however, Catholic biblical interpretation has yet to embrace an anticipatory view of the cosmos and critique a distorting tradition. It needs to focus on what religion means in the context of cosmic drama.

An Anticipatory Approach

Catholic biblical interpretation is called to an anticipatory approach "that can accommodate in one wide vision both biblical hope and contemporary science's unfinished universe" (*RF*, 22). This anticipatory vision (metaphysics of the future) offers cosmic hope as a framework.[35] While theologically

35. Haught (*RF*, 22–28) distinguishes this from an analogical vision (metaphysic of the eternal present) and from an archaeological vision (metaphysics of the past). In his *New Cosmic Story* (32–41), the latter is named as archaenomic.

we can only sketch our understanding of God, science is also unsure of what is to come. However, if Catholic thought is both scientifically awake and stirred by Abrahamic faith, "we are a forward-looking species whose vitality, intellectual passion, and moral seriousness require our acknowledging the fundamentally anticipatory orientation of our existence" (*RF*, 159). From a biblical point of view, human existence is an exodus journey, a pilgrimage, a desert wandering. This sense of being on a spiritual journey does not uproot us from nature but moves humanity from anthropocentric stewardship to care of our common home.[36]

Cosmic hope is a hope that is grounded in the Abrahamic, prophetic religious traditions in which the central biblical theme of promise sees all events in nature and history as a path *toward* the living God who is "up ahead, calling the temporal world into being from out of the future" (*RF*, 121). Cosmic hope—waiting hope—"stays with the world process, waiting patiently across the generations . . . for the dramatic flow of events to carry the whole of creation, and not just our personal lives, towards fulfilment in God" (*RF*, 122). This awareness of an unfinished universe raises questions about suffering. Within the Christian tradition, suffering has been viewed as expiation. A theology of expiation "tries to make sense of suffering by attributing it solely to sin." Where there is guilt, a matching penalty must be "paid in the currency of suffering" (*RF*, 95). Another theological proposal tries to make sense of suffering by moving it from expiation to education, where suffering is meaningful as being part of a divine discipline to develop the character or soul in a way essential to growth (*RF*, 96). Within the anticipatory hope of Abrahamic expectation, such views have no legitimate place because suffering is part of an unfinished universe, which is in the process of becoming through "divine love [that] as revealed in Jesus opens up the possibility of new life unceasingly" (*RF*, 97–99). Cosmic hope is an anticipatory approach, an anticipatory vision of nature. A posture of waiting hope is the fundamental biblical virtue (*RF*, 36).

Abrahamic hope permeates Scripture and the teachings of Jesus. Reading with Abrahamic hope invites us toward the horizon of fuller being to which God, up ahead, is calling us.[37] Jesus invites us to live with hope into the

36. See my "Beyond the Paradigm of Stewardship: Making Right Relationship Happen with God, People and Earth," in *Habitats of the Basileia: Essays in Honour of Elaine M. Wainwright*, ed. Caroline Blyth, Emily Colgan, and Robert Myles (Sheffield: Sheffield Phoenix Press, forthcoming).

37. On Luke 12:32–34, see my "Living into Our Future," *Tui Motu InterIslands* 273 (August 2022): 24–25.

promise of God's unfolding future. The Pauline understanding of a universe in Christ (Col 1:13–20; Eph 1:9–10) reflects the scientific understanding of a universe becoming more. Abrahamic hope evokes one who, against hope, believes in hope (Rom 4:18). Insights such as these in Scripture have been struggling to emerge from the shadows.

The Evolutionary Achievement of Jesus

In the light of evolution, death is a biological necessity and a fact of evolutionary life. No further explanation is needed. This departs from the explanation found in the Jewish and Christian account of the fall.[38] In traditional Christianity, death is seen as a penalty. The 1994 *Catechism of the Catholic Church* ignores evolutionary science and its explanations of human origins. It repeats and expands the teaching of the Council of Trent (1545–1563) that through procreation everyone inherited the original sin of Adam, whose guilt is forgiven through the sacrament of baptism while sinful desires yet persist fomenting sin in human persons.[39] Going beyond the traditional atonement approach, others view the death of Jesus as "a striking moral example of the extent to which altruism could draw one."[40]

Within God's purpose of creation, Jesus in his death-resurrection saved humanity from the evolutionary destiny of individual death rather than from sin. Mahoney refers to this as "the evolutionary achievement of Jesus."[41] Benedict XVI spoke of the resurrection being like "an explosion of light . . . a qualitative leap in the history of 'evolution' and of life in general toward a new future life, toward a new world which, starting from Christ, already continuously permeates this world of ours, transforms it and draws it to itself."[42]

38. On Catholic responses to evolution, see Jack Mahoney, *Christianity in Evolution: An Exploration* (Washington, DC: Georgetown University Press, 2011), 2–6.

39. Jack Mahoney, *Christianity in Evolution*, 55–60. Note Mahoney's comments on "what Paul meant in Romans 5:12 when he used the Greek phrase *eph' hō* relating to Adam's action. Augustine and others, including the council fathers at Trent, relying on the Old Latin translations, took this to mean in Latin *in quo*, or 'in whom,' with the clear implication that everyone had sinned in Adam. Most exegetes today understand this phrase as using the common Greek preposition *epi* to imply succession rather than inclusion, thus giving the meaning 'since when' rather than 'in whom' all have sinned." Mahoney, *Christianity in Evolution*, 55. See *CCC* §§379–421.

40. Mahoney, *Christianity in Evolution*, 51.

41. Mahoney, *Christianity in Evolution*, 49–70.

42. Benedict XVI, "Easter Vigil Homily" (15 April 2006). https://www.vatican.va/con

The questions that emerge about traditional Christian teachings that focus on an original sin, which "for many Christians is the most difficult religious teaching to square with Darwinian evolution,"[43] invite us to return to the concentric circle of our Christian story. There we reflected how in evolutionary consciousness, "religion" indicates an awakening to the dawn of "rightness" whereby a new, continuing movement began making ever more clear distinctions between a right way and a wrong way to live, think, act, work, and pray. What is traditionally called original sin is "the brokenness of the world into which each of us is born, a condition to which we humans have contributed throughout history" (*RF*, 40–41). In his encyclical *Sollicitudo rei socialis*, or *On Social Concerns*, John Paul II names structures of injustice as "structures of sin" that "are rooted in personal sin, and thus always linked to the concrete acts of individuals who introduce these structures, consolidate them and make them difficult to remove."[44] This sinful condition affects the entire creation, which is exploited by human greed and violence. According to Denis Edwards, "We need to retrieve [original sin] and bring it alive for the twenty-first century."[45] This calls for a redemption as extensive as the whole created world. Haught points out that our actual sins are "rebellions against God's passionate call and creative longing for the universe to become more than it is at present." He continues: "Only God, whom we believe to have become incarnate in the Christ, can bring ultimate healing and meaning to life's evolution, to the individual's misery, to a history distorted by human sin, and ultimately, to the entire restless universe" (*RF*, 40–41). In addition, the violent death of Jesus, freely undertaken because of the moral program to which he committed himself, which met with resistance from religious leaders and the Roman Empire, can sharpen the focus of the gospel and give it more vitality and relevance today. This is not about people today losing a sense of sin but living with a sense of maturity, reality, and discovery in the concentric circle of our earth story.

---

tent/benedict-xvi/en/homilies/2006/documents/hf_ben-xvi_hom_20060415_veglia-pasquale.html.

43. John F. Haught, *God after Darwin: A Theology of Evolution* (Philadelphia: Westview, 2008), 145–46.

44. John Paul II, Encyclical Letter *Sollicitudo rei socialis* (December 30, 1987) §36. https://www.vatican.va/content/john-paul-ii/en/encyclicals/documents/hf_jp-ii_enc_30121987_sollicitudo-rei-socialis.html.

45. Edwards, *God Acts*, 129.

Our Earth Story

In *Laudato si'*, Pope Francis refers to our "common home" (§6). All belong to the household (οἶκος) of God. "Ecology" and "ecumenism" (οἰκουμένη), along with "economics," which is so linked with hearing "*both the cry of the earth and the cry of the poor*" (*LS* §49), are also derived from this Greek word.[46] Integral ecology affirms the deep connections found in the biblical creation accounts, which "suggest that human life is grounded in three fundamental and closely intertwined relationships: with God, with our neighbour and the earth itself" (*LS* §66). This resonates in my context, where Māori have an expression in verbal form, *whakawhanaungatanga*, or "making right relationship happen." The causative prefix *whaka* suggests "making" and turns the noun *whanaungatanga* (right relationship) into the verb *whakawhanaungatanga*, meaning "making right relationship" in a series of interconnected relationships with God (*Atua*), people (*tangata*), and land (*whenua*).[47] We are called to live an integral ecology, aware that "everything is interconnected" (*LS* §138) and ready "*to hear both the cry of the earth and the cry of the poor*" (*LS* §49). The fundamental ecological virtue is hope (*RF*, 158).

According to Ann Braudis, ecology presupposes evolution. She understands that evolutionary biology is woven into *Laudato si'* (e.g., *LS* §§18, 81).[48] For her, "the value of this document lies in its harmony with evolutionary consciousness," which refers to the capacity of human beings to be conscious participants in the evolution of their cultures and human society in order to "contribute, both as one human family and each one in our own modest way, to the ongoing creation of a now-awaking universe."[49] Braudis identifies five ways in which this is so. First, *Laudato si'* is informed not only by Scripture and other spiritual insights but by the results of scientific research (e.g., *LS* §§62, 201). Second, it is inclusive in character: "I would like to enter into dialogue with all people about our common home" (*LS* §3). Third, it has awareness of a shifting worldview. Francis refers explicitly to

46. Ecology is from Greek οἶκος (household) and λόγος (word).

47. Henare Tate, "Stepping into Māori Spirituality," in *He Kupu Whakawairua Spirituality in Aotearoa New Zealand: Catholic Voices*, ed. Helen Bergin and Susan Smith (Auckland: Accent Publications, 2002), 41–43. On indigenous people, see *LS* §§146, 179.

48. Ann Braudis, "*Laudato Si'* and Evolutionary Consciousness," in *NewsNotes*, 41, no. 3 (2016): 3. https://maryknollogc.org/sites/default/files/newsnotes/attachments/MayJune2016_NewsNotes.pdf.

49. Braudis, "*Laudato Si'* and Evolutionary Consciousness," 3.

"a strategy for real change" that requires "rethinking processes in their entirety, for it is not enough to include a few superficial ecological considerations while failing to question the logic which underlies present-day culture" (*LS* §197). Fourth, the keyword "integral" is often found: "What is needed is a politics which is far-sighted and capable of a new, integral and interdisciplinary approach to handling different aspects of the [environmental] crisis" (*LS* §197). Finally, there is an understanding of the qualities of truth, beauty, and goodness. These express the longings of the human heart, where "the human spirit and consciousness are ceaselessly touched by and yearn for the Infinite and from which cultural change flows."[50] Such are central to spiritual experience from which emerges the development of consciousness and cultural change.

Jesus's inherited belief in the gift of the land is the backdrop to his role in God's call. His imagination was grounded in the natural world and the human struggle with it. Sean Freyne suggests that the potential blessedness of life in the land so moved Jesus to see the present as a graced moment that influenced the direction of his ministry.[51] Halvor Moxnes highlights the importance of three dimensions of place for understanding an incident or saying or action in the life of Jesus as he participated in God's mission in the context of the changing face of Galilee: the experience of place, specifically how it is managed and controlled; the legitimation of place, that is, the ideological underpinning of the dominant controlling view; and the imagination of place, or the way in which an alternative vision of place can be developed and strategies conceived to implement the new, evolving vision.[52]

In summary, by moving through the interconnected concentric circles of my personal story, my family story, our Christian story, our human story, our Earth story, and our cosmic story, I have offered a way for Catholic biblical interpretation to foster a new synthesis of Catholic spirituality with contemporary science and biblical hope.

Denis Edwards summarizes the stance from which, as a biblical interpreter, I shall take steps toward an anticipatory reading of the Gospel according to John by considering aspects of the Prologue (John 1:1–18), which will plunge me into the story in new, unfolding ways in order to participate

50. Braudis, "*Laudato Si'* and Evolutionary Consciousness," 3.

51. Sean Freyne, *Jesus, A Jewish Galilean: A New Reading of the Jesus-Story* (London: T&T Clark, 2004), 42.

52. Halvor Moxnes, *Putting Jesus in His Place: A Radical Vision of Household and Kingdom* (Louisville: Westminster John Knox, 2003), 1–21.

with Jesus in completing the works of God by hearing "*both the cry of the earth and the cry of the poor*" (*LS* §49). Edwards writes: "When twenty-first century cosmology describes the emergence and expansion of our universe, and when contemporary biology describes the evolution of life on Earth, the [biblical interpreter] takes these scientific findings seriously, because she interprets the history of the universe that cosmology describes, and the story of life that biology articulates, as the fruit of the divine action of creation."[53]

Toward an Anticipatory Reading of the Prologue of the Gospel according to John

An anticipatory reading, as we have seen, is grounded in Abrahamic hope, which sees nature and history as part of the world of becoming into which we may confidently insert our lives and particular callings as we journey *toward* the living God who is up ahead, calling all creation into being in an unfinished and evolving universe. Among the ways in which John's Gospel tells an old story in a new way is to begin with the Prologue (1:1–18), which sets the tone, introduces concepts and characters, and contains clues to what will unfold in the story that follows. In this cosmological framework, Jesus is inserted into the unfolding drama of God's unfinished, evolving story both by reinterpreting the biblical cosmologies of Genesis 1 and the Wisdom literature and by drawing on understandings of ancient Hellenistic cosmology to describe the life and death-resurrection of Jesus.[54]

Ancient understandings of the cosmos are very different from our contemporary views. While the ecological concerns that face twenty-first century readers were not ancient preoccupations, Rémi Brague identifies that at the heart of ancient and medieval cosmologies, with their links to anthropology, was a wisdom that led to ethics. He identifies four aspects of a cosmological framework: (1) it articulates the link between cosmology and the human person; (2) it considers "the world" as the resting place for hu-

53. Edwards, *God Acts*, 1.

54. Space does not permit me to go into detail here. For further information, see my "The Cosmology of John 1:1–14 and Its Implications for Ethical Action in This Ecological Age," *Colloquium* 45, no. 2 (2013): 137–53; Kathleen P. Rushton, RSM, "The Implications of the Cosmology of the Prologue for Johannine Eschatology," *InterfaceTheology* 1, no. 1 (2015): 37–54; Kathleen P. Rushton, RSM, *The Cry of the Earth and the Cry of the Poor: Hearing Justice in John's Gospel* (London: SCM, 2020), 3–15.

manity; (3) it links cosmology to wisdom; and (4) it leads to contemplation as the precursor to ethical action.[55] I shall look briefly at three terms in the Prologue (ἐν ἀρχῇ, ὁ λόγος, and πάντα) that evoke nuances in both biblical and Hellenistic cosmologies, thereby creating new rhetorical and theological nuances in the Johannine symbolic world.[56]

"In the beginning" (ἐν ἀρχῇ) in John 1:1 recalls the Genesis creation account, where the Spirit hovered over the waters and creation is presented as the garden of God.[57] John ends with, "Now there was a garden in the place where he was crucified, and in the garden, there was a new tomb" (John 19:41). Incarnation and death-resurrection are linked with ongoing creation. 'Eν ἀρχῇ also conveyed a multiplicity of Hellenistic philosophical and cosmological notions. The ἀρχῇ is a "beginning," although it does not have a beginning or an end. It also "surrounds" and "steers" all that is, "containing the whole and in some way responsible for and explaining its direction."[58] It is the basic "stuff" of the world. "The *archē* of the early philosophers names what there was before there was anything else; it has a role as providing a causal explanation for the world and its phenomena, but does not have to be explained itself."[59]

The term for "the Word," ὁ λόγος, also echoed many Hellenistic concepts that enabled the evangelist to express the central truth of the life and death-resurrection of Jesus in the context of an understanding that saw the wonders of the world as living and moving images of the eternal. For the Jewish philosopher Philo of Alexandria, ὁ λόγος contains the world of ideas and is the instrument of creation and the principle of cosmic cohesion.[60] The extent of this term is shown by Philo, who according to Brague "uncovered the principle of creation and gave it a Greek name that evokes a thousand res-

55. Rémi Brague, *The Wisdom of the World: The Human Experience of the Universe in Western Thought*, trans. Teresa Lavender Faga (Chicago: University of Chicago Press, 2003). For a summary, see my "Cosmology of John," 140–43.

56. On these terms, see my "Cosmology of John," 143–52.

57. Margaret Daly-Denton, *John: An Earth Bible Commentary; Supposing Him to Be the Gardener* (London: Bloomsbury T&T Clark, 2017), 27–41, who from an ecological perspective sets out extensively the biblical echoes related to the garden of God in the Prologue.

58. M. R. Wright, *Cosmology in Antiquity*, Sciences of Antiquity (London: Routledge, 1995), 167.

59. Wright, *Cosmology in Antiquity*, 167.

60. Edward Adams, "Graeco-Roman and Ancient Jewish Cosmology," in *Cosmology and New Testament Theology*, ed. Jonathan T. Pennington and Sean M. McDonough, LNTS 355 (London: T&T Clark, 2008), 26.

onances: *logos*."[61] Calling Jesus "the Word" evokes the dynamic energy and power of the word and deed of the biblical "word of God." Word and deed go together. "God said" is repeated ten times as God creates (Gen 1:3–26). In the prophetic tradition, "the word of God came" to prophets, challenging and propelling action (e.g., Joel 1:1; Hos 1:1). The word of God is a life-giving factor (Deut 32:46–47), has power to heal (Ps 107:20), is a light for the people (Ps 119:105), and has a creative function (Ps 33:6). Several times, the word of God is presented as having an apparent existence of its own, carrying out an independent personal function (Isa 55:11).

The term λόγος is not found beyond the Prologue with this sense. The familiar philosophical and biblical intertextuality of ἐν ἀρχῇ and the continuity this suggests with John 1:1 give way to discontinuity, for the λόγος is ascribed qualities of Wisdom/Sophia. By the end of the Prologue, it is firmly established that the male Word/λόγος is Jesus, who is imaged as the female figure of Wisdom. This continues as the Gospel unfolds.[62] The word of God theology has a common heritage in the Wisdom literature.

By Plato's time (c. 428–347 BCE), the word πάντα ("all things") was one of several ways of naming the universe.[63] In the Wisdom traditions, this refers to the wider-than-human creation (Wis 7:15–22). God is addressed by the narrator: you "have made all things by your word, and by your wisdom have formed humankind" (Wis 9:1–2).[64] Thus, the word and wisdom, along with humankind and "all things," are linked. Wisdom "pervades and penetrates all things" (7:24) and "can do all things" and "renews all things" (7:27). Wisdom, reaching from one end of the earth to the other, "orders all things well" (8:1). Because "she is an initiate in the knowledge of God," Wisdom is "the active cause of all things" (8:4–5). This biblical use of the phrase "all things" to convey a sense of the cosmos matches a similar phrase, "holds all things together," found in ancient Stoic philosophy to express the concept of a divine bond that unifies the world.[65] In summary, in the rich preexistent divine Wisdom/Sophia tradition, the Hellenistic intellectual tradition of a unified cosmos is expressed in biblical terms.

61. Brague, *Wisdom of the World*, 47.

62. For an overview of the scholarship on Wisdom/Sophia in this Gospel, see my *Parable of the Woman in Childbirth*, 214–18.

63. Adams, "Graeco-Roman and Ancient Jewish Cosmology," 6–7.

64. Citations from the book of Wisdom in this paragraph are taken from the NRSV.

65. Ernest G. Clarke, *The Wisdom of Solomon*, CBC (Cambridge: Cambridge University Press, 1973), 18.

In summary, the cosmological horizon of the Prologue and that of present-day readers, informed by twenty-first-century cosmologies and evolutionary biology, can meet in a biblically inspired shift to a vision that integrates more deliberately the biblical themes of promise and liberation, embracing prophetic justice and covenantal promises that Scripture associates with a creative and renewing God (*RF*, 171). Thus, present-day Christians are affirmed and challenged to live with a wisdom that inspires a transforming spirituality and ethical action in our complex, evolving, beautiful, suffering, and interconnected world in which the works of God are unfinished. Imagination plays a vital role in our understanding of reality—ourselves, the world, the universe, and God. Our understanding of the "world" is rich and multilayered. We are missioned to the *good world*,[66] which is always being made new and coming into being. Our action in the world contributes to the deeper incarnation of God and the redemptive gathering of the whole world into the body of Christ (*RF*, 52). We confront the *evil world*, resisting all subjection to earthly masters who exploit the Earth, human beings, and the other-than-human. We seek the *alternative world* of God's new, unfolding future in which we are called to participate with Jesus in God's work of ongoing creation by hearing "*both the cry of the earth and the cry of the poor*" (*LS* §49).

66. On these three worlds, see Sandra M. Schneiders, IHM, *Buying the Field: Catholic Religious Life in the Mission to the World* (New York: Paulist, 2013), 37.

What Does It Mean to Read Scripture as the Word of God?

Navigating Authority and Normativity

Luke Timothy Johnson

In this essay, I propose to think about what it might mean to read Scripture as the word of God.[1] The topic embraces two distinct but interrelated questions pertinent to those seeking to practice their scholarship as believers. First, what is the meaning of the designation "word of God" when applied to the compositions of the Christian canon?[2] Second, what does this designation mean—that is, imply—for how these compositions are read? In brief, how do (or how should) convictions concerning the character of Scripture determine the dispositions of readers? The second of these questions is the one that I want most to engage, but the first question, for reasons of clarity, demands to be dealt with first.

You will notice that I speak of "Scripture" (γραφή) rather than "the Bible" (τὰ βιβλία) for the simple but important reason that "Scripture" designates the collection of writings that the church has determined should be read liturgically in the assembly to the faithful precisely as "the word of God" and which alone should be used in ecclesial debates concerning right belief and right practice, whereas "the Bible" simply identifies the same compositions as a historically defined collection that can be engaged by believers and unbelievers alike in any fashion they choose, as they might engage the collection of Plato's dialogues or the Upanishads. To employ the term "Scripture" for these writings, then, is to place ourselves within the context of ecclesial life—the context shaped by the commitment of faith—rather than the con-

1. This essay builds on, but goes in a different direction than, my contributions to the volume coauthored by myself and William S. Kurz, *The Future of Catholic Biblical Scholarship: A Constructive Conversation* (Grand Rapids: Eerdmans, 2002). For part of the discussion that book engendered, see the symposium in *Nova et Vetera* 4, no. 1 (2006): 95–200.

2. See Luke Timothy Johnson, *The Writings of the New Testament: An Interpretation*, 3rd ed. (Minneapolis: Fortress, 2010), 525–41.

text of the academy. It is Scripture precisely as the church's book that we choose to designate as the word of God.

This ecclesial context is, first and above all, a liturgical context. From as early as the Council of Carthage in 397, the canon of Scripture was defined in terms of the writings that were to be read in the assembly.[3] In contemporary Catholic usage, readings from the prophets and epistles are concluded with the ritual declaration "The word of the Lord," to which the people respond, "Thanks be to God." This pronouncement and its response provide the structure of my reflection.

Preliminary Observations

The liturgical formula echoes the usage of Scripture itself, which, especially in the prophets (beginning with the first and greatest prophet, Moses) and in the apostle Paul, daringly attaches the tag "word of God" to the statements made by humans (see 1 Thess 2:13). The prophets claimed that the "word of God" came to them through auditions or visions, and they gave linguistic expression to what they heard and saw. Prophets are human beings who hear what other people hear and see what other people see, but within what they hear and see, they apprehend a deeper reality.[4] They are called to enunciate for others God's vision for the world, a vision (or "word") that otherwise would be inaccessible.

God's vision for the world, moreover, consistently challenges the world as constructed by humans on their own terms, making the pronouncement of God's word a dangerous enterprise. The prophetic word met with resistance and violent rejection. But the disciples of the prophets, who attended to the human words that spoke a divine challenge, preserved the oral pronouncements in writing so that what began as an oral intervention in the tangled circumstances of the past became, through reading, the permanent possibility of intersecting human experience in ever-changing circumstances.

Paul and the other apostles continued the mission of the prophets before them.[5] They were witnesses who proclaimed the presence and power of God

3. "Apart from the canonical scriptures nothing is read in church under the name of the divine Scriptures . . . let the church across the sea [i.e., Rome] be consulted for the confirmation of this canon" (Article 39).

4. See "The Character of the Prophet," in Luke Timothy Johnson, *Prophetic Jesus, Prophetic Church: The Challenge of Luke-Acts to Contemporary Christians* (Grand Rapids: Eerdmans, 2011), 39–51.

5. Although the designations differ, prophet and apostle are phenomenologically

in the death and resurrection of Jesus, not only as an event of the recent past but as an existential reality of the present: the work of the Holy Spirit among believers (in "signs and wonders") certified the "power" of the word of the cross (1 Cor 1:17–18; 2:4; cf. Rom 15:19). The "word" of the kerygma was good news (εὐαγγέλιον) from and about God that disclosed for those open to hearing a new vision of reality and a capacity for a new way of living "in Christ." The gospel was, in the preaching of the apostles, the direct heir of the "word of God" proclaimed by the prophets of old. By extension, the letters, visions, and narratives that believers composed could function in the same manner as prophetic compositions: they could mediate to readers in subsequent ages the promise and challenge of God's vision for humanity.

What Scripture itself shows us is that the expression "word of God" is a kind of shorthand (or synecdoche, if you prefer) for God's presence and power in the world, displayed through God's ongoing creation of all things visible and invisible, through the speech and actions of the prophets, and above all through Jesus, who is that Word made flesh (John 1:14). Scripture itself teaches us that God's word is "living and active" (Heb 4:12) in the human experience of God's presence before it finds expression in writing—writing, moreover, whose singular purpose is bearing witness to that living and active experience. Thus, Luke describes the expansion of the first Christian mission under the impetus and direction of the Holy Spirit as the spread of "the word" through proclamation and through signs and wonders worked by God (see Acts 6:7; 8:4; 11:1; 12:24; 13:49; 16:6; 19:20).

By no means, then, can Scripture be regarded as the sole source of God's self-disclosure. Even that passage from Paul that is sometimes cited as evidence for such an exclusive claim (2 Tim 3:15–17) stresses the functional character of all "God-inspired γραφή": it makes believers wise unto salvation, educates and trains them, equips them "for every good work" (2 Tim 3:17; cf. Titus 3:8, 14).[6] But Scripture itself makes abundantly clear that God's continuing self-revelation happens above all within and through human experience of God's world. It is difficult to improve on the excellent distinction made by Sandra Schneiders: Scripture does not so much contain

similar in their being sent to bear witness to God's presence and power in the world. See Luke Timothy Johnson, *Constructing Paul*, vol. 1 of *The Canonical Paul* (Grand Rapids: Eerdmans, 2020), 125–44.

6. For analysis and discussion, see Luke Timothy Johnson, *The First and Second Letters to Timothy*, AB 35A (New York: Doubleday, 2001), 416–26.

revelation as *participate* in revelation.[7] Such clarification does not diminish the significance of the written text but rather enhances it. For believers today—including Catholic scholars—Scripture has a privileged place within the hermeneutical dialectic that can be termed "revelation."[8]

First, without the symbols of Scripture, humans could never perceive, in the welter of their experience, the presence and power of the living God and, above all, the presence and power of the risen Christ through his Holy Spirit. Scripture faithfully read—in the liturgical assembly first of all, then in devotional meditation and then in disciplined study—shapes those who read into a scriptural construction of reality, enabling them to "imagine the world that Scripture imagines."[9] Scripture's ability to make readers "wise unto salvation" begins with this fundamental formative function: believers can perceive their experience in terms of idolatry and faith, of sin and grace, precisely and solely because Scripture has provided the lens to perceive it so.

Second, the experience of the world as suffused with God's presence and power often confirms believers' understanding of Scripture, but because the extratextual word of God that presses upon them at every moment is "living and active" and capable of genuine surprise, sometimes shaking believers' prior understanding of Scripture (and even of the God with whom they have to do), Scripture itself must be reread and understood anew in light of the experience of God in the world. The written text does not dictate to God or control God's possible activity. The obedience of faith is directed not at scriptural precedent but at the living God continuously active in the world. This does not imply the abandonment of Scripture. It merely confirms the role that Scripture itself adopts, as it constantly points outside itself to God's activity in the world.[10]

Third, this hermeneutical dialectic is what can properly be called "revelation," and it requires of believers the employment of critical intelligence

7. Sandra M. Schneiders, IHM, *The Revelatory Text: Interpreting the New Testament as Sacred Scripture*, 2nd ed. (Collegeville, MN: Liturgical Press, 1999).

8. For "Revelation as a Process of Interpretation," see Luke Timothy Johnson, *Faith's Freedom: A Classic Spirituality for Contemporary Christians* (Minneapolis: Fortress, 1990), 47–59.

9. See my discussion in Johnson and Kurz, *The Future of Catholic Biblical Scholarship*, 119–42. Richard B. Hays has similarly stressed the imagination as the cognitive/dispositional faculty that best engages the mystery of God's presence and power; see his *The Conversion of the Imagination: Paul as the Interpreter of Israel's Scriptures* (Grand Rapids: Eerdmans, 2005).

10. The argument is made in multiple ways in Luke Timothy Johnson, *The Revelatory Body: Theology as Inductive Art* (Grand Rapids: Eerdmans, 2015).

in a common effort to discern how God's word in the world and God's word in the text can be made creatively to converse, to discover the ways in which the tension between "what Scripture says" (or what we thought Scripture to be saying) and "what God is doing" (or what we hope we discern of God's mysterious activity) might be relieved, through new and possibly better understandings both of Scripture and of the living God.[11]

In a never-ending process of reciprocal shaping and influence, then, a process that involves the entire ecclesial community, the word of God expressed through the human experience of the world and the word of God as mediated by ancient and God-inspired texts summon all believers—and all believing scholars—into the asceticism of attentiveness that is an essential dimension of faith understood as creative fidelity.

A Critical Distinction

What weight, then, should believers give Scripture when they read it as the word of God? On this point, I think it is helpful to make a distinction between what is normative and what is authoritative. Scripture is clearly *normative* in the manner suggested above: in its liturgical and devotional reading, it fundamentally shapes the perceptions and dispositions of believers into a scriptural imagination. The world imagined by Scripture is the one that believers choose to adopt, embody, and enact.

But Scripture is also clearly not normative in the sense that everything proposed or commanded in Scripture must, or even should, be adopted, embodied, or enacted by faithful Christians. All of the limitations, inconsistencies, contradictions, and even flat errors identified already by patristic readers prohibit such a robotic "following" of Scripture. As every careful reader acknowledges, such difficulties make delusional the claim to "follow Scripture" in every respect. There are cases, indeed, in which the church must, under the guidance of the Holy Spirit, say no to explicit statements or directives in Scripture.

If the language of normativity tends in the direction of reducing Scripture to a set of rules or prescriptions, and fidelity to Scripture to the obedient

11. In my *Scripture and Discernment: Decision Making in the Church* (Nashville: Abingdon, 1996), I pay close attention to the way Luke's narrative of the church's decision to include gentiles without demanding the observance of the law provides a scriptural *exemplum* of this very interpretive dynamic.

fulfillment of such rules and prescriptions, the term *authoritative* opens the possibility of a more nuanced ascription of importance to Scripture. To say that Scripture as the word of God is authoritative is to acknowledge that believers choose to stand within the world that is unimaginable apart from Scripture, owe allegiance to the vision of God's world disclosed by Scripture, and engage Scripture in all its parts as they seek to discern the dimensions of their obedience to the living God.

The authority of Scripture for believing readers has at least three distinct aspects.[12] The first is the most important: Scripture as a whole and in all its parts *authors* a certain identity among readers, and it does so reliably. Those who attend faithfully to the teachings of Torah and the prophets, and who sing the psalms together and apart, perceive the world and their own existence as graciously given by the one God and as directed by God's wisdom. Those who attend to the writings of the New Testament are slowly fashioned according to "the mind of Christ" (1 Cor 2:16). They not only view the world through the lens of the crucified and exalted Christ but also seek to live according to the pattern of radical obedience and loving service embodied by Jesus (Phil 2:1–11). Liturgically proclaimed and devotionally pondered, Scripture authors (shapes) readers into people of faith rather than atheists, into Christians rather than Muslims or Buddhists, into compassionate servants of the poor and weak rather than elite despisers of the oppressed of the earth. It is this dimension of Scripture, its "authoring of identity," that can most properly be termed "normative."

A second aspect of Scripture's authority is the way it "authorizes" its own reinterpretation. The presence of Christ in the Holy Spirit gifts believers with an ἐξουσία (authority/freedom) and παρρησία (boldness/freedom/courage) that was so powerfully displayed by Jesus (Matt 7:29; 10:1; 28:18; Luke 4:32, 36; 5:24; John 5:27; 7:18; 12:49) and the apostles (Acts 4:13, 29; 28:31; 2 Cor 7:4; 10:2), that can find expression in the courage to reinterpret the accepted readings of Scripture. The very composition of the New Testament serves as a sustained exemplum of such boldness, in the first instance by reinterpreting the death of an executed criminal "cursed" by the explicit words of Torah as the obedient death of God's servant who gave life to the world (Gal 3:10–14)—a reinterpretation that was accomplished so quickly that Paul can already speak of Jesus's shocking death as "according to the

12. For the following, see Luke Timothy Johnson, "The Bible's Authority for and in the Church," in *Engaging Biblical Authority: Perspectives on the Bible as Scripture*, ed. William P. Brown (Louisville: Westminster John Knox, 2007), 62–72.

Scriptures" (1 Cor 15:3). The experience of the Holy Spirit forced a rereading of Scripture that found antecedents for the proclamation of him as "Christ and Lord" (Acts 2:14–36).[13]

A second powerful example of rereading Scripture under the impetus of the experience of God's presence and power through the Holy Spirit is the decision—narrated in Acts 10–15—to accept gentiles into the people without requiring that they be circumcised or observe the law. Note that at the Jerusalem Council's critical moment, James provides in Acts 15:16–18 a dramatic rereading of the prophet Amos in support of this decision—using the LXX version rather than the MT, which goes in quite a different direction—introducing the citation with "the words of the prophets agree with this thing (τούτῳ)," not "this thing agrees with the words of the prophets." It is the "thing" that is the experience of God that leads to the reinterpretation of Scripture.[14]

A third aspect of Scripture's authority lies in its collection of commands, prescriptions, declarations, and directions found in Torah and Wisdom literature in the Old Testament, and in the Gospels and Letters of the New Testament. I use the term *auctoritates* (authorities) for these disparate propositions and mandates. As in the practice of law, they represent antecedents that responsible interpretation must take into account in the process of decision-making. It is at this level that Scripture presents readers with a wide range of lacunae (things not addressed), of errors (due to ignorance or bias), of inconsistencies (arising from differences in time, place, and circumstance), of disagreement (does God test [πειράζειν] or not? Are you reading the Psalms or James?),[15] and even of contradiction (is the state God's instrument to ensure moral order or the embodiment of evil? Are you reading 1 Peter or Revelation?). It is here that the exercise of a properly critical intelligence comes into play. Unfortunately, present-day readers tend to focus on these "norms" rather than on the first two dimensions of authority, which are far more important to "making wise unto salvation." By treating Scripture primarily as a rule book, such readers reveal an immaturity, a failure to grow into genuine Christian adulthood (1 Cor 3:1; 13:11; 14:20).

13. See Johnson, *The Writings of the New Testament*, 111–33.

14. See Johnson, *Scripture and Discernment*, 98–106; also Luke Timothy Johnson, *The Acts of the Apostles*, SP 5 (Collegeville, MN: Liturgical Press, 1992), 258–81.

15. For the seriousness with which this "contradiction in Scripture" was taken by patristic writers, see my chapter "Journeying East with James," in Luke Timothy Johnson, *Brother of Jesus, Friend of God: Studies in the Letter of James* (Grand Rapids: Eerdmans, 2004), 61–83, especially 74–75.

Here is a homely analogy. When we are children, our parents seem godlike in their omniscience and power. Their actions are the model for our own; their word on every subject is supreme. We do what they say; we imitate what they do. The Ford is the best of all cars because "we" have a Ford; Democrats are the best political party because "we" vote Democratic. In the eyes of children, parents combine authority and normativity. In the process of growing into the world, however, young adults not only become aware of other norms and authorities—some friends drive Subarus, some vote Libertarian—but we can see that some of our parents' "norms" are inadequate or even wrong—we realize, perhaps, how homophobic and even racist our families were. They correctly suspect that if they keep driving a Ford simply because their family always drove one, or remain sexist "because that's the way we were raised," they may have failed to reach full adulthood.

Does this suggest that the authority of parents is denied? Far from it. If we truly are adult, then we recognize how our parents formed us in our values and perceptions, a service for which they can never fully be repaid. We recognize as well that part of their rearing of us was freeing us to make our own adult decisions in the way they did. Finally, we continue to turn to them—as the source of our identity and tradition—for wisdom and counsel in our difficult adult decisions. They remain *authoritative* for us in all these ways even if we make life decisions quite different from their own. But we seek from them wisdom and genuine liberty more than we seek a decision on what we should do.

In similar fashion, I suggest that reading Scripture as "the word of God" requires of present-day believers a mature and complex apprehension of Scripture's authority. Christians have the ability to discern the subtle working of God's Holy Spirit in the tangle of human experience because they are formed in the first place by God's word in Scripture. And when the experience of God among them leads to an aporia with regard to an earlier understanding of Scripture (or even of how God works), they are authorized by the example of Scripture itself to reinterpret both their experience and the text of Scripture. In this process of discernment and reinterpretation, all of Scripture that is pertinent to the subject must be taken into account, that is, treated as authoritative even if not normative. Decisions by believers to treat one text as more normative than another, finally, must be guided by that prior and persistent formation of their imaginations according to "the mind of Christ."

Believers do not "cancel" passages that they reject as normative, or, finding them inadequate or offensive, banish them from any further consideration. Instead, they embrace such "authorities" as opportunities for a deeper "wisdom unto salvation." To read Scripture as the word of God means to expect from ancient texts a promise and challenge that exceeds the capacity of the ancient authors to issue but that is a dimension of God's constant presence and power, a promise and challenge always relevant to our own existence. Present-day Christians unite with the earliest interpreters of Scripture by reading with the assumption that the God who presses on us at every moment seeks to instruct us, to communicate a wisdom that we by ourselves are incapable of reaching. The problem, we assume, lies less in the text of Scripture than in us. We must learn to read in a way that enables God's promise and challenge to transform us.[16] In short, to read Scripture as the word of God means to adopt the premises of premodern interpretation rather than the premises of modernity.[17] The choice is both real and necessary.

The Inadequacy of "Historical-Critical" Reading

The term "modernity" is applied to the world constructed on the basis of the European Enlightenment and the technological wonders to which it gave rise.[18] The Enlightenment based itself on the rejection of the world constructed on the basis of scriptural imagination, above all Scripture's persistent claim that God is present and powerful within creation, that, indeed, "the world is charged with the grandeur of God."[19] For modernity to triumph, miracles must be defeated—hence the energy put to this question by Locke, Hume, and Spinoza.[20] But if the living God is either denied or reduced to the status of cosmic clockmaker, then speaking of the religious writings of ancient and benighted people as "the word of God" is meaning-

16. See my "Origen and the Transformation of the Mind" in Johnson and Kurz, *The Future of Catholic Biblical Scholarship*, 64–90.

17. I sketch the premises of premodern interpretation in Johnson and Kurz, *The Future of Catholic Biblical Scholarship*, 35–63.

18. See the extensive analysis and critique in Luke Timothy Johnson, *Miracles: The Presence and Power of God in Creation*, Resources for the Interpretation of the Bible in the Church (Louisville: Westminster John Knox, 2018).

19. Gerard Manley Hopkins, "God's Grandeur," in *The Poems of Gerard Manley Hopkins*, ed. W. H. Gardner and N. H. Mackenzie, 4th ed. (London: Oxford University Press, 1967), 66.

20. Johnson, *Miracles*, 12–25.

less, and any persistent claim of that sort must be regarded as superstition and a willful resistance to human progress.[21]

The so-called historical-critical approach to the Bible—please note my use of the distancing noun "Bible"—is the perfect exemplification of modernity, with its premises deriving from seventeenth- and eighteenth-century British deists and its "*wissenschaftlich*" pretenses shaped by nineteenth-century German universities. Interpretation of the Bible cannot allow any talk of divine inspiration or divine revelation; the Bible is simply a collection of historical artifacts of no greater intrinsic merit than Gilgamesh. The ancient compositions are to be read exclusively as human productions of a certain time and place whose meaning must be gained from the circumstances of their composition. Amos and Isaiah may speak of a "word of God" and even claim to speak it, but such locutions are to be understood in much the same way as their talk of divine visions and auditions, that is, within the boundaries of an ancient religious outlook that is by no means necessarily shared by the interpreter.

But the interpretive approach of modernity is not content with descriptive history. It must also be "critical," meaning that the modern reader stands in judgment on biblical texts. At the most benign level, such judgment involves deciding issues of dating, authorship, and literary integrity. I say "benign," but it is difficult to calculate just how much distancing from the voice of Scripture is accomplished by the massive efforts expended by "biblical critics" in such dismemberment. At a far more insidious level, however, "critical" means judging the contents of the Bible on the basis of modern sensibilities: the worth of the biblical witness is measured by its conformity to present-day standards of theology and ethics.

In those German and then American universities and seminaries that championed the historical-critical paradigm, the sway of "Protestant presuppositions" was obvious, pitting the prophets against the law and Paul against James.[22] In more recent decades, a variety of other ideological stances—all of them extensions of the historical-critical approach—has dictated what in the Bible might be worthwhile to contemporary readers and what must be jettisoned because it fails in ideological conformity: feminist, liberationist,

21. The shift in cultural dominance is obvious in the tone adopted by the Bible's "cultured despisers," from the cautious arguments made in the eighteenth century to the strident mockery found among the "new atheists" of the twentieth century.

22. While disagreeing on most everything else, J. Z. Smith and I agree on the pervasive influence of such presuppositions in historical-critical scholarship; see Luke Timothy Johnson, *Religious Experience in Earliest Christianity* (Minneapolis: Fortress, 1998), 1–68.

postcolonialist hermeneutics proceed on the basis of an assumed superiority to the biblical witness. The *norma normans non normata* is the "experience/ social location/ideology" of the readers. Here, there is not the hermeneutical dialectic between Scripture and experience I described above. Here, the ideological commitment serves as an absolute criterion. Texts that do not "correspond" are rejected totally.

The seeds of distrust sown by Enlightenment critics have grown into the brambles of hermeneutical suspicion cultivated by contemporary ideological criticism. Increasingly, the texts of Scripture are regarded as "toxic," and biblical interpretation is seen as therapeutic. Now, authority is assumed to belong to the interpreter more than to Scripture. Rather than standing under the judgment of the word of God, interpreters stand in judgment on the ancient compositions gathered into the Bible. It should cause no surprise that exercises in "biblical theology" that start with the premise that such theology is a "historical discipline" turn out to be profoundly disappointing.

The Creed as "Ideology"

I do not suggest that a presuppositionless interpretation of Scripture is possible or even desirable. Instead, I propose that believing interpreters gladly embrace the ideological standpoint (or hermeneutical framework) that is distinctive to the church, found in the living tradition of sanctity displayed by the saints, in the teaching office of the magisterium, and above all in the creed, while also rejecting the narrow ideological bases that have, within the academy, replaced the hermeneutical context of the church and pass themselves off as both more scientific and more humane than the ecclesial tradition. The Nicene Creed recited by Catholic worshipers every Sunday professes the faith of the assembly and provides a rule for that faith. It narrates the Christian myth, thereby constructing the imaginative world (derived from Scripture) within which believers can live and guiding their practices. The creed not only derives from Scripture; it "unobtrusively but effectively supplies the Christian people with the code for understanding its sacred text."[23]

Most pertinent to the present reflection, the creed proclaims—and all believing interpreters of Scripture profess with their fellow worshipers—that the Holy Spirit is "Lord and Giver of Life" (here echoing the conviction running through

23. See Luke Timothy Johnson, *The Creed: What Christians Believe and Why It Matters* (New York: Doubleday, 2003), 59, see further 58–64.

the New Testament that the Holy Spirit mediates the presence and power of the risen Lord Jesus) and "spoke through the prophets." This highly cryptic pronouncement provides the creedal basis for discerning the word of God active in every age through the prophets and for gladly receiving the writings of Scripture as the word of God, as "God breathed" through the Holy Spirit (2 Tim 3:16).

For the believing interpreter, then, the presupposition that "God's word" is somehow communicated through the canonical writings—that God seeks to make us "wise unto salvation" through the reading of these texts—is met by the dispositions associated with obediential faith itself: an eager attentiveness, a willingness to hear, a trust that one's openness will not be in vain, a willingness to be taught, a refusal to give up even on what appear to be the most recalcitrant of passages. Approaching Scripture as the word of God, in short, demands that a disposition of generous hospitality governs interpretation rather than an attitude of suspicion.[24]

Critical inquiry finds its place within this commitment to receptivity. Critical inquiry enables the interpreter to discern the manner in which Scripture teaches and instructs unto salvation. Critical inquiry demands distinctions and qualifications, not least in regard to the difference between normativity and authority. Critical thinking allows us to discern within obscurity, and even apparent impossibility, the markings of God's wisdom. The combination of generous hospitality and critical inquiry will find, to be sure, a variety of specific expressions.[25] Before concluding this essay, I offer an illustration of such a generous, yet critical, reading in 1 Tim 2:11–15.

Engaging the Difficult Text of 1 Timothy 2:11–15

Few today would dispute the designation of 1 Tim 2:11–15 as "difficult." Even those who take Paul's forbidding women from speech in the assembly as

24. The term "hermeneutics of suspicion" derives from Paul Ricoeur, *Freud and Philosophy: An Essay on Interpretation*, trans. Denis Savage (New Haven: Yale University Press, 1965). I first became aware of "the hermeneutics of generosity" in conversation with L. Gregory Jones sometime in the 1990s. See L. Gregory Jones, *Embodying Forgiveness: A Theological Analysis* (Grand Rapids: Eerdmans, 1995).

25. Precisely this combination characterized much of premodern interpretation, most spectacularly in the work of Origen. Nobody has ever been more rigorous in the analysis of the text's literal meaning than he; nobody has ever been as daring in the search for a wisdom that the literal sense appeared to lack or even betray. See Johnson and Kurz, *The Future of Catholic Biblical Scholarship*, 64–90.

normative for their own rules of ministry—allowing only males to be ordained—must (unless they are themselves captive to the most profound sort of misogyny) find themselves, in moments of self-honesty, troubled by the harshness of Paul's judgment,[26] the rashness of his theological rationalization,[27] and the obscurity of his final affirmation.[28] By contrast, those who reject its normativity typically relieve any possible struggles by canceling the text altogether. Once canceled as normative, the passage is no longer read, liturgically or devotionally. It is effectively removed from Scripture.

Such cancellation of the passage is based on two critical principles. The first is classically historical-critical: the passage, indeed, the entire three letters called the Pastorals, were written not by Paul but by a later imitator who betrayed Paul's best instincts.[29] In the most radical version of this position, it is the later author of the Pastorals who interpolated the troublesome sex-

26. It is no harsher, however, than Paul's command in 1 Cor 14:34–35, which calls women speaking in church "shameful," consistent with his language concerning women prophesying or praying without veils in 1 Cor 11:3–16.

27. Basing women's subordination on the order of creation ("Adam was made first, then Eve") is consistent with the same appeal to Gen 2:7 in 1 Cor 11:8, though here there is no corresponding statement concerning gender equality "in the Lord" (1 Cor 11:11–12). Similarly, the statement that Eve was deceived and fell into transgression echoes 2 Cor 11:3 but contrasts with Paul's insistence elsewhere on Adam's sin (Rom 5:12–21).

28. The statement that "woman will be saved through childbirth [τεκνογονία] if they remain [ἐὰν μείνωσιν] in faith and love and holiness with moral discretion" is loaded with purely exegetical issues. Is "salvation" here meant to be eternal salvation, membership in the community of the "saved," or "brought safely (through childbirth)"? Does the plural "if they remain" connect to the common noun γυνή, so that it represents a condition of women being saved, or does it refer to the children's moral character (here dependent on the mother!)? Patristic and medieval interpreters alike were simply uncertain as to what Paul *meant*, and were troubled by inferences in either direction; see, for example, the tenth-century commentator Oecumenius of Tricca, *Pauli Apostoli ad Timotheum Prior Epistola* (PG 119:133–96). In the nineteenth century, J. A. Bengel declared that Paul could not have meant eternal salvation, since "multae quae pariunt tamen pereunt, quae non pariunt, tamen salvantur" (many women who give birth nevertheless perish, while many women who don't give birth nevertheless are saved). *Gnomon Novi Testamentum*, 3rd ed. (Stuttgart: Steinkopf, 1860), 822.

29. The pseudonymous character of Paul's letters to his delegates is one of the "dogmas" of historical-critical scholarship, virtually unchallenged in present-day scholarship. It is not a conclusion that is reached by means of inquiry; it is rather the premise that initiates inquiry. See, e.g., Robin Scroggs, "Paul and the Eschatological Woman," *JAAR* 40, no. 3 (1972): 282–303; and most elaborately, Yann Redalié, *Paul après Paul: Le temps, le salut, la morale selon les épîtres à Timothée et à Tite* (Geneva: Labor et Fides, 1994). See also the full discussion in Johnson, *First and Second Letters to Timothy*, 55–99.

ist passages in 1 Cor 11:3–16 and 14:32–35.[30] On the basis of pseudonymity, the passage lacks any normative claim on Christians. Unfortunately for this position, there is every reason to consider the Pastorals as Pauline, certainly within the sense that they were written during Paul's ministry under his authorization.[31] There is no real evidence, furthermore, to support the fantasy of interpolations in 1 Corinthians.[32] More fatally, the authority of Scripture has nothing to do with authorship and everything to do with canonicity.[33] If it depended on certainty concerning human authorship, consistency would demand that most of the Old and the New Testaments be abandoned. Like it or not, the reason the Pastorals are (or should be) read in the liturgical assembly is that they are, like the rest of Scripture, considered in some fashion to communicate the word of God.

The second critical principle supporting cancellation of 1 Tim 2:11–15 is ideological. Since the appearance of *The Women's Bible* sponsored by nineteenth-century feminists,[34] this passage has been considered the prime New Testament example of the "texts of terror" that have led to the oppression of women.[35] On the principle that only texts supporting the legitimate rights of women can be regarded as "authoritative,"[36] and that texts suppressing those rights are to be rejected, the passage is regarded as toxic and not authentically "Scripture." In this view, whether the historical "Paul" or a pseudepigrapher consciously sought to suppress a nascent women's movement in the church,[37] the effect of his words served to marginalize women,

30. For a standard statement of the positions, see Hans Conzelmann, *1 Corinthians: A Commentary on the First Epistle to the Corinthians*, trans. J. W. Leitch, Hermeneia (Philadelphia: Fortress, 1975), 246; also, Jerome Murphy-O'Connor, "Interpolations in 1 Corinthians," *CBQ* 48, no. 1 (1986): 81–96.

31. See Johnson, *Constructing Paul*, 33–41, 62–92.

32. See especially Antoinette Clark Wire, *The Corinthian Women Prophets: A Reconstruction through Paul's Rhetoric* (Minneapolis: Fortress, 1990), 149–52.

33. Luke Timothy Johnson, *A Catholic Consciousness: Scripture, Theology, and the Church* (New York: Paulist, 2021), 17–32.

34. Elizabeth Cady Stanton, *The Women's Bible* (New York: European, 1895).

35. The expression comes from Phyllis Trible, *Texts of Terror: Literary-Feminist Readings of Biblical Narratives* (Philadelphia: Fortress, 1984).

36. See especially Rosemary Radford Ruether, "The Feminist Critique in Religious Studies," *Soundings* 64, no. 4 (1981): 388–402; Rosemary Radford Ruether, *Sexism and God-Talk* (Boston: Beacon, 1983). Ruether uses "authoritative" in the sense that I use "normative." See also Elisabeth Schüssler Fiorenza, *Bread Not Stone: The Challenge of Feminist Biblical Interpretation* (Boston: Beacon, 1984), 23–63.

37. See, e.g., Jouette M. Bassler, "The Widow's Tale: A Fresh Look at 1 Timothy 5:3–16," *JBL* 103, no. 1 (1984): 23–41; Joanna Dewey, "1 Timothy," in *The Women's Bible*

and, precisely because they were read as "Scripture," led subsequent generations to perpetuate unequal and prejudicial treatment of women in the church and in society.[38] Accordingly, suspicion and resistance must characterize any interpretation.

The option of censorship or cancellation—which is actually a rejection of hermeneutics—has, however, at least two major problems. First, the assumption that the church should hear only those texts that confirm present-day perceptions and practices is fraught with peril. There are, after all, few passages in Scripture that, when examined closely enough, do not collide with one contemporary premise or another; where does the process of purgation stop? It is surely the case, moreover, that the salutary character of Scripture has at least as much to do with its capacity to shock and challenge us as it does with its ability to soothe and comfort us. Already in Origen, the scandal of the literal meaning of the text drove this great and exemplary interpreter to seek greater wisdom. If we do not likewise acknowledge the scandal, we may also miss the opportunity to discover God's wisdom.

Contemporary readers, then, must be willing and able to state how and why they stand against texts that conflict with their own views and practices. But they should also be open to the possibility of learning something important precisely from the cognitive dissonances generated by the disparities in outlook and practice. Just as it is an error to grant the ancient text absolute normativity, so is it an error to deny its continuing authority or to assume that a contemporary ethos (or social arrangement) has absolute normative value.

The second problem with cancellation is that it does not work. Preventing texts from being read in worship does not remove them from all reading. Failing to engage them creatively does not keep others from employing them destructively. Difficult passages continue to be read and acted on despite their rejection by scholars. And outside the framework of constructive preaching and critical scholarship, in the hands of those already driven by prejudice and even violence, these passages can continue to have negative effects. Only if texts that have scandalous or even harmful potential are confronted and engaged by public discourse within the assembly of believers can their dangerous aspects be exorcised and their healing aspects be reclaimed.

Commentary, ed. Carol A. Newsom and Sharon H. Ringe (Louisville: Westminster John Knox, 1992), 355–57.

38. For the fascinating way in which some patristic commentators sought to mitigate the effect of the passage, insisting on the authority of women to instruct men "in private" (as Priscilla instructed Apollos), see Johnson, *First and Second Timothy*, 26–33.

Seeking Wisdom

To read Scripture as the word of God, then, is to read it in the search for God's wisdom in all of Scripture, refusing to jettison passages that do not please us. In cases such as 1 Tim 2:11–15, this search requires of us, first, dispositions of hospitality (generosity) more than dispositions of suspicion: however difficult the passage is for us to read, we are convinced that wisdom is to be found in it. It requires of us, second, the use of a critical intelligence that can discern—in life as well as in the reading of texts—"what is the will of God, what is good and pleasing and perfect" (Rom 12:2). Finally, it demands of us that we understand and apply the distinction between what is normative and what is authoritative in the passage that is read as God's word.

There is more than enough justification for a community of believers to refuse normative force to Paul's command, to declare in the presence of God and led by the Holy Spirit that women who speak in the assembly are not acting contrary to "God's word" and should not, on the basis of this passage, be suppressed from expressing their God-bestowed gifts of leadership. This passage (like those in 1 Cor 11:3–16 and 14:32–35) presents an inadequate and even erroneous standard if applied simply to decide who should practice ministry within the church.[39] I have already noted elements in the text that are problematic: it is gratuitous in context,[40] it is based solely on Paul's own authority ("I do not allow") rather than a principle grounded in the gospel, and the warrant for the injunction is, in fact, a faulty reading of Torah. It is appropriate as well to recognize the harm that the normative understanding of the passage has done in the history of the church. That female believers, above all, should be "suspicious" of passages like this one is completely understandable and should be acknowledged.

There are other reasons for rejecting the passage's normative status. The essentialist treatment of gender here stands in tension with Paul's liberative and empowering vision of there being "in Christ" no more female or male (Gal 3:28)[41] and Paul's own practice concerning the public role of women

39. The case is roughly the same as with the rules for purity demanded by Leviticus, which determine who can and who cannot remain in the camp, who can and who cannot serve as priests. See Johnson, *The Revelatory Body*, 180–205.

40. The instructions for men in worship to avoid anger and disputation and for women in worship to display virtue rather than finery are well-balanced. The admonition concerning women's speaking disrupts this balance.

41. We should note as well the way in which in 1 Cor 7:1–7 Paul assigns mutual ἐξουσία to both woman and man in marriage. The fallacious movement from literary text to

like Priscilla and Phoebe.[42] It seems clear that Paul was comfortable with the ministry of women "in the field," but when the context of the οἶκος (where the ἐκκλησία met) was involved, he fell back on the conventional roles that Mediterranean culture assigned to women.[43] We have, then, a classic "contradiction in Scripture" that calls for resolution. In my discussion above, I stated that in the search for what is normative in Scripture, the statements that most conform to "the mind of Christ" (1 Cor 2:16), that is, to the truth of the gospel (Gal 2:5, 14), must govern interpretation. In this case, the principled statement of gender equality in Christ must surely take precedence over a casual ascription of gender roles and proclivities.

But there is still another and most important consideration: the "word of God" that is God's presence and power in creation has shown us in the lives of real women through the centuries (above all in the saints) how women are not weaker and more susceptible to deception, but are in truth powerful leaders and teachers, among them "doctors of the church"![44] This "experiential" criterion is dispositive, precisely because it is based solidly on the work of the Holy Spirit.

But if the community of believers decides (as I think it should) that 1 Tim 2:11–15 is not "normative," that as church we are in fact going to recognize the leadership of women despite Paul's clear command to the contrary, does this mean that the passage is not "authoritative" in the sense I have previously defined? No, this passage, like every passage in Scripture, is an "authority" that demands of us careful reading and creative interpretation. The believing interpreter is driven to this careful and creative engagement because of the conviction that in one way or another God's word and wisdom can be communicated in the present day through these fallible words from antiq-

ontological status with regard to gender occurs repeatedly in a prominent stream of contemporary theology, Catholic and Protestant. On sex and the image of God, see Johnson, *A Catholic Consciousness*, 147–61.

42. The discrepancy is noted by such patristic interpreters as Theodore of Mopsuestia, *I Thessalonians—Philemon*, vol. 2 of *In Epistolas B. Pauli commentarii: The Latin Edition with Greek Fragments*, ed. H. B. Swete (Cambridge: Cambridge University Press, 1882), 93–96; Oecumenius of Tricca (PG 119:153–240); Theophylact (PG 125:47). Some point not only to the example of Priscilla but also to women in Scripture who exercised authority over men, like Judith!

43. See Johnson, *Constructing Paul*, 272–98.

44. The recognition by the Vatican that Teresa of Avila, Catherine of Siena, Thérèse of Lisieux, and Hildegard of Bingen are doctors of the church has, to be sure, not in the least been matched by the logical implication concerning the leadership capacity of all women in the church.

uity. Rather than "cancel" the passage and never read it again, we are driven by this conviction to return to the passage again and again in the quest for wisdom.

But how can this be done? We are, alas, now incapable of the sort of moral and allegorical interpretations that enabled our ancestors in the faith to negotiate passages that at the literal level confused or offended the interpreter's sense of what was worthy of God.[45] For better or worse, we find ourselves in the position of seeking wisdom precisely through the literal sense. How, then, can we proceed?

One technique that I have employed is to degenderize the passage. By thus removing the major stumbling block, we (?) open the way to a new appreciation for all of 1 Tim 2, which concerns aspects of worship for those whose "love comes from a pure heart and a good conscience, and a sincere faith" (1 Tim 1:5), aspects of worship that are not ritual but moral and that summon us, in turn, to a reading that likewise focuses on the moral dispositions that are appropriate to common prayer and that are "pleasing in the sight of our savior God, who wants all people [πάντας ἀνθρώπους] to be saved and to come to the recognition of truth" (2:4). The one mediator between God and humans, after all, is the human Christ Jesus, "who gave himself as a ransom on behalf of all" (2:5–6). Such moral dispositions are not distributed by gender.

We see that the passage, taken as a whole, advocates moral dispositions in worship that are the opposite of arrogance, display, competition, and self-assertion. Thus, the prayers said for all people, including rulers of every sort, are pleasing to God but are also said with an eye toward living "a peaceful and quiet life [ἤρεμον καὶ ἡσύχιον βίον] in complete piety and dignity" (2:2).[46] The lifting up of hands in prayer should be "removed from anger and argument" (2:8).[47] Clothing worn in public worship should be simple, not an occasion for the display of wealth, but instead should suggest the virtues of "modesty and discretion" appropriate to those "dedicated to the service of God through good works" (2:9–10).

By bracketing the question of gender, then, we find there is much to be

45. In contrast to present-day readers who are scandalized by texts that appear to harm humans, Origen stumbled over texts that appeared to diminish the truth about God; his spiritual interpretations sought above all "a meaning worthy of God" (*Princ.* 4.1, 15).

46. The ἡσυχίᾳ that is the goal of life in 2:2 is repeatedly stated as a quality of learning (ἐν ἡσυχίᾳ) in 2:11–12.

47. For the context of disputation, see Luke Timothy Johnson, *Interpreting Paul*, vol. 2 of *The Canonical Paul* (Grand Rapids: Eerdmans, 2021), 428–48.

learned from the passage. We learn that God wills the salvation of all humans and that Jesus gave himself for all humans and that, correspondingly, the community should pray for all people without discrimination, especially those "over them" and in a position to oppress them. We learn that behavior in the assembly is to be marked by distinct moral qualities associated with "quiet and peace" rather than competition and rancor, with good works rather than outward display.

Can we also learn anything valuable by degenderizing 1 Tim 2:11–15? In fact, 2:11–12 reminds us that "learning" in the context of worship demands "quiet" (ἡσυχίᾳ) and "complete subordination" (πάσῃ ὑποταγῇ).[48] And if we ignore the business of one person "having authority over another" simply because of one's gender, it is possible to agree that all in the assembly should hear God's word with quiet submission. Worship is not the place or time for self-assertion but for obedient faith, which always requires submissive listening, not to each other but to God. A degenderized reading of 2:15, in turn, can lead to an appreciation of τεκνογονία by both parents as demanding of them persistence in "faith and love and holiness with moral discretion" in the hope that their children also will "remain in faith and love and holiness with moral discretion."

I am happy to acknowledge that this technique of degenderizing can take us only so far. But it does, I hope, illustrate how a decision to say no to a passage at the level of normativity can be accompanied by a yes to the passage as an authoritative source of wisdom.

A passage such as 1 Tim 2:11–15 can also serve the church as a source of wisdom, and therefore as "God's word," by standing as a warning. Thus, insight can be gained into the harmful potential of 2:13–14 through the simple technique not of degenderizing but of reverse gendering, a technique that is particularly helpful when studying with a predominantly male group of readers, because it enables them to hear the negative impact of Paul's gratuitous statements. It is startling for males to hear that they are not to have authority over women, because women are superior in the order of creation and because men are more susceptible to being deceived than are women. Women should be in charge because they are better and smarter than men! Men should shut up and let women teach them!

The "wisdom" thus conveyed is twofold. First, it can reveal to men the true import of sexist premises and language. The shock of having Scripture

48. It is not accidental, I think, that the Orthodox Hesychastic tradition stresses in particular the necessity of quiet and complete submission in prayer.

declare (in this reverse reading) that women are essentially and functionally superior to men should lead to greater self-awareness among male readers and an appreciation of why women have always felt oppressed by this passage. They might even appreciate that the ascription of ontological and functional superiority does no real benefit to males, either. It is not a good thing to assume that one occupies a higher link on the chain of being and is incapable of being deceived. A second lesson is that any essentialist rationalizing of social arrangements is dangerous and probably wrong. Leadership in the Christian community ought to be based on the gifts distributed by the Holy Spirit, not on the conventional assumptions of the social order.

Reading for Wisdom

I have proposed that reading Scripture as the word of God does not foreclose but rather demands the exercise of critical thinking, not in service of reducing but rather enhancing Scripture's essential role in the hermeneutical process we call revelation. For believing readers, the dispositions of trust and generosity that belong to obedient faith should always precede and condition attitudes of distrust and suspicion. By no means do such dispositions prevent the interpreting community from distinguishing between what is normative and what is simply authoritative in Scripture. At times, Christians must, in the name of the truth of the gospel, say no to a passage as normative for ecclesial life, but even as they do so, they are impelled by faith to seek what wisdom God conveys through the passages that are most difficult for them and, even when their own search for wisdom seems inadequate, remain confident that God will raise up other and better readers than they who can find how every passage of Scripture "makes wise unto salvation."

Biblical Inspiration and Textual Criticism

God's Word and the Texts of Jude

JAMES B. PROTHRO

Amid his advocacy for rigorous historical analysis within and for the sake of Christian faith, one aspect of Père Lagrange's legacy is his interest in textual criticism, especially of the New Testament and the Gospels. His historical perspective disposed him to address not merely the ancient cultures, genres, and events behind and in the biblical text but also the history of the text itself. He wrote, opined, and researched on text-critical methodology, critical editions, ancient versions, and material discoveries, like the Chester Beatty Papyri.[1] This was pioneering work at a time when numerous discoveries and influential critics (such as Westcott, Hort, and von Soden) were ushering New Testament textual criticism to assume fresh relevance and take new shapes.[2] It was difficult work also, when classrooms and pulpits continued to use standard versions (e.g., the King James or the Vulgate) and many suspected textual critics of impiety—a charge against which Lagrange had to defend himself.[3] For Lagrange, however, the piety due to the sacred texts

1. E.g., Marie-Joseph Lagrange, OP, "Une nouvelle édition du Nouveau Testament," *RB* 47, no. 2 (1939): 163–83; "L'Origene de la version syro-palestinienne des Évangiles," *RB* 34, no. 4 (1925): 481–504; "La revision de la Vulgate par Saint Jérome," *RB* 27, nos. 1–2 (1918): 254–57; "L'ancienne version syriaque des Évangiles," *RB* 29, no. 3 (1920): 321–52; "Un nouveau papyrus contenant un fragment des Actes," *RB* 36, no. 4 (1927): 549–60; "La seconde parole d'Oxyrhynque," *RB* 31, no. 3 (1922): 427–33; "Le manuscript sinaitique," *RB* 35, no. 1 (1926): 89–93; "Le groupe dit césaréen des manuscrits des Évangiles," *RB* 38, no. 4 (1929): 481–512; "Les papyrus Chester Beatty pour les Évangiles," *RB* 43, no. 1 (1934): 5–41; "Projet de critique textuelle rationelle du N. T.," *RB* 42, no. 4 (1933): 481–98; "Un nouveau papyrus évangélique," *RB* 38, no. 2 (1929): 161–77; "Deux nouveaux textes relatifs à l'Évangile," *RB* 44, no. 3 (1935): 321–43.

2. See Lagrange's overview of the "current situation" in his day in "Projet de critique textuelle," 488–92.

3. See Marie-Joseph Lagrange, OP, "Iterum Mt. 11,19: *A Filiis* an *Ab Operibus*?," *Bib* 6, no. 4 (1925): 461–63.

is precisely what calls for editorial alterations: if we aim to hear Scripture as God inspired it, we should desire that not a syllable be lost or corrupted, and this calls us not to rest on the texts we know but to correct our knowledge and in some cases to revise our texts.[4]

The value of textual criticism received robust confirmation in Pius XII's 1943 encyclical *Divino afflante Spiritu* (hereafter *DAS*).[5] In 1893, Leo XIII had called exegetes to attend to the original languages and to consult "the more ancient manuscripts," though not intending to replace the public, official use of the Sixto-Clementine Vulgate, which he maintained "substantially" rendered the originals' meaning.[6] Pius XII sounded a louder and more programmatic call to study the original languages and the original text, including a call for revised critical editions for Catholics. The Vulgate, Pius wrote, had proven itself free from error "in matters of faith and morals," and it "may be safely quoted" as a functional "juridical" authority (*DAS* §21). But the "critical" authority lies with the originals. Indeed, "the original text," he ventures, "having been written by the inspired author himself, has more authority and greater weight than any of even the very best translations, whether ancient or modern" (*DAS* §16).

The rationale for this call is grounded in the encyclical's vision of biblical inspiration and the purpose of exegesis, one reaffirmed and developed strongly in the Dogmatic Constitution *Dei Verbum* at Vatican II. The inspiration of Scripture is correlated not merely with the subsequent ecclesial reception of the texts—as though the church's approval or use of the canon is what makes it inspired—but with the process of composition itself.[7] God inspired the biblical authors as true "authors," who make assertions and teach truth in communicative modes embedded in the generic and linguistic conventions of their time.[8] This implies a need to understand such communica-

4. Compare Lagrange, "Projet de critique textuelle," 495–96.

5. Pius XII, Encyclical Letter *Divino afflante Spiritu* (September 30, 1943). Translations in this essay from papal encyclicals are from Dean P. Béchard, SJ, ed. and trans., *The Scripture Documents: An Anthology of Official Catholic Teachings* (Collegeville, MN: Liturgical Press, 2002).

6. Leo XIII, Encyclical Letter *Providentissimus Deus* (November 18, 1893) §13. (Béchard labels this as paragraph no. 25.)

7. See, already, the constitution on revelation from Vatican I, *Dei Filius* §2: "These [books] the Church holds to be sacred and canonical, not because, having been composed by simple human industry, they were later approved by her own authority, nor merely because they contain revelation without error, but because, having been written by the inspiration of the Holy Spirit, they have God for their author and were delivered as such to the Church" (in Béchard, *Scripture Documents*, 17).

8. Vatican Council II, Dogmatic Constitution *Dei Verbum* (November 18, 1965) §11. Hereafter, all references to this source will appear in the text as *DV*.

tive conventions in order to understand the divine word (*DV* §12; *DAS* §§33–38). As Lagrange put it, "To know what God teaches, we must determine the thought of the human teacher."[9] If this desire to know how the inspired author communicated applies at the level of language structure or genre, it certainly applies at the level of wording. As Pius XII put it, "It is the duty of the exegete to lay hold, so to speak, with the greatest care and reverence of the very least expressions which, under the inspiration of the Divine Spirit, have flowed from the pen of the sacred writer, so as to arrive at a deeper and fuller knowledge of his meaning" (*DAS* §15). To this end, textual criticism is "rightly employed in the case of the sacred Books" precisely "because of that very reverence that is due to the divine oracles. For its very purpose is to insure that the sacred text be restored as perfectly as possible, be purified from the corruptions due to the carelessness of the copyists . . . and from all other kinds of mistakes that are wont to make their way gradually into writings handed down through the centuries" (*DAS* §17).

As a Catholic exegete interested in hearing and expounding the biblical message for others, I take seriously this call to the critical task. However, one must also recognize the bare fact that even our best critical tools cannot guarantee that a "critical" text gives us access to precisely what an original author or editor prepared for the text's initial audience. And this fact can lead some to question the validity of the critical enterprise or, if one locates "inspiration" *only* in an ancient author's original wording, to question whether we even have access to the inspired word of God at all. In this paper, I aim first to illustrate these tensions with the Letter of Jude as a sample case, and thereafter to offer a perspective on biblical inspiration that can reaffirm but reframe the role of textual criticism within the task of ecclesial theological interpretation.

Inspiration and the Challenge of Textual Criticism

According to Pius XII, a call to reconstruct the original text for interpretation is not a novelty or rejection of tradition, even if it sounded that way to some Catholics in his day. Patristic authors often engaged in the adjudication of divergent manuscripts, and even those who approved the Vulgate at the Council of Trent called for corrected editions not only of their inaccurate

9. Marie-Joseph Lagrange, OP, *The Meaning of Christianity according to Luther and His Followers in Germany*, trans. W. S. Reilly, SS (New York: Longmans, Green, 1920), 96.

copies of the Vulgate but also of the original languages (*DAS* §§17, 20–21). Yet the pope discerned a divine "invitation" for twentieth-century exegetes to engage in this enterprise even more ardently. New manuscript discoveries and methodological advances are gifts of "divine providence" (*DAS* §12), and "gratitude to the God of all providence" demands "urgently" that the faithful respond by using these gifts to better our knowledge of Scripture (*DAS* §19).

Since Pius XII's encyclical, the field of textual criticism has not been idle. New discoveries such as the Bodmer Papyri offer important early evidence for the New Testament text, not least the earliest (and complete!) Greek manuscript of Jude in P^{72} (P.Bodmer VII). Indeed, whereas Lagrange reported a wealth of about four thousand Greek manuscripts, that number is conservatively about five thousand today.[10] Technological advances enable new discoveries and also afford a better understanding of old discoveries.[11] And New Testament critics continue to update their methods and tools to better adjudicate the increasingly complex data set.[12]

Nonetheless, such advances have not brought about utter confidence in today's printed editions. Pius XII had consoled readers that textual criticism had "rules so firmly established and secure" that "any abuse" of the text or of the rules of criticism "can easily be discovered" (*DAS* §18). But subsequent methodological advances, while increasing confidence in what we can know, have more starkly shown what we cannot know given the available data. Some new discoveries reinforce confidence about our critical texts or provide a missing link that helps emend them, but others only complexify the history of transmission of the New Testament—not to mention the Hebrew Bible, where some Judean desert findings cast uncertainty about the earliest recoverable form of entire books.[13] Further, even where one is confident about a particular textual decision, one cannot trace the transmission

10. Cf. Lagrange, "Une nouvelle édition," 483; Jacob W. Peterson, "Math Myths: How Many Manuscripts We Have and Why More Isn't Always Better," in *Myths and Mistakes in New Testament Textual Criticism*, ed. Elijah Hixson and Peter J. Gurry (Downers Grove, IL: IVP Academic, 2019), 48–69.

11. E.g., Conrad Thorup Elmelund, "The Undertext of Greek NF MG 99 from Sinai (GA 0289)," *TC: A Journal of Biblical Textual Criticism* 27 (2022): 51–68.

12. See Tommy Wasserman and Peter J. Gurry, *A New Approach to Textual Criticism: An Introduction to the Coherence-Based Genealogical Method*, RBS 80 (Atlanta: Society of Biblical Literature, 2017).

13. See, e.g., Eugene Ulrich, *The Dead Sea Scrolls and the Developmental Composition of the Bible*, VTSup 169 (Leiden: Brill, 2015).

tradition beyond the point of our earliest evidence, and we cannot have absolute certainty that our best printed texts represent precisely what an author or editor composed.[14] Critical methods can allow *reasonable* certainty that, barring a significant new data point, we have no reason to doubt our printed text. But this means that we are potentially always one discovery or methodological change away from placing the same degree of certainty in a different text. Moreover, the "rules" of criticism pertain especially to the realms of probability, and these rules are not applied without subjectivity, as critics disagree about what did or could have happened in the transmission of the texts.[15] Recent editions of the New Testament have introduced a new diamond-shaped siglum, often nicknamed the "diamond of uncertainty," which marks passages in the printed text where the editors themselves regard two readings as of equal value. This means that, at these points, even the editorial committee (not to mention other critics and commentators) does not claim that the reading printed is superior to an alternative. In other passages, the committee is quick to remind us that the lack of a diamond "does not mean that the editors regard the text as definitively established," only that they viewed the printed text as the best of several readings.[16]

There are a number of ways in which the difficulties could be illustrated. Not all of them are of the same type, and not all of them can be manageably addressed in this essay. Cases in which a whole book existed in two forms in antiquity (e.g., Esther, Jeremiah) call for a philosophical decision by editors about how to define that book and what to print. Official Catholic materials may also require consideration of the extent and overall shape of the books affirmed as canonical by the Council of Trent (e.g., the inclusion of Mark 16:9–20 and John 7:53–8:11)—though it would not necessarily preclude interpretations of both forms of the books.[17] The considerations below will

14. The language above about absolute and reasonable certainty parallels, though also bypasses, debates around whether the goal of criticism should be the "original" text (as the author wrote or dispatched it) or the "initial" text (the most likely text from which all known text-forms stem). See Peter J. Gurry, *A Critical Examination of the Coherence-Based Genealogical Method in New Testament Textual Criticism*, NTTSD 55 (Leiden: Brill, 2017), 90–101.

15. History, including textual history, must of necessity rely on what is likely to have happened when in doubt about a particular matter, and likelihood takes commonality into account. Nonetheless, Robert Jewett's caution is notable: "History, after all, is the arena of the unique rather than the average." *Dating Paul's Life* (London: SCM, 1979), 54.

16. From the introduction to the Nestle-Aland *Novum Testamentum Graece*, 28th rev. ed., ed. Barbara Aland et al. (Stuttgart: Deutsche Bibelgesellschaft, 2012), 55.

17. See further Stephen Ryan, OP, "The Word of God and the Textual Pluriformity of

be relevant to such issues. In this essay, however, I would like to focus on a New Testament text whose shape is not in doubt but whose specific wording is notoriously difficult to reconstruct: the Letter of Jude.

The Texts of Jude

Jude is frequently used as a sample for text-critical work in New Testament studies due to its manageable size, the relative paucity of manuscripts, and its numerous textual problems.[18] Some textual conundrums in Jude pertain to Christology. In v. 4, most modern editions read in a way that identifies Christ himself as "our only sovereign and Lord" (τὸν μόνον δεσπότην καὶ κύριον ἡμῶν Ἰησοῦν Χριστόν). This might indicate a fairly high Christology, if the author assumes a single divine lordship that Christ here must share with God. In many manuscripts, however, one finds language that seems to clarify the distinction as well as the unity of the persons: "the only sovereign God and our Lord Jesus Christ" (τὸν μόνον δεσπότην θεὸν καὶ κύριον ἡμῶν Ἰησοῦν Χριστόν).[19] Far more debated is the text of v. 5, where the person who delivered Israel out of Egypt is identified differently in the manuscripts. One can see the differences reflected in the translations of the NRSV and NRSVue.[20]

---

the Old Testament," in *"Verbum Domini" and the Complementarity of Exegesis and Theology*, ed. Scott Carl (Grand Rapids: Eerdmans, 2015), 123–50; Stephen Ryan, OP, "The Text of the Bible and Catholic Biblical Scholarship," *Nova et Vetera* 4, no. 1 (2006): 132–41. Regarding the extent of the books printed in Catholic Bibles, Session IV of the Council of Trent affirmed the canonicity of the Western canonical books "in their entirety and with all their parts, as they have been customarily read in the Catholic Church and preserved in the ancient Latin Vulgate edition" (in Béchard, *Scripture Documents*, 4). Trent's intent regarding the macro-level shape of books like Esther (with additions) and Mark (including Mark 16:9–20) is fairly clear, though the textual problems of the Vulgate (due to which the Tridentine fathers asked for a critical edition to be made!) seem to leave the canonicity of many smaller insertions and other corruptions in different editions of the Vulgate before and after Trent open to doubt (e.g., inclusions of the Prayer of Manasseh in 2 Chronicles or the longer readings of 1 John 5:7–8).

18. See Charles Landon, *A Text-Critical Study of the Epistle of Jude*, JSNTSup 135 (Sheffield: Sheffield Academic, 1996); Tommy Wasserman, *The Epistle of Jude: Its Text and Transmission*, ConBNT 43 (Stockholm: Almqvist and Wiksell, 2006).

19. This latter reading is not widely adopted, but see arguments in its favor in Landon, *Text-Critical Study*, 63–67.

20. These translations also reflect a difference regarding the placement of ἅπαξ (here "once for all").

> Now I desire to remind you, though you are fully informed, that the Lord, who once for all saved a people out of the land of Egypt, afterward destroyed those who did not believe. (Jude 5 NRSV)

> Now I desire to remind you, though you are fully informed, once and for all, that Jesus, who saved a people out of the land of Egypt, afterward destroyed those who did not believe. (Jude 5 NRSVue)

Most manuscripts read "the Lord" (κύριος), which might be interpreted as referring to either the Father or the Son, while others differentiate: some have "God" (θεός), while a significant minority read "Jesus" ('Ιησοῦς). Several scholars and recent editions opt for "Jesus" as the harder reading, one more likely to have been corrected by scribes, as it identifies the preincarnate Christ as active in Israel's deliverance (cf. 1 Cor 10:4) but uses a name more proper to Christ after the incarnation.[21] However, a large number of scholars continue to favor "Lord" as the reading that best explains the rise of the others and fits with Jude's style and theology.[22] Jude otherwise refers to Jesus with further titles like "Lord" and "Christ," not merely as "Jesus," and it is easy to imagine the *nomen sacrum* abbreviation KC (κύριος) being confused with IC ('Ιησοῦς) in early stages of transmission.

These textual decisions are pertinent to Christology and theology in Jude and, therewith, in earliest Christianity. Nevertheless, in terms of theological data, the difference is not so much whether Jude conceived of Christ as preexistent or identified him closely with the Father (compare vv. 4, 14–15, 21, 25) but what words Jude used to do so. More consequential for interpretation and the application of Jude are the textual problems in vv. 22–23, where variant wording affects one's understanding of the author's message and how the letter means to address God's people in times of crisis.

21. Opting for "Jesus" here, with different arguments, compare Jerome H. Neyrey, SJ, *2 Peter, Jude: A New Translation with Introduction and Commentary*, AB 37C (New Haven: Yale University Press, 1993), 62; Henning Paulsen, *Der Zweite Petrusbrief und der Judasbrief*, KEK 12/2 (Göttingen: Vandenhoeck & Ruprecht, 1992), 60–61; Philipp F. Bartholomä, "Did Jesus Save the People out of Egypt? A Re-examination of a Textual Problem in Jude 5," *NovT* 50, no. 2 (2008): 143–58.

22. Wasserman, *Epistle of Jude*, 263–66; Jörg Frey, *Der Brief des Judas und der zweite Brief des Petrus*, THKNT 2/15 (Leipzig: Evangelische Verlagsanstalt, 2015), 68–70; Peter H. Davids, *The Letters of 2 Peter and Jude*, Pillar New Testament Commentary (Grand Rapids: Eerdmans, 2006), 48; Anton Vögtle, *Der Judasbrief, der zweite Petrusbrief*, EKKNT 22 (Neukirchen-Vluyn: Neukirchener Verlag, 1994), 37–40; Richard J. Bauckham, *Jude, 2 Peter*, WBC 50 (Waco, TX: Word Books, 1983), 43.

Jude opens by calling his addressees, the "beloved," to "contend for the faith" (vv. 1, 3), as "ungodly" people (v. 4) have crept in and are polluting the community by their behavior and their teaching. Jude offers several exempla that remind the beloved of God's track record for punishing rebellion, and he warns that Christ will return to carry out such a judgment in the future (vv. 5–19). Thereafter, the letter's *peroratio* comes in the imperatives of vv. 20–23. The beloved are to keep themselves in the faith, waiting for Christ's mercy at his return (vv. 20–21), and they are to work for the salvation of those who are currently in eschatological danger (vv. 22–23).

In the context of the letter, then, Jude 20–23 affects the very "point" Jude means to make and what Jude means his audience to *do* in this situation. Unfortunately, the manuscripts show significant variation in this latter call to have mercy on others. Indeed, Jude 22–23 is "undoubtedly one of the most corrupt passages in NT literature."[23] There are numerous smaller units of variation and more than one major alteration in terms of the structure and order of material, and commentators and editors are divided. We can present only a limited and broad overview here. At base, we have a choice between a two-clause or three-clause text in Jude 22–23.

A *three-clause reading* is adopted in several editions, not least the current Nestle-Aland edition.

> καὶ οὓς μὲν ἐλεᾶτε διακρινομένους, οὓς δὲ σῴζετε ἐκ πυρὸς ἁρπάζοντες, οὓς δὲ ἐλεᾶτε ἐν φόβῳ μισοῦντες καὶ τὸν ἀπὸ τῆς σαρκὸς ἐσπιλωμένον χιτῶνα.
> And on some who doubt have mercy; save others by snatching them from the fire; on others have mercy with fear, hating even the garment stained by the flesh.

This is the passage's structure as found in the corrected text of Sinaiticus. Alexandrinus has the same except that instead of the first imperative, ἐλεᾶτε (have mercy), it reads ἐλέγχετε (rebuke). Here and throughout the early history of transmission, the participle διακρινομένους seems to have caused some confusion. In several passages, the term seems to indicate "doubt," some internal dispute or distinction about an impression or truth-claim.[24] More regularly, however, it means to "dispute" outwardly with others, as

23. Carroll D. Osburn, "The Text of Jude 22–23," *ZNW* 63, no. 1 (1972): 139.

24. BDAG lists, for "doubt," Matt 21:21; Mark 11:23; Luke 11:38; Rom 4:20; 14:23; Jas 1:6; 2:4.

indeed it does earlier in Jude (v. 9).[25] Some scribes seem to have altered the imperative to make it more appropriate as a response to "disputers," with a call not to have mercy but to "rebuke" them (as in the Sixto-Clementine Vulgate). Other texts have an alternate for this participle, putting it in the nominative plural (διακρινομένοι), commanding the beloved to make distinctions or perhaps be internally discerning *while* they have mercy on some.[26]

The interpretation of διακρινομένους as "disputers" brings us to the *two-clause reading*. The shortest iteration of a two-clause text, with probably the best claim to originality, is that found in P⁷².

> οὓς μὲν ἐκ πυρὸς ἁρπάσατε, διακρινομένους δὲ ἐλεεῖτε ἐν φόβῳ μισοῦντες καὶ τὸν ἀπὸ τῆς σαρκὸς ἐσπιλωμένον χιτῶνα. (P⁷²)
> Snatch some out of the fire, and on those who dispute have mercy with fear, hating even the garment stained by the flesh.

This shorter text, rather than a list of three objects with three imperatives, is a juxtaposition of two objects (μέν/δέ) and two imperatives. The text issues first a general call to save people ("some") from the fire. Then, in the particular case of those who "dispute"—perhaps the rebels or those who side with them—the text calls the beloved to have mercy but with a conscious awareness not to become entangled in their sin. This shorter text has been known from a wide array of early versions—Latin, Syriac, Coptic—as well as from citations in Jerome (*Comm. Ezek.*, book 6, 18:5–9) and, already in the second century, in Clement of Alexandria (*Strom.* 6.8.65). Charles Bigg in fact opted for nearly exactly this reading already in 1901.[27] But the discovery of P⁷² in the mid-twentieth century demonstrated that it is a Greek manuscript reading and not a loose quotation by Clement or a non-Greek corruption in the versions, and many commentators now opt for its text as original.

Nonetheless, the evidence is complicated, and the choice is not simply between the corrected Sinaiticus or the papyrus. Several manuscripts offer readings that are intermediate between these forms. The corrected text of

25. See particularly Peter Spitaler, "Doubt or Dispute (Jude 9 and 22–23): Rereading a Special New Testament Meaning through the Lense [*sic*] of Internal Evidence," *Bib* 87, no. 2 (2006): 201–22.

26. Some also seem to have taken it as a true passive rather than a middle participle, calling for mercy on those who are "being judged" (as in some Latin versions), potentially referring to divine judgment or ecclesiastical penance.

27. See Charles Bigg, *A Critical and Exegetical Commentary on the Epistles of St. Peter and St. Jude*, ICC (Edinburgh: T&T Clark, 1901), 340–42.

Ephraemi Rescriptus (C) has essentially the reading of P^{72} but reversed, with the snatching clause now after the clause about the "disputers," and with the imperative "save" (σώζετε) added to the "snatching" clause. Others have the same but with the alterations we noted above related to διακρινομένους: some with the imperative "rebuke" replacing the command to have mercy on the disputers, while others (K L P S) and the Byzantine text have this reversed two-clause text but with διακρινομένους in the nominative: "And on some (οὓς μέν) have mercy as you make judgments; but on others (οὓς δέ) have mercy with fear, snatching them from the fire, hating even the garment stained by the flesh."[28] And there are many more minor variations.[29]

We are clearly dealing with a confused transmission tradition. Several smaller units can be explained by interpretive changes related to διακρινομένους or perhaps to an accidental omission or repetition of οὓς. But the variety and spread of the shorter and longer two-clause readings suggest that one must reckon with some kind of evolution or devolution, and likely a combination of intentional and accidental corruptions that led to the one or the other even at the same point of variation. If the three-clause reading is original, with its two commands to have "mercy" and διακρινομένους in the first clause, one may explain some of the intermediate forms by a scribe skipping accidentally over a οὓς δέ and a few words thereafter, shortening it intentionally out of interpretive confusion or omitting the imperative "save" as unnecessary.[30] If P^{72} represents the initial text, one may explain the intermediate forms as resulting from corrective or interpretive additions ("save" as an added gloss), accidental or intentional doubling of οὓς δέ, or a scribe who knew of another version of the text with "mercy" or διακρινομένους in the first clause and expanded the passage by conflating them.[31]

What of the readings' consistency with Jude's style and argument? Again there is disagreement. On one hand, the three-clause reading might seem the harder reading and more likely to be changed, particularly since the clauses

28. Vaticanus apparently exhibits a hybrid, with all the words of the three-clause reading above and its two imperatives to "have mercy," but with only one οὓς δέ.

29. See Wasserman, *Epistle of Jude*, 197; Sakae Kubo, "Jude 22–23: Two-Division Form or Three?," in *New Testament Textual Criticism: Its Significance for Exegesis; Essays in Honor of Bruce M. Metzger*, ed. Eldon Jay Epp and Gordon D. Fee (Oxford: Oxford University Press, 1981), 239–41.

30. See the three-clause arguments in Wasserman, *Epistle of Jude*, 324–29; Kubo, "Jude 22–23"; Vögtle, *Der Judasbrief*, 102–5; Davids, *Letters of 2 Peter and Jude*, 98–100.

31. For two-clause arguments, see Landon, *Text-Critical Study*, 131–34; Osburn, "Text of Jude 22–23"; Bauckham, *Jude*, 108–11; Frey, *Der Brief des Judas*, 119–21.

begin with a differentiation of objects (οὓς μέν . . . οὓς δέ . . . οὓς δέ) but ultimately offer three distinct actions, with only one clause giving any information about its object ("disputing"). Likewise, the three-clause reading seems to fit the author's rhetorical penchant for triads (three verbs in v. 8, three participles in vv. 20–21, etc.).[32] However, there are strong arguments in favor of the two-clause reading found in P^{72}. The two-clause reading distinguishes the actions commanded based on the disposition of their objects, whether or not they actively "dispute" and pose a danger, and this seems to be what one should expect in such a juxtaposition with the objects fronted: among the ungodly, some (οὓς μέν) are simply to be snatched from the fire, while those who dispute (διακρινομένους δέ) should be given mercy with caution due to the danger they may pose to one's own sanctity. This fits Jude's examples depicting ungodly people of negative influence—such as Korah and Balaam, for instance, whose destruction was (mercifully) delayed but whose continued influence brought the downfall of many (v. 11). Further, the triads in Jude hardly speak against the shorter reading. A penchant for triads did not preclude Jude from a mere two-part μέν / δέ in v. 10. Indeed, if we count the *actions* called for in P^{72} rather than only counting imperative mood verbs, the two-clause structure is also triadic, as it calls believers to (a) snatch people from the fire and (b) have mercy on those who dispute while (c) consciously avoiding any impurity.[33]

A decision is difficult. The "rules" of criticism to which Pius XII appeals do not settle the issue objectively, as the external and internal evidence admit of different interpretations. More than one commentator has declared the problem virtually insoluble.[34] "This is one of the places in the NT in which

32. See J. D. Charles, "Literary Artifice in the Epistle of Jude," *ZNW* 82, no. 1–2 (1991): 122–23.

33. Indeed, not all of Charles's examples of Jude's triads are grammatically neat ("Literary Artifice," 122–23). Charles counts three participles linked to the imperative in vv. 20–21 as a triad, excluding the imperative itself. But in v. 9, Charles counts the three verbals in Michael's actions by including one that is only an infinitive complement and not a separate action at all: Michael "did not *dare* [ἐτόλμησεν] pronounce [ἐπενεγκεῖν] a judgment of blasphemy, but *said* [εἶπεν]." In v. 13, Charles counts "wild," "foaming," and "shame" as further evidence of Jude's penchant for triads. Yet only the first two are descriptions of the ungodly as "waves"; "shame" is that with which they foam.

34. Opting for the three-clause reading, compare Paulsen, *Der Zweite Petrusbrief und der Judasbrief*, 82: "Das Verständnis der Verse wird erheblich erschwert durch die Unsicherheit des Textes, dessen Probleme sich nicht mehr überzeugend lösen lassen." Frey, who opts for two clauses, writes: "Die textkritischen Probleme dieser Aussage . . . lassen sich nicht mehr eindeutig lösen" (*Der Brief des Judas*, 119).

scholars simply cannot state with any assurance what the original text was."[35] Nonetheless, a decision is necessary. Out of twenty-five verses, in only four (vv. 20–23) does Jude explicitly tell the beloved what they should *do*, and vv. 22–23 comprise the only explicit indication in the letter as to how the beloved should respond to those who, amid the crisis, have already strayed into the inferno that Jude's fiery rhetoric has been foretelling. God did not inspire Jude to write all these forms of the text to the letter's first audience. One preparing a critical edition must choose something to print, and one interested in what Jude meant to say must make a decision here about which words Jude wrote. Significantly, for theological interpretation, one intending to hear and actualize this message today will be affected by whether Jude calls the faithful in crisis first to rebuke the "disputers" or to have mercy on them, and by whether Jude's final caution to avoid contamination is general or names a specific danger in showing mercy to the dissident.

I find the shorter reading, and particularly that found in P^{72}, more compelling. Nothing speaks against it on internal grounds, and its fit with Jude's argument and style tilts the scales in its favor. Its external attestation, though rare among Greek manuscripts, is strengthened by the date of the papyrus and its use in patristic and versional sources. Nonetheless, while I must make a decision for the sake of exegesis, it would be overconfident to hold my decision with anything like absolute certainty. One can have reasonable confidence that one has made the best decision possible based on one's understanding of the available evidence. Critics endeavoring to reconstruct the text for the sake of hearing the inspired Scripture should strive for nothing less, but we should not pretend to anything more. How, then, should we understand the text and interpretation of God's word when a textual decision is meaningful but ultimately uncertain?

A Communicative Teleology of God's Inspired Word

In the vision of exegesis and inspiration espoused by Pius XII and *Dei Verbum*, a desire to hear the words of Scripture as God originally inspired them calls for text-critical reconstruction. But the methods of criticism cannot necessarily guarantee that result. Does this invalidate the critical enterprise? Or, from a different perspective, might it undermine confidence in the possibility of hearing the inspired word of God at all?

35. Davids, *Letters of 2 Peter and Jude*, 98.

As I see it, a solution can be found in looking again at the theology of inspiration itself in relation to biblical text-forms. First, we need not locate inspiration *exclusively* in a single text-form, as though one cannot access the inspired Scripture through imperfect copies.[36] To limit inspiration to "the" singular autographic text is impracticable and, as we will see below in 2 Timothy, biblically counterevidenced. In cases where a book's contents are composed and edited by different people, such a restriction would either deny God's inspiring work in the meaningful process of editing and arranging of material or in the composition of the material later edited. We would have to choose either whether God inspired the original psalmists and sages or the wording as later edited (compare, e.g., Prov 25:1).[37] Moreover, since even in antiquity no assembly possessed "originals" of more than a few books (at most!) and only imperfect handmade copies of the others, to restrict inspiration only to perfectly accurate forms of the text would be to affirm that the church has never possessed a fully inspired Bible.

It is instructive here to return to two of the primary passages employed in Christian theologies of inspiration, one from 2 Peter and one from 2 Timothy:

> 2 Pet 1:21: For no prophecy was ever brought about through human will; rather, people spoke from God as they were carried by the Holy Spirit.
>
> 2 Tim 3:15–17: From infancy you have known the sacred writings, which are able to make you wise unto salvation through faith in Christ Jesus. All scripture is divinely inspired and useful for teaching, for rebuke, for correction, for training in justice, in order that the person of God might be ready, prepared for every good work.

36. See the fuller argument (and dialogue with other views) in James B. Prothro, "Inspiration and Textual Preservation: A Catholic Essay," *ProEccl* 30, no. 2 (2021): 141–62.

37. If we appeal to the text's "final form" as the only inspired version (as many do), we must still address the problems of textual variation in the transmission and preservation of those texts. Too tight a correlation of inspiration to canonical form risks implying that ecclesial reception confers inspiration on the texts rather than merely recognizing texts already inspired (a view rejected already in Vatican I, *Dei Filius* §2, noted above). However, if one can attribute inspiration to more than one form of a text, as I argue, there is room to say that two texts are inspired, while only one is received as prototypical for translation into lectionaries or use in dogmatic judgments (see further Prothro, "Inspiration and Textual Preservation," 149–62).

The passage from 2 Peter affirms the inspiration of prophecy—and theological tradition has taken this to extend to the work of "hagiographers," inspired writers of every stripe—in its earliest and even pretextual stages. People spoke as they were moved by the Spirit in the very composition of the message, making their message "not the word of humans but, as is truly the case, the word of God" (1 Thess 2:13). In writing, too, God's movements to inspire what would become a canonical book of Scripture are at work in the beginning stages of its composition, from what was said to the way it was remembered, written, and edited.[38] This datum is balanced, however, by the passage from 2 Timothy, for the affirmation that "all Scripture" is inspired is clearly referring to the books of the Old Testament *in forms that Timothy can read and has read* (the writings Timothy has known since his pre-Christian childhood). That is, 2 Tim 3:16—a main text for the inspiration of Scripture—predicates inspiration not of ideal "originals" but of real, accessible copies that have undergone centuries (in many cases) of manual corruption. Indeed, given the use of the Old Testament in the Pauline tradition, it likely predicates inspiration of copies not in the original languages but in Greek translation.

If these texts can teach us about biblical inspiration, they suggest that inspiration occurs *throughout* the compositional process and that it is not compromised by the production and use of later, imperfect, real text-forms. This means that we should be able to affirm more than one form of the biblical text as inspired, even when we can be reasonably certain that its wording is imperfect. One might ask how two different text-forms, at least one of which must be inaccurate to the wording originally inspired, can be considered inspired. Here 2 Tim 3:15–17 comes to our aid again, as it correlates inspiration not with a text's flawlessness or exact wording but with its purpose as a text. While much ink has been spilled on Scripture's being "in-spired" or "God-breathed" (θεόπνευστος) and what that implies about its inherent qualities, "the weight of the sentence" in 2 Tim 3:16 falls on what the text is

38. See, already, Marie-Joseph Lagrange, OP, *Historical Criticism and the Old Testament*, trans. Edward Myers (London: Catholic Truth Society, 1905), 96–98. Further, with psychological and Thomistic insights, Benoit distinguishes helpfully between the ways in which divine inspiration operates at different compositional stages on different persons. See Pierre Benoit, OP, *Aspects of Biblical Inspiration*, trans. Jerome Murphy-O'Connor, OP, and S. K. Ashe, OP (Chicago: Priory, 1965); cf. Denis Farkasfalvy, OCist, *A Theology of the Christian Bible: Revelation, Inspiration, Canon* (Washington, DC: Catholic University of America Press, 2018), 111–20.

inspired to *do*.[39] God's goal in inspiring texts is not merely to get the perfect words onto a page. Inspired texts are "able," as such, to make one wise *unto* (εἰς) salvation and are useful *for* (πρός) teaching and reproof *so that* (ἵνα) one might be prepared *for* (πρός) every good work.

Not every text-form can represent precisely the wording compiled for dispatch by the original author or editor, the precise form in which "everything and only those things which [God] wanted written" is printed with singular exactness.[40] But more than one text-form can serve God's purpose to *communicate* God's intended message, form the faithful in justice, and make them "wise unto salvation through faith in Christ Jesus" (2 Tim 3:15).[41] The texts are inspired to participate in God's economy of self-disclosure, to reveal and communicate God's person and God's saving will, supremely in Jesus Christ (cf. Heb 1:1–2; *DV* §§2–4). As in any act of communication, this revelation is disclosed in the individual parts of the divine message but most fully through the whole. Each word in a sentence can have meaning on its own, yet as words combine into the whole, one can perceive how each is meant to signify in relation to the others. Something similar can be said of the many books and differing voices found in Scripture as they come together into the communicative whole of the canon. The recent *Catechism* summarizes insights from Bernard and Augustine here: "Through all the words of Sacred Scripture, God speaks only one single Word, his one Utterance in whom he expresses himself completely."[42] God inspires the message of each text, with

39. Christopher R. Hutson, *First and Second Timothy and Titus*, Paideia (Grand Rapids: Baker Academic, 2019), 195. The meaning of "inspiration" in 2 Timothy as related to a divine outbreathing of a text has been questioned recently by John C. Poirier, *The Invention of the Inspired Text: Philological Windows on the Theopneustia of Scripture*, LNTS 640 (London: T&T Clark, 2021). Poirier argues that it should be understood to mean that the text is "life-giving" and concludes by critiquing certain evangelical hermeneutics. To my understanding, Catholic tradition affirms Scripture's life-giving potential because it speaks a divinely sourced message through which the life-giving Spirit operates, the latter conviction being based not solely on the term θεόπνευστος but on other passages and theological convictions (e.g., Matt 22:43; 2 Pet 1:21; Heb 1:1; 3:7).

40. Vatican Council II, Dogmatic Constitution *Dei Verbum* (November 18, 1965) §11 (in Béchard, *Scripture Documents*, 24).

41. Compare Jeannine K. Brown, *Scripture as Communication: Introducing Biblical Hermeneutics*, 2nd ed. (Grand Rapids: Baker Academic, 2021); William M. Wright IV and Frances Martin, *Encountering the Living God in Scripture: Theological and Philosophical Principles for Interpretation* (Grand Rapids: Baker Academic, 2019), 37–99.

42. *CCC* §102. Compare Augustine, *Ennarrat. Ps.* 103.4.1; Bernard of Clairvaux, *Sermones de diversis* 5.2; Farkasfalvy, *Theology of the Christian Bible*, 60–62.

its particular authorial tone and language and modes of expression, to speak a word to its initial audience, and each has meaning on its own. Yet God intended, beyond the purview of those text's authors and first readers, that these should all interrelate to convey a whole in which Genesis and Obadiah and Romans and Matthew become messages within the message, words that convey the word. It is this act of communication within which individual words and statements and even whole books possess their fullest value as "the word of the Lord." And if we trust that God continues to speak through Matthew or Daniel even after those books' composers ceased to write, we can posit that divine providence has not ceased to guide the church to hear the same word through differing and even imperfect wordings of their texts as new generations copied or translated them.

Juridical Sufficiency and the Critical Difference

If two forms of a text can be considered inspired, a communicative and teleological perspective on the inspired "word" helps to understand how this can be the case. Two text-forms, whether at the level of a particular wording or even the shape of a book (e.g., Esther, Jeremiah), can be inspired inasmuch as they both contribute what they are meant to contribute to the communication of that greater "word" within the canon. Uncertainties about particular individual wordings today, or certainties about corruptions in the texts used in former days, do not compromise God's goal to communicate that word through Scripture or the ability of imperfect texts to achieve the formative and revelatory goal for which they were inspired. In any act of human communication, while individual words are important, the message can still be conveyed correctly "even when some of the words are drowned out in ambient noise," as happens often when two friends speak to each other across a noisy street or through the static of a radio.[43] And, like any human reiterating the same message to a friend at different times, God can speak the same word with more than one wording, even if God is calling the church today to hear that word in a more ancient and more precise form through critical reconstruction. This allows us to affirm the sufficiency and goodness of texts to which Pius XII would accord "juridical" authority—the Sixto-Clementine Vulgate in his day, the *Nova Vulgata* (1979) and approved

43. Dirk Jongkind, *An Introduction to the Greek New Testament, Produced at Tyndale House, Cambridge* (Wheaton, IL: Crossway, 2019), 103.

vernacular translations or lectionaries today. Read within a communicative model of revelation as a whole, these texts do not teach error—though all of them have wordings that are not accurate when compared to the original compositions—and God uses these texts to speak to the church. They "may be quoted safely and without fear of error in disputations, in lectures, and in preaching" (*DAS* §21).[44]

Returning to Jude, the christological variations in vv. 4–5 are not insignificant, but they also do not affect the broader witness of the New Testament to the person of Christ, his preexistence, or his close identification with the saving and judging actions of God. Regarding the call to mercy in vv. 22–23, the teaching that believers in Christ should intervene for the salvation of those in danger of judgment, and even that "rebuking" them can be part of such saving intervention, is not compromised no matter which text one chooses (cf. Matt 18:15–35; Gal 6:1–2; 2 Thess 3:13–15; Jas 5:20–21; 1 John 5:16). I can read more than one form of these texts from a lectionary as "the word of the Lord" without crossing my theological fingers behind my back. I can regard them as "safe" and even, as argued above, as inspired for the purpose of fulfilling their role within the greater divine message.

However, the possibility that a text-form is critically incorrect and still "inspired" or "safe" does not mean that we should not strive to restore the text to the best of our abilities. Not every form of the text is inspired for the uses to which we subject the Bible. This is obviously the case in matters of mere history. A text that does not intend to represent what Jude wrote at v. 5—or one that does so incorrectly—is not useful to answer questions about the book's author or about the history of Christology, even if the reading does not ultimately alter Catholic doctrine about Christ.

44. Pius XII does not appeal to a communication model per se, but he does claim the Vulgate's inerrancy within the church's reception of the whole of Scripture's witness "in the sense in which the Church has understood and understands it" (*DAS* §21). Given passages in the Bible depicting incomplete standards of faith and morality, however, to claim the text is free from error in doctrine or morals seems already to assume a hermeneutical tradition by which the moral or doctrinal implications of certain passages or books are relativized and subjected to the message of the whole as received by the church's living tradition. A communication model does not restrict inerrancy or inspiration only to statements about doctrine and morals, but it does subordinate all specific claims to the greater Word. See more recently the discussions of truth and error in Farkasfalvy, *Theology of the Christian Bible*, 121–58. Contrast, from an evangelical perspective, the arguments by Peter J. Gurry, who restricts inspiration to one text-form but argues that multiple text-forms can be sufficiently inerrant in "Inerrancy and the Initial Text," *Presbyterion* 49, no. 1 (2023): 54–67.

Beyond mere history, however, not every text is best suited to theological interpretation. A communicative view of Scripture's message that subordinates all the parts to the whole necessarily, at the same time, reminds us that each part is important, and the clarity and effect of the whole is enhanced by the clarity of each part. A sentence is more than the sum of its parts, but it cannot communicate the same thing without its parts, and distorted details can create misunderstandings in content.[45] This is all the more true given the particular role Scripture is meant to play in the life of God's people. There are many texts beyond those in the canon that have the goal of edifying and forming the faithful unto salvation. But other edifying texts are not divinely purposed to nourish and guide the faithful with the same universal and perpetual authority as Scripture. Likewise, within Scripture itself, each book's contents are meant to contribute to the whole. If critics or bishops were to cut out an unpopular verse from printings of Matthew or Genesis, we can perhaps be comforted by the fact that this would not invalidate the ability of those editions to communicate the greater divine message. But such a removal would affect the way in which God meant Matthew and Genesis to contribute to that greater message, and enough removals of material—like a large amount of "noise" drowning out a friend's words—could indeed compromise a printed Bible's ability to communicate the "word of the Lord."

Further, even where a difference in wording is small and does not affect the message of a particular chapter or book within the canon, a communicative model reminds us that smaller elements of a message are not inconsequential. If a person can communicate the same content in more than one wording, the *way* in which a friend says what she says can affect how we understand what she means or what "point" she means to make by saying it. Indeed, such details can enhance our encounter not just with the message but with the person who relates to us in conveying it. In Scripture, the textual details are not immaterial in matters of specifics or in our encounter with the God who speaks through the text. If we want to read the text for *all* its worth as a communicative act, we should strive to comprehend the message with all its enhancements and details where possible.

These critical communicative differences are significant for theological

45. Using a more aesthetic analogy, one can compare the whole of Scripture with a symphony, the value of which is greater than but irreducibly constituted and therefore affected by the way each part is played. Clearly hearing each note and line in this symphony, then, requires literary, historical, philological, and text-critical analysis *within* "theological" interpretation. See James B. Prothro, "Theories of Inspiration and Catholic Exegesis: Scripture and Criticism in Dialogue with Denis Farkasfalvy," *CBQ* 83, no. 2 (2021): 307–14.

interpretation, further, because of the way that Scripture is meant to address the faithful. We can come to the Bible with systematic questions and scour it for relevant answers, but its nature as a collection of communicative texts means that we are not primarily meant to consult it as an encyclopedia but to hear its books as texts that *address* us. We should read each text in light of the whole, but God's address to us through the long and complex canon happens in smaller communicative units at particular times—whether preached from the lectionary or in personal or communal study. We are to hear ourselves addressed by particular books and through the voices and arguments and examples of their authors. And hearing God's word through particular ancient texts for the way that they address us, or at least doing so responsibly, involves considering the way in which the author addressed the text's initial audience, not just hearing things authors happened to say but the points they meant to make and the effects they intended.[46]

Such considerations are relevant particularly to exhortative texts like Jude 22–23. If my community is to hear the Letter of Jude, and if we hear our own crises of morality or leadership in Jude's descriptions of the "ungodly," then Jude's tone and the particularities of his instruction are directly relevant and even divinely given for us to hear. To be sure, other passages inform believers about how to respond within crisis, and if taken together they will all point to the same truth in Christ. But among such passages, we are to be moved and instructed and rebuked by *this* address, to experience how this book—as opposed to any other—speaks to people in such situations to form them in faith and love and endurance. And the illocution, the "point" of what Jude means people to do and therefore also the address we hear in the text, is affected by the wording of these verses. We will hear Jude's peroration differently if we hear a call to "rebuke" those who dispute or simply to "have mercy," if we hear Jude's caution to keep oneself unstained while having mercy as a general caution or as one particularly and warningly appended in the case of dealing with those who oppose the truth. Among other texts that inform Christians about faithful responses to scandal and crisis, God inspired the Letter of Jude to pack its own punch and contribute its own voice, and that punch is softened if Jude's commands about how the faithful should respond are replaced by later scribes' alterations or misrepresentations of it.

We need not believe that only perfect reconstructions provide reliable

46. On the role of speech acts and illocution in Catholic hermeneutics, see, among others, James B. Prothro, "History, Illocution, and Theological Exegesis: Reading Paul's Letter to Philemon," *Nova et Vetera* 18, no. 4 (2020): 1341–63.

access to the divine message or bear the Spirit's power to form God's people. But the lack of absolute perfection does not devalue or undermine the attempt to achieve the best text that we can. If God speaks the one great word through many smaller acts of human communication, better—though imperfect—knowledge of what those humans communicated allows us better to hear Scripture's teaching, rebukes, and consolations so that by them we may be trained in wisdom and justice—the purpose for which it was inspired (2 Tim 3:15–17).

Bibliography

Abbott, Walter. *The Documents of Vatican II*. London-Dublin: Geoffrey Chapman, 1966.

Abrams, M. H. *The Mirror and the Lamp: Romantic Theory and the Critical Tradition*. Oxford: Oxford University Press, 1971.

Ackerman, Susan. "At Home with the Goddess." Pages 455–68 in *Symbiosis, Symbolism, and the Power of the Past: Canaan, Ancient Israel, and Their Neighbors, from the Late Bronze Age through Roman Palaestina: Proceedings of the Centennial Symposium, W. F. Albright Institute of Archaeological Research and American Schools of Oriental Research, Jerusalem, May 29/31, 2000*. Edited by W. G. Dever and S. Gitin. Winona Lake, IN: Eisenbrauns, 2003.

Adams, Edward. "Graeco-Roman and Ancient Jewish Cosmology." Pages 5–27 in *Cosmology and New Testament Theology*. Edited by Jonathan T. Pennington and Sean M. McDonough. LNTS 355. London: T&T Clark, 2008.

Aḥituv, Shmuel. *Canaanite Toponyms in Ancient Egyptian Documents*. Jerusalem: Magnes, 1984.

Aland, Barbara, Kurt Aland, Johannes Karavidopoulos, Carlo M. Martini, and Bruce M. Metzger, eds. *Novum Testamentum Graece*. 28th rev. ed. Stuttgart: Deutsche Bibelgesellschaft, 2012.

Albertz, Rainer. "Welche Art von Individualität förderte die altisraelitische Familienreligion?" Pages 133–51 in *Religionspraxis und Individualität: Die Bedeutung von persönlicher Frömmigkeit und Family Religion für das Personkonzept in der Antike*. Edited by Alexandra Grund-Wittenberg. Leiden: Brill, 2021.

Albright, W. F. *Yahweh and the Gods of Canaan*. Garden City: Doubleday, 1968.

Allison, Dale C., Jr. "Behind the Temptations of Jesus: Q 4:1–13 and Mark 1:12–

13." Pages 195–214 in *Authenticating the Activities of Jesus*. Edited by Bruce Chilton and Craig A. Evans. NTTS 2/28. Leiden: Brill, 1999.

———. *Constructing Jesus: Memory, Imagination, and History*. Grand Rapids: Baker Academic, 2010.

———. *The Historical Christ and the Theological Jesus*. Grand Rapids: Eerdmans, 2009.

———. "How to Marginalize the Traditional Criteria of Authenticity." Pages 3–30 in *How to Study the Historical Jesus*. Vol. 1 of *The Handbook for the Study of the Historical Jesus*. Edited by Tom Holmén and Stanley E. Porter. Leiden: Brill, 2010.

———. "It Don't Come Easy: A History of Disillusionment." Pages 186–99 in *Jesus, Criteria, and the Demise of Authenticity*. Edited by Chris Keith and Anthony Le Donne. London: T&T Clark, 2012.

———. "Jesus and the Victory of Apocalyptic." Pages 126–41 in *Jesus and the Restoration of Israel: A Critical Assessment of N. T. Wright's "Jesus and the Victory of God."* Edited by Carey C. Newman. Downers Grove, IL: InterVarsity Press, 1999.

———. *Jesus of Nazareth: Millenarian Prophet*. Minneapolis: Fortress, 1998.

Anagwo, Emmanuel Chinedu. "Cult of the Ancestors and Saints from the Igbo (Nigerian) Experience: A Liturgical Evaluation." *Grace & Truth* 35, no. 2 (2018): 8–23.

Anderson, Janice Capel. *Matthew's Narrative Web: Over, and Over, and Over Again*. JSNTSup 91. Sheffield: JSOT Press, 1994.

Anthonioz, Stéphanie. "Chérubins / *keruvim*: Évolutions et mutation." Pages 93–114 in *Les chérubins /* Keruvim *dans l'antiquité: Approche historique et comparée*. Kasion 6. Edited by Philippe Abrahami and Stéphanie Anthonioz. Münster: Zaphon, 2021.

Anyumba, Godfrey, and Mkateko Nkuna. "Lake Fundudzi: A Sacred Lake in South Africa That Is Not Open for Tourism Development." *African Journal of Hospitality, Tourism and Leisure* 6 (2017): 1–20.

Aquino, María Pilar. "Latina Feminist Theology: Central Features." Pages 133–60 in *A Reader in Latin Feminist Theology: Religion and Justice*. Edited by María Pilar Aquino, Daisy L. Machado, and Jeanette Rodriguez. Austin: University of Texas Press, 2002.

———. "Latin American Feminist Theology." *JFSR* 14, no. 1 (1998): 89–107.

———. *Our Cry for Life: Feminist Theology from Latin America*. Maryknoll, NY: Orbis, 1992.

Avigad, Nahman, and Benjamin Sass. *Corpus of West Semitic Stamp Seals*. Publications of the Israel Academy of Sciences and Humanities, Section of Humanities. Jerusalem: Israel Academy of Sciences and Humanities, 1997.

Ayres, Lewis. *Nicaea and Its Legacy: An Approach to Fourth-Century Trinitarian Theology.* Oxford: Oxford University Press, 2004.

Ba, Amadou Hampate. "Présentation des religions traditionnelles africaines." Pages 65–87 in *Les religions africaines comme source de valeurs de civilisation.* Edited by Alioune Diop. Paris: Présence Africaine, 1972.

Bailey, Kenneth E. *Jesus through Middle Eastern Eyes: Cultural Studies in the Gospels.* London: SPCK, 2008.

Bajeux, Jean-Claude. "Mentalité noire et mentalité biblique." Pages 57–82 in *Des prêtres noirs s'interrogent.* Présence Africaine with Msgr. Lefebvre. Paris: Éditions du Cerf, 1956.

Balthasar, Hans Urs von. *Martin Buber & Christianity: A Dialogue between Israel and the Church.* Translated by Alexander Dru. New York: Macmillan, 1961.

———. *Schau und Gestalt.* Vol. 1 of *Herrlichkeit: Eine theologische Ästhetik.* Freiburg: Johannes, 2019.

Baly, Denis. "The Geography of Monotheism." Pages 253–78 in *Translating and Understanding the Old Testament: Essays in Honor of Herbert Gordon May.* Edited by Harry T. Frank and William L. Reed. Nashville: Abingdon, 1970.

Balz, H. "στενάζω." *EDNT* 3:272–73.

Bar, Shaul. "Resheph in the Hebrew Bible." *JBQ* 45, no. 2 (2017): 119–26.

Barber, Michael Patrick. *The Historical Jesus and the Temple: Memory, Methodology, and the Gospel of Matthew.* Cambridge: Cambridge University Press, 2023.

Barker, Margaret. *The Great Angel: A Study of Israel's Second God.* Louisville: Westminster John Knox, 1992.

Barnett, Jon, and John Campbell. *Climate Change and Small Island States: Power, Knowledge and the South Pacific.* London: Earthscan, 2010.

Barré, Jean-Luc. *François Mauriac – Biographie intime.* 2 vols. Paris: Fayard, 2009–2010.

Bartholomä, Philipp F. "Did Jesus Save the People out of Egypt? A Reexamination of a Textual Problem in Jude 5." *NovT* 50, no. 2 (2008): 143–58.

Bartlett, John. *Bartlett's Familiar Quotations.* 9th ed. Boston: Little, Brown, and Co., 1909.

Barton, George A. "Native Israelitish Deities." Pages 86–115 in *Oriental Studies: A Selection of the Papers Read before the Oriental Club of Philadelphia, 1888–1894.* Boston: Ginn & Company.

Bassler, Jouette M. "The Widow's Tale: A Fresh Look at 1 Timothy 5:3–16." *JBL* 103, no. 1 (1984): 23–41.

Bauckham, Richard J. *Jude, 2 Peter*. WBC 50. Waco, TX: Word Books, 1983.

Beasley-Murray, G. R. *Jesus and the Kingdom of God.* Grand Rapids: Eerdmans, 1986.

Beattie, John. *Bunyoro: An African Kingdom.* Case Studies in Cultural Anthropology 3. New York: Holt, Rinehart and Winston, 1960.

Béchard, Dean P., SJ, ed. and trans. *The Scripture Documents: An Anthology of Official Catholic Teachings.* Collegeville, MN: Liturgical Press, 2002.

Becking, Bob. "The Boundaries of Israelite Monotheism." Pages 9–27 in *The Boundaries of Monotheism*. Edited by Anne-Marie Korte and Maaike de Haardt. Studies in Theology and Religion 13. Leiden: Brill, 2008.

———. "More Than One God?" Pages 60–76 in *Divine Doppelgängers: YHWH's Ancient Look-Alikes.* Edited by Collin Cornell. Winona Lake, IN: Eisenbrauns, 2020.

Behr, John. *The Nicene Faith.* Crestwood, NY: St. Vladimir's Seminary Press, 2004.

Bendemann, Reinhard von. "Auditus et Testamentum: Die Heilung des Tauben/Stummen in der Dekapolis (Mk 7, 31–37)." Pages 55–69 in *Systematisch Praktisch: Festschrift für Reiner Preul zum 65. Geburtstag.* Edited by Wilfried Härle, Bernd-Michael Haese, Kai Hansen, and Eilert Herms. ThSt 80. Marburg: N. G. Elwert Verlag, 2005.

Benedict XVI (Pope)/Joseph Ratzinger. "Biblical Interpretation in Crisis: On the Question of the Foundations and Approaches of Exegesis Today." Pages 1–23 in *Biblical Interpretation in Crisis: The Ratzinger Conference on Bible and Church.* Edited by Richard John Neuhaus. Grand Rapids: Eerdmans, 1989.

———. *Called to Communion: Understanding the Church Today.* Translated by Adrian Walker. San Francisco: Ignatius, 1996.

———. "Chapter II, The Transmission of Divine Revelation." Pages 181–98 in vol. 3 of *Commentary on the Documents of Vatican II.* Edited by Herbert Vorgrimler. Translated by William Glen-Doepel, Hilda Graef, John Michael Jakubiak, and Simon and Erika Young. New York: Herder and Herder, 1968.

———. "Easter Vigil Homily" (15 April, 2006). https://www.vatican.va/content/benedict-xvi/en/homilies/2006/documents/hf_ben-xvi_hom_20060415_veglia-pasquale.html.

———. "Intervention in the Fourteenth General Congregation of the Synod." In *Insegnamenti* 4, no. 2 (October 14, 2008).

———. *In the Beginning: A Catholic Understanding of Creation and Fall.* Translated by Boniface Ramsey, OP. Ressourcement. Grand Rapids: Eerdmans, 1995.

———. *Jesus of Nazareth: From the Baptism in the Jordan to the Transfiguration.* Translated by Adrian J. Walker. New York: Doubleday, 2007.

———. *Jesus of Nazareth, Part Two: Holy Week; From the Entrance into Jerusalem to the Resurrection.* Translated by Philip J. Whitmore. San Francisco: Ignatius, 2010.

———. Post-synodal Apostolic Exhortation *Verbum Domini.* September 30, 2010.

———. *Zur Lehre des Zweiten Vatikanischen Konzils: Formulierung, Vermittlung, Deutung.* Gesammelte Schriften 2/7. Freiburg: Herder, 2012.

Bengel, J. A. *Gnomon Novi Testamentum.* 3rd ed. Stuttgart: Steinkopf, 1860.

Benoit, Pierre, OP. *Aspects of Biblical Inspiration.* Translated by Jerome Murphy-O'Connor, OP, and S. K. Ashe, OP. Chicago: Priory, 1965.

Ben Zvi, Ehud. *Hosea.* FOTL 1/21A. Grand Rapids: Eerdmans, 2005.

Bernard, Penny S. "Ecological Implications of Water Spirit Beliefs in Southern Africa." *USDA Forest Service Proceedings* 27 (2003): 148–54.

Beumer, Johannes. *Die katholische Inspirationslehre zwischen Vaticanum I und II.* SBS 20. Stuttgart: Katholisches Bibelwerk, 1966.

Biebuyck, Daniel, and Kahombo C. Mateene, eds. and trans. *The Mwindo Epic from the Banyanga.* Berkeley: University of California Press, 1971.

Bigg, Charles. *A Critical and Exegetical Commentary on the Epistles of St. Peter and St. Jude.* ICC. Edinburgh: T&T Clark, 1901.

Bobertz, Charles A. *The Gospel of Mark: A Liturgical Reading.* Grand Rapids: Baker Academic, 2016.

Bockmuehl, Markus. *Seeing the Word: Refocusing New Testament Study.* STI. Grand Rapids: Baker Academic, 2006.

Bodnar, John. *Remaking America: Public Memory, Commemoration, and Patriotism in the Twentieth Century.* Princeton: Princeton University Press, 1992.

Bond, Helen K. *The Historical Jesus: A Guide for the Perplexed.* London: T&T Clark, 2012.

Bonnet, Corinne. "Que fait le genre aux dénominations divines, entre mondes grecs et sémitiques?" *Archimede* 8 (2021): 1–16.

Borger, Rylke. *Die Inschriften Asarhaddons,* Königs von Assyrien. Archiv für Orientforschung 9. Graz: Ernst F. Weidner, 1956.

Brague, Rémi. *The Wisdom of the World: The Human Experience of the Universe in Western Thought.* Translated by Teresa Lavender Faga. Chicago: University of Chicago Press, 2003.

Bratcher, Robert G., and Eugene A. Nida. *A Handbook on the Gospel of Mark*. UBS Handbook Series. New York: United Bible Societies, 1961.

Braudis, Ann. "*Laudato Si'* and Evolutionary Consciousness." *NewsNotes* 41, no. 3 (2016). https://maryknollogc.org/sites/default/files/newsnotes/attachments/MayJune2016_NewsNotes.pdf.

Braun, F.-M., OP. *L'oeuvre du Père Lagrange: Étude et bibliographie*. Fribourg en Suisse: St. Paul, 1943.

———. *The Work of Père Lagrange*. Edited and translated by Richard T. A. Murphy, OP. Milwaukee: Bruce, 1963.

Brenner, Athalaya. "The Hebrew God and His Female Complements." Pages 48–63 in *The Feminist Companion to Mythology*. Edited by Carolyne Larrington. London: Pandora, 1992.

Brown, Jeannine K. *Scripture as Communication: Introducing Biblical Hermeneutics*. 2nd ed. Grand Rapids: Baker Academic, 2021.

Brown, Raymond E., SS. "Counterreply." *CBQ* 18, no. 1 (1956): 47–53.

———. *The Death of the Messiah: From Gethsemane to the Grave; A Commentary on the Passion Narratives in the Four Gospels*. 2 vols. ABRL. New York: Doubleday, 1994.

———. "Père Lagrange and the *Sensus Plenior*." *CBQ* 17, no. 3 (1955): 451–55.

Brown, Raymond E., SS, and Thomas Aquinas Collins, OP. "Church Pronouncements." Pages 1166–74 in *The New Jerome Biblical Commentary*. Edited by Raymond E. Brown, SS, Joseph A. Fitzmyer, SJ, and Roland E. Murphy, OCarm. Englewood Cliffs, NJ: Prentice Hall, 1990.

Brown, Robert McAfee. *Gustavo Gutiérrez: An Introduction to Liberation Theology*. New York: Orbis, 1990.

Buccellati, Giorgio. "Yahweh, the Trinity: The Old Testament Catechumenate (Part 1)." *Communio* 34 (2007): 38–75.

Burtchaell, James Tunstead, CSC. *Catholic Theories of Biblical Inspiration since 1810: A Review and Critique*. Cambridge: Cambridge University Press, 1969.

Burton, Keith A. "Numbers." *EDB*, 973–74.

Caquot, André. "Sur quelque démons de l'Ancien Testament (Reseph, Qeteb, Deber)." *Sem* 6 (1956): 53–68.

Carl, Scott, ed. *"Verbum Domini" and the Complementarity of Exegesis and Theology*. Catholic Theological Formation Series. Grand Rapids: Eerdmans, 2015.

CELAM (Consejo Episcopal Latinoamericano in Medellín). *Documentos finales de Medellín*. 1968. http://www.celam.org/doc_conferencias/Documento_Conclusivo_Medellin.pdf.

Certeau, Michel de. *Heterologies: Discourse on the Other*. Theory and History of Literature 17. Minneapolis: University of Minnesota Press, 1986.

Chaine, Joseph. "The Old Testament – Semitism." Pages 11–53 in *Père Lagrange and the Scriptures*. Translated by Richard T. A. Murphy, OP. Milwaukee: Bruce, 1946.

Charles, J. D. "Literary Artifice in the Epistle of Jude." *ZNW* 82, no. 1–2 (1991): 106–23.

Chiu, José Enrique Aguilar, Richard J. Clifford, SJ, Carol J. Dempsey, OP, Eileen M. Schuller, OSU, Thomas D. Stegman, SJ, and Ronald D. Witherup, PSS, eds. *The Paulist Biblical Commentary*. New York: Paulist, 2018.

Choi, John H. "Resheph and Yhwh Ṣĕbāʾôt." *VT* 54, no. 1 (2004): 17–28.

Chouraqui, André. *Paroles: Deutéronome*. Paris: J.-C. Lattès, 1993.

Chrétien, Jean-Louis. *The Ark of Speech*. Translated by Andrew Brown. London: Routledge, 2004.

Clarke, Ernest G. *The Wisdom of Solomon*. CBC. Cambridge: Cambridge University Press, 1973.

Clement of Alexandria. *Excerpts of Theodotus*. Translated by William Wilson. Waterford, Ireland: CrossReach, 2019.

Coco, Pierre-Dominique. "Notes sur la place des morts et des ancêtres dans la société traditionnelle." Pages 226–42 in *Les religions africaines comme source de valeurs de civilisation*. Edited by Alioune Diop. Paris: Présence Africaine, 1972.

Cohen, Mark E. *The Cultic Calendars of the Ancient Near East*. Bethesda, MD: CDL, 1993.

Collins, John J., Gina Hens-Piazza, Barbara Reid, OP, and Donald Senior, CP. "Introduction." Pages ix–xiii in *The Jerome Biblical Commentary for the Twenty-First Century*. 3rd ed. Edited by John J. Collins et al. London: T&T Clark, 2022.

Collins, John J., Gina Hens-Piazza, Barbara Reid, OP, and Donald Senior, CP, eds. *The Jerome Biblical Commentary for the Twenty-First Century*. 3rd ed. London: T&T Clark, 2022.

Comparetti, Domenico. *Vergil in the Middle Ages*. Hamden, CT: Archon, 1966.

Cone, James H. *A Black Theology of Liberation*. Philadelphia: Lippincott, 1970.

Congar, Yves M.-J., OP. *Tradition and Traditions: A Historical and Theological Essay*. London: Macmillan, 1967.

Congregation for the Doctrine of the Faith. Instruction *Libertatis nuntius*. August 6, 1984.

Conzelmann, Hans. *1 Corinthians: A Commentary on the First Epistle to the Co-*

rinthians. Translated by J. W. Leitch. Hermeneia. Philadelphia: Fortress, 1975.

Cooper, Jerrold. “Sacred Marriage and Popular Cult in Early Mesopotamia.” Pages 81–96 in *Papers of the First Colloquium on the Ancient Near East – The City and Its Life Held at the Middle Eastern Culture Center in Japan (Mitaka, Tokyo)*. Edited by Eiko Matsushima. Heidelberg: Winter, 1993.

Couturier, Guy, ed. *Les patriarches et l'histoire: Autour d'un article inédit du Père M.-J. Lagrange, O. P.* LD. Paris: Éditions du Cerf-Fides, 1998.

Croatto, J. Severino. *Liberación y Libertad: Pautas hermenéuticas*. Buenos Aires: Mundo Nuevo, 1973.

Crossley, James G. *The Date of Mark's Gospel: Insight from the Law in Earliest Christianity*. JSNTSup 266. London: T&T Clark, 2004.

———. *Jesus and the Chaos of History: Redirecting the Life of the Historical Jesus*. Oxford: Oxford University Press, 2015.

Daley, Brian E., SJ. *God Visible: Patristic Christology Reconsidered*. Changing Paradigms in Historical and Systematic Theology. Oxford: Oxford University Press, 2018.

Daly-Denton, Margaret. *John: An Earth Bible Commentary; Supposing Him to Be the Gardener*. London: Bloomsbury T&T Clark, 2017.

Davids, Peter H. *The Letters of 2 Peter and Jude*. Pillar New Testament Commentary. Grand Rapids: Eerdmans, 2006.

Davies, Graham I. *Ancient Hebrew Inscriptions: Corpus and Concordance*. 2 vols. Cambridge: Cambridge University Press, 1991.

Davies, W. D., and Dale C. Allison Jr. *The Gospel according to St. Matthew*. ICC. 3 vols. Edinburgh: T&T Clark, 1988–1997.

Davis, Natalie Zemon. “From ‘Popular Religion’ to Religious Cultures.” Pages 321–41 in *Reformation Europe: A Guide to Research*. Edited by Steven Ozment. St. Louis: Center for Reformation Research, 1982.

———. “Some Tasks and Themes in the Study of Popular Religion.” Pages 307–37 in *The Pursuit of Holiness in Late Medieval and Renaissance Religion*. Edited by Charles Edward Trinkaus and Heiko Augustinus Oberman. Studies in Medieval and Reformation Thought 10. Leiden: Brill, 1974.

Day, John. *Yahweh and the Gods and Goddesses of Canaan*. JSOTSup 265. London: Sheffield Academic Press, 2002.

Dazet-Brun, Philippe. “Mauriac et sa *Vie de Jésus*: le romancier devenu biographe.” *Anabasis* 28 (2018): 241–52.

De Moor, Johannes C. “‘O Death, Where Is Thy Sting?’” Pages 99–107 in *Ascribe to the Lord: Biblical and Other Studies in Memory of Peter C. Craigie*. Edited by Lyle Eslinger and Glen Taylor. JSOTSup 67. Sheffield: Sheffield Academic, 1988.

Deppe, Dean B. *The Theological Intentions of Mark's Literary Devices: Markan Intercalations, Frames, Allusionary Repetitions, Narrative Surprises, and Three Types of Mirroring.* Eugene, OR: Wipf & Stock, 2015.

Dewart, Joanne M. "'Moral Union' in Christology before Nestorius." *Leval théologique et philosophique* 32 (1976): 283–99.

Dewey, Joanna. "1 Timothy." Pages 353–58 in *The Women's Bible Commentary.* Edited by Carol A. Newsom and Sharon H. Ringe. Louisville: Westminster John Knox, 1992.

———. "Mark as Interwoven Tapestry: Forecasts and Echoes for a Listening Audience." *CBQ* 53, no. 2 (1991): 221–36.

Di Palma, Gaetano. "'Lia disse: "Per fortuna!" E lo chiamó Gad' (Gen 30, 11)." *Aisthema* 1, no. 2 (2014): 46–69.

Doak, Brian R. "The Giant in a Thousand Years." Pages 14–32 in *Ancient Tales of Giants from Qumran and Turfan: Contexts, Traditions, and Influences.* Edited by Matthew Goff, Loren T. Stuckenbruck, and Enrico Morano. WUNT 360. Tübingen: Mohr Siebeck, 2016.

———. *The Last of the Rephaim: Conquest and Cataclysm in the Heroic Ages of Ancient Israel.* Ilex Foundation Series 8. Washington, DC: Harvard University Center for Hellenic Studies, 2012.

Donahue, John R., SJ, and Daniel J. Harrington, SJ. *The Gospel of Mark.* SP 2. Collegeville, MN: Liturgical Press, 2002.

Dujardin, Édouard. "Le Jésus de M. Mauriac." *Europe* (June 15, 1936).

Dunn, James D. G. *Jesus Remembered.* Vol. 1 of *Christianity in the Making.* Grand Rapids: Eerdmans, 2003.

Dyssel, Allan. "Behemoth, Beast of the Negev? A Fusion of Animals, Mythical Beasts and Monsters in Isaiah 30:6." *Pharos Journal of Theology* 99 (2018): 1–13.

Edwards, Denis. *How God Acts: Creation, Redemption, and Special Divine Action.* Hindmarsh: ATF Theology, 2010.

Ehrlich, Uri. "The Ancestors' Prayers for the Salvation of Israel in Early Rabbinic Thought." Pages 249–56 in *Jewish and Christian Liturgy and Worship: New Insights into Its History and Interaction.* Edited by Albert Gerhards and Clemens Leonhard. Jewish and Christian Perspectives 15. Leiden: Brill, 2007.

Elmelund, Conrad Thorup. "The Undertext of Greek NF MG 99 from Sinai (GA 0289)." *TC: A Journal of Biblical Textual Criticism* 27 (2022): 51–68.

Episcopal Conference of the Pacific. *Synod Synthesis CEPAC Conference.* August 14, 2022. https://synod.org.pl/pacific-region-episcopal-conference-of-the-pacific-c-e-pac.

Escallier, Claude. "La spiritualité de François Mauriac." *Etudes de langue et littérature françaises* 60 (1992): 108–23.

———. *Mauriac et l'évangile*. Paris: Beauchesne, 1993.

Esposito, Thomas. *Jesus' Meals with Pharisees and Their Liturgical Roots*. AnBib 209. Rome: Gregorian and Biblical Press, 2015.

Eve, Eric. *Behind the Gospels: Understanding the Oral Tradition*. Minneapolis: Fortress, 2014.

Ezeanya, Stephen N. "God, Spirits and the Spirit World." Pages 30–46 in *Biblical Revelation and African Beliefs*. Edited by Kwesi A. Dickson and Paul Ellingworth. Maryknoll, NY: Orbis, 1969.

Farkasfalvy, Denis, OCist. "The Case for Spiritual Exegesis." *Communio* 10 (1983): 332–50.

———. *Inspiration and Interpretation: A Theological Introduction to Sacred Scripture*. Washington, DC: Catholic University of America Press, 2010.

———. *A Theology of the Christian Bible: Revelation, Inspiration, Canon*. Washington, DC: Catholic University of America Press, 2018.

Fillion, L.-C. *Les étapes du rationalisme dans ses attaques contre les Évangiles et la vie de Jésus-Christ: Exposition historique et critique*. Paris: P. Lethielleux, 1914.

Fischer, Steven Roger. *A History of the Pacific Islands*. 2nd ed. Basingstoke: Palgrave Macmillan, 2013.

Fish, Stanley. *Is There a Text in This Class? The Authority of Interpretive Communities*. Cambridge, MA: Harvard University Press, 1982.

Fitzmyer, Joseph A., SJ. *The Acts of the Apostles: A New Translation with Introduction and Commentary*. AB 31. New York: Doubleday, 1998.

———. *The Biblical Commission's Document "The Interpretation of the Bible in the Church": Text and Commentary*. SubBi 18. Rome: Pontifical Biblical Institute, 1995.

———. *First Corinthians: A New Translation with Introduction and Commentary*. AB 32. New Haven: Yale University Press, 2008.

———. *The Gospel according to Luke: A New Translation with Introduction and Commentary*. 2 vols. AB 28–28A. New York: Doubleday, 1981–1985.

———. *The Interpretation of Scripture: In Defense of the Historical-Critical Method*. New York: Paulist, 2008.

———. *The Letter to Philemon: A New Translation with Introduction and Commentary*. AB 34C. New York: Doubleday, 2000.

———. *Romans: A New Translation with Introduction and Commentary*. AB 33. New York: Doubleday, 1993.

———. *Scripture, the Soul of Theology*. New York: Paulist, 1994.

Flannery, Austin, OP, ed. *Vatican Council II: The Basic Sixteen Documents*. Rev. ed. Northport, NY: Costello, 1996.

Fleddermann, Harry. "'And He Wanted to Pass by Them' (Mark 6:48c)." *CBQ* 45, no. 3 (1983): 389–95.

Fogarty, Gerald P., SJ. *American Catholic Biblical Scholarship: A History from the Early Republic to Vatican II*. San Francisco: Harper and Row, 1989.

Foster, Benjamin R. "Epic of Creation." Pages 390–402 in *Canonical Compositions from the Biblical World*, vol. 1 of *The Context of Scripture*. Edited by William W. Hallo and K. Lawson Younger Jr. Leiden: Brill, 1997.

Fouchet, Max-Pol. "François Mauriac: Vie de Jésus." *Esprit* 44 (1936): 228–29.

Fouda, Basile-Juléat. *La philosophie négro-africaine de l'existence: Herméneutique des traditions orales africaines*. Pensée africaine. Paris: L'Harmattan, 2013.

France, R. T. *The Gospel of Mark: A Commentary on the Greek Text*. NIGTC. Grand Rapids: Eerdmans, 2002.

Francis (Pope). Apostolic Letter issued "motu proprio" *Aperuit illis*. September 30, 2019.

———. Apostolic Letter *Scripturae sacrae affectus*. September 30, 2020.

———. Encyclical Letter *Fratelli tutti*. October 3, 2020.

———. Encyclical Letter *Laudato si'*. May 24, 2015.

———. "Foreword." Pages vii–viii in *The Jerome Biblical Commentary for the Twenty-First Century*. 3rd ed. Edited by John J. Collins et al. London: T&T Clark, 2022.

Franzelin, J. B. *Tractatus de divina Traditione et Scriptura*. Rome: Typographia Polyglotta, S. C. de Propaganda Fide, 1870.

Frayer-Griggs, Daniel. "Spittle, Clay, and Creation in John 9:6 and Some Dead Sea Scrolls." *JBL* 132, no. 3 (2013): 659–70.

Fredriksen, Paula. *When Christians Were Jews: The First Generation*. New Haven: Yale University Press, 2018.

Freedman, David Noel. "'Who Is Like Thee among the Gods?' The Religion of Early Israel." Pages 383–405 in *History and Religion*. Edited by John R. Huddlestun. Vol. 1 of *Divine Commitment and Human Obligation: Selected Writings of David Noel Freedman*. Grand Rapids: Eerdmans, 1997.

Frevel, Christian. "Beyond Monotheism? Some Remarks and Questions on Conceptualising 'Monotheism' in Biblical Studies." *Verbum et Ecclesia* 34, no. 2 (2013): 1–7.

Frey, Jörg. *Der Brief des Judas und der zweite Brief des Petrus*. THKNT 2/15. Leipzig: Evangelische Verlagsanstalt, 2015.

Freyne, Sean. *Jesus, A Jewish Galilean: A New Reading of the Jesus-Story*. London: T&T Clark International, 2004.

García Arenas, Paula Andrea, and Juan Alberto Casas Ramírez. "Una visión panorámica sobre la hermenéutica bíblica latinoamericana." Pages 303–19 in *80 Años de Exégesis Bíblica en América Latina: Actas del Congreso Internacional de Estudios Bíblicos organizado con ocasión del 80º aniversario de Revista Bíblica*. Edited by Eleuterio R. Ruiz. RevistBSup 7. Estella: Verbo Divino, 2019.

Gathercole, Simon J. *The Preexistent Son: Recovering the Christologies of Matthew, Mark, and Luke*. Grand Rapids: Eerdmans, 2006.

Gerstenberger, Erhard. "Weiblich von Gott Reden?" Pages 37–52 in *Christlicher Glaube und religiöse Bildung: Frau Prof. Dr. Friedel Kriechbaum zum 60. Geburtstag am 13. August 1995*. Edited by Hermann Deuser and Gerhard Schmalenberg. Giessen: Fachbereich Evangelische Theologie und Katholische Theologie und deren Didaktik, 1995.

Giambrone, Anthony, OP. "Aux sources du petit livre rouge de Loisy." *Codex* 23 (April, 2022).

———. *A Quest for the Historical Christ: Scientia Christi and the Modern Study of Jesus*. Washington, DC: Catholic University of America Press, 2022.

Gibson, Jeffrey B. "Jesus' Refusal to Produce a Sign (Mk. 8:11–13)." *JSNT* 12, no. 38 (1990): 37–66.

Gillespie, Justin E. *The Development of the Belief in the Resurrection within the Old Testament*. Pontificia Università della Santa Croce Dissertationes Series Theologica 26. Rome: Edizioni Santa Croce, 2009.

Gilmour, Garth. "Iconism and Aniconism in the Period of the Monarchy: Was There an Image of the Deity in the Jerusalem Temple?" Pages 91–103 in *Visualizing Jews through the Ages: Literary and Material Representations of Jewishness and Judaism*. Edited by Hannah Ewence and Helen Spurling. London: Routledge, 2015.

Goldberg, Oskar. *Die Wirklichkeit der Hebräer*. Revised and edited by Manfred Voigts. Jüdische Kultur 14. Wiesbaden: Harrassowitz, 2005.

Golub, Mitka R. "Israelite and Judean Theophoric Personal Names in the Hebrew Bible in the Light of the Archaeological Evidence." *ANES* 54 (2017): 35–46.

Gonçalves, Francolino J. "Deux systèmes religieux dans l'Ancien Testament: De la concurrence à la convergence." *Annuaire EPHE, Sciences religieuses* 115 (2007): 117–22.

Goodacre, Mark. “Scripturalization in Mark’s Crucifixion Narrative.” Pages 33–47 in *The Trial and Death of Jesus: Essays on the Passion Narrative in Mark*. Edited by Geert Van Oyen and Tom Shepherd. CBET 45. Leuven: Peeters, 2006.

Görg, Manfred, and Bernhard Lang, eds. *Neues Bibel-Lexikon*. 3 vols. Zürich: Benziger, 1991.

Gray, Timothy. *The Temple in the Gospel of Mark: A Study in Its Narrative Role*. WUNT 2/242. Tübingen: Mohr Siebeck, 2008.

Green, Douglas J. *“I Undertook Great Works”: The Ideology of Domestic Achievements in West Semitic Royal Inscriptions*. FAT 2/41. Tübingen, Mohr Siebeck, 2010.

Grillmeier, Alois. “Chapter III, The Divine Inspiration and the Interpretation of Sacred Scripture.” Pages 199–246 in vol. 3 of *Commentary on the Documents of Vatican II*. Edited by Herbert Vorgrimler. Translated by William Glen-Doepel, Hilda Graef, John Michael Jakubiak, and Simon and Erika Young. New York: Herder and Herder, 1968.

Grover, Emma. “The Saint and the Swan: Animal Interactions in the Hagiography of Hugh of Avalon.” *Quidditas* 41 (2020): 7–16.

Gundry, Robert H. *Mark: A Commentary on His Apology for the Cross*. Grand Rapids: Eerdmans, 1993.

Gurry, Peter J. *A Critical Examination of the Coherence-Based Genealogical Method in New Testament Textual Criticism*. NTTSD 55. Leiden: Brill, 2017.

———. “Inerrancy and the Initial Text.” *Presbyterion* 49, no. 1 (2023): 54–67.

Gurtner, Daniel M. *The Torn Veil: Matthew’s Exposition of the Death of Jesus*. SNTSMS 139. Cambridge: Cambridge University Press, 2007.

Gutiérrez, Gustavo. *The Density of the Present: Selected Writings*. Maryknoll, NY: Orbis, 1999.

———. *The God of Life*. Translated by Matthew J. O’Connell. Maryknoll, NY: Orbis, 1991.

———. *A Theology of Liberation: History, Politics, and Salvation*. Rev. ed. Translated and edited by Caridad Inda and John Eagleson. Maryknoll, NY: Orbis, 1988.

———. “Towards a Theology of Liberation.” Pages 62–76 in *Liberation Theology: A Documentary History*. Edited by Alfred T. Hennelly. Maryknoll, NY: Orbis, 1990.

Hadley, Judith M. *The Cult of Asherah in Ancient Israel and Judah: Evidence for a Hebrew Goddess*. University of Cambridge Oriental Publications 57. Cambridge: Cambridge University Press, 2000.

Halpern, Baruch. *From Gods to God: The Dynamics of Iron Age Cosmologies.* FAT 63. Tübingen: Mohr Siebeck, 2009.

Hammond-Tooke, W. D. "World View I: A System of Beliefs." Pages 298–329 in *The Bantu-Speaking Peoples of Southern Africa*. Edited by W. D. Hammond-Tooke. London: Routledge & Kegan Paul, 1974.

Harding, D. E. *The Hierarchy of Heaven and Earth: A New Diagram of Man in the Universe.* Gainesville: University of Florida Press, 1979.

Haught, John F. *God after Darwin: A Theology of Evolution.* Philadelphia: Westview, 2008.

———. *The New Cosmic Story: Inside Our Awakening Universe.* New Haven: Yale University Press, 2017.

———. *Resting on the Future: Catholic Theology for an Unfinished Universe.* New York: Bloomsbury Academic, 2015.

Hau'ofa, Epeli. "Our Sea of Islands." *The Contemporary Pacific* 6, no. 1 (1994): 148–61.

Hays, Christopher B. "How Many Histories of Death Does the Hebrew Bible Contain?" *CBQ* 81, no. 4 (2019): 679–91.

Hays, Richard B. *The Conversion of the Imagination: Paul as the Interpreter of Israel's Scriptures.* Grand Rapids: Eerdmans, 2005.

Hazoumé, Paul. "L'âme du Dahoméen animiste révélée par sa religion." *Présence Africaine* 14–15, nos. 3–4 (1957): 233–51.

Healy, Mary. *The Gospel of Mark.* Catholic Commentary on Sacred Scripture. Grand Rapids: Baker Academic, 2008.

Heereman, Nina Sophie. *Behold King Solomon on the Day of His Wedding: A Symbolic Diachronic Reading of Song 3,6–11 and 4,12–5,1.* BETL 321. Leuven: Peeters, 2021.

———. "'Where Is Wisdom to Be Found?' Rethinking the Song of Songs' Solomonic Setting." *ZAW* 130, no. 3 (2018): 418–35.

Heil, John Paul. *The Gospel of Mark as Model for Action: A Reader-Response Commentary.* Eugene, OR: Wipf & Stock, 2001.

———. *Jesus Walking on the Sea: Meaning and Gospel Functions of Matt 14:22–33, Mark 6:45–52 and John 6:15b–21.* AnBib 87. Rome: Biblical Institute Press, 1981.

———. "The Narrative Strategy and Pragmatics of the Temple Theme in Mark." *CBQ* 59, no. 1 (1997): 76–100.

Henderson, Suzanne Watts. "'Concerning the Loaves': Comprehending Incomprehension in Mark 6:45–52." *JSNT* 24, no. 83 (2001): 3–26.

Hennelly, Alfred T., SJ. *Liberation Theologies: The Global Pursuit of Justice.* Mystic, CT: Twenty-Third Publications, 1995.

Henry, Michel. "Speech and Religion: The Word of God." In *The Michel Henry Reader*. Edited by Scott Davidson and Frédéric Seyler. Translated by Leonard Lawlor, Joseph Rivera, George Faithful, Scott Davidson, Michael Tweed, Peter T. Connor, Karl Hefty, Pierre Adler, Justin Boyd, Crina Gschwandtner, and Jeffery L. Kosky. Northwestern University Studies in Phenomenology and Existential Philosophy. Evanston, IL: Northwestern University Press, 2019.

Herring, George. *An Introduction to the History of Christianity: From the Early Church to the Enlightenment*. London: Continuum, 2006.

Hodgson, Peter C. *The Formation of Historical Theology: A Study of Ferdinand Christian Baur*. Makers of Modern Theology. New York: Harper & Row, 1966.

Hooker, Morna D. *The Signs of a Prophet: The Prophetic Actions of Jesus*. Harrisburg, PA: Trinity Press International, 1997.

Hopkins, Gerard Manley. "God's Grandeur." In *The Poems of Gerard Manley Hopkins*, edited by W. H. Gardner and N. H. Mackenzie. 4th ed. London: Oxford University Press, 1967.

Horowitz, Isaiah. *Bereshit*. Vol. 1 of *Shney Luchot Habrit*. 2nd ed. Translated by Eliyahu Munk. Jerusalem: Lambda, 1999.

Hossfeld, Frank-Lothar, and Erich Zenger. *Die Psalmen: Psalm 1–50*. NEchtB 29. Würzburg: Echter, 1993.

Hrůša, Ivan. *Ancient Mesopotamian Religion: A Descriptive Introduction*. Münster: Ugarit-Verlag, 2015.

Human, Dirk J. "Portraits of 'Angels': Some Ancient Near Eastern and Old Testament Perspectives in Relation to ATR Belief System(s)." *Pharos Journal of Theology* 102, Special Edition 1 (2021): 1–11.

Hunsberger, David R. "Theophoric Names in the Old Testament and Their Theological Significance." PhD diss., Temple University, 1969.

Hurowitz, Victor Avigdor. *I Have Built You an Exalted House: Temple Building in the Bible in Light of Mesopotamian and Northwest Semitic Writings*. JSOTSup 115. Sheffield: JSOT Press, 1992.

———. "'Solomon Built the Temple and Completed It': Building the First Temple according to the Book of Kings." Pages 281–302 in *From the Foundations to the Crenellations: Essays on Temple Building in the Ancient Near East and Hebrew Bible*. Edited by Mark J. Boda and Jamie Novotny. AOAT 366. Münster: Ugarit-Verlag, 2010.

Hutson, Christopher R. *First and Second Timothy and Titus*. Paideia. Grand Rapids: Baker Academic, 2019.

Hutton, Jeremy M. "Southern, Northern and Transjordanian Perspectives."

Pages 679–92 in *Religious Diversity in Ancient Israel and Judah*. Edited by Francesca Stavrakopoulou and John Barton. London: T&T Clark, 2010.

Iqbal, Muhammad. *The Development of Metaphysics in Persia*. Lahore: Bazm-i-Iqbal, 1954.

Japhet, Sarah. *The Ideology of the Book of Chronicles and Its Place in Biblical Thought*. BEATAJ 9. Frankfurt: Lang, 1989.

Jensen, Adolf E. *Myth and Cult among Primitive Peoples*. Chicago: University of Chicago Press, 1963.

Jewett, Robert. *Dating Paul's Life*. London: SCM, 1979.

John Paul II (Pope). Encyclical Letter *Sollicitudo rei socialis*. December 30, 1987.

———. "Letter of His Holiness John Paul II to Reverend George V. Coyne, SJ, Director of the Vatican Observatory." June 1, 1988. https://www.vatican.va/content/john-paul-ii/en/letters/1988/documents/hf_jp-ii_let_19880601_padre-coyne.html.

———. Post-synodal Apostolic Exhortation *Ecclesia in Africa* (September 14, 1995).

Johnson, Luke Timothy. *The Acts of the Apostles*. SP 5. Collegeville, MN: Liturgical Press, 1992.

———. "The Bible's Authority for and in the Church." Pages 62–72 in *Engaging Biblical Authority: Perspectives on the Bible as Scripture*. Edited by William P. Brown. Louisville: Westminster John Knox, 2007.

———. *Brother of Jesus, Friend of God: Studies in the Letter of James*. Grand Rapids: Eerdmans, 2004.

———. *A Catholic Consciousness: Scripture, Theology, and the Church*. New York: Paulist, 2021.

———. *Constructing Paul*. Vol. 1 of *The Canonical Paul*. Grand Rapids: Eerdmans, 2020.

———. *The Creed: What Christians Believe and Why It Matters*. New York: Doubleday, 2003.

———. *Faith's Freedom: A Classic Spirituality for Contemporary Christians*. Minneapolis: Fortress, 1990.

———. *The First and Second Letters to Timothy*. AB 35A. New York: Doubleday, 2001.

———. *Interpreting Paul*. Vol. 2 of *The Canonical Paul*. Grand Rapids: Eerdmans, 2021.

———. *The Letter of James*. AB 37A. New York: Doubleday, 1995.

———. *Miracles: The Presence and Power of God in Creation*. Resources for the Interpretation of the Bible in the Church. Louisville: Westminster John Knox, 2018.

———. *Prophetic Jesus, Prophetic Church: The Challenge of Luke-Acts to Contemporary Christians.* Grand Rapids: Eerdmans, 2011.

———. *Religious Experience in Earliest Christianity.* Minneapolis: Fortress, 1998.

———. *The Revelatory Body: Theology as Inductive Art.* Grand Rapids: Eerdmans, 2015.

———. *Scripture and Discernment: Decision Making in the Church.* Nashville: Abingdon, 1996.

———. *The Writings of the New Testament: An Interpretation.* 3rd ed. Minneapolis: Fortress, 2010.

Johnson, Luke Timothy, and William S. Kurz, SJ. *The Future of Catholic Biblical Scholarship: A Constructive Conversation.* Grand Rapids: Eerdmans, 2002.

Jones, L. Gregory. *Embodying Forgiveness: A Theological Analysis.* Grand Rapids: Eerdmans, 1995.

Jongkind, Dirk. *An Introduction to the Greek New Testament, Produced at Tyndale House, Cambridge.* Wheaton, IL: Crossway, 2019.

Joseph, Simon J. *Jesus and the Temple: Crucifixion in Its Jewish Context.* SNTSMS 165. Cambridge: Cambridge University Press, 2016.

Just, Felix, SJ. "Lectionary Statistics." Updated January 2, 2009. https://catholic-resources.org/Lectionary/Statistics.htm.

Kalimi, Isaac. "The Rise of Solomon in the Ancient Israelite Historiography." Pages 7–44 in *The Figure of Solomon in Jewish, Christian and Islamic Tradition: King, Sage and Architect.* Edited by Joseph Verheyden. TBN 16. Leiden: Brill, 2013.

Kampen, John. *Matthew within Sectarian Judaism.* AYBRL. New Haven: Yale University Press, 2019.

Kaufmann, Yehezkel. "The Bible and Mythological Polytheism." *JBL* 70, no. 3 (1951): 179–97.

———. *The Religion of Israel: From Its Beginnings to the Babylonian Exile.* Translated by Moshe Greenberg. Chicago: University of Chicago Press, 1960.

Kayode, J. O. *Understanding African Traditional Religion.* Ile-Ife: University of Ife Press, 1984.

Keener, Craig S. *A Commentary on the Gospel of Matthew.* Grand Rapids: Eerdmans, 1998.

———. *The Historical Jesus of the Gospels: Jesus in Historical Context.* Grand Rapids: Eerdmans, 2009.

Keith, Chris. "The Indebtedness of the Criteria Approach to Form Criticism and Recent Attempts to Rehabilitate the Search for an Authentic Jesus." Pages 25–48 in *Jesus, Criteria, and the Demise of Authenticity.* Edited by Chris Keith and Anthony Le Donne. London: T&T Clark, 2012.

———. *Jesus' Literacy: Scribal Culture and the Teacher from Galilee.* LNTS 413. London: T&T Clark, 2011.

———. "Social Memory Theory and Gospels Research: The First Decade (Part Two)." *Early Christianity* 6, no. 4 (2015): 526–27.

Kertelge, Karl. *Die Wunder Jesu im Markusevangelium: Ein redaktionsgeschichtliche Untersuchung.* Munich: Kösel, 1970.

Kessy, Marcel G. "Death Rituals among the Chagga of Tanzania." BA Thesis, Tangaza College/Catholic University of Eastern Africa, 2002.

Kim, Sun Wook. "An Investigation of a Cyclic Pattern in Mark 4:35–8:21 and Its Theological Significance." *BTB* 47, no. 4 (2017): 205–15.

Kirk, Alan. *Memory and the Jesus Tradition.* RJFTC. London: Bloomsbury T&T Clark, 2018.

———. "Social and Cultural Memory." Pages 1–24 in *Memory, Tradition, and Text: Uses of the Past in Early Christianity.* Edited by Alan Kirk and Tom Thatcher. SemeiaSt 52. Atlanta: Society of Biblical Literature, 2005.

Kittel, Gerhard, and Gerhard Friedrich, eds. *Theological Dictionary of the New Testament.* Translated by Geoffrey W. Bromiley. 10 vols. Grand Rapids: Eerdmans, 1964–1976.

Klein, Jacob. "Building and Dedication Hymns in Sumerian Literature." *ASJ* 11 (1989): 27–67.

Kloppenborg, John S. *The Formation of Q: Trajectories in Ancient Wisdom Collections.* 2nd ed. SAC. Harrisburg, PA: Trinity Press International, 2000.

Knorn, Bernhard, SJ. "Johann Baptist Franzelin (1816–86): A Jesuit Cardinal Shaping the Official Teaching of the Church at the Time of the First Vatican Council." *Journal of Jesuit Studies* 7, no. 4 (2020): 592–615.

Koen, Lars. "Partitive Exegesis in Cyril of Alexandria's Commentary on the Gospel according to St. John." *StPatr* 25 (1993): 115–21.

Konradt, Matthias. *The Gospel according to Matthew: A Commentary.* Translated by M. Eugene Boring. Waco, TX: Baylor University Press, 2020.

Kremser, Konrad. *Die Hochzeit des Königs: Exegetisch theologische Untersuchungen zu Psalm 45.* Österreichische Bibel Studien 51. Berlin: Peter Lang, 2019.

Krüger, René. *Dios o el Mamón: Análisis semiótico del proyecto económico y relacional del Evangelio de Lucas.* Buenos Aires: Lumen, 2009.

Kubo, Sakae. "Jude 22–23: Two-Division Form or Three?" Pages 239–53 in *New Testament Textual Criticism: Its Significance for Exegesis; Essays in Honor of Bruce M. Metzger.* Edited by Eldon Jay Epp and Gordon D. Fee. Oxford: Oxford University Press, 1981.

Kurtz, Lester R. *The Politics of Heresy: The Modernist Crisis in Roman Catholicism.* Berkeley: University of California Press, 1986.

Laban, Luamanuvau Winnie. “Closing Remarks.” Page 191 in *Resilience in the Pacific: Addressing the Critical Issues*, ed. Brian Lynch and Graham Hassall. Wellington: New Institute of International Affairs, 2011.

Lado, Ludovic. “The Roman Catholic Church and African Religions: A Problematic Encounter.” *The Way* 45, no. 3 (2006): 7–21.

Lagrange, Marie-Joseph, OP. “A propos de l’encyclique ‘Providentissimus.’” *RB* 4, no. 1 (1895): 48–64.

———. “Avant-propos.” *RB* 1, no. 1 (1892): 1–16.

———. “Bulletin: L’interprétation de la Sainte Écriture par l’Église.” *RB* 9, no. 1 (1900): 135–42.

———. *Christ and Renan: A Commentary on Ernst Renan’s “The Life of Jesus.”* Translated by Maisie Ward. London: Sheed & Ward, 1928.

———. “Deux nouveaux textes relatifs à l’Évangile.” *RB* 44, no. 3 (1935): 321–43.

———. *Études sur les religions sémitiques.* EBib. Paris: Lecoffre, 1903.

———. *Historical Criticism and the Old Testament.* Translated by Edward Myers. London: Catholic Truth Society, 1905.

———. “Inspiration des Livres Saints.” *RB* 5, no. 2 (1896): 199–220.

———. “Iterum Mt. 11,19: *A Filiis* an *Ab Operibus*?” *Bib* 6, no. 4 (1925): 461–63.

———. *La méthode historique, surtout à propos de l’Ancien Testament.* Paris: Lecoffre, 1903.

———. “L’ancienne version syriaque des Évangiles.” *RB* 29, no. 3 (1920): 321–52.

———. “La Prophétie de Jacob.” *RB* 7, no. 4 (1898): 525–40.

———. “La revision de la Vulgate par Saint Jérome.” *RB* 27, nos. 1–2 (1918): 254–57.

———. “La seconde parole d’Oxyrhynque.” *RB* 31, no. 3 (1922): 427–33.

———. “La *Vie de Jésus* par M. François Mauriac.” *RB* 45, no. 3 (1936): 321–45.

———. *L’Écriture en Église: Choix de portraits et d’exégèse spirituelle (1890–1937).* Edited by Maurice Gilbert. LD 142. Paris: Éditions du Cerf, 1990.

———. “Le groupe dit césaréen des manuscrits des Évangiles.” *RB* 38, no. 4 (1929): 481–512.

———. “Le manuscript sinaitique.” *RB* 35, no. 1 (1926): 89–93.

———. *Le sens du christianisme d’après l’exégèse allemande.* EBib. Paris: Gabalda, 1918.

———. “Les papyrus Chester Beatty pour les Évangiles.” *RB* 43, no. 1 (1934): 5–41.

———. *L’Évangile de Jésus Christ avec la synopse évangelique.* Edited by Ceslas Lavergne, OP. Paris: Perpignan Artège Lethielleux, 2017.

———. *L'Évangile selon saint Marc*. EBib. Paris: Lecoffre, 1911.
———. "L'innocence et le péché (Gen. II,4–III)." *RB* 6, no. 3 (1897): 341–79.
———. "L'inspiration et les exigences de la critique." *RB* 5, no. 4 (1896): 496–518.
———. "L'Origene de la version syro-palestinienne des Évangiles." *RB* 34, no. 4 (1925): 481–504.
———. *The Meaning of Christianity according to Luther and His Followers in Germany*. Translated by W. S. Reilly, SS. London: Longmans, Green, 1920.
———. *Monsieur Loisy et le modernisme: A propos des "Mémoires."* Paris: Éditions du Cerf, 1932.
———. "Pascal et les prophéties messianiques." *RB* 3, no. 4 (1906): 533–60.
———. *Personal Reflections and Memoirs*. Translated by Henry Wansbrough, OSB. New York: Paulist, 1985.
———. "Projet de critique textuelle rationelle du N. T." *RB* 42, no. 4 (1933): 481–98.
———. "Projet d'un commentaire complet de l'Écriture Sainte." *RB* 9, no. 3 (1900): 414–23.
———. *Saint Paul: Épitre aux Romains*. EBib. Paris: Gabalda, 1916.
———. "Une nouvelle édition du Nouveau Testament." *RB* 47, no. 2 (1939): 163–83.
———. "Une pensée de saint Thomas sur l'inspiration scripturaire." *RB* 4, no. 4 (1895): 563–71.
———. "Un nouveau papyrus contenant un fragment des Actes." *RB* 36, no. 4 (1927): 549–60.
———. "Un nouveau papyrus évangélique." *RB* 38, no. 2 (1929): 161–77.
Landon, Charles. *A Text-Critical Study of the Epistle of Jude*. JSNTSup 135. Sheffield: Sheffield Academic, 1996.
Lane, Dermott A. *The Experience of God: An Invitation to Do Theology*. New York: Paulist, 2003.
Lane, William L. *Commentary on the Gospel of Mark*. NICNT. Grand Rapids: Eerdmans, 1975.
Larson, Thomas J. "Nyambi, the High God of the Hambukushu." *South African Journal of Ethnology* 7, no. 1 (1984): 9–13.
Laurentin, René. *Les évangiles de l'enfance du Christ: Vérité de Nöel au-déla des mythes; Exégèse et sémiotique, historicité et théologie*. 2nd ed. Paris: Desclee, 1983.
Law, William. *Liberal and Mystical Writings of William Law*. Edited by Williams Scott Palmer. London: Longmans, Green, 1908.
Lebreton, Jules. "La Vie de Jésus de F. Mauriac: Le témoignage d'un chrétien." Études 227 (April, 1936): 56–62.

Le Donne, Anthony. *The Historiographical Jesus: Memory, Typology, and the Son of David.* Waco, TX: Baylor University Press, 2009.

Lemaire, André. *Les ostraca: Introduction, traduction, commentaire.* Vol. 1 of *Inscriptions hébraïques.* Paris: Éditions du Cerf, 1977.

Leo XIII (Pope). Encyclical Letter *Providentissimus Deus.* November 18, 1893.

Levine, Amy-Jill. *The Misunderstood Jew: The Church and the Scandal of the Jewish Jesus.* San Francisco: HarperOne, 2006.

Lewallen, Jason. "Interpreting Conversion: Hermeneutic Training in François Mauriac's *Le noeud de vipères.*" *Christianity & Literature* 68, no. 2 (2019): 213–32.

Lincicum, David. "F. C. Baur's Place in the Study of Jewish Christianity." Pages 137–66 in *The Rediscovery of Jewish Christianity: From Toland to Baur.* Edited by F. Stanley Jones. HBS 5. Atlanta: Society of Biblical Literature, 2012.

Lincoln, Bruce. "À la recherche du Paradis Perdu." *HR* 43, no. 2 (2003): 139–54.

Linton, Olaf. "The Demand for a Sign from Heaven (Mark 8.11–12 and par.)." *ST* 19, nos. 1–2 (1965): 112–29.

Litwa, M. David. *Hermetica II: The Excerpts of Stobaeus, Papyrus Fragments, and Ancient Testimonies in an English Translation with Notes and Introductions.* Cambridge: Cambridge University Press, 2018.

Loisy, Alfred. *The Gospel and the Church.* Translated by Christopher Home. New York: Charles Scribner's Sons, 1904.

Lonergan, Bernard. *The Ontological and Psychological Constitution of Christ.* Collected Works of Bernard Lonergan 7. Toronto: University of Toronto, 2014.

López, Elisa Estévez. "'Y todos los que lo tocaban quedaban sanados': El cuerpo como espacio de gracia." *Sal Terrae* 100 (1997): 323–36.

Lowie, Robert H. *Primitive Religion.* New York: Liveright, 1948.

Lubac, Henri de. *History and Spirit: The Understanding of Scripture according to Origen.* Translated by Anne Englund Nash. San Francisco: Ignatius, 2007.

———. *Scripture in the Tradition.* Milestones in Catholic Theology. Translated by Luke O'Neill. New York: Crossroad, 2000.

Lufuluabo, François-Marie. *Valeur des religions africaines selon la Bible et selon Vatican II.* Kinshasa: Éditions St. Paul Afrique, 1967.

Lugira, Aloysius Muzzanganda. *African Religion.* World Religions. New York: Facts on File, 1999.

———. *African Religion: A Prolegomenal Essay on the Emergence and Meaning of African Autochthonous Religions.* Nyangwe: Omenana, 1981.

Luz, Ulrich. *Matthew.* 3 vols. Hermeneia. Minneapolis: Fortress, 2001–2007.

———. "Matthew's Interpretive 'Tendencies' and the 'Historical' Jesus." Pages 577–99 in *Jesus Research: New Methodologies and Perceptions; The Second Princeton-Prague Symposium on Jesus Research*. Edited by James H. Charlesworth with Brian Rhea and Petr Pokorný. Grand Rapids: Eerdmans, 2014.

M., Mulago gwa Cikala. *La religion traditionnelle des Bantu et leur vision du monde*. Bibliothèque du centre d'études des religions africaines 5. Kinshasa: Faculté de Théologie Catholique, 1980.

MacDonald, Nathan. "The Origin of 'Monotheism.'" Pages 204–15 in *Early Jewish and Christian Monotheism*. Edited by Loren T. Stuckenbruck. JSNTSup 263. London: T&T Clark, 2004.

Machinist, Peter B. "Once More: Monotheism in Biblical Israel." *JISMOR* 1 (2005): 25–39.

Madigan, Kevin. "Catholic Interpretation of the Bible." Pages 73–87 in *The Catholic Study Bible*. 3rd ed. Edited by Donald Senior, John J. Collins, and Mary Ann Getty. New York: Oxford University Press, 2016.

Maduro, O. "Christian Democracy and the Liberating Option for the Oppressed in Latin American Catholicism." *Concilium* 193 (1987): 106–19.

Mahoney, Jack. *Christianity in Evolution: An Exploration*. Washington, DC: Georgetown University Press, 2011.

Malbon, Elizabeth Struthers. "Echoes and Foreshadowings in Mark 4–8: Reading and Rereading." *JBL* 112, no. 2 (1993): 211–30.

Mapara, Jacob. *Shona Sentential Names*. Mankon: Langaa, 2013.

Marcus, Joel. *Mark: A New Translation with Introduction and Commentary*. 2 vols. AB 27–27A. New Haven: Yale University Press, 2000–2009.

Martin, Dale B. *Pedagogy of the Bible: An Analysis and Proposal*. Louisville: Westminster John Knox, 2008.

Martin, Francis. "Revelation and Its Transmission." Pages 54–75 in *Vatican II: Renewal within Tradition*. Edited by Matthew L. Lamb and Matthew Levering. Oxford: Oxford University Press, 2008.

Martín-Asensio, Gustavo. "Dicho y hecho: Las palabras de institución como acto de habla en Marcos 14." *EstBib* 73, no. 1 (2015): 25–44.

Mauriac, François. *Les paroles restent*. Paris: Grasset, 1985.

———. *1968–1970*. Vol. 5 of *Bloc-notes*. Edited by Jean Touzot. Paris: Seuil, 1993.

———. *Nouvelles lettres d'une vie 1906–1970*. Paris: Grasset, 1989.

———. *Vie de Jésus*. Paris: Flammarion, 1936.

McIntosh, Jonathan S. *The Flame Imperishable: Tolkien, St. Thomas, and the Metaphysics of Faërie*. Kettering, Ohio: Angelico, 2017.

McKenzie, John L. *Second Isaiah*. AB 20. Garden City, NY: Doubleday, 1968.

Mesters, Carlos. *Defenseless Flower: A New Reading of the Bible.* Maryknoll, NY: Orbis, 1989.

Míguez, Néstor O. "Latin American Reading of the Bible: Experiences, Challenges and Its Practice." *ExpTim* 118, no. 3 (2006): 120–29.

Milgrom, Jacob. *Leviticus 17–22.* AB 3A. New Haven: Yale University Press, 2007.

Miller, Robert D., II, OFS, ed. *Between Israelite Religion and Biblical Theology: Essays on Archaeology, History, and Hermeneutics.* CBET 80. Leuven: Peeters, 2016.

———. *Chieftains of the Highland Clans: A History of Israel in the 12th and 11th Centuries B. C.* Grand Rapids: Eerdmans, 2005.

———. *Covenant and Grace in the Old Testament: Assyrian Propaganda and Israelite Faith.* PHSC 16. Piscataway, NJ: Gorgias Press, 2012.

———. *The Dragon, the Mountain, and the Nations: An Old Testament Myth, Its Origins and Afterlives.* EANEC 6. Winona Lake, IN: Eisenbrauns, 2018.

———. *Finding Beauty in the Bible: An Aesthetic Commentary on the Song of Songs.* McMaster Biblical Studies Series. Eugene, OR: Pickwick, 2023.

———. "Iron Age Medicine Men and Old Testament Theology." Pages 87–128 in *Between Israelite Religion and Biblical Theology: Essays on Archaeology, History, and Hermeneutics.* Edited by Robert D. Miller II. CBET 80. Leuven: Peeters, 2016.

———. "Lineamenta for an Understanding of Israelite Monotheism." *Bible Bhashyam* 32 (2006): 124–34.

———. *Many Roads Lead Eastward: Overtures to Catholic Biblical Theology.* Eugene, OR: Cascade, 2016.

———. *Oral Tradition in Ancient Israel.* Biblical Performance Criticism 4. Eugene, OR: Cascade, 2011.

Mitarev, Alexander, and Leonid Kogan. *Animal Names.* Vol. 2 of *Semitic Etymological Dictionary.* AOAT 278. Münster: Ugarit-Verlag, 2005.

Mojola, Aloo Osotsi. "The Chagga Scapegoat Purification Ritual and Another Re-Reading of the Goat of Azazel in Leviticus 16." *Melita Theologica* 50, no. 1 (1999): 57–83.

Moller, Philip, SJ. "What Should They Be Saying about Biblical Inspiration? A Note on the State of the Question." *Theological Studies* 74, no. 3 (2013): 605–31.

Moloney, Francis J. *A Body Broken for a Broken People: Divorce, Remarriage, and the Eucharist.* 3rd ed. Mulgrave: Garratt Publishing, 2015.

Montagnes, Bernard, OP. *The Story of Father Marie-Joseph Lagrange: Founder of Modern Catholic Bible Study.* Translated by Benedict Viviano, OP. New York: Paulist, 2006.

Morales, Isaac Augustine, OP. "Père Lagrange and the Historical Study of the Bible: Faith, Reason, and Sacred Scripture." *Dominicana* 57, no. 1 (2014): 18–26.

Morgan, Jonathan. "Number Symbolism in Cyril of Alexandria's Interpretation of Scripture." *Phronema* 34, no. 1 (2019): 85–103.

Morris, Michael J. *Warding off Evil: Apotropaic Tradition in the Dead Sea Scrolls and Synoptic Gospels.* WUNT 2/451. Tübingen: Mohr Siebeck, 2017.

Morrow, Jeffrey L. *Alfred Loisy and Modern Biblical Studies.* Washington, DC: Catholic University of America Press, 2019.

Moxnes, Halvor. *Putting Jesus in His Place: A Radical Vision of Household and Kingdom.* Louisville: Westminster John Knox, 2003.

Mtuze, P. T. *The Essence of Xhosa Spirituality and the Nuisance of Cultural Imperialism: Hidden Presences in the Spirituality of the AmaXhosa of the Eastern Cape and the Impact of Christianity on Them.* Florida Hills: Vivlia, 2003.

Münnich, Maciej M. *The God Resheph in the Ancient Near East.* Orientalische Religionen in der Antike 11. Tübingen: Mohr Siebeck, 2013.

———. "What Did the Biblical Goat-Demons Look Like?" *UF* 38 (2006): 525–35.

Murphy, Richard T. A., OP. "Lagrange, Marie Joseph." *NCE* 8:281.

———. "Mémorial—Lagrange." *CBQ* 3, no. 2 (1941): 134–44.

Murphy-O'Connor, Jerome. "Interpolations in 1 Corinthians." *CBQ* 48, no. 1 (1986): 81–96.

Mwanaka, Tendai R. *Language, Thought, Art and Existence: Creative Nonfictions.* Mankon: Langaa, 2017.

Nanko, Carmen. "Elbows on the Table: The Ethics of Doing Theology, Reflections from a U. S. Hispanic Perspective." *Journal of Hispanic/Latino Theology* 10 (2003): 52–77.

Neuner, J., SJ, and J. Dupuis, SJ. *The Christian Faith: Doctrinal Documents of the Catholic Church.* New York: Alba House, 1990.

Newman, John Henry. "Secret Faults." Pages 31–40 in *Parochial and Plain Sermons.* San Francisco: Ignatius, 1997.

Newman, Judith H. *Before the Bible: The Liturgical Body and the Formation of Scriptures in Early Judaism.* Oxford: Oxford University Press, 2018.

Neyrey, Jerome, SJ. "Interpretation of Scripture in the Life of the Church." Pages 33–46 in *Vatican II: The Unfinished Agenda: A Look to the Future.* Edited by Lucien Richard, OMI, with Daniel Harrington, SJ, and John W. O'Malley, SJ. New York: Paulist, 1987.

———. *2 Peter, Jude: A New Translation with Introduction and Commentary.* AB 37C. New Haven: Yale University Press, 1993.

Noegel, Scott B. "The Women of Asherah: Weaving Wickedness in 2 Kings 23:7." *CBQ* 83, no. 2 (2021): 208–19.

Ntumba, Tshiamalenga. "Mythe et religion en Afrique." *Cahiers des religions africaines* 18, no. 36 (1984): 179–95.

Nürnberger, Klaus. *The Living Dead and the Living God: Christ and the Ancestors in a Changing Africa.* Pretoria: C. B. Powell Bible Centre, 2007.

Nyirenda, Kingsley. *Mbande Hill Sacredness.* Mzuni Documents 186. Mzuzu: Mzuni, 2018.

O'Collins, Gerald, SJ. *Inspiration: Towards a Christian Interpretation of Biblical Inspiration.* New York: Oxford University Press, 2018.

O'Connell, Marvin R. *Critics on Trial: An Introduction to the Catholic Modernist Crisis.* Washington, DC: Catholic University of America Press, 1994.

Ogiozee, Olena P. "The Value of the Continuity between African and Old Testament Worldviews." MA Thesis, Regent University, 2009.

O'Malley, John W. "Councils, Church." In *Encyclopedia of the Bible and Its Reception Online.* Edited by Constance M. Furey, Peter Gemeinhardt, Joel LeMon, Thomas Römer, Jens Schröter, Barry Dov Walfish, and Eric Ziolkowski. Berlin: de Gruyter, 2012. https://doi.org/10.1515/ebr.councilschurch.

Opoku, Kofi Asare. "African Traditional Religion: An Enduring Heritage." Pages 67–82 in *Religious Plurality in Africa: Essays in Honour of John S. Mbiti.* Edited by Jacob K. Olupona and Sulayman S. Nyang. Religion and Society 32. Berlin: de Gruyter, 1993.

Ornan, Tally. "Ištar as Depicted on Finds from Israel." Pages 235–55 in *Studies in the Archaeology of the Iron Age in Israel and Jordan.* Edited by Amihai Mazar. JSOTSup 331. Sheffield: Sheffield Academic Press, 2001.

Osburn, Carroll D. "The Text of Jude 22–23." *ZNW* 63, no. 1 (1972): 139–44.

Painter, John. *Theology as Hermeneutics: Rudolf Bultmann's Interpretation of the History of Jesus.* Historic Texts and Interpreters in Biblical Scholarship 4. Sheffield: Almond, 1987.

Paoli, Arturo. *La perspectiva política de San Lucas.* Buenos Aires: Siglo XXI, 1973.

Pastrone, Pablo Nazareno. "Juan Straubinger, pionero del movimiento bíblico argentino." Pages 17–32 in *80 años de exégesis bíblica en América Latina: Actas del Congreso Internacional de Estudios Bíblicos organizado con ocasión del 80º aniversario de Revista Bíblica.* Edited by Eleuterio R. Ruiz. RevistBSup 7. Estella: Verbo Divino, 2019.

Paulsen, Henning. *Der Zweite Petrusbrief und der Judasbrief.* KEK 12/2. Göttingen: Vandenhoeck & Ruprecht, 1992.

Peterson, Jacob W. "Math Myths: How Many Manuscripts We Have and Why

More Isn't Always Better." Pages 48–69 in *Myths and Mistakes in New Testament Textual Criticism*. Edited by Elijah Hixson and Peter J. Gurry. Downers Grove, IL: IVP Academic, 2019.

Pidel, Aaron, SJ. *The Inspiration and Truth of Scripture: Testing the Ratzinger Paradigm*. Verbum Domini. Washington, DC: Catholic University of America Press, 2023.

Pilarski, Ahida Calderón. "Los estudios de género: La investigación feminista y la perspectiva Latino/a/x en la hermenéutica bíblica en los Estados Unidos." Pages 151–70 in *80 años de exégesis bíblica en América Latina: Actas del Congreso Internacional de Estudios Bíblicos organizado con ocasión del 80º aniversario de Revista Bíblica*. Edited by Eleuterio R. Ruiz. RevistBSup 7. Estella: Verbo Divino, 2019.

Pitre, Brant. *Jesus and the Last Supper*. Grand Rapids: Eerdmans, 2015.

———. *Jesus, the Tribulation, and the End of the Exile: Restoration Eschatology and the Origin of the Atonement*. WUNT 2/204. Tübingen: Mohr Siebeck, 2005.

———. "*Verbum Domini* and Historical-Critical Exegesis." Pages 26–40 in *"Verbum Domini" and the Complementarity of Exegesis and Theology*. Edited by Scott Carl. Catholic Theological Formation Series. Grand Rapids: Eerdmans, 2015.

Pius X (Pope). Encyclical Letter *Pascendi Dominici gregis*. September 8, 1907.

Pius XII (Pope). Encyclical Letter *Divino afflante Spiritu*. September 30, 1943.

Plankey, Raymond. "Conference Looks to Future of Liberation Theology." *National Catholic Reporter*. November 23, 2011.

Poirier, John C. *The Invention of the Inspired Text: Philological Windows on the Theopneustia of Scripture*. LNTS 640. London: T&T Clark, 2021.

Pontifical Biblical Commission. *In generali consessu*. *AAS* 54 (1961): 507–8.

———. *The Interpretation of the Bible in the Church*. Rome: Libreria Editrice Vaticana, 1993.

———. *The Jewish People and Their Sacred Scriptures in the Christian Bible*. Rome: Libreria Editrice Vaticana, 2002.

Pontifical Council for Interreligious Dialogue. *Pastoral Attention to Traditional Religions*. November 21, 1993.

Pritchard, James B., ed. *Ancient Near Eastern Texts Relating to the Old Testament*. 3rd ed. Princeton: Princeton University Press, 1969.

Prothro, James B. "History, Illocution, and Theological Exegesis: Reading Paul's Letter to Philemon." *Nova et Vetera* 18, no. 4 (2020): 1341–63.

———. "Inspiration and Textual Preservation: A Catholic Essay." *ProEccl* 30, no. 2 (2021): 141–62.

———. "Theories of Inspiration and Catholic Exegesis: Scripture and Criticism in Dialogue with Denis Farkasfalvy." *CBQ* 83, no. 2 (2021): 294–314.

Przanowski, Mateusz. "Christ as *Deus Absconditus* in Thomas Aquinas's Theology." *Nova et Vetera* 16, no. 3 (2018): 881–98.

Rad, Gerhard von. "Es ist noch eine Ruhe vorhanden dem Volke Gottes." Pages 101–8 in *Gesammelte Studien zum Alten Testament.* TB 8. Munich: Kaiser, 1958.

Radl, W. "ἔρημος." *EDNT* 2:51–52.

Ramage, Matthew J. *Jesus, Interpreted: Benedict XVI, Bart Ehrman, and the Historical Truth of the Gospels.* Washington, DC: Catholic University of America Press, 2017.

Ramírez, Juan Alberto Casas. "*Effatha*: Aproximación exegética al relato de curación del tartamudo sordo en Mc 7,31–37." *Fran* 58, no. 166 (2016): 149–77.

Rapaport, Moshe, ed. *The Pacific Islands: Environment and Society*. Rev. ed. Honolulu: University of Hawaii Press, 2013.

Redalié, Yann. *Paul après Paul: le temps, le salut, la morale selon les épîtres à Timothée et à Tite.* Geneva: Labor et Fides, 1994.

Regev, Eyal. *The Temple in Early Christianity: Experiencing the Sacred.* AYBRL. New Haven: Yale University Press, 2019.

Reid, Barbara E., OP. "The What, Why, and How of Feminist Biblical Interpretation." *The Bible Today* 57, no. 3 (May 2019).

———. *Wisdom's Feast: An Invitation to Feminist Interpretation of the Scriptures.* Grand Rapids: Eerdmans, 2016.

Renz, Johannes. *Die althebräischen Inschriften.* Vol. 2, pt. 1 of Handbuch der althebräischen Epigraphik. Darmstadt: Wissenschaftliche Buchgesellschaft, 1995.

Rey, Pierre-Louis. "Vie de Jésus, un roman idéaliste." *Oeuvres & Critiques* 26, no. 2 (2001): 48–58.

Ricoeur, Paul. *Freud and Philosophy: An Essay on Interpretation.* Translated by Denis Savage. New Haven: Yale University Press, 1965.

Robinson, Robert Bruce. *Roman Catholic Exegesis since Divino Afflante Spiritu: Hermeneutical Implications.* SBLDS 111. Atlanta: Scholars Press, 1988.

Rodríguez, Rafael. "Authenticating Criteria: The Use and Misuse of a Critical Method." *JSHJ* 7, no. 2 (2009): 152–67.

———. *Structuring Early Christian Memory: Jesus in Tradition, Performance and Text.* LNTS 407. London: T&T Clark, 2010.

Rosenstock-Huessy, Eugen. *Practical Knowledge of the Soul.* Eugene, OR: Wipf & Stock, 2015.

Rountree, Te Aroha. "Once Was Colonised: Jesus Christ." Pages 161–75 in *Theol-*

ogy as Threshold: Invitations from Aotearoa New Zealand. Edited by Jione Havea, Emily Colgan, and Nāsili Vaka'uta. Decolonizing Theology. Lanham, MD: Lexington Books/Fortress Academic, 2022.

Royo, Antonio, OP, and Jordan Aumann, OP. *Theology of Christian Perfection*. Dubuque: Priory, 1962.

Rubin, David C. *Memory in Oral Traditions: The Cognitive Psychology of Epic Ballads, and Counting-out Rhymes*. Oxford: Oxford University Press, 1995.

Ruether, Rosemary Radford. "The Feminist Critique in Religious Studies." *Soundings* 64, no. 4 (1981): 388–402.

———. *Sexism and God-Talk*. Boston: Beacon, 1983.

Ruiz, Jean-Pierre. *Readings from the Edges: The Bible and People on the Move*. Maryknoll, NY: Orbis, 2011.

Runesson, Anders. *Divine Wrath and Salvation in Matthew: The Narrative World of the First Gospel*. Minneapolis: Fortress, 2016.

Runesson, Anders, and Daniel M. Gurtner, eds. *Matthew within Judaism: Israel and the Nations*. ECL. Atlanta: Society of Biblical Literature, 2019.

Rushton, Kathleen P., RSM. "Beyond the Paradigm of Stewardship: Making Right Relationship Happen with God, People and Earth." In *Habitats of the Basileia: Essays in Honour of Elaine M. Wainwright*. Edited by Caroline Blyth, Emily Colgan, and Robert Myles. Sheffield: Sheffield Phoenix, forthcoming.

———. "The Cosmology of John 1:1–14 and Its Implications for Ethical Action in This Ecological Age." *Colloquium* 45, no. 2 (2013): 137–53.

———. *The Cry of the Earth and the Cry of the Poor: Hearing Justice in John's Gospel*. London: SCM, 2020.

———. "The Implications of the Cosmology of the Prologue for Johannine Eschatology." *InterfaceTheology* 1, no. 1 (2015): 37–54.

———. "Living into Our Future." *Tui Motu InterIslands* 273 (August, 2022): 24–25.

———. "On the Crossroads between Life and Death: Reading Birth Imagery in John in the Earthquake Changed Regions of Otautahi Christchurch." Pages 57–72 in *Bible, Borders, Belonging(s): Engaging Readings from Oceania*. Edited by Jione Havea, David Neville, and Elaine Wainwright. SemeiaSt 75. Atlanta: Society of Biblical Literature, 2014.

———. "Pacific Island Peoples: Resilience and Climate Change." *Concilium* 3 (2017): 105–12.

———. *The Parable of the Woman in Childbirth of John 16:21: A Metaphor for the Death and Glorification of Jesus*. Lewiston, NY: Mellen, 2011.

———. "Rediscovering Forgotten Features: Scripture, Tradition and Whose

Feet May Be Washed on Holy Thursday Night." Pages 91–112 in *Reinterpreting the Eucharist: Explorations in Feminist Theology and Ethics*. Edited by Anne Elvey, Carol Hogan, Kim Power, and Claire Renkin. Sheffield: Equinox Publishing, 2013.

Ryan, Stephen, OP. "The Text of the Bible and Catholic Biblical Scholarship." *Nova et Vetera* 4, no. 1 (2006): 132–41.

———. "The Word of God and the Textual Pluriformity of the Old Testament." Pages 123–50 in *"Verbum Domini" and the Complementarity of Exegesis and Theology*. Edited by Scott Carl. Grand Rapids: Eerdmans, 2015.

Sanders, E. P. *The Historical Figure of Jesus*. New York: Penguin, 1993.

———. *Jesus and Judaism*. Philadelphia: Fortress, 1985.

Sanders, Seth L. "'The Mutation Peculiar to Hebrew Religion': Monotheism, Pantheon Reduction, or Royal Adoption of Family Religion?" *JANER* 14, no. 2 (2014): 217–27.

———. "When the Personal Became Political: An Onomastic Perspective on the Rise of Yahwism." *HBAI* 4, no. 1 (2015): 78–105.

Schille, Gottfried. "Das Leiden des Herrn: Die evangelische Passionstradition und ihr 'Sitz im Leben.'" *ZTK* 52, no. 2 (1955): 161–205.

Schmid, Konrad. "Gibt es 'Reste hebräischen Heidentums' im Alten Testament? Methodische Überlegungen anhand von Dtn 32,8f und Ps 82." Pages 105–20 in *Primäre und sekundäre Religion als Kategorie der Religionsgeschichte des Alten Testaments*. Edited by Andreas Wagner. Berlin: de Gruyter, 2012.

Schmidt, Brian B. *Israel's Beneficent Dead: Ancestor Cult and Necromancy in Ancient Israelite Religion and Tradition*. Winona Lake, IN: Eisenbrauns, 1996.

Schmidtkunz, Petra. *Das Moselied des Deuteronomiums: Untersuchungen zu Text und Theologie von Dtn 32,1–43*. FAT 2/124. Tübingen: Mohr Siebeck, 2020.

Schneiders, Sandra M., IHM. *Buying the Field: Catholic Religious Life in the Mission to the World*. New York: Paulist, 2013.

———. *The Revelatory Text: Interpreting the New Testament as Sacred Scripture*. 2nd ed. Collegeville, MN: Liturgical Press, 1999.

———. *Written That You May Believe: Encountering Jesus in the Fourth Gospel*. Rev. ed. New York: Crossroad, 2003.

Schroeder, Roger, SVD. "Interculturality as a Paradigm of Mission." Pages 155–70 in vol. 2 of *Intercultural Mission*. Edited by Lazar T. Stanislaus, SVD, and Martin Ueffing. Sankt Augustin, Germany: Steyler Missionwissenschaftliches Institute, 2015.

Schroer, Silvia. "Gender and Iconography from the Viewpoint of a Feminist Biblical Scholar." *Lectio Difficilior* 2 (2008): 1–25.

Schudson, Michael. "Dynamics of Distortion in Collective Memory." Pages

346–64 in *Memory Distortion: How Minds, Brains, and Societies Reconstruct the Past.* Edited by D. L. Schachter. Cambridge: Harvard University Press, 1995.

Schüssler Fiorenza, Elisabeth. *Bread Not Stone: The Challenge of Feminist Biblical Interpretation.* Boston: Beacon, 1984.

———. "The Ethics of Biblical Interpretation: Decentering Biblical Scholarship." *JBL* 107, no. 1 (1988): 3–17.

Schwartz, Barry. *Abraham Lincoln and the Forge of National Memory.* Chicago: University of Chicago Press, 2000.

Scott, R. B. Y. *The Relevance of the Prophets.* New York: Macmillan Company, 1960.

Scroggs, Robin. "Paul and the Eschatological Woman." *JAAR* 40, no. 3 (1972): 282–303.

Secretariat for Non-Christians. *The Attitude of the Church towards the Followers of Other Religions: Reflections and Orientations on Dialogue and Mission.* 1984. https://www.dicasteryinterreligious.va/dialogue-and-mission-1984.

Segovia, Fernando. "Latin American Biblical Interpretation in the Diaspora: Latinx American Biblical Criticism." Pages 171–93 in in *80 años de exégesis bíblica en América Latina: Actas del Congreso Internacional de Estudios Bíblicos organizado con ocasión del 80º aniversario de Revista Bíblica.* Edited by Eleuterio R. Ruiz. RevistBSup 7. Estella: Verbo Divino, 2019.

———. "Towards a Hermeneutics of Diaspora: A Hermeneutics of Otherness and Engagement." Pages 57–74 in *Social Location and Biblical Interpretation in the United States.* Vol. 1 of *Readings from This Place.* Edited by F. F. Segovia and M. A. Tolbert. Minneapolis: Fortress, 1995.

Segundo, José Luis, SJ. *Liberación de la teología.* Buenos Aires: Carlos Lohlé, 1975.

———. *The Liberation of Theology.* Translated by John Drury. Maryknoll, NY: Orbis, 1976.

Senior, Donald, CP. *The Gospel of Matthew.* Interpreting Biblical Texts. Nashville: Abingdon, 1997.

———. "Interpreting the Scriptures – the Church and the Modern Catholic Biblical Renewal." Pages 1923–49 in *The Jerome Biblical Commentary for the Twenty-First Century.* 3rd ed. Edited by John J. Collins et al. London: T&T Clark, 2022.

———. *Jesus: A Gospel Portrait.* Rev. ed. New York: Paulist, 1992.

———. *The Landscape of the Gospels: A Deeper Meaning.* New York: Paulist, 2020.

———. *Matthew.* ANTC. Nashville: Abingdon, 1998.

———. *Raymond E. Brown and the Catholic Biblical Renewal.* New York: Paulist, 2018.

———. "Viewing the Jewish Jesus of History through the Lens of Matthew." Pages 81–96 in *Soundings in the Religion of Jesus: Perspectives and Methods in Jewish and Christian Scholarship.* Minneapolis: Fortress, 2012.

Senior, Donald, CP, John J. Collins, and Mary Ann Getty, eds. *The Catholic Study Bible.* 3rd ed. New York: Oxford University Press, 2016.

Seow, C. L. *Job 1–21: Interpretation and Commentary.* Illumination Commentaries Series. Grand Rapids: Eerdmans, 2013.

Serequeberhan, Tsenay. *The Hermeneutics of African Philosophy: Horizon and Discourse.* London: Routledge, 1994.

Sim, David C. "Matthew and Jesus of Nazareth." Pages 155–72 in *Matthew and His Christian Contemporaries.* Edited by David C. Sim and Boris Repschinski. LNTS 333. New York: T&T Clark, 2008.

Small, Jocelyn Penny. *Wax Tablets of the Mind: Cognitive Studies of Memory and Literacy in Classical Antiquity.* Abingdon: Routledge, 1997.

Smith, Mark S. *God in Translation: Deities in Cross-Cultural Discourse in the Biblical World.* FAT 57. Tübingen: Mohr Siebeck, 2008.

———. *The Ugaritic Baal Cycle: Introduction with Text, Translation & Commentary of KTU I.I–I.2.* VTSup 55. Leiden: Brill, 1994.

Smith, William Robertson. *Lectures on the Religion of the Semites: Second and Third Series.* Edited by John Day. JSOTSup 183. Sheffield: Sheffield Academic Press, 1995.

Sommer, Benjamin D. "The Babylonian Akitu Festival: Rectifying the King or Renewing the Cosmos?" *Journal of the Ancient Near Eastern Society* 27, no. 1 (2000): 81–95.

Sonnet, Jean-Pierre. "Côté cour, côté jardin: Salomon, L'Adam royal." Pages 247–60 in *Le roi Salomon, un héritage en question: Hommage à Jacques Vermeylen.* Edited by Claude Lichert and Dany Nocquet. Le Livre et le Rouleau 33. Brussels: Lessius 2008.

Soumaho, Mesmin-Noël. *Éléments de méthodologie pour une lecture critique.* Recherches gabonaises. Libreville: CERGEP, 2002.

Sourou, Jean-Baptiste. "African Traditional Religion and the Catholic Church in the Light of the Synods for Africa: 1994 and 2009." *African Human Rights Law Journal* 14, no. 1 (2014): 142–49.

Spitaler, Peter. "Doubt or Dispute (Jude 9 and 22–23): Rereading a Special New Testament Meaning through the Lense [*sic*] of Internal Evidence." *Bib* 87, no. 2 (2006): 201–22.

Stalder, Kurt. *Sprache und Erkenntnis der Wirklichkeit Gottes: Texte zu einigen wissenschaftstheoretischen und systematischen Voraussetzungen für die exegetische und homiletische Arbeit.* Edited by Urs von Arx. Ökumenische Beihefte zur Freiburger Zeitschrift für Philosophie und Theologie 38. Freiburg: Universitätsverlag, 2000.

Stanton, Elizabeth Cady. *The Women's Bible.* New York, European, 1895.

Stein, Robert H. *Mark.* BECNT. Grand Rapids: Baker Academic, 2008.

Steinmann, Jean. *La Vie de Jésus.* Paris: Les Libraires Associés, 1959.

Sullivan, Francis A., SJ. *Magisterium: Teaching Authority in the Catholic Church.* New York: Paulist, 1983.

Suriano, Matthew. *A History of Death in the Hebrew Bible.* Oxford: Oxford University Press, 2018.

Svartvik, Jesper. *Mark and Mission: Mk 7:1–23 in Its Narrative and Historical Contexts.* ConBNT 32. Stockholm: Almqvist and Wiksell, 2000.

Synod of Bishops. "The Word of God in the Life and Mission of the Church." October 28, 2008. https://www.ncronline.org/news/synod-final-propositions-synod-bishops-bible.

Talar, Charles J. T. "Modernism." Pages 793–99 in vol. 2 of *New Catholic Encyclopedia: Supplement 2010.* Edited by Robert L. Fastiggi. Detroit: Gale, 2010.

Tanner, Norman P., SJ. *Decrees of the Ecumenical Councils.* 2 vols. London: Sheed and Ward, 1990.

Tate, Henare. "Stepping into Māori Spirituality." Pages 34–53 in *He Kupu Whakawairua Spirituality in Aotearoa New Zealand: Catholic Voices.* Edited by Helen Bergin and Susan Smith. Auckland: Accent Publications, 2002.

Taylor, Vincent. *The Gospel according to Saint Mark.* New York: St. Martin's, 1963.

Tempels, Placide. *Bantu Philosophy.* Translated by Margaret Read. Collection Présence Africaine. Orlando: HBC, 2010.

Theissen, Gerd. *Sociología del movimiento de Jesús: El nacimiento del cristianismo primitivo.* Translated by José Antonio Jauregui. Santander: Sal Terrae, 1979.

Theodore of Mopsuestia. *I Thessalonians—Philemon.* Vol. 2 of *In Epistolas B. Pauli commentarii: The Latin Edition with Greek Fragments.* Edited by H. B. Swete. Cambridge: Cambridge University Press, 1882.

Thiessen, Matthew. *Jesus and the Forces of Death: The Gospels' Portrayal of Ritual Impurity within First-Century Judaism.* Grand Rapids: Baker Academic, 2020.

Toorn, Karel van der. "Goddesses in Early Israelite Religion." Pages 83–97 in

Ancient Goddesses: The Myths and the Evidence. Edited by Lucy Goodison and Christine Morris. Madison: University of Wisconsin Press, 1998.

———. *Scribal Culture and the Making of the Hebrew Bible*. Cambridge: Harvard University Press, 2007.

Topor, Wolor. "The Concept of God in the African Philosophy." *Journal of African Religion and Philosophy* 1, no. 2 (1990): 1–6.

Tosato, Angelo. *The Catholic Statute of Biblical Interpretation*. Edited by Monica Lugato. Rome: Gregorian and Biblical Press, 2021.

Töyräänvuori, Joanna. "An Iconographic Allusion to the Northwest Semitic Sea Deity Yamm from 8th Century BC Jerusalem?" Pages 193–202 in *"My Spirit at Rest in the North Country" (Zechariah 6.8): Collected Communications to the XXth Congress of the International Organization for the Study of the Old Testament, Helsinki 2010*. Edited by Hermann Michael Miemann and Matthias Augustin. BEATAJ 57. New York: Peter Lang, 2011.

Trible, Phyllis. *Texts of Terror: Literary-Feminist Readings of Biblical Narratives*. Philadelphia: Fortress, 1984.

Trinka, Eric. *Cultures of Mobility, Migration, and Religion in Ancient Israel and Its World*. Routledge Studies in the Biblical World. New York: Routledge, 2022.

Tshibangu, T. *Le propos d'une théologie africaine*. Kinshasa: Presses Universitaires du Zaire, 1974.

Uffenheimer, Benjamin. "Myth and Reality in Ancient Israel." Pages 135–68 in *The Origins and Diversity of Axial Age Civilizations*. Edited by Shmuel N. Eisenstadt. New York: State University of New York Press, 1986.

Ulrich, Eugene. *The Dead Sea Scrolls and the Developmental Composition of the Bible*. VTSup 169. Leiden: Brill, 2015.

Valkenberg, Wilhelmus G. B. M. *Words of the Living God: Place and Function of Holy Scripture in the Theology of St. Thomas Aquinas*. Publications of the Thomas Instituut te Utrecht 2/6. Leuven: Peeters, 2000.

Vall, Gregory. *Ecclesial Exegesis: A Synthesis of Ancient and Modern Approaches to Scripture*. Verbum Domini. Washington, DC: Catholic University of America Press, 2022.

Van Dijk, J. "Canaanite God Horon and His Cult in Egypt." *Göttinger Miszellen* 107 (1989): 59–68.

Vatican Council I. Dogmatic Constitution *Dei Filius*. April 24, 1870.

Vatican Council II. Declaration on the Relation of the Church to Non-Christian Religions *Nostra aetate*. October 28, 1965.

———. Decree *Ad gentes*. December 7, 1965.

———. Dogmatic Constitution *Dei Verbum*. November 18, 1965.

———. Pastoral Constitution *Gaudium et spes*. December 7, 1965.
Venard, Olivier-Thomas. *A Poetic Christ: Thomist Reflections on Scripture, Language and Reality*. Translated by Kenneth Oakes and Francesca Aran Murphy. Illuminating Modernity. London: T&T Clark, 2019.
Verman, Mark. "The Power of Threes." *JBQ* 36, no. 3 (2008): 171–81.
Villamán, Marcos. *Leyendo el evangelio de Lucas*. México: CAM, 1982.
Vincent, Louis-Hugues. *Le Père Marie-Joseph Lagrange: Sa vie et son œuvre*. Paris: Parole et silence, 2013.
Viviano, Benedict Thomas, OP. *Catholic Hermeneutics Today: Critical Essays*. Eugene, OR: Cascade, 2014.
Vögtle, Anton. *Der Judasbrief, der zweite Petrusbrief*. EKKNT 22. Neukirchen-Vluyn: Neukirchener Verlag, 1994.
Voorwinde, Stephen. *Jesus' Emotions in the Gospels*. London: T&T Clark, 2011.
Walton, John H., and D. Brent Sandy. *The Lost World of Scripture: Ancient Literary Culture and Biblical Authority*. Downers Grove, IL: IVP Academic, 2013.
Warner, Marina. *Signs and Wonders: Essays on Literature and Culture*. London: Chatto & Windus, 2003.
Wasserman, Tommy. *The Epistle of Jude: Its Text and Transmission*. ConBNT 43. Stockholm: Almqvist and Wiksell, 2006.
Wasserman, Tommy, and Peter J. Gurry. *A New Approach to Textual Criticism: An Introduction to the Coherence-Based Genealogical Method*. RBS 80. Atlanta: Society of Biblical Literature, 2017.
Wazana, Nili. "Anzu and Ziz: Great Mythical Birds in Ancient Near Eastern, Biblical, and Rabbinic Traditions." *JANES* 31, no. 1 (2009): 111–35.
Wcela, Emil A. "What Is Catholic about a Catholic Translation of the Bible?" *CBQ* 71, no. 2 (2009): 247–63.
Weinfeld, Moshe. "Sabbath, Temple and the Enthronement of the Lord: The Problem of the Sitz im Leben of Genesis 1:1–2:3." Pages 501–12 in *Mélanges bibliques et orientaux en l'honneur de M. Henri Cazelles*. Edited by André Caquot and Matthias Delcor. AOAT 212. Kevelaer: Butzon & Bercker, 1981.
Westerlund, David. "Spiritual Beings as Agents of Illness." Pages 152–69 in *African Spirituality: Forms, Meanings, and Expressions*. Edited by Jacob Obafẹmi Kẹhinde Olupọna. World Spirituality 3. New York: Crossroad, 2000.
Whitekettle, Richard. "Bugs, Bunny, or Boar? Identifying the Zîz Animals of Psalms 50 and 80." *CBQ* 67, no. 2 (2005): 250–64.
Wilder, Thornton, and Joseph Cermatori. "The Barock; or, How to Recognize a

Miracle in the Daily Life." *Proceedings of the Modern Language Association of America* 136, no. 2 (2021): 246–53.

Williams, Charles. *The English Poetic Mind*. New York: Russell & Russell, 1963.

———. *Witchcraft*. Cleveland: World, 1959.

Williams, Joel F. "Foreshadowing, Echoes, and the Blasphemy at the Cross (Mark 15:29)." *JBL* 132, no. 4 (2013): 913–33.

Williams, Logan. "The Stomach Purifies All Foods: Jesus' Anatomical Argument in Mark 7.18–19." *NTS* (forthcoming).

Wink, Walter. *The Bible in Human Transformation: Toward a New Paradigm for Biblical Study*. Philadelphia: Fortress, 1973.

Wire, Antoinette Clark. *The Corinthian Women Prophets: A Reconstruction through Paul's Rhetoric*. Minneapolis: Fortress, 1990.

Witherup, Ronald D., SS. "The Bible in the Life of the Church." Pages 1615–21 in *The Paulist Biblical Commentary*. Edited by José Enrique Aguilar Chiu, Richard J. Clifford, SJ, Carol J. Dempsey, OP, Eileen M. Schuller, OSU, Thomas Stegman, SJ, and Ronald Witherup, PSS. New York: Paulist, 2018.

———. *Scripture: Dei Verbum*. Rediscovering Vatican II. New York: Paulist, 2006.

Wood, Alice. *Of Wings and Wheels: A Synthetic Study of the Biblical Cherubim*. BZAW 385. Berlin: de Gruyter, 2008.

Woodroof, Tim. "The Church as Boat in Mark: Building a Seaworthy Church." *ResQ* 39, no. 4 (1997): 231–49.

Wright, M. R. *Cosmology in Antiquity*. Sciences of Antiquity. London: Routledge, 1995.

Wright, William M., IV, and Frances Martin. *Encountering the Living God in Scripture: Theological and Philosophical Principles for Interpretation*. Grand Rapids: Baker Academic, 2019.

Wyatt, Nicolas. "Grasping the Griffin: Identifying and Characterizing the Griffin in Egyptian and West Semitic Tradition." *Journal of Ancient Egyptian Interconnections* 1, no. 1 (2009): 29–39.

———. "The Rumpelstiltskin Factor: Explorations in the Arithmetic of Pantheons." Pages 88–128 in *Some Wine and Honey for Simon: Biblical and Ugaritic Aperitifs in Memory of Simon B. Parker*. Edited by A. Joseph Ferrara and Herbert B. Huffmon. Eugene, OR: Pickwick, 2020.

Yoshiko Reed, Annette. *Demons, Angels, and Writing in Ancient Judaism*. Cambridge: Cambridge University Press, 2020.

Zevit, Ziony. *The Religions of Ancient Israel: A Synthesis of Parallactic Approaches*. London: Continuum, 2001.

Contributors

Kelly Anderson (PhD, The Catholic University of America) is associate professor and chair of the Department of Sacred Scripture for the Major Seminary at Saint Charles Borromeo Seminary. She coauthored the volume *James, First, Second, and Third John* for the Catholic Commentary on Sacred Scripture (Baker Academic).

Michael Patrick Barber (PhD, Fuller Theological Seminary) is professor of scripture and theology at the Augustine Institute Graduate School of Theology. He is the author of various academic publications, including *The Historical Jesus and the Temple: Memory, Methodology, and the Gospel of Matthew* (Cambridge University Press) and the forthcoming *The Bible and Anointing of the Sick* (Baker Academic).

Laurie Brink, OP (PhD, University of Chicago) is professor of New Testament studies at Catholic Theological Union and New Testament book review editor for *The Bible Today*. Her current research and pedagogical interests include contextualization and hermeneutics and particularly the intersection of science, theology, and religious life. Her recent publications include *The Heavens Are Telling the Glory of God: An Emerging Chapter for Religious Life; Science, Theology, and Mission* (Liturgical Press) and *What Does the Bible Say about Friendship?* (New City Press).

Anthony Giambrone, OP (SSL, Pontifical Biblical Commission; PhD, University of Notre Dame) is professeur ordinaire and vice director at the École biblique et archéologique de Jérusalem. He is visiting professor for the University of Notre Dame (Jerusalem campus), Ludwig-Maximilians-Universität (Munich), and the Angelicum (Rome).

Mark Giszczak (PhD, The Catholic University of America) is professor of Sacred Scripture at the Augustine Institute Graduate School of Theology. He is the author of *Wisdom of Solomon* in the Catholic Commentary on Sacred Scripture (Baker Academic).

Nina Sophie Heereman (SSD, École biblique et archéologique française de Jérusalem) is associate professor of Sacred Scripture at St. Patrick's Seminary and University. She is the author of *"Behold King Solomon on the Day of His Wedding!": A Symbolic-Diachronic Reading of Song 3:6–11 and 4:12–5:1* (Peeters).

Luke Timothy Johnson (PhD, Yale University) is the Robert W. Woodruff Distinguished Professor of New Testament and Christian Origins Emeritus at Emory University. Among numerous books and articles, he is coauthor of *The Future of Catholic Biblical Scholarship* (Eerdmans) and author of *Imitating Jesus: The Disputed Character of Christian Discipleship* (Eerdmans).

J. L. Manzo (PhD, The Catholic University of America) is associate professor of Scripture and coordinator of the Spanish Master of Pastoral Studies Program at the Mexican American Catholic College for Incarnate Word University. She is working on a volume on Ben Sira for the Wisdom Commentary Series.

Robert D. Miller II, OFS (PhD, University of Michigan) was Ordinary Professor of Old Testament at The Catholic University of America and Research Affiliate at the University of Pretoria. He wrote many books and articles on biblical interpretation, including *Many Roads Lead Eastward: Overtures to Catholic Biblical Theology* (Cascade).

Isaac Augustine Morales, OP (PhD, Duke University) is associate professor of theology at Providence College. He is the author of *The Bible and Baptism: The Fountain of Salvation* (Baker Academic) and the coeditor of *A Scribe Trained for the Kingdom of Heaven: Essays on Christology and Ethics in Honor of Richard B. Hays* (Fortress Academic).

Brant Pitre (PhD, University of Notre Dame) is Distinguished Research Professor of Scripture at the Augustine Institute Graduate School of Theology. He is the author of *Jesus and the Last Supper* (Eerdmans) and coauthor with Michael P. Barber and John A. Kincaid of *Paul, a New Covenant Jew: Rethinking Pauline Theology* (Eerdmans).

James B. Prothro (PhD, University of Cambridge) is associate professor of Scripture and theology at the Augustine Institute Graduate School of Theology. He teaches and writes in the fields of ancient Greek, biblical hermeneutics, and exegesis. His recent books include *The Apostle Paul and His Letters: An Introduction* (Catholic University of America Press) and *The Bible and Reconciliation: Confession, Repentance, and Restoration* (Baker Academic).

Kathleen P. Rushton, RSM (PhD, Griffith University) is an independent researcher, adjunct lecturer in Biblical Studies at Trinity Methodist Theological College, Auckland, and former lecturer at the Christchurch Campus of the Catholic Institute of Aotearoa New Zealand (now Te Kupenga – Catholic Theological College). She is the author of *The Cry of the Earth and the Cry of the Poor: Hearing Justice in John's Gospel* (SCM Press).

Donald P. Senior, CP (PhD, KU Leuven) was a Passionist priest and scholar who served as professor and longtime president at the Catholic Theological Union in Chicago. As an academic, he taught widely and edited study Bibles and commentaries. His publications include *Raymond E. Brown and the Catholic Biblical Renewal* (Paulist Press) and the Abingdon New Testament Commentary on the Gospel of Matthew.

Index of Authors

Abbott, Walter, 229, 234
Abrams, M. H., 117
Ackerman, Susan, 107–8
Adams, Edward, 243–44
Aḥituv, Shmuel, 96
Albertz, Rainer, 97
Albright, W. F., 99
Allison, Dale C., Jr., 124, 170–71, 174, 178, 180
Anagwo, Emmanuel Chinedu, 114–15
Anderson, Janice Capel, 177
Anthonioz, Stéphanie, 111
Anyumba, Godfrey, 104, 106
Aquino, María Pilar, 212, 224–25
Aumann, Jordan, 103
Avigad, Nahman, 109
Ayres, Lewis, 205

Ba, Amadou Hampate, 102, 105
Bailey, Kenneth E., 232–33
Bajeux, Jean-Claude, 101, 115
Balthasar, Hans Urs von, 113, 208
Baly, Denis, 97–98
Balz, H., 154
Bar, Shaul, 109
Barber, Michael Patrick, 4, 169, 171, 176
Barker, Margaret, 100
Barnett, Jon, 231
Barré, Jean-Luc, 186
Bartholomä, Philipp F., 272
Bartlett, John, 184, 200
Barton, George A., 98
Bassler, Jouette M., 259
Bauckham, Richard J., 272, 275
Beasley-Murray, G. R., 124, 137–38
Beattie, John, 102
Béchard, Dean P., 30, 32, 34, 267, 271, 280
Becking, Bob, 94, 97, 99–100
Behr, John, 206
Bendemann, Reinhard von, 152
Benedict XVI, 7, 26, 33, 35, 38, 71, 78, 87, 121, 124, 238–39
Benoit, Pierre, 279
Ben Zvi, Ehud, 132
Bernard, Penny S., 104
Beumer, Johannes, 5
Biebuyck, Daniel, 102, 104
Bigg, Charles, 274
Bobertz, Charles A., 148
Bockmuehl, Markus, 78
Bodnar, John, 167
Bond, Helen K., 178–79
Bonnet, Corinne, 100
Borger, Rykle, 126
Brague, Rémi, 243–44
Bratcher, Robert G., 151
Braudis, Ann, 240–41
Braun, F.-M., 9–12, 14, 24, 81, 83, 184
Brenner, Athalaya, 94
Brink, Laurie, 42
Brown, Jeannine K., 280
Brown, Raymond E., 6, 11, 30, 39, 144
Brown, Robert McAfee, 220

Buccellati, Giorgio, 100
Bultmann, R., 144
Burtchaell, James Turnstead, 5
Burton, Keith A., 146

Campbell, John, 231
Caquot, André, 110
Carl, Scott, 27
Cermatori, Joseph, 115
Certeau, Michel de, 97
Chaine, Joseph, 11, 16
Charles, J. D., 276
Chiu, Jose Enrique Aguilar, 29
Choi, John H., 109
Chouraqui, André, 112
Chrétien, Jean-Louis, 116
Cikala M., Mulago gwa, 104–5
Clarke, Ernest G., 244
Coco, Pierre-Dominique, 105
Cohen, Mark E., 127
Collins, John J., 8, 17, 29, 41, 50
Collins, Thomas Aquinas, 6, 30
Comparetti, Domenico, 118
Cone, James H., 219
Conzelmann, Hans, 259
Cooper, Jerrold, 125
Couturier, Guy, 85
Croatto, J. Severino, 220
Crossley, James G., 173, 179, 181

Daley, Brian E., 205
Daly-Denton, Margaret, 243
Davids, Peter H., 272, 275, 277
Davies, Graham I., 109
Davies, W. D., 174, 180
Davis, Natalie Zemon, 97–98
Day, John, 99, 107
Dazet-Brun, Philippe, 189
De Moor, Johannes C., 110
Deppe, Dean B., 145, 148–49, 156
Dewart, Joanne M., 205
Dewey, Joanna, 145, 259–60
Dibelius, M., 144
Di Palma, Gaetano, 109
Doak, Brian R., 111–12
Donahue, John R., 151, 153–54, 156
Dujardin, Édouard, 191–92
Dunn, James D. G., 178
Dupuis, J., 221
Dyssel, Allan, 110

Edwards, Denis, 235, 239, 241–42
Ehrlich, Uri, 115
Elmelund, Conrad Thorup, 269
Escallier, Claude, 186–87
Esposito, Thomas, 144
Eve, Eric, 167
Ezeanya, Stephen N., 102–6

Farkasfalvy, Denis, 8, 32, 41, 143, 279, 282
Fillion, L.-C., 62
Fiorenza, Elisabeth Schüssler, 211, 259
Fischer, Steven Roger, 231
Fish, Stanley, 58
Fitzmyer, Joseph A., 7, 25–26, 38–39, 143, 179, 221
Flannery, Austin, 28, 161
Fleddermann, Harry, 149
Fogarty, Gerald P., 84
Foster, Benjamin R., 125
Fouchet, Max-Pol, 191
Fouda, Basile-Juléat, 104
France, R. T., 149, 152–53, 155
Francis, 7–8, 41, 118, 227
Franzelin, J. B., 162
Frayer-Griggs, Daniel, 153
Fredriksen, Paula, 178
Freedman, David Noel, 100
Frevel, Christian, 93, 98, 100–101
Frey, Jörg, 272, 275–76
Freyne, Sean, 241

García Arenas, Paula Andrea, 215
Gathercole, Simon J., 207
Gerstenberger, Erhard S., 99
Getty, Mary Ann, 17
Giambrone, Anthony, 192–93, 207–8
Gibson, Jeffrey B., 156
Gillespie, Justin E., 112
Gilmour, Garth, 108–9
Goldberg, Oskar, 98
Golub, Mitka R., 95
Gonçalves, Francolino J., 127–28

Goodacre, Mark, 144
Gray, Timothy, 157–58
Green, Douglas J., 130
Grillmeier, Alois, 29, 31, 33, 36, 40
Grover, Emma, 117
Gundry, Robert H., 154–55
Gurry, Peter J., 270, 282
Gurtner, Daniel M., 172, 175, 178
Gutiérrez, Gustavo, 217, 221

Hadley, Judith M., 108
Halpern, Baruch, 108–9
Hammond-Tooke, W. D., 104
Harding, D. E., 115
Harrington, Daniel J., 151, 153–54, 156
Haught, John F., 4, 227–28, 230, 235–37, 239–40
Hau'ofa, Epeli, 231
Hayes, Richard B., 249
Hays, Christopher B., 98, 100
Hazoumé, Paul, 102, 104–5
Healy, Mary, 152, 156
Heereman, Nina Sophie, 126–27, 130, 132
Heil, John Paul, 148–49, 151–52, 154, 156, 158
Henderson, Suzanne Watts, 149
Hennelly, Alfred T., 218
Henry, Michael, 116
Herring, George, 46
Hodgson, Peter C., 72
Hooker, Morna D., 177
Hopkins, Gerard Manley, 254
Horowitz, Isaiah, 110
Hossfeld, Frank-Lothar, 136
Hrůša, Ivan, 100
Human, Dirk J., 101
Hunsberger, David R., 96
Hurowitz, Victor Avigdor, 131
Hutson, Christopher R., 280
Hutton, Jeremy M., 98

Iqbal, Muhammed, 116

Japhet, Sarah, 133
Jaroš, K., 110
Jensen, Adolf E., 102–3, 105–6
Jewett, Robert, 270
John Paul II, 113, 229–30, 239
Johnson, Luke Timothy, 4, 7, 16, 25, 38, 54, 246–52, 254–63
Jones, L. Gregory, 257
Jongkind, Dirk, 281
Joseph, Simon J., 176
Just, Felix, 88

Kalimi, Isaac, 133
Kampen, John, 172
Kaufmann, Yehezkel, 99–100
Kayode, J. O., 103–4
Keener, Craig S., 174, 181
Keith, Chris, 169–71
Kertelge, Karl, 152
Kessy, Marcel G., 105, 114
Kim, Sun Wook, 145
Kirk, Alan, 167–68
Klein, Jacob, 131
Kloppenborg, John S., 172
Knorn, Berhard, 162
Koen, Lars, 205–6
Konradt, Matthias, 174
Kremser, Konrad, 136
Krüger, René, 220
Kubo, Sakae, 275
Kurtz, Lester R., 90
Kurz, William S., 4, 7, 16, 25, 38, 54, 246, 249, 254, 257

Laban, Luamanuvau Winnie, 230–31
Lado, Ludovic, 114
Lagrange, Marie-Joseph, 10–12, 14, 24, 27, 43–44, 61–69, 72–77, 79, 81–86, 92–93, 95–96, 100–101, 107, 111–12, 116, 118, 122–23, 163–65, 183, 185, 193–200, 204, 207, 209, 266, 268–69, 279
Landon, Charles, 271, 275
Lane, Dermott A., 233
Lane, William L., 152, 154
Larson, Thomas J., 102, 104
Laurentin, René, 25
Law, William, 118
Lebreton, Jules, 191
Le Donne, Anthony, 166–69
Lemaire, André, 96, 109

Leo XIII, 5–6, 32, 89–90
Levine, Amy-Jill, 4
Lewallen, Jason, 187–88
Lincicum, David, 72
Lincoln, Bruce, 130
Linton, Olaf, 156
Litwa, M. David, 118
Loisy, Alfred, 123
Lonergan, Bernard, 203
López, Elisa Estévez, 153
Lowie, Robert H., 103
Lubac, Henri de, 120–23
Lufuluabo, François-Marie, 102–3, 105
Lugira, Aloysius Muzzaganda, 101–3, 105–6
Luz, Ulrich, 172, 174–75, 179

MacDonald, Nathan, 93, 99
Machinist, Peter B., 98–99
Madigan, Kevin, 49–50
Maduro, O., 213
Mahoney, Jack, 238
Malbon, Elizabeth Struthers, 145
Marcus, Joel, 148–49, 154, 173, 179
Martin, Dale B., 54–55
Martin, Francis, 8, 29, 32
Martín-Asensio, Gustabo, 157
Mateene, Kahombo C., 102, 104
Mauriac, François, 185–86, 188, 190, 194–97
McIntosh, Jonathan S., 115, 117
McKenzie, John L., 135
Mesters, Carlos, 221
Míguez, Néstor O., 214
Milgrom, Jacob, 112
Miller, Robert D., II, 17–18, 25, 41, 94, 100, 113
Mitarev, Alexander, 111
Mojola, Aloo Osotsi, 105
Moller, Philip, 165
Moloney, Francis J., 234
Montagnes, Bernard, 9–10, 13, 24, 44, 46–49, 80
Morales, Isaac Augustine, 81
Morgan, Jonathan, 146
Morris, Michael J., 110
Morrow, Jeffrey L., 5–6
Moxnes, Halvor, 241
Mtuze, P. T., 103, 105
Münnich, Maciej M., 109–10
Murphy, Richard T. A., 46–48, 50, 58
Murphy-O'Connor, Jerome, 259
Mwanaka, Tendai R., 104

Nanko, Carmen, 59
Neuner, J., 221
Newman, John Henry, 201
Newman, Judith H., 144
Neyrey, Jerome, 29, 272
Nida, Eugene A., 151
Nkuna, Mkateko, 104, 106
Noegel, Scott B., 108
Ntumba, Tshiamalenga, 105
Nürnberger, Klaus, 101, 104–5, 114, 116
Nyirenda, Kingsley, 102, 104, 106

O'Collins, Gerald, 8
O'Connell, Marvin R., 5
Ogiozee, Olena P., 101, 104, 109
O'Malley, John W. O., 51
Opoku, Kofi Asare, 102–3, 105
Ornan, Tally, 107
Osburn, Carroll D., 273, 275

Painter, John, 218
Paoli, Arturo, 220
Pastrone, Pablo Nazareno, 212–13
Paulsen, Henning, 272, 276
Peterson, Jacob W., 269
Pidel, Aaron, 8
Pilarski, Ahida Calderón, 222, 226
Pitre, Brant, 34–35, 157, 176–77, 179
Pius X, 6, 49, 90
Pius XII, 6, 30, 32, 50, 267–69, 282
Plankey, Raymond, 225
Poirier, John C., 280
Prothro, James B., 7, 232, 278, 283–84
Przanowski, Mateusz, 205

Rad, Gerhard von, 131
Radl, W., 155
Ramage, Matthew J., 8
Ramírez, Juan Alberto Casas, 152, 215
Rapaport, Moshe, 231

Ratzinger, Joseph, 38, 60–66, 78, 123, 139, 234–35
Redalié, Yann, 258
Reid, Barbara E., 56–57
Rengstorf, K. H., 156
Renz, Johannes, 94, 108
Rey, Pierre-Louis, 202
Ricoeur, Paul, 257
Robinson, Robert Bruce, 6, 11
Rodríguez, Rafael, 168–70
Rosenstock-Huessy, Eugen, 118
Rountree, Te Aroha, 232
Royo, Antonio, 103
Rubin, David C., 167
Ruether, Rosemary Radford, 259
Ruiz, Jean-Pierre, 58, 223–24
Runesson, Anders, 172, 174, 176
Rushton, Kathleen P., 230–31, 233–34, 237, 242–44
Ryan, Stephen, 270–71

Sanders, E. P., 168–69, 179, 181
Sanders, Seth L., 95
Sandy, D. Brent, 89
Sass, Benjamin, 109
Schille, Gottfried, 144
Schmid, Konrad, 99
Schmidt, Brian B., 112
Schmidt, K. L., 144
Schmidtkunz, Petra, 109–10
Schneider, John, 154
Schneiders, Sandra M., 4, 55–56, 245, 248–49
Schroeder, Roger, 57
Schroer, Silvia, 108
Schudson, Michael, 166–67
Schwartz, Barry, 167–68
Schweitzer, Albert, 67, 69
Scott, R. B. Y., 177
Scroggs, Robin, 258
Segovia, Fernando, 57–58, 213–14, 222–23
Segundo, José Luis, 218–19
Senior, Donald, 17, 19, 29, 40–41, 51, 174
Seow, C. L., 109
Serequeberhan, Tsenay, 101
Sim, David C., 173–74
Small, Jocelyn Penny, 167
Smith, Mark S., 93–95, 106, 125
Smith, William Robertson, 98
Sommer, Benjamin D., 126–27
Sonnet, Jean-Pierre, 133
Soumaho, Mesmin-Nöel, 102–3
Sourou, Jean-Baptiste, 113–14
Spitaler, Peter, 274
Stalder, Kurt, 119
Stanton, Elizabeth Cady, 259
Stein, Robert H., 154, 156
Steinmann, Jean, 209
Sullivan, Francis A., 32
Suriano, Matthew, 112
Svartvik, Jesper, 173

Talar, Charles J. T., 49
Tanner, Norman P., 42, 160, 162
Tate, Henare, 240
Taylor, Vincent, 154
Tempels, Placide, 113
Thiessen, Matthew, 173
Toorn, Karel van der, 89, 108
Topor, Wolor, 101, 103, 105–6, 114
Tosato, Angelo, 8, 93
Töyräänvuori, Joanna, 108
Trible, Phyllis, 259
Trinka, Eric, 94
Tshibangu, T., 101

Uffenheimer, Benjamin, 98
Ulrich, Eugene, 269

Valkenberg, Wilhelmus G. B. M., 8
Vall, Gregory, 39
Van Dijk, J., 96
Venard, Oliver-Thomas, 8
Verman, Mark, 146
Villamán, Marcos, 220
Vincent, Louis-Hugues, 62
Viviano, Benedict Thomas, 7, 25
Vögtle, Anton, 272, 275
Voorwinde, Stephen, 154

Walton, John H., 89
Wasserman, Tommy, 269, 271–72, 275
Wazana, Nili, 111
Wcela, Emil A., 4

Weinfeld, Moshe, 125, 127, 129
Weisengoff, John P., 11
Westerlund, David, 104–6
Whitekettle, Richard, 111
Wilder, Thornton, 115
Williams, Charles, 117, 119
Williams, Joel F., 145
Williams, Logan, 173
Wink, Walter, 25
Wire, Antoinette Clark, 259
Witherup, Ronald D., 29–30, 33, 39–40
Wood, Alice, 111
Woodroof, Tim, 148, 159–60
Wright, M. R., 243
Wright, William W., IV, 8, 280
Wyatt, Nicolas, 100, 110–11

Yoshiko Reed, Annette, 100–101

Zenger, Erich, 136
Zevit, Ziony, 96–97

Index of Subjects

Abraham, 2, 93, 132, 223–24, 228
Abrahamic hope, 228, 237–38, 242. *See also* cosmic hope
Adam, 133, 238, 258n27
Adapa, 92
Ad gentes, 52, 58, 59
African Traditional Religions (ATR), 15, 18, 92–119. *See also* Old Testament: and African Traditional Religions
Akan, 102, 103, 105
Akkadian, 81, 92
Albert the Great, 117, 118
Alexandrian exegesis, 3, 205, 211
allegorical interpretation, 2, 3, 49, 211, 263
Allison, Dale, 170–71, 180, 183
Amarna letters, 92
Amat, Felix Torres, 212
Amos, 252, 255
anagogical interpretation, 3
ancestors, 102, 103, 105–6, 111–12, 113–15
angels, 115, 117, 138, 180
Antiochene exegesis, 3, 211
Anzu, 92, 111
apologetics, 10–11
Aquinas, Thomas, 3, 4, 8, 11, 45, 115, 117, 164, 184
Aquino, María Pilar, 222, 224–25
Arad, 108
archaeology, 5, 17, 20–21, 48, 49, 50, 59, 80, 88, 93–95, 98, 101, 107–8, 212, 236n35
Arinze, Francis, 113
Aristotle, 3, 117
Asherah, 92, 94, 99, 107–8, 116, 131–32
Ashtoret, 96, 107. *See also* Astarte
Assyria, 95n21, 125, 126, 220
Astarte, 107, 116
Augustine, 2, 3, 66, 117–18, 207, 238n39, 280
authority of Scripture, 80, 87, 89, 91, 250–54, 256–57, 259, 260, 261–62, 264, 265, 283; and the Vulgate, 267, 281

Baal, 94, 95, 96, 97, 99, 107–9, 128
Baal Cycle, 125, 128
Babylon, 93, 125–27, 134–35, 163, 220
Baila, 102
Bailey, Kenneth, 232–33
Bajeux, Jean-Claude, 115
Bantu, 112–13
base community, 215–16, 221
Bassa, 103
Baur, Ferdinand Christian, 71–73, 118
Bea, Augustin, 20–21
Bemba, 102
Benedict XVI, 7–8, 15, 19, 21–23, 26, 29, 33–38, 41, 42, 121, 123, 138, 234n31; and Lagrange, 60–66, 71, 73, 77n27, 78. *See also Verbum Domini*
Ben Zvi, Ehud, 132
Bernard, 3, 280
"biblical Docetism," 41, 166

"biblical question," 5, 7–8
Bigg, Charles, 274
Bodmer Papyri, 269. *See also* P^{72}
Bonaventure, 3
Brague, Rémi, 242–43
Braudis, Ann, 240–41
Braun, F.-M., 12
Brown, Raymond E., 6, 17, 22–23, 29, 53
Bultmann, Rudolf, 144n3, 218
Byzantine text, 275

Calvinism, 197
Canaanite religion, 92, 94, 99, 125, 128, 131
canon, 11, 88, 232; and inspiration, 162–63, 246–47, 257, 259, 267, 270, 278n37, 279–80, 281, 283–84; and interpretation, 15, 26, 31–32, 33, 35, 37, 39–40, 41, 58
capitalism, 213–14, 225
Catholic biblical renewal, 23, 51, 52–53, 55, 59, 73
CELAM. *See* Council of Latin American Bishops
Chagga, 105, 114
Chalcedonian definition, 191, 203, 205
chaos, 125–26, 128, 129, 135, 137, 138–39
cherubim, 110–11, 115
Chester Beatty Papyri, 266
circumcision, 2, 73
Clement of Alexandria, 2, 4, 115, 117, 163, 274
Codex Alexandrinus, 273
Codex Ephraemi Rescriptus, 275
Codex Sinaiticus, 273, 274
Codex Vaticanus, 275n28
colonialism, 101n61, 118–19, 212, 214, 215, 220, 222–23, 225, 226, 230, 231–32
concentric circles of interpretation, 227, 241; Christian view, 233–35; cosmic view, 227–30; earth view, 240–42; human view, 235–39; personal and family view, 230–33
Cone, James, 219
Cormier, Hyacinth M., 83–84, 85
cosmic hope, 236–37. *See also* Abrahamic hope
cosmology, 135n46, 228, 233–34, 242–43, 245
Couchoud, Paul-Louis, 192–93
Council of Carthage, 247
Council of Elvira, 117
Council of Jerusalem, 252
Council of Latin American Bishops (CELAM), 215–16, 219, 220n22, 221, 226
Council of Trent, 5, 119n184, 160n53, 238, 268, 270
covenant, 17, 129, 132, 136–37, 141, 157n48, 233, 245
Cox, Harvey, 219
Coyne, George V., 229
creation, 56–57, 80, 103, 115, 125–27, 129, 130n36, 134–36, 137, 138, 140, 141, 147, 153, 163, 228, 230, 233, 237, 238–39, 240, 242, 243–45, 248, 254, 258n27, 262, 264
Croatto, José Severino, 219–20
cross. *See* crucifixion
crucifixion, 67, 72, 122, 140, 141–42, 144n3, 146n9, 153–54, 157, 177, 188, 190, 224, 243, 248, 251
Cuban revolution, 214, 222
Cyril of Alexandria, 118, 146n10, 205

Daniel, 68, 88, 137, 176, 178–79, 281
Dante, 185
Dao De Jing. *See* Tao Te Ching
David, 129, 130–31, 133, 136, 138–39
death, 238
deism, 66–68, 73, 75, 78, 255
Dei Verbum, 6, 11, 19, 21–22, 24–43, 48, 51–52, 55, 59, 87, 120–21, 161, 165–66, 214, 228, 234, 267, 277. *See also* Second Vatican Council
demigods, 101, 107, 116
demons, 110, 114, 139, 148, 151, 171
demythologization, 118, 138
Didymus the Blind, 118
disciples of Jesus, 68, 70, 77, 140, 144n3, 145, 147–50, 151, 153–57, 158, 159–60, 176, 177–78, 180, 202, 207
Divino afflante Spiritu, 6, 11, 19, 20–21, 30, 32, 50, 51, 87, 267. *See also* Pius XII
Dogon, 102

Dominican order, 9, 13, 14, 15, 20, 44–47, 50, 59, 81, 83, 196, 209, 217
Dominic de Guzman, 45–46
Dor, 110
dragon, 116, 117, 129, 134, 135n46, 138–40, 142. *See also* chaos
Dujardin, Édouard, 191, 193

Ea, 126n27, 131
École biblique, 9–10, 14, 20, 44, 47–48, 61, 82, 184, 191
Eden, 130n36, 134, 228
Edward, Lord Herbert, 66–67
Edwards, Denis, 239, 241–42
El, 94, 95, 107
Elijah, 107, 113, 117, 149, 199
Enlightenment, 5, 60–61, 63–64, 68, 254–56. *See also* rationalism
Enuma Elish, 92, 125–27
epigraphy, 10, 94–95, 185
Epimenides of Cnossos, 117
Esagila. *See* temple: Esagila
Esposito, Thomas, 143–44
Esther, 270, 281
Etana, 92
eucharistic hermeneutics, 15, 143–60
Evangelii gaudium, 19, 23
evolution, 80, 238–39, 240, 242. *See also* science
exile, 108, 134–36, 163–64
exodus, 135n46, 136, 157, 219
Exodus, book of, 128, 219–21
Ezekiel, 95, 116, 136
Ezra, 52–53, 163

family religion. *See* popular religion
Farkasfalvy, Denis, 41n51, 143–44, 282n44
feminist criticism, 54, 55–57, 255, 259–60
feminist theology, 224–25
First Vatican Council, 80, 162, 267n7, 278n37
Fish, Stanley, 58
Fitzmyer, Joseph, 22, 25–26, 39, 143
folk religion. *See* popular religion
Fon, 102, 104, 105
form criticism, 30, 143–45, 165

Francis, 7–8, 19, 23, 41, 45, 118, 161, 240. *See also Evangelii gaudium*
Franzelin, Johann Baptist, 162, 163–64, 165
Freyne, Sean, 241
Frühwirth, Andreas, 84
Fula, 102

Gad, 96, 109, 116
Gathercole, Simon, 207
Gaudium et spes, 215, 228
Genesis, 15, 20, 83–86, 91, 111, 115, 163, 242–43, 281, 283
gentiles, 72, 73, 77, 150–52, 154–55, 157, 159, 174, 176, 224, 250n11, 252
giants, 111, 116
Gilgamesh, 92, 255
Goethe, 185
Gospel of John, 34, 70, 72, 73, 140–41, 168, 190, 206–8, 210, 241, 242–45
Gospel of Luke, 72, 73, 141, 176, 207, 220, 248
Gospel of Mark, 15, 72, 73, 74, 75, 85, 135n48, 143–60, 172–73, 174, 207, 224, 271n17
Gospel of Matthew, 17, 70, 72, 73, 148, 151, 168, 171, 172–83, 207, 281, 283
grace, 52, 112, 160n53, 185, 186, 188, 189–90, 196, 197, 209, 228, 241, 249
Grebo, 103
Gregory of Nazianzus, 118, 206
Grillmeier, Alois, 29, 31, 36
Gutiérrez, Gustavo, 217–18, 219, 225

Harnack, Carl Gustav Adolf, 192
Haught, John, 228–30, 235–36, 239
Hebrew Bible. *See* Old Testament
Hebrew language, 2, 44, 81, 135, 153n33, 155. *See also* Semitic languages
Hegel, Georg Wilhelm Friedrich, 66, 71–73, 74, 75
henotheism, 93, 98–99, 106
Herder, John Gottfried, 185
Herod Antipas, 156, 159
Hinduism, 101
historical-critical method, 1, 5–6, 7, 19,

20–23, 24–30, 33–43, 47–52, 53, 54–55, 59, 60, 86–91, 120–22, 143, 193, 194, 211, 212–13, 231–33, 254–56; and Lagrange, 10–13, 20, 24–25, 27, 45, 47–50, 60–78, 79, 82–83, 85, 92, 183, 185; and Pastoral Epistles, 258–59; philosophical underpinnings, 66–78, 80–81; and reader-response, 211, 218–19
Historical Criticism and the Old Testament (Lagrange), 11, 24–25
historical Jesus, 15, 67–71, 162, 166–83, 192–94, 202–3, 209–10
Hobbes, Thomas, 117
Holtzmann, Heinrich Julius, 75
Holy Spirit, 46, 58, 65, 139, 141, 162, 164, 211, 248, 249, 250, 251–52, 253, 256–57, 261–62, 265, 267n7, 278
Homer, 64
Hosea, 95, 132, 175
hospitality, 257, 261
Hugh of Avalon, 117n174
Hugh of St. Cher, 46
Hugh of St. Victor, 3, 4n8
human authorship, of Scripture, 11, 15, 27–28, 31, 33, 34n35, 37, 40, 51, 161–69, 182, 211, 259
Hume, David, 254

Iberian Catholicism, 212
Igbo, 102, 103, 104
Innocent III, 118
inspiration, 6, 8, 10–11, 16, 49, 161, 162–66, 211, 216, 232–33, 246–65, 267–71, 277–85. *See also* human authorship, of Scripture; magisterial teaching, on Scripture
intercultural criticism, 52, 54, 55, 57–59
Interpretation of the Bible in the Church, The, 22, 28n15, 34, 36, 51, 53, 56, 59
interpretive community, 58–59
interreligious dialogue, 112–19
Irenaeus, 163
Isaiah, 110, 134–36, 164, 198–99, 255
Isidore of Seville, 117, 163

Jacob of Edessa, 118
James, 2, 73, 252, 255
Jansenism, 188, 198
Jeremiah, 95, 97, 107, 116, 136, 270, 281
Jerome, 2, 4, 163, 274
Jerusalem, 2, 73, 77, 81–82, 92, 107, 108, 126, 137, 141, 168, 174, 176, 181–82, 195
Jews. *See* Judaism
John XXIII, 21
John Chrysostom, 163
John Paul II, 113, 229, 230, 239
Johnson, Luke Timothy, 25, 26, 38n42, 54
John the Baptist, 75, 156, 169, 202
Judaism, 4, 22, 63, 67, 70, 73, 79, 110, 124, 133, 143, 146n10, 155, 199, 224, 238; and the Gospel of Matthew, 171–74, 177, 178, 180–81, 183
Judaizing, 72
Judas, 201
Jude, 2, 118, 268, 269, 271–77, 282, 284

Kant, Immanuel, 66, 70
kathenotheism, 93
Kaufmann, Yehezkel, 99, 119
Kavango, 102, 104
Keith, Chris, 169–70, 171
Kessy, Marcel, 114
Khirbet el-Qom, 94, 108
kingdom of God, 69, 75–77, 122–25, 127–30, 132, 135–36, 138–42, 173, 180, 195, 204, 217
King James Version, 266
kingship, 122, 123, 124, 125–31, 133, 135, 137, 138–42
Konkomba, 105
Kpelle, 103
Kuntillet Ajrud, 94, 108

La Plata Seminary, 212
La Revista Bíblica, 212, 225
Latin America, 211, 212–15, 220–21, 222–23, 224–26; and the United States, 213–14, 222–26
Laudato si', 240–41
Lebreton, Jules, 191
Le Donne, Anthony, 166–69
Le noeud de vipères, 188–89
Leo XIII, 5–6, 20, 32, 49, 82–83, 86, 89–90, 92, 267. *See also Providentissimus Deus*
Lessing, Gotthold Ephraim, 67

liberal theology, 74–76, 78
liberation theology, 59, 211, 214–21, 222–26, 255; and feminism, 56, 57, 224–25
Lilith, 99
literal interpretation, 3, 4, 6, 11, 40, 49, 123n15, 211, 257n25, 260, 263
liturgical sequence, 145–47, 150, 153, 157, 159
liturgical use of Scripture, 143–44, 145, 146–47, 160, 246–47, 249, 250–51, 258–59
Lobedu, 104
Locke, John, 254
logos, 203, 205, 243–44
Loisy, Alfred, 5–6, 11, 13, 20, 82, 122–23, 192, 193, 204
Lombard, Peter, 115
Lonergan, Bernard, 203–4
Lubac, Henri de, 120–21, 122, 123
Luther, Martin, 61, 62, 64, 66, 74. *See also* Lutheranism
Lutheranism, 11, 66, 69, 79. *See also* Protestantism
Luz, Ulrich, 172–73, 175

Maasai, 106
magic, 93, 105, 117–18
magisterial teaching: on Scripture, 15, 16, 19–23, 32–34, 38, 40, 42, 49, 52, 80, 87, 90, 120, 161, 165–66, 233–36, 256. *See also* *Dei Verbum*; *Divino afflante Spiritu*; *Evangelii gaudium*; *Pascendi dominici gregis*; *Providentissimus Deus*; *Verbum Domini*
Manyika Shona, 104
Māori, 230, 240
Marcionism, 124
Marduk, 126–27, 128, 131
Maritain, Jacques, 186, 188
Martin, Dale, 54–55
Marxism, 214, 215, 219
Mary (mother of Jesus), 10, 139, 199–200, 209, 212
Mary Magdalene, 201
massevoth, 92, 108
Mauriac, François, 15, 185–210; on the nature of Jesus, 190–91, 192–93, 194–96, 198, 199, 201–8
Meaning of Christianity (Lagrange), 61–78
Medellín. *See* Council of Latin American Bishops
medieval thought, 33, 42, 45, 81, 232, 242, 258n28
memory research, 11, 15, 161, 166–72, 178, 182–83
Mende, 104, 105
messianism, 68, 69, 74, 75, 76–77, 123, 136–38, 139, 140, 204
Middle Ages, 45. *See also* medieval thought
modernist crisis, 7, 10, 45, 49, 79, 80, 82, 86, 90, 190, 254–56
monolatry, 93, 98, 106. *See also* monotheism
monotheism, 15, 93–107, 114n157, 116. *See also* henotheism; monolatry; polytheism
Mosaic authorship, 13, 84, 90, 163–64
Moses, 118, 149, 157n48, 163, 199, 247
Mossi, 102
Mot, 96, 109
Moxnes, Halvor, 241
Mpondomise, 104
Murphy, Roland, 22
myth, 17, 55, 64, 74, 75, 93, 103, 109, 110–11, 116, 124, 125–27, 128–30, 132, 134–35, 137, 138, 140, 256

Nabu, 131
Nanko-Fernández, Carmen, 58–59
narrative criticism, 1, 144–45; applied to Mark, 147–58
Nestorianism, 203n63, 205
Nicene Creed, 256–57
normativity of Scripture, 250–51, 253, 257–60, 261–62, 264, 265. *See also* authority of Scripture
Nürnberger, Klaus, 114, 115–16
Nyakyusa, 102, 104
Nyambi, 102, 104
Nyambo, 102
Nyanga, 102, 104, 105

Old Testament, 1, 2, 17, 41, 50, 92–94, 99, 101n61, 121–24, 140, 149–50, 252, 259, 269, 279; and African Traditional

Religions, 109, 113–14, 116–17; and the kingdom of God, 127–38; and Lagrange, 11, 13, 15, 24, 79–91, 92
Ongo, 102
onomastics, 95–96, 107
Origen, 2, 4, 120, 138, 148n18, 163, 257n25, 260, 263n45
original sin, 238–39. *See also* sin

P72, 269, 274–77
parables, 76, 77, 124, 141, 198
partitive exegesis, 205–6
Pascendi dominici gregis, 6, 20, 49–50. *See also* Pius X
Passover, 122, 157–58, 159, 160, 177–78
Pastoral Epistles, 72, 258–59
Paul VI, 22, 229
Paul of Tarsus, 2, 9, 71–73, 115, 118, 164, 238, 247–48, 251, 255, 257–59, 261–62, 264, 279
Paulus, Heinrich, 68, 69–70, 71
Pelagianism, 197
Pentateuch, 13, 49, 84, 163–64. *See also* Mosaic authorship
Peter, 66n18, 71, 73, 74, 144n3, 252, 278–79
Pharisees, 150, 155–56, 157, 159, 172–73, 181
philology, 10, 21, 48, 61, 62n10, 63, 74, 80, 210, 212, 283n45
Philo of Alexandria, 243
Phla-Pherá-speakers, 104
Phoebe, 262
Phoenician, 92, 109
phoenix, 117–18
Pius X, 6, 20–21, 45, 49–50, 84, 90, 92. *See also Pascendi dominici gregis*
Pius XII, 6, 19, 20–21, 30, 32, 50, 51, 87, 267–69, 276, 277, 281–82. *See also Divino afflante Spiritu*
Plato, 2, 74, 236, 244, 246
Poels, Henri, 21, 84
polytheism, 93–94, 96, 98, 100, 101, 106, 131
popular religion, 94, 97–98
postcolonial criticism, 1, 15, 52, 57, 211–26, 256
Priscilla, 260n38, 262
prophets, 107–8, 113, 118, 136, 181–82, 220, 240, 247–48, 251, 252, 255, 257
Protestantism, 22, 42, 48, 53, 54, 63, 65, 67, 70, 74, 76, 192, 222, 255
Providentissimus Deus, 5, 20, 49, 50. *See also* Leo XIII
Pseudo-Dionysius, 115

Q source, 74
Quodvultdeus of Carthage, 118

rationalism, 5, 10, 19, 27, 42, 62, 68–71, 73, 75, 78, 81, 90. *See also* Enlightenment
Ratzinger, Joseph. *See* Benedict XVI
reader-response approach, 211, 223. *See also* historical-critical method: and reader-response
Reid, Barbara, 56–57
Reimarus, Hermann Samuel, 67–68, 71
Reinhard, Franz Volkmar, 68–69
religion, 10, 49, 67, 93, 97–98, 118, 121, 132, 187–88, 229–30, 235–36
Renan, Ernest, 93, 192, 193, 202
repentance, 124, 179–81
Rephaim, 92, 96, 111
Resheph, 96, 99, 109
resurrection of Jesus, 34, 67–68, 71, 80, 140–41, 158, 233, 238, 242–43, 248
Revelation of John, 72, 142, 149, 220, 252
Revue biblique, 9–10, 13, 20, 49, 82, 84
Rigaux, Béda, 29
Rite Zaïros, 115
Roman Empire, 231, 239
Romans, 72, 85, 238n39, 281
Ruiz, Jean-Pierre, 58, 222, 223–24

sacred marriage, 125, 127, 131–32, 139, 140–41
sacrifice, 103, 146n10, 153–54, 158, 160; in Matthew, 175–76, 177–78, 181
Samaria, 112
San, 104, 105
Satan, 138–39, 171, 206
Schleiermacher, Friedrich, 68, 70–71, 93
Schneiders, Sandra, 55, 248–49
Schudson, Michael, 166

Schwartz, Barry, 167–68
Schweitzer, Albert, 67n20, 75, 76, 204
science, 4, 15, 47, 48–49, 65n14, 80–81, 228–29, 235–36, 237–38, 240–41. *See also* evolution
Second Council of Nicaea, 208
Second Vatican Council, 5, 6–7, 19, 21–22, 23, 24–43, 48, 51–53, 87, 161, 164, 165–66, 214, 228–30, 267. *See also Dei Verbum*
secularism, 10n30, 13n43, 21, 27, 42, 79, 81, 85, 119n186, 213
Segovia, Fernando, 57–58, 214, 222–23, 224
Segundo, José Luis, 218–19
seirim, 99, 110, 115
Semitic languages, 44, 81, 82, 185
Semitic religions, 92–97, 99–101, 121, 122
Septuagint, 2, 110n135, 155, 252
seraphim, 110, 115
Shakandanga. *See* Nyambo
Shamash, 96, 109, 116
Shemesh. *See* Shamash
sin, 133, 154n36, 180–82, 186–90, 201, 208, 215, 219, 237, 238–39, 249, 258n27, 274. *See also* original sin
Sinai, 44, 128, 132, 233
Sirach, 88
social memory. *See* memory research
Socrates, 75
Solomon, 131–33, 134, 136–37
Songhai, 102, 117
South America. *See* Latin America
Spinoza, Baruch, 66, 69, 254
spirits, 102, 103–6, 107, 109–10, 111, 113, 114, 115–17, 142
Straubinger, Johannes "Juan," 212–13
Strauss, David Friedrich, 68, 71, 74–75, 78, 192
Swazi, 104
Synoptic Gospels, 77, 139, 143–44, 171, 175, 177, 179, 206–7
Syrophoenician woman, 150, 151, 157, 159, 223, 224

Taanach cult stand, 108
Tao Te Ching, 236
Tempels, Placide, 112–13
temple, 125, 126, 127, 128–29, 130–32, 138; and the church, 140–42, 158; Esagila, 126, 127; of Jerusalem, 107, 132–33, 134, 136, 140, 147, 173n44, 195, 199; in Matthew, 175–82, 183
Tertullian, 2, 93, 163
textual criticism, 6, 10, 16, 34, 80, 88, 266–85; and Lagrange, 266–68
theological interpretation, 1, 4, 7, 11, 15, 26–27, 31–43, 52, 120–42, 228, 256, 283–84
Thérèse Desqueyroux, 187
Thérèse of Lisieux, 188
Thomism, 165, 197, 279n38
Tiamat, 126, 128
Tobit, 88, 110n135, 112
Torah, 132, 148, 151n26, 157n47, 163, 173–74, 251, 252, 261. *See also* Pentateuch
translation, 2, 3, 42, 51, 55, 110, 153, 211, 212, 232, 238n39, 267, 271, 278n37, 279, 282
typology, 2, 168–69
Tyre, 151, 174

Ugarit, 109, 135n46
University of Chicago, 54
Upanishads, 236, 246

Vai, 103
Vatican I. *See* First Vatican Council
Vatican II. *See* Second Vatican Council
Venda, 104, 105
Verbum Domini, 7, 21, 23, 26–27, 33–35, 37, 87n15, 121. *See also* Benedict XVI
Vergil, 117–18, 185
Vie de Jésus (Mauriac), 15, 185–86, 189–210
Vincent, Hugues, 62, 120
Vulgate, 212, 266, 267, 268–69, 271n17, 274, 281, 282n44

Weber, Max, 219
Weiss, Johannes, 76, 192, 204
Wisdom (personified), 244
Wisdom literature, 242, 244, 252
Wisdom of Solomon, 116
women in ministry, 257–65

word of God, 3, 7, 10, 34n35, 36, 38, 41, 48, 51, 53, 56, 59, 152, 159, 161, 211, 212, 215–16, 218, 221, 226, 244, 246–57, 259, 261–62, 265, 268, 277, 279

Xenophon, 74
Xhosa, 104

Yahweh, 93–94, 95–96, 98, 99, 107, 108–9, 135n46
Yoruba, 104

Zephaniah, 95
Zulu, 104

Index of Scripture

Old Testament

Genesis

1–2 163
1:2 129
1:3–26 244
1:6–9 129
1:26–27 153
1:31 152–53
2:7 258n27
6:1–4 111
12:1–20 223
12:10–20 223
12:17 224
13:18 107
14:15 111
15 132
15:6 2
15:9 146n10
15:20 111
21:33 107
28:18 118
31:53 99
32:24–30 107
35:14 118
35:19 96

Exodus

9:24 109
12:15 156
12:19 156
13:3 156
13:7 156
15 127–28
15:1 128
15:4 128
15:6–7 128
15:13 128
15:17–18 128
18:21 148
18:25 148, 155
20:1–2 99
23:14–19 146n10
24:8 157n48
29:37 181
33:19 149
33:22 149
34:6 149

Leviticus

4:7 158
4:18 158
4:25 158
4:30 158
4:34 158
17:7 110

Numbers

13 111
21 110n140
21:14 163

Deuteronomy

1:28 111
1:46–2:1 111
2:11 111
2:14 111
2:20 111
3:11 111
3:13 111
4:19 96, 99
6:4 152
6:4–5 99
7:13 107
8 110n149
12:10 131
17:3–5 96
18:9–14 112
26:14 112
28:4 107
28:18 107
28:51 107
32:3 152
32:8–9 94, 99
32:24 110
32:39 99, 149n23
32:46–47 244
34:6 163

Joshua

5:20 110
6:1 96
11–15 111

12:4 111
13:12 111
17:14–18 111
17:15 111
19:27 96
21:22 96

Judges
9:37 107
11:24 99

1 Samuel
1:24 146n10
6:9–11 96
9:16 130
14:2 107
16–17 139
17 111
18:13 114
22:6 107
28 112

2 Samuel
5:24 107
7:1 131
7:11–16 131
18:8 111
18:18 112
22:11 111

1 Kings
1:9 118
4:20–5:1 132
5–9 132
5:5 132
6:2–22 146n10
8 131–32
10:21 132
10:24 133
11 133
11:5 107
11:33 107
15:13 107, 132
15:28 139n53
16:33 132
18 99, 107
18:19 132
19:11 149

2 Kings
13:6 132
13:21 114
16:4 94
17:11–12 94
17:16–17 94
18:4 107
21:6–7 94
23:4 132
23:4–7 107
23:8 110
23:8–14 94
23:11 109
23:13 107
23:14 107
23:15 107

1 Chronicles
14:9 96
14:11 96
22:9–10 134
29:23 133

2 Chronicles
11:15 110

Nehemiah
8 52
8:3 52
8:12 53, 59

Job
5:7 109
7:12 135n46
9:8 149n21
9:11 149n21
9:13 135n46
18:20 154n36
24:12 153n36, 154n36
26:12 129, 135n46
30:25 154n36
31:38 154n36
38:31–32 110

Psalms
2:7 139
2:9 140
9:3 132
18 94
20 94
23:2 148n13, 155
29 100, 129n34
29:1–2 94
33:6 244
45 132, 135
48:2 94
48:2–3 135
50 111
50:10–12 111
55:17 146n10
58 100
58:6 117
58:12 94n10
74:13 135n46
76:4 109
78:48 109
80 111
82 94n10, 99
82:1 94
82:1–6 100
85:2 132
88:11 111
89 126n24, 129
89:5–10 94
89:6–8 100
89:6–9 112
89:11 135n46
89:12–13 129
89:15 136
89:20–22 129–30
89:26–30 129–30
89:36–38 129–30
89:40 136
91:5–6 100
91:6 110
93 129

93:1 129
93:2 129
95 110n135
106:28 112
107:20 244
110 2
118:26 182
119:105 244
145:6 152
145:16 148

Proverbs

2:18 111
9:18 111
21:16 111
23:32 111
24:23 163
25:1 278

Ecclesiastes

10:11 117

Song of Songs

8:6 109

Isaiah

6 110
6:1–8 94
6:9 198
8:19–20 112
9:3 136
9:5–6 136
11:6–9 135
13:21 110
14:9 111
14:13 94
14:29 107
17:5 96
19:8 153n36
21:2 153n35
24:7 153–54
26:14 111
26:19 111
27:1 135n46
28:2 110
28:8–14 232n19
29:3 112
29:4 112, 114
30:6 110
30:22 94
34:14 110
40:1–11 134n45
40:9 139
41:4 149n23
41:17–20 134n45
41:21–24 99
43:1–7 134n45
43:10 149n23
43:10–13 99
43:25 149n23
44:24–28 134n45
45:18 149n23
46:4 149n23
48:6–13 134n45
51:9–10 129
51:9–11 134–35
51:12 149n23
52:6–7 135
52:7 139
52:10 136
54:5 136
55:3 136
55:11 244
57:6–9 112
59:15–20 135
61:1 139
62:5 136
63:1–6 135
65–66 135
65:11 109
65:17–25 136
65:25 135
66:22–23 136

Jeremiah

2:23 94
16:5–8 112
16:7 112
20:15 135n48
23:6 137
31:33 136
32:29 95
33:15–16 137
44 107
44:17 132

Lamentations

1:8 154n36
1:21 154n36

Ezekiel

6:13 95
8:16 109
10:9 115
21:11 154n36
26:15 154n36
26:16 154
29:3 135n46
34 136
34:23 155
37 136
37:26–28 137
47 135
47:1–12 141

Daniel

3:25 100
6:10 146n10
7 137
7:3 179
7:13 179
7:13–14 137
7:17 179
7:25 179
8:10 179
8:13–14 178
9:26–27 176, 178
9:27 179
11:3 178
11:31 176, 179
12:1 179
12:11 176, 179

Hosea

1–3 132

1:1 244
2 94
2:19 95
6:2 110
6:6 175
9:3 132
13:14–15 110

Joel
1:1 244
4:17–21 135

Amos
2:9 111

Obadiah
17–21 135

Jonah
1:17 146n10

Micah
4:4 132
5:3 137

Nahum
3:7 153n36

Habakkuk
3:5 109–10

Zephaniah
1:4–5 95

Zechariah
9:9 168
9:10 137
13:7 155
14:6–11 135
14:8 141

New Testament

Matthew
1:21 181
3:17 139
4:1–11 171
4:2 206
4:17 180
5:19 173
5:21–26 175
5:23–24 175
6:12 175
7:29 251
8:1–4 175
8:24 206
8:27 199
8:34 174
9:13 175
10:1 251
11:19 86
11:21 180
12:7 175
12:28 77, 139
12:40 146n10
12:41 180
13 141
13:24–30 77, 142
13:31–32 77
13:33 77n27, 142
14:24 148
15:22 174
15:28 151
15:33 155n42
18:3–4 180
18:15–35 282
21:4 168
21:21 273n24
21:42–46 195
22:3 142
22:43 280n39
23 177, 181–82
23:16–22 175–76
23:19–21 181
23:29–39 182
23:38 176, 178
24 176
24:2 175
24:7 179
24:9 179
24:15 176, 179
24:21 179
24:29 179
24:30–31 179
24:36 206
26 177
26:2 177
26:19 177
26:39 206
27:28 174
27:51 176
27:53 176
28:18 251

Mark
1:1–14:11 146n9
1:1–14:21 159
1:14 124
1:14–15 139
1:15 124, 180
1:40–45 175
1:41 151n26, 154
2:5 157n48
2:5–12 151n25
2:26 147n8
3:5 149
3:13–19 148
3:15 150
3:20 147n8
3:22 171
3:27 139
4 141
4:3 150
4:3–9 77n27
4:9 150
4:11 141
4:12 150, 198
4:23 150
4:26–29 77n27
4:30–32 77n27
4:35–41 148
5:7 149
5:28–29 151n26
5:37–43 152
5:41 151n26, 153
5:43 152–53
6:11 180
6:12 180
6:32–44 154

6:34 146, 154, 159
6:34–44 145, 147
6:34–56 146–47
6:34–8:21 145n8, 157, 160
6:37 147n8, 148
6:38 147n8, 148
6:39 148
6:41 145, 147n8, 148, 150
6:42 148, 151
6:43 155
6:44 147n8
6:45–52 148
6:45–56 147
6:50 149
6:52 147n8, 149–51, 156, 159
7:1–23 150
7:1–8:21 146, 150
7:2 147n8, 150
7:3 173
7:5 147n8, 150
7:7–13 150
7:14–15 150
7:18 150–51, 173
7:19 151n26, 157n48, 173
7:24 174
7:24–30 151, 154, 159, 223
7:24–8:9 150
7:25–30 150
7:27 147n8, 150–51
7:29 151
7:31–37 146, 150, 152, 159
7:32 152
7:33 152
7:34 150, 153
7:35 152
7:37 152
8:1–9 145, 151–53
8:1–10 150, 154, 174
8:4 147n8, 150, 155
8:5 147n8, 150
8:6 145, 147n8, 150
8:8 155
8:11–21 155
8:14 147n8, 155–57, 159
8:14–21 155–56
8:16 147n8, 155–56
8:17 147n8, 155–56, 159
8:17–18 156
8:19 147n8, 155
8:19–20 157
10:40 206
10:45 153–54
11:1–11 168
11:15–17 158n49
11:23 273n24
12:33 158n49
12:35–37 2, 195
13:2 175
13:8 179
13:9 179
13:14 179
13:19 179
13:24 179
13:25 179
13:26 179
13:33 77
14:8 157
14:12 158n49
14:12–16:20 146n9
14:17 144n3
14:22 145, 147n8, 153, 157n49
14:22–24 145–46, 157n49
14:24 158
14:33 206
14:58 178
14:72 144n3
15:1 144n3
15:17 174
15:25 144n3
15:33 144n3
15:34 144n3, 153
15:42 144n3
16:9–20 270n17

Luke

2:46 206
2:51 206
2:52 206
4:32 251
4:36 251
5:12–16 175
5:23 251
5:32 180
6:12 206
7:21 139
10:13 180
11 207
11:32 180
11:38 273n24
12:32–34 237
13:3 180
13:5 180
13:18–19 77
13:20 77n27
15:7 180
15:10 180
16:30 180
17:3–4 180
19:28–40 168
21:6 175
21:10 179
21:20 176, 179
22:41–44 195
23:45 176
24:47 180
24:52 176

John

1:1 206, 243
1:1–18 241
1:14 34, 138, 140, 226, 248
1:18 205, 206
1:27 231
2:1–22 140
2:19 140
2:21 140
4:6 206
5 207
5:7–8 271n17
5:19 139, 206
5:24 180
5:27 251
6:27 206
7:18 251
7:39 122
7:53–8:11 270
8:12 206

8:15 206
9:4 206
9:39 180
10:18 206
11:35 206
12:14 168
12:40 149
12:47–48 180
12:49 206, 251
14:6 206
14:28 206
15:15 206
15:24 180
18:9 206
19:41 243
20:17 206
20:19 140
20:21 140

Acts
2:1–36 141
2:14–36 252
2:32–36 2
4:13 251
4:29 251
6:7 248
8:4 248
10–15 252
10:15 151n26
10:38 140
11:1 248
12:24 248
13:49 248
15:16–18 252
16:6 248
19:20 248
21:17–26 174
28:31 251

Romans
2:4–5 181
4:3–10 2
4:18 238
4:20 273n24
5:12 238
5:12–21 258n27
8:19–23 141
8:23 154n36
8:38–39 114
11:7 149
11:25 149
12:2 261
14:23 273n24
15:4 2
15:19 248

1 Corinthians
1:17–18 248
2:4 248
2:16 251, 262
3:1 252
6:19 141
7:1–7 261n41
10:1–22 181
10:4 272
10:10–11 1
10:11 2
11:3–16 258n26, 259, 261
11:8 258n27
11:11–12 258n27
11:27–34 181
12:12–26 141
13:11 252
14:20 252
14:32–35 259, 261
14:34–35 258n26
15:3 252
15:22–23 114
15:26 140

2 Corinthians
1:20 2
3:14 149
5:2 154n36
5:4 154n36
7:4 251
10:2 251
11:2 141
11:3 258n27
11:26 155n42

Galatians
2 73
2:5 262
2:12 174
2:14 262
3:10–14 251
3:28 261
4:21–31 2
6:1–2 282

Ephesians
1:9–10 238
1:20–22 2
2:19–20 141
4:10 140
4:14 148n17
5:27 141
6:12 142

Philippians
1:21–24 114
2:1–11 251
2:10 146n10

Colossians
1:13 138
1:13–20 238
1:15 130, 139

1 Thessalonians
1:9–10 181
2:13 247, 279
4:13–18 114

2 Thessalonians
3:13–15 282

1 Timothy
1:5 263
2 263
2:2 263
2:4 263
2:5–6 263
2:9–10 263
2:11–12 264n46

2:11–15 257, 259, 261–62, 264
2:13–14 264

2 Timothy
3:15 280
3:15–17 248, 278–79, 285
3:16 257, 279
3:17 248

Titus
1:12 117
3:8 248
3:14 248

Hebrews
1:1 280n39
1:1–2 280n39
2:14–15 140
3:7 280
4:12 248
11:38 155n42
12 114
12:5–6 2

James
1:6 273n24
1:22 59
2:4 273n24
2:21–23 2
4:6 2
5:20–21 282

1 Peter
3:22 2
4:18 2

2 Peter
1:21 278, 280n39
2:11 118

1 John
5:7–8 271
5:16 282
5:19 141

Jude
1 273
3 273
4 271–73
4–5 282
5 271–72, 282
5–19 273
8–10 118
9 273
10 276
11 276
14–15 272
14–16 2
20–21 273, 276
20–23 273, 277
21 272
22–23 272–73, 277, 282, 284
25 272

Revelation
9:5 149
11:10 149
12:5 140
12:7–18 138
12:9 138
12:17 142
14:10 149
19:1 142
20:10 149
21–22 142
22:17 142
22:20 142

DEUTERO-CANONICAL WORKS

Judith
8:3 96

Wisdom of Solomon
7:15–22 244
7:24 244
7:27 244
8:1 244
8:4–5 244
9:1–2 244
13:3–7 116

Sirach
16:7 111
30:18–19 112
30:20 153n36
48:13–14 114

1 Maccabees
1:26 153n36

2 Maccabees
9:21 153n36

Index of Other Ancient Sources

Pseudepigrapha

Jubilees
1:4 177

Apostolic Fathers

1 Clement
25 117

Didache
9.1 148n15
9.3–4 148n15
9.5 148n15

Dead Sea Scrolls

1QH[a]
XX, 24–27 153n35
XX, 31–32 153n35

1QS
10:20 181n75

4Q171
3:1–3 181n75

4Q264
8–10 153n35

4Q511
28–29 153n35

Damascus Document (CD)
4:2 180n75
6:4–5 180n75
8:16 181n75
19:16 181n75
20:17 181n75

Josephus

Antiquities
13.297 173

Rabbinic Texts

Genesis Rabbah
82.10 115

b. Bava Metzi'a
85b 114–15

b. Sotah
34b 115

b. Ta'anit
16a 115

Midrash Tanhuma
179 114–15

Early Christian Texts

Augustine

Epistles
137 118n177

Tractates on John
36.1 207

Clement of Alexandria

Stromata
1.22 163n9
6.8.65 274

Cyril of Alexandria

Adversus Julian
1.4.8.14–1.4.9.7 118n179

Didymus the Blind

Commentary on the Psalms
22–26.10 118n179
88.8–18 118n179

Gregory of Nazianzus

Orations
28.4 118n179
29.17 206
29.18 206

Irenaeus

Against Heresies
3.21.2 163n9

Isodore of Seville

Origines
6.3.1–2 163n9

Jacob of Edessa

Hexameron
149b11–150a17 118n179

Jerome

Commentary on Ezekiel
6, 18:5–9 274

Helvidius
7 163n9

John Chrysostom

Homilies on Hebrews
8 163n9

Origen

Commentary on Matthew
11.5 148

On First Principles
4.1 263n45
4.15 263n45

Quodvultdeus

Against Five Heresies
3.4 118n179

Tertullian

De cultu feminarum
1.3 163n9

De testimonio animae
100.2 93

Akkadian Texts

Amarna Letters
EA 197 96n23
EA 256 96n23

Enuma Elish
IV.138–139 126
VI.54 126
VI.61–66 126n27
VI.112 126

Ugaritic Texts

Keilalphabetische Texte aus Ugarit (KTU)
1.14.i.16–20 109n128
1.82.2 109n128
1.148.18 107n115

Inscriptions and Ostraca

Tel Qasile Ostraca
2 96

Egyptian Texts

Execration Texts
E60 96

Greco-Roman Texts

Aristotle

De animalibus
2.367r 117
409v 117
416v–420v 117

Vergil

Fourth Eclogue
13–14 118

Muslim Texts

Qur'an
23:14 115

Medieval Authors

Bernard of Clairvaux

Sermones de diversis
5.2 280n42

Hugh of St. Victor

De Scripturis
5 3nn1–3

Thomas Aquinas

Summa theologiae
I, q. 44, art. 2 115
III, q. 40, art. 1–2 46

Papal Documents

Ad gentes
§22 52, 233

Aperuit illis
§2 161

Catechism of the Catholic Church
§102 280
§114 32
§121 87
§§379–421 238n39
§1128 160
§2818 142

Dei Filius
§2 162, 267n8, 278n37

Dei Verbum
§§2–4 280

§9 234n31
§11 48, 267, 280
§§11–13 6n17
§12 26–33, 35–43, 48, 120, 165, 268
§13 166
§23 51

Divino afflante Spiritu
§§11–19 6n16
§12 269
§15 268
§16 267
§17 268–69
§18 269
§19 30, 269
§§20–21 269
§21 267, 282n44
§24 32
§33 30
§§33–38 268
§40 50
§§46–48 6n16

Ecclesia in Africa
§67 113

Fratelli tutti
§§13–14 118

Gaudium et spes
§5 229
§21 229
§34 229

Laudato si'
§3 240
§6 240
§18 240
§49 227, 240, 242, 245
§62 240
§66 240
§81 240
§138 240
§146 240n47
§179 240n47
§197 241
§201 240

Pascendi dominici gregis
§9 6n13
§§13–14 6n13
§22 6n13
§26 6n13
§§30–34 6n13
§34 49
§42 90

Providentissimus Deus
§10 89
§13 267n6
§17 90
§28 32

Sententiae in IV libris distinctae
4.5.3 115

Sollicitudo rei socialis
§36 239

Verbum Domini
§32 26n11, 33–34, 87–88
§34 26n11, 27, 33, 35–37, 40, 121
§35 43
§38 37
§39 37
§44 34–35
§47 37–38